Lebor G

The book of the taking of Ireland

(Part I)

Editor

R. A. Stewart Macalister

Alpha Editions

This edition published in 2020

ISBN : 9789354036323

Design and Setting By
Alpha Editions
www.alphaedis.com
email - alphaedis@gmail.com

LEBOR GABÁLA ÉRENN

THE BOOK OF THE TAKING OF IRELAND

PART I

EDITED AND TRANSLATED, WITH NOTES, ETC.

BY

R. A. STEWART MACALISTER, D. LITT.

DUBLIN:

PUBLISHED FOR THE IRISH TEXTS SOCIETY
BY THE EDUCATIONAL COMPANY OF IRELAND, LTD.
89 TALBOT STREET

1938

CONTENTS.

CORRIGENDA.

p. xiii, line 23 : *after* R² *add*—traceable in some quotations in R³.

p. xv, line 20 : *add*—At the top of the first page of E there are two old library class-marks, A. 1. 8 and B. 35. Above the 8 there is the invocation *Emanuel*, faint but decipherable : between the two marks there is an illegible note, dia dui (?) . . . ib, with a date ending (1)753.

p. xvi, line 10 : *add*—P was probably meant to complete an acephalous copy already in its writer's possession : hence the abrupt ending.

p. xxiii, line 6 : *after* manuscripts *add*—I dare not flatter myself that these complex lists of variants contain no errors or omissions, but I feel confident that nothing of importance has been overlooked.

p. xxxiv, line 2 : for √A read √V.

p. 8, line 6, below the table : *for* eleventh *read* twelfth. In line 8, *after* Madrid, *add*—Σᴹ, likewise at Madrid, is of the eleventh century.

p. 12, line 21 : *delete* whether . . . importance. In line 24, *after* edge, *add*— The tear would have run in the opposite direction if it had been inflicted in the original act of pillage ; it must have been a later misdemeanour, to remove from the leaf matter not germane to its new context.

p. 163, line 14 : *for* Dula *read* Dala.

p. 223, footnote (²⁹) : *after* version *add* of the Irenaeus text.

p. 239, line 15 : *add*—This poem is printed, *Todd Lectures*, iii, p. 46.

TABLE OF ABBREVIATIONS AND CRITICAL SYMBOLS.

1. *Notation for Redactions* : —

   R^1, R^2, R^3, the First, Second, Third Redactions.
   Min or μ, the version called *Miniugud*.
   K, the modernised version of Micheál ó Cléirigh.

2. *Notation for the Extant Manuscripts* :—

A : Stowe A.2.4.	Λ : Book of Leean, first text.
B : Book of Ballymote.	**M** : Book of Leean, second text.
β : H.2.4 in T.C.D.	
β^1 : H.1.15 in T.C.D.	**P** : P.10266 in National Library, Dublin.
β^2 : Stowe D.* 3.2.	
D : Stowe D.4.3.	**R** : Rawl.B.512 in Bodleian Library.
E : E.3.5. no. 2 in T.C.D.	
F¹ : Book of Fermoy.	V^1 : Stowe D.5.1.
F² : Stowe D.3.1.	V^2 : Stowe D.4.1.
H : H.2.15 no. 1 in T.C.D.	V^3 : Stowe D.1.3.
L : Book of Leinster.	

   R^1 is contained in **L**, **F**.
   R^2 ,,   ,,   ., **A, D, E**, Λ **P, R, V**.
   R^3 ,,   ,,   ,, **B**, β, β^1, β^2, **H,M**.
   Min is suffixed to the copies of R^2 in Λ, **R, V**. To distinguish the portions of these MSS. containing the Min text from those containing the R^2 text, the symbols $\mu\Lambda$, μR, μV are used for the former.
   K is contained in a number of paper MSS., but for purposes of reference the authoritative autograph (23 K 32 in R.I.A.) has been considered sufficient.

---

*For the sake of brevity the shelf-marks of the Stowe collection are here stated in Arabic numerals, though Roman numerals are used in the Library.

Where it is necessary to refer to any combination of two of the β MSS., or to all three of them, the formula β^{012} (varied as required) is used for brevity.

$\mathbf{F^1}$, $\mathbf{F^2}$, are parts of one dismembered MS. collectively denoted by $\mathbf{F}$.

$\mathbf{V^1}$, $\mathbf{V^2}$, $\mathbf{V^3}$, are parts of one dismembered MS. collectively denoted by $\mathbf{V}$.

3. *Notation for Lost Manuscripts of Critical Importance* :—

$$*\mathbf{Q}, \quad *\mathbf{X}, \quad *\mathbf{W}, \quad *\mathbf{Z}.$$

$\sqrt{}\,\mathbf{B}$,   the exemplar from which $\mathbf{B}$ was copied.

$\overset{2}{\sqrt{}}\,\mathbf{B}$,   the exemplar from which $\sqrt{}\mathbf{B}$ was copied.

$\overset{n}{\sqrt{}}\,\mathbf{B}$,   a MS. in the ancestry of $\mathbf{B}$ at an unspecified number of steps back from it.

(Analogous symbolism for the ancestry of the other MSS.)

$\sqrt{}\mathbf{BH}$,   the common ancestor of $\mathbf{B}$ and $\mathbf{H}$. [But $\mathbf{H}\sqrt{}\mathbf{B}$ means the extant MS. $\mathbf{H}$ in combination with $\sqrt{}\mathbf{B}$.]

$\infty\,\mathbf{R^3}$,   the *autograph* of the Third Redaction, or the *compiler* of the Third Redaction, according to the context.

$\infty\,\mathbf{L}$,   the Manuscript in which the tradition represented by $\mathbf{L}$ was differentiated from the other MSS. of the same Redaction.

$\sqrt{}\mathbf{R^3}$,   the Manuscript from which all the *extant* Manuscripts of the Third Redaction are derived (which may or may not be identical with $\infty\mathbf{R^3}$).

(Analogous symbolism for the ancestry of other MSS. and Versions.)

Note.—$\mathbf{R}$ *alone* denotes the Bodleian MS. ; $\mathbf{R}$ with a superscript numeral is to be read " Redaction."

4. *Miscellaneous abbreviations* :—

c : Correction, corrector (according to context).

g : Gloss, glossator ; a gloss *incorporated* in the text.

g^2: a secondary gloss, or gloss upon a gloss, also incorporated in the text.

ɔ: a gloss which remains external to the text, superscript (**sprs**), subscript (**sbs**), or in the margin (**marg**) of the MS.

s: Scribe: **s¹**, **s²**, the first, second, scribe of a **MS.**

y: Interpolation, interpolator. **yc M** is to be read "interpolated by a corrector of **M**." **y sprs s M** "interpolated, above the line, by the original scribe of M". (**y** is used in preference to **i** as being a more distinctive letter.)

LG: The name of the text, *Lebor Gabála*.

s., d.: *in the translation*, to be read "son of," "daughter of."

om, ins, in the lists of *variae lectiones*, to be read "omit(s)," "insert(s)."

sec. man. = *secunda manu*.

R.I.A.: Royal Irish Academy.

T.C.D.: Trinity College, Dublin.

§: The *sections* of the book.

¶: The *paragraphs* of the book.

The glossarial or other interpolated matter in the text is denoted by the signs ⁺... ‖ . secondary glosses being marked ⁺¹... ‖¹: these symbols are more fully elucidated, where necessary, in the notes.

The columns on each folio of the MS. are denoted in the usual way by the Greek letters a β γ δ, the *recto* and *verso* being numbered thus continuously. In most cases a β are on the recto, γ δ on the verso. Except in the case of the MSS. H, β, β^1, β^2 the numeration is by folios, *not* by pages.

In the translation, glossarial matter is enclosed in square brackets [ ]; the restoration of lost matter in angled brackets < >.

INTRODUCTION.

Lebor Gabála Érenn, a title which we can best translate literally, "the Book of the Taking of Ireland," is a compilation which professes to narrate the history of the successive colonists of that country. The earlier Redactions have come down to us, in whole or in part, in fifteen MSS. (counting F, V, as one each, but counting separately the two versions in the *Book of Lecan*). These have been enumerated in the foregoing table, and are more fully described below.

For critical purposes, however, the number has to be reduced to eleven. A is a direct (and very poor) copy of D, and gives us nothing that D cannot supply: while β β^1 β^2 are all derivatives from B, and are thus of no use except to restore one folio, which B lost at some time after they were written.

Although these manuscripts agree, on the whole, in the facts, or alleged facts, which they set forth, the words in which they state them differ profoundly. They fall into redactional groups, essentially at variance in the selection and order of presentment of the narratives, and in the language in which these are expressed. The editor has no alternative but to print them *in extenso,* independently of one another.[1] A single composite text, with an unmanageably cumbrous sediment of *variae lectiones* at the bottom of the page, would be perfectly useless for any critical student of this important document and of its complex history. It may be said that this conclusion has not been reached without experiment.

---

[1] There are a few places in which this is not necessary, but these are exceptional.

The work is primarily paedagogic, for which purpose it is interspersed with mnemonic sets of verses, intended to be learned off by heart. To the modern reader these verses are an unmitigated nuisance, rarely adding anything to what he has already learnt from the prose text; nevertheless it is clear that they are the foundation on which the whole work, *in its present form*, is based. The *corpus* of historical verse became the common reservoir of knowledge upon which the prose compilers drew; and the selections which they made therefrom dictated the selection of facts which they set forth in the several redactions.

For this reason, the treatment of the verse has to be different from that of the prose: it has been found most convenient (again after experiment) to separate the verse texts from the prose, and to print them independently.

It is probable, indeed, that this is a return to the practice of the original prose redactors; that they did not write out the verse compositions in full, but merely jotted down as cues the opening words of each in the margins of their MSS., in the confidence that their readers would already have these texts securely in their heads, as they themselves had. In fact, the manuscript R gives us no more than such jottings, incorporated, it is true, in the text, but not extending beyond the first quatrain of any poem. It is conceivable that this is *not* the mere shirking of a lazy scribe, but that it is an actual survival of a traditional custom.[2] This suggestion is corroborated by the diversity of the formulae introducing the poems, even in MSS. which otherwise have close verbal similarity. *As dia chuimniugud-sain: de quibus hoc carmen:* [so-and-so] *cecinit*—these and similar expressions are used, even in nearly related MSS., at random, making it clear that in this matter the scribes had no stereotyped exemplars to keep their copies uniform. We infer, therefore, that in the autographs these formulae of introduction were not present; and that they were inserted only after the scribes had realized that human memory is untrustworthy, and that it was wiser to write out the poems in full. The same conclusion is

---

[2] Some few of the poems are written in full in μR.

indicated by the divergent forms of proper names sometimes appearing in the verse texts and in the associated prose. Thus in B, ¶ 156 *ff.*, we find several times the name "Caithear," but in the parallel poem no. XIV it appears as "Caicher."

The Extant Manuscripts.

There are in all five redactions of the text: *Min*, R¹, R², R³, and K, the last being O'Clery's[3] modernised version. Postponing the questions of their contents, origins, and mutual relationships, we may here briefly describe the manuscripts upon which an edition of the text has to be based.

Owing to the convenience of denoting a manuscript by a single letter only, I have taken the liberty of adopting symbols for certain well-known codices, different from those in ordinary use. Thus, I call the *Book of Leinster* L, not LL: the *Book of Ballymote* B, not BB: and for the two texts in the *Book of Lecan*, instead of *Lec¹* and *Lec²* (which would be too clumsy for constant reference), I have adopted the symbols A and M. The latter may be read and explained (at the reader's pleasure) not as "em," but as "lambda two."

The First Redaction.

Only two MSS. of R¹ survive, namely, L and F.

L. *The Book of Leinster* (T.C.D. Library, H.2.18), c. 1150 A.D. In this codex, which is too well-known to need description, our text occupies folios 1–13.

The folios measure about 12·7 × 9 inches[4]; and bear four columns, with about 51–53 lines of writing in each. The *recto* of the first folio must have for long remained unprotected by a binding, in consequence of which the writing is rendered partly illegible by dirt, wear, and other injury.

---

[3] I use the anglicised form here, because the genitive case of the native form cannot be accommodated to an English context: "ó Cléirigh's" is gibberish.

[4] In this and the other MSS. these measurements vary slightly from folio to folio; the vellum is not cut with mechanical uniformity.

The rest, as a whole, is readable enough; though the edges of
some of the folios are frayed, and, throughout, many of the
words and letters are thus damaged or lost. A transcript of
the first 115 pages of the MS., line for line and page for page,
was made in 1852 by Eugene O'Curry (L.5.20 in T.C.D.
Library). This is often useful in restoring writing that has
become illegible since his time; but it cannot be trusted with
full confidence, and he has shirked the task of trying to
decipher the first page, where his help would have been of the
utmost value.

F. *The Book of Fermoy* (R.I.A. Library, 23 E. 29). The
connexion of this copy of LG with the Book of Fermoy is
factitious and partial only. It is written upon twenty-two
folios of vellum, of which the first eight form a gathering,
bound into the front of the Book of Fermoy: the remaining
fourteen I had the good fortune to identify in one of the
Stowe MSS. (R.I.A. Library, D.3.1). The folios measure on
an average 10·5 × 8 ins. There are 31 lines of writing in
each column, and two columns on each page. The Fermoy
fragment, and the first two folios of the Stowe fragment, are
written upon in a coarse, bold hand, using very black ink
and a broad-pointed pen on which the writer leans heavily.
Dr. Best identifies the handwriting as that of Adam
ó Cianáin of Lisgoole, County Fermanagh, whose *obit* is
recorded in the *Annals of the Four Masters* at A.D. 1373.
On the third folio of the Stowe fragment (fol. 11 of the
complete book), in column *a*, after line 27, the handwriting
appears to change abruptly: but careful comparison shows
that the same scribe continues to work, using a pen with a
finer point. On the same folio, however, column δ, after
line 4, there is actually a change of scribe. s^2 F has a
rounder, and, on the whole, a better style of handwriting than
s^1 F. At first he decorates his capital letters with blobs of
colour, though not on the later pages: he is fond of ending
them with crudely drawn animal heads, which s^1 F never
does. After the change of the pen in the hand of s^1 F, the
number of lines in the column increases to 39. The whole
work ends abruptly at 22 γ 10, with the reign of Eochaid
Uairches in the "Roll of the Kings." The remainder of

column γ, and the whole of column δ, of this folio were left blank, suggesting that the copy stopped at this point because the remainder was lost from √F : an irrelevant anecdote about King David and a beggar has at some later time been scribbled into the empty space.[5] An additional leaf, possibly part of the earliest binding of the book, originally blank, is also now covered with scribbling. As in the case of L, the *recto* of the first folio of F is in a very bad condition from wear, tear, and dirt. It was cleaned chemically during the progress of the present work by Professor Ditchburn, of T.C.D., with the satisfactory result that most of the text, which I had abandoned as hopelessly illegible, proved recoverable. It should be noted that the folios in the Stowe MS., as at present bound, are misplaced. The first, which follows immediately after the last folio of the Fermoy fragment, is bound in as the seventh folio of the Stowe book.[6] The text carries on from there to the present end of the volume (eight folios) : then continues on the prefixed folios in this order— 6, 1, 2, 3, 4, 5.[7]

Of the lost MSS. of the First Redaction, *Q and *X, which are of considerable critical importance, we shall speak when occasion arises. *Q was the copy used by ∞ R³, *X was used by one of the glossators of R².

The redaction called *Míniugud*, which is a form of R¹, is more fully discussed below.

The Second Redaction.

The majority of the MSS. of LG belong to R². These are V, E, P, R, D, Λ, and A.

---

[5] Edited by S. H. O'Grady from two other MSS.; see *Mélusine* iv (1888), col. 163.   See also K. Meyer in *Arch. für Celt. Lex.* iii 321 for a different version.

[6] The bottom margin of this leaf has been clipped off, apparently to remove some scribbled matter : there is similar scribbling on the bottom margin of the following folio, *recto*.

[7] In references to this MS. in the present edition, the folios are numbered in their *true* order, not in the haphazard order in which they are bound.

V, a MS. in the Stowe collection (R.I.A. Library), now divided into three volumes (V¹ = D.5.1, V² = D.4.1, and V³ = D.1.3). V¹ consists of nine folios, with four columns of writing on each; size of leaves 11.8×8 ins., 51–55 lines of writing in each column. At the beginning there is an elaborately coloured interlaced monogram of the word IN: and throughout there are well-drawn initial letters. The whole is written in a beautiful neat hand, which, however, is rather cramped, and not perfectly easy to decipher. The MS. has undergone extensive re-inking, and it is not always certain that the restorer has done his work accurately. At the top of folio 1a of V¹ there are two faint, worn lines of writing in Gothic lettering—apparently a library mark; under ultra-violet light they seem to read *Monasterii Insi Patraic*, but they are too far gone to yield with assurance even to that powerful solvent of palæographical difficulties. V² has eight, V³ six folios: they are on the whole better preserved than V², which has suffered severely from wear. In V² the writing stops abruptly at 8 δ 9 (end of the poem *Fland for Ērind hi tigh*), after which the rest of the column is blank. We must infer that a gathering had been lost from √V, and that the scribe of V was unable to find means of filling the lacuna.[8] The gap extends to the end of the 13th quatrain of the poem *Gáedel glas* in Min: with the 14th quatrain the text resumes abruptly, on the first folio of V³, and runs on to the end of *Ēriu ardinis na rīgh*, which finishes the MS. There are coloured initials in V¹ and V², but not in V³: but the style of the writing, the size of the folios, and the number of lines in the column, leave no room for doubt that the three volumes originally formed one book. Fragments of other books, in vellum and in paper, quite irrelevant in contents, are now bound up with the two later volumes.

---

[8] The lacuna does not exist in the closely cognate copy A; the text here runs on intact over rather more than 8 leaves of A which have no equivalent in V. This clearly shows that A is not, as has been supposed, a transcript of V: it must be derived from √ V at latest. In μV the Roll of the Kings originally stopped at Sirna Sōeglach, and has been continued in a different but contemporary hand: μA knows nothing of this, and breaks off at Sirna—another demonstration that the two MSS. are not in "mother-and-daughter" relationship.

E, a manuscript once bound up in separate folios scattered through a miscellany of scraps class-marked E.3.5 in T.C.D. Library (Gwynn's *Catalogue*, no. 1433, p. 308): now collected once more into a single volume, and class-marked E.3.5., no. 2. It contains 16 folios, measuring 11.4×8.25 ins., with four columns of 48 lines of writing on each. There is hardly any ornamentation. The handwriting was recognised long ago by O'Curry (*Battle of Magh Leana,* p. 35, footnote) as that of Tórna ō Maeil-Chonaire, poet and historian to the earls of Desmond at the beginning of the fifteenth century: and this is confirmed by a scribal note at the bottom of folio 2 γ. He wrote carelessly; haplographies are frequent, usually corrected in the margin by himself or by a later reader. Many of the lenited letters, which were not dotted by the original scribe, have been dotted by a later meddler. On the other hand, there are many good readings, and the MS. is of considerable critical importance. A note at the bottom of fo. 9 verso claims ownership of the book for Muirges *ruadh* ua Maoil-Chonaire (a different person from the scribe of D), "wherever it may be found."

P, formerly in the Phillips Collection at Cheltenham, now in the National Library of Ireland, class-marked P. 10266. It has been described by Whitley Stokes,[9] who has, however, not observed that the fragment of LG (which he does not appear to have identified as such) is only by accident a part of the book. It is a single quaternion, 10×7.3 ins., prefixed to a fragment from another MS. with folios of a rather larger size. Only the first two folios contain LG material, and there does not appear ever to have been any more of the text. The writing is minute, running across the whole page in a single column of 41 lines. Folio 1 *recto* is utterly illegible, the whole page having been reduced with gallic acid and dirt to a uniform dead brownish black. A large monogram of IN, extending down the whole height of the page on the left-hand side, and followed (apparently) by PRI, in unusually large characters, can be traced; but nothing further. The rest of

---

[9] *Martyrology of Oengus* (Henry Bradshaw Soc. edition), p. ix ff.

the text is clear, extending from ⁊ *ní derna fáilte* (¶ 5A) to *risin mac mbec ragad* (¶ 119), where the scribe ceased abruptly from his work. Some parts of Folio 1 *verso* (the first nine lines and the poem No. 1) have been re-inked, not quite accurately. Though so fragmentary, the text is useful, as it helps considerably in the decipherment of some obscure passages in VE, the only other MSS. which have preserved the first folio of the text of R². There is no colophon : but Arabic figures are freely used in the text, and this and other indications suggest a date of about 1480–1520.

R, the only MS. of the older versions not in Dublin, is an early fifteenth-century copy contained in the well-known miscellany, Rawl. B. 512, in the Bodleian Library. This MS. has been described, and its contents catalogued, by Whitley Stokes[1] ; and it is here needless to go over the same ground. The text of LG occupies foll. 76 *recto*–100 *verso*. The beginning of the book is lost : calculation shows that two leaves are gone ; possibly three, if (as is improbable) the text contained the Nel-Moses pericope (¶ 118 ff.) and the long poem V written out in full. Another leaf has disappeared between ¶¶ 272–288. These defects took place before the addition of pagination to the MS., which ignores them. Two folios are numbered 76, the second being distinguished as 76 A : the first two folios are transposed in the binding. There are two columns upon each page, with 37 lines of writing in each column. At the end of the text of R² there comes the copy of *Míniugud* here called μR.

D, class-marked Stowe D.4.3 in the R.I.A. Library. This is a vellum MS., the pages being 9 × 7·5 inches, with two columns of writing upon every page except the *recto* of fol. 7, and the lower part of the *recto* of fol. 21, in which the writing runs across the page with about 56 letters in each line. The book seems to have been exposed to fire at some time : the lower and outer edges, and especially the lower

---

[1] *Tripartite Life of St. Patrick* (Rolls Series), vol. i, p. xiv ff.

outer angles, of most of the folios are badly scorched, and
the writing on the parts affected is often difficult to read.
The lines of writing are very irregularly disposed; so far as
I have counted them, they range in number from 29 to 41 in
the column. Appropriately to this irregularity, the handwriting is poor, sometimes not very legible. Forty-two folios
remain : two have been lost from the beginning, and the end
is also imperfect. The MS. is of considerable critical value,
and has some remarkable readings[11] : the scribe's name,
Muirges (or Muirgius) mac Pāidīn, appears in scribbles at
17 γ bottom, 25 β 14, and 35 δ bottom. In the last place
only has he given his father's name, and this has been partly
burnt away. He is a grumbler : at the bottom of 8 γ, in a
note now difficult to decipher, he appears to complain that
his ruler is too broad; on 11 γ he is troubled because his
light is bad; at 17 γ he has mislaid his *cailc*, that is, presumably, the pumice with which he smoothed the surface of
his vellum; and on 11 *recto* the shears of a bookbinder have
silenced a reference derogatory, as we may suppose, to his
parchment. In the present work the two lost initial leaves
are counted in, in references to this MS.; the first extant folio
being numbered "3," in accordance with the old pagination.
In the MS. a new pagination, starting from the first extant
folio, has been substituted in roughly written numerals, the
old pagination being sometimes either scratched out or written
over.

The scribe was certainly the Muirges mac Pāidīn ua
Maoil-Chonaire who made the transcript of the Book of
Fenagh in the R.I.A. Library in 1517, and who died in 1543.
Though the writing in the Fenagh volume is much more
careful, comparison of the two books leaves no room for
doubt that they come from the same hand. This being so,
we may infer that this MS. is the same as "The Book of

---

[11] Among these are a number of interpolations, evidently borrowed
from a copy of R¹, and all marked in the margin of the page as *Slicht
Libuir na Huidri*, "An extract from (literally, [following in] The track
of) *Lebor na Huidri*." This records the fact that a copy of LG, in the
R¹ Redaction, was included among the (now missing) contents of that
MS.

Baile ui Maoil-Chonaire, written by Muirghes mac Paidīn
ui Maoil-Chonaire out of Leabhar na Huidhri," which
O Clēirigh specifies as one of the sources of his own work.
The marginal notes referred to in the footnote have misled
him into supposing that the whole book was copied from LU.
See further on the MS. A, below.

A, the first text in *The Book of Lecan* (R.I.A. Library,
23.P.2). The impending publication of a facsimile of this
important volume makes it unnecessary to describe it here:
in the published catalogue of the Royal Irish Academy's
collection of MSS. there is a full analysis of its contents.
This text is at the beginning of the book, and has lost the
first nine folios: they were already gone in 1724.[12]   In
consequence the copy begins abruptly in the section relating
to the FirBolg (in the middle of the poem appended to
¶ 292). The complete text, including the copy of *Min.*
appended to R² (here called μA), covered 30 folios, with two
columns on each page, containing 41–55 lines of writing, so
far as they have been tested. It ends in the middle of
column 30 δ, with the following colophon, repeated immediately below by a later hand in a different ink: *Finit.
Adam o Cuirnin do sgrib do Gilla Isu mac Firbissigh .i.
d'ollam o Fiachrach, Anno. Do', M° CCCC° xuiij°.* "It
endeth. Adam ō Cuirnīn wrote it, for Gilla Isu mac Fir
Bisigh, the man of learning of the Ui Fiachrach, A.D. 1418."
This is the most exactly dated copy of the text which we
possess. Many of the folios have become semi-transparent
by contamination with some greasy substance, and the writing
on the one side shows through to the other, making decipherment difficult.

A is the only extant paper MS. (excluding some eighteenth
century copies, mentioned below) of any of the pre- O Clēirigh
redactions. It is Stowe A.2.4 in the R.I.A. Library, and

___

[12] Bishop Nicolson, *Irish Historical Library*, p. 38. The leaves from
this MS. now bound into H 2 17. in the library of T.C.D., are not
those missing from the beginning of the codex, as is stated by an
oversight in the catalogue of the T.C.D. Irish Manuscripts, p. 112.

apparently belongs to the seventeenth century. There are
47 leaves, 7.8×5.8 ins., some of them much tattered. I
have collated this copy sufficiently to assure myself that it is
a direct transcript of D. It reproduces slavishly the ortho-
graphical and other peculiarities of D, except for the not
infrequent mistakes of its own copyist. Some of these mistakes can be explained, on reference to D, by obscurities in
the script of the earlier MS. A is imperfect at both ends,
and has no independent value for the criticism of the text:
it has just the slight importance that in a few cases it does
not reproduce corrections that have been made *secunda manu*
in D, suggesting that these may have belonged to a time later
than its own transcription. But sA was so incompetent that
we cannot be sure even of this : he may have overlooked them,
or omitted them intentionally. In the present edition of LG,
A has been left out of consideration altogether.

Assuming that D was one of the sources followed by
O Clērigh, A was probably prepared for his use—not, however, *by* him, as it is not in his handwriting. Some leaves
of a different text, which though roughly scribbled appear
actually to be in O'Clery's writing, are bound up in the same
volume.

A lost MS. of this redaction, *Z, will be referred to as
occasion arises. It was the copy of R² used by a *glossator*
of R³ (*g* R³). The Manuscript of R² used by the *compiler*
of R³ (∞ R³) we shall call *W.

The Third Redaction.

R³ is contained in two MSS., B and M; and an important
fragment of a third, H, is extant.

B, *The Book of Ballymote* (R.I.A. Library, 23 P 12). In
this codex LG occupies folios 8–34 : on each page there are
two columns of writing, with 55–57 lines in each. Folios 9,
and 24–30 inclusive, are missing. The latter defect is of long
standing; but folio 9 must have been lost after the middle
of the eighteenth century, when two transcripts of the text

were made from this MS. One of these, written in 1728 by
Richard Tipper, here called β, is fairly good, though not
perfect; and it is of great value for restoring the text of the
missing folio. It is labelled on the binding "Book of Ballymote," and class-marked H.2.4 in T.C.D. Library (Gwynn's
Catalogue, 1295). The other is apparently lost, but two
copies were made from it: β^1, in a MS. written by Tadhg
Ó Neachtain, in or about the year 1745, and dubbed upon its
title-page *Psaltair na Teamhrach*, "The Psalter of Tara,"
though the binding is more soberly labelled "Miscellanea
Hibernica, transcribed by T. Ó Naghtan"; also in T.C.D.
Library (H.1.15, Gwynn's Catalogue, 1289): and β^2, a
pitifully illiterate production, class-marked Stowe D.3.2 in
the R.I.A. Library. These two MSS. share a considerable
number of mistakes and peculiar spellings, showing their
descent from a common more or less inaccurate original
($\sqrt{\beta^{12}}$) interposed between them and the ancestral B[13]; and
they are both so much inferior to β, that their only use is to
corroborate some of its peculiar readings, and to show that
these were really to be found in the missing leaf of B. In
very few cases can we accept a divergent reading of $\sqrt{\beta^{12}}$
in preference to β. Where we have B intact, these three
copies are useless, and are here ignored. Folios 24–30 were
lost from B before any of them was made: β does not
attempt to supply the deficiency; but $\sqrt{\beta^{12}}$ has filled it by
copying from the still extant μV, for collation shows beyond
the possibility of doubt that $s\sqrt{\beta^{12}}$ has here and there been
misled by peculiarities in μV (misspellings, a badly set-out
cor fá chasán, imperfectly legible writing, etc.). The version
of this missing portion in β^1 and β^2 is, therefore, of no value.

---

[13] I allow this to stand, because it is still possible as a statement of
the facts; but on subjecting my collations to a final revision, when I
considered the relationship between these two MSS. more closely, and
noted a number of places where a peculiar error in β^2 could be accounted
for by careless penmanship in β^1, I became more inclined to regard β^1
as a direct (though poor) copy of B, and β^2 a yet worse copy of β^1.
The hypothethical $\sqrt{\beta^{12}}$ thus disappears altogether, and β^2 loses all the
little value that it might have had.

M is the second text in *The Book of Lecan*, occupying folios 264–312.[14] It is a very peculiar text, having some interpolations (notably the story of Partholon's faithless wife Delgnat) not found in any other ancient version. √M was apparently imperfect: certainly the latter half of the "Roll of the Kings" was missing from it, and s M was compelled to supply the deficiency by a makeshift adaptation of a version of the saga of the *Bōrama* Tribute, differing in some respects from that in the Book of Leinster. The important lacuna in the first section of LG, to be described later, was also a serious imperfection in √M. The problems connected with this copy must, however, be considered as they arise.

The copyist of M was working against time. Even when he was called away for a few minutes, a deputy (s² M) took his place, and wrote during his absence. The text is, so to speak, punctuated by short groups of lines in the very distinctive handwriting of s² M, which alternate with the work of the main scribe (s¹ M), changing sometimes even in the middle of a line. There is never any crowding or over-running, as would be the case if s² M were a later scribe, filling in gaps that for any reason had been left by a predecessor. Presumably the writers of M could not obtain the use of √M for more time than was just sufficient for their work. As in such a case they would not have leisure to hunt for extraneous matter, it seems probable that the interpolations and other peculiarities of M were all transferred to that ms. bodily from √M. It is further possible that they were deprived of it before they were able to copy the whole of the Roll of the Kings, and that this, rather than a deficiency in √M, is the explanation of the peculiarity noticed in the preceding paragraph.

H is a fragment of five folios, 13·5 × 9·6 ins., with two columns on each page, and 56 lines of writing in the column. It is bound into a volume of miscellaneous fragments (H.2.15, no. 1, in T.C.D., Gwynn's Catalogue, 1316).

[14] Throughout this edition the old *foliation* of the Book of Lecan, in the upper right-hand corner of the *recto* of each folio, is used for reference, instead of the more recent *pagination* in square brackets in the bottom margin.

Four of these folios belong to the first section of LG, and contain matter nowhere else extant. The fifth has a version of the end of the Nemed section, cognate with that in K, and differing profoundly from every other text of this part of the book. With this the H copy of LG appears to have ended, the remainder of the folio being occupied with other matter. At the end of this folio there is a colophon which would seem to date the MS. to some time before 1252 (see Gwynn's Catalogue, p. 91), but the interpretation of the note is uncertain, and the date seems, if anything, too early for the language and especially the orthography of the MS. It is the pages, not the folios, in this miscellany which are numbered (as under, in pencil).[15] The first portion of LG occupies pp. 97–104, but the folios are not in their right order—they should run thus, 103–104, 97–98, 101–102, 99–100. The Nemed fragment is in the first column of page 67. About one-third of the upper portion of folio 103–104 has been torn away and lost.

In preparing for publication the three prose texts, I have chosen L, V, and B as the standard copies of R¹, R², and R³ respectively; and the book is printed as it appears in those MSS., except where some other fills a lacuna, or corrects an obvious error. Numerals, as well as the ordinary abbreviations and contractions, are expanded silently; and the marking of long vowels, which is quite haphazard in the MSS., is reduced to some sort of order (with horizontal strokes). In the tables of variants, and in places where a passage depends on one MS. only, the marking of prolongation (with accent-like strokes), is reproduced as in the original[16]: except on the

---

[15] There is an older, now obsolete, pagination in ink, which we may ignore.

[16] In a few cases marks of prolongation, inserted before I decided to give without such interference passages depending on a single MS., have evaded deletion and appear on the printed page. I have allowed them to stand, to avoid needless proof-correction: but these apart, the absence of such marks will be a useful indication to the reader that the text before him survives in one MS. only. In *English* contexts, meticulous accentuation has not been considered necessary.

letter *i*, where the accent-like mark is usually nothing more
than a distinguishing mark, like the dot in ordinary print.
This is here left out. I also omit the *punctum delens* placed
over "eclipsed" letters. By repeated collations an effort has
been made to attain to the ideal of recording every variant,
however trifling, presented by the manuscripts. The three
MSS. specified have been chosen, less because they are the
best copies of their respective redactions than because they
are the most complete. In fact, F probably is nearer to
∞ R¹ than L; and the late MSS. of R², DER, often give
readings preferable to those in V. M is admittedly more
complete than B, but it has too many eccentric readings and
interpolations to justify its being selected as the standard
for R².

The verse texts cannot be classified into "redactions,"
and they have to be treated in a different way. Of these I
have endeavoured to construct a text, giving the reader as
full an *apparatus criticus* of variant readings as possible, to
enable him to test, and, it may be, to improve upon it. I
have not, however, attempted to standardize the orthography,
which would involve an interference with the testimony of
the MSS. that I felt would be too drastic. The text does not
need to be treated like a Greek classical composition, where
it is of the first importance to recover the exact words of the
literary master who wrote it. The ideal which I have set
before myself is the humbler one, of making it possible for
a scholar to whom the MSS. are inaccessible to reconstruct the
text of any one of them, except in the matter of abbreviations
and marks of vowel prolongation. To have attempted to
reproduce all of these would have more than doubled the
bulk of the lists of *variae lectiones*, with no very apparent
advantage. This is not to say that they are unimportant :
on the contrary, I have gleaned some valuable hints on the
affiliation of MSS. from a comparison of such extraneous
matters as the ornamentation of initial capital letters, and
the abbreviations or other peculiarities of the caligraphy (or
cacography) of individual words.

In this connexion it may be said here that it is especially
interesting to compare the initial letters scattered throughout
V with those in D. In V they are neatly drawn and coloured,

EXAMPLES OF INITIAL LETTERS FROM D AND V.

though in design they show only too clearly that the art to
which they belong was already moribund or dead : in D they
are badly drawn, in an ink outline only. But it is obvious that
they are the same designs. As D cannot possibly be a copy
of V, it is clear that the two MSS. derive their ornamentation,
like their text, from a common original. This fact, which
gives us a new criterion for determining the affinity of
manuscripts, may be illustrated by the specimens here reproduced,[16a] from tracings made with the kind consent of the
Council of the R.I.A.

O'Clery's Redaction.

K has already been published as far as the *Roll of the
Kings*, and need not here be repeated. It is of little critical
value, having been much manipulated editorially, but there
is enough to show that its compiler had access to MSS. no
longer extant. He has a long version of the Partholón-
Delgnat story, differing from that in M almost throughout :
and his Nemed text, though it has affinities with the unique
text in H, displays a like independence. The chief importance of this version is its rich glossarial matter.

The last degeneration of the text is found in two nineteenth
century MSS. in the British Museum (Egerton, 101, 105), which
give us O'Clery's version with some of the difficulties cut out
and easy bits of Keating's History substituted.

THE CONTENTS OF THE BOOK.

The book in its present form, in all the principal
redactions, falls into ten separate and independent sections,
as under—

[16a] The small ᵹ, to the left, and the upper O, O, R are from V;
the lower O, O, R and the large ᵹ are from the corresponding paragraphs in D. (Notice the broken lines and loose ends in the first of

C

—and notwithstanding the profound differences in detail
between the different redactions, they agree in the main lines
of their contents.

Prof. A. C. Clark, in a work to whose teaching I gladly
acknowledge my indebtedness,[17] has laid it down as a principle
that "a text is like a traveller who goes from one inn to
another, losing an article of luggage at each halt." By this
he means, that the text sheds passages piecemeal as it is
copied from manuscript to manuscript; so that when delivered
to its reader at the end of a succession of transcriptions, it
is shorter—often considerably so—than when it left the
author's hand, to run the gauntlet of scribal carelessness,
sleepiness, incompetence, and laziness. Other things being
equal, a longer text is, therefore, to be preferred, by the
critical editor, to a shorter text. That this principle is sound
when applied to classical literature no one who has made a
careful study of Prof. Clark's work can doubt: but it breaks
down when applied to Irish texts. In Ireland, the philomath,
eager to air his stock of erudite inanity, early made his baleful
appearance. To adapt the formula of Prof. Clark's analogy,
an Irish text is like a traveller who, as he passes from inn
to inn, stuffs his portmanteau with the china dogs, the waxen
fruits, the crochet-work antimacassars, and all the other
futilities with which his successive lodgings are adorned. It
is quite possible that when LG was drawn up by its first
compiler, it was not longer than what would fill three or four
sheets of notepaper. It has grown to its present dimensions
by an extraordinary accretion of glosses, interpolations, and
other amplifications. Certainly the old canon of New Testament criticism, *brevior lectio praeferenda verbosiori*, is here
applicable!

It does not require any great insight to see that the book
is in reality a combination of two originally independent
documents. The block of material, sections III to VII, has
been interpolated: sections II and VIII run on continuously,
and were no doubt at one time in immediate connexion. If
we cut the interpolated sections out, we find ourselves left

---

these letters, showing that the artist, though a fair draughtsman, did
not understand the principles which regulated designs such as this.)
  [17] *The Descent of Manuscripts* (Oxford, 1918), at p. 23.

with a *History of the Gaedil*, based upon the history of the Children of Israel as it is set forth in the Old Testament, or (perhaps more probably) in some consecutive history paraphrased therefrom. The parallelism, which can be displayed in tabular form as below, is too close to be accidental.

Old Testament.	*Lebor Gabála.*

The biblical history from the Creation to the Sons of Noah is borrowed by the Irish historians : after which—

Shem is selected and his genealogy is followed out . . .	Japhet is selected and his genealogy is followed out . . .
until we reach Terah and his son Abram, upon whose family the historian specializes . . .	until we reach Nēl and his son Gāedel, upon whose family the historian specializes . . .
down to the two wives and the numerous sons of Jacob.	down to the two wives and the numerous sons of Mīl.
A servitude in Egypt begins with a friendly invitation from an Egyptian king . . .	An oppression in Egypt begins with a friendly invitation from an Egyptian king . . .
and the children of Israel are delivered by the adopted son of an Egyptian princess.	and the children of Nēl are delivered by the son-in-law of the Egyptian king. This deliverer meets and almost joins forces with his prototype Moses.[18]
They wander for a long time, beset by enemies . . .	They wander for a long time, beset by enemies . . .
and sojourn at a mountain (Sinai) where they receive the doom that not they but their children shall reach the Promised Land; so they wander . . .	and sojourn at a mountain (Riphi) where they receive the doom that not they but their children shall reach the Promised Land; so they wander . . .
till their leader sees the Promised Land from the top of a mountain afar off.	till their leader sees the Promised Land from the top of a tower afar off.

---

[18] Some portions of this incident are probably due to later interpolation: it is in essence, however, at least as old as Nennius.

Old Testament—con.	*Lebor Gabāla*—con.
He dies: but his successor conducts the people to a subjugation of the former inhabitants of Canaan, amid circumstances of marvel and mystery . . .	He dies: but his successors conduct the people to a subjugation of the former inhabitants of Ireland, amid circumstances of marvel and mystery . . .
and to a successful colonization of the country.	and to a successful colonization of the country.
The history then concludes with a brief record of the successive kings (beginning with a partition of the country), allotting in most cases not more than a single paragraph to individual kings.	The history then concludes with a brief record of the successive kings (beginning with a partition of the country), allotting in most cases not more than a single paragraph to individual kings.

We infer that the book originally described only a single "taking"—that of the Celtic Irish, to whom the author himself belonged, and in whom he was chiefly interested. This is why *Gabāla*, in the singular number, still remains in the title of the book: it is not the "Book of Takings of Ireland," but "The Book of The Taking."

The intruded matter (§§ III-VII) may have had some historical basis, but much of it partakes rather of the nature of a *Theogonia*: see the introductions prefixed to each of the sections, where their relation to mythology and history is discussed. We shall see later that this group of sections is itself capable of further analysis into separate component elements.

These different histories appear to have been in existence, and (even if their combination had already been effected) to have been still available in their separate form, when Nennius wrote his *Historia Britonum*, about the end of the eighth century.[19] He must have been able to refer to a literary source of information about the Pre-Milesian invasions: but for the history of the Milesians themselves he apparently had

---

[19] *Historia Nennii*, ed. Petrie in *Materials for the History of Great Britain*, p. 56: ed. Faral in *La Légende arthurienne* (Paris, 1929), vol. iii, pp. 11, 12. For convenience I assume the historical existence of "Nennius": after all, *someone* must have written the book which bears his name. Also for convenience I call him by the old-established form of his name, rather than by the less familiar "Nemnius."

to depend on the oral information conveyed to him by persons described as *peritissimi Scottorum* (and condemned by some of his glossators with the words, *nulla certa historia originis Scottorum continetur*). His abstract of the Pre-Milesian invasions is analysed at a later stage of our work; the only point about it which we need notice here is the single word "Damhoctor" [20]—which Nennius wrongly supposes to be a personal name, denoting the leader of one of the invading troops whose progeny was supposed to be still in Ireland at the time when Nennius wrote. But evidently it is nothing but the Irish for "a company of eight persons": this misunderstood word is a valuable testimony that for *this* part of the history Nennius had a written text in the Irish language at his elbow.

The Relation between the Redactions.

The relationship existing between (*a*) the Manuscripts and (*b*) the Redactions has been discussed by Thurneysen[21] and Van Hamel.[22] I may say that I refrained from making a close study of these most important contributions to the subject till I had formed my own conclusions, so as to arrive at an independent opinion.

The very simple *stemma* of the MSS. drawn up by Van Hamel (*op. cit.*, p. 115) is hardly an adequate representation of their inter-relationship. The facts, which are more complex, must be allowed to develop themselves as we proceed: for the moment it is sufficient to advise readers of Van Hamel's most valuable study, that the *Míniugud* appendix of V (which Van Hamel calls "S") is *not* lost: and that A (which Van Hamel calls "Lec 1") is not a daughter MS. of his S, but, if we may further develop the genealogical terminology, a sort of "niece." Two of the many proofs of this have been given already. Likewise, F cannot be considered a direct copy of L; in many places it

---

[20] We need not trouble ourselves with the variant reading *Clamhoctor* adopted in Petrie's edition.

[21] "Zur irischen Handschriften und Litteraturdenkmälern, zweite Serie": *Abhandl. der k. Gesellschaft der Wissenschaften zu Göttingen*, neue Folge, xiv, no. 3, 1913.

[22] "On Lebor Gabála." Z.C.P. x (1915), p. 97.

preserves an older and purer text. Moreover, V (Van
Hamel's S) is not an original text, but a faulty copy; in
some places even the late MSS., E and P, give preferable
readings.

As to the Redactions, both Thurneysen and Van Hamel
recognise the five different versions, R¹, R², R³, Min, and K,
as they are here called. Thurneysen calls them A, B, C,
B III, and D respectively (B II being the synchronistic
matter appended to R²). Van Hamel uses a similar
symbolism—A, Ba, C, Bb, D. Their distribution of the
MSS. among the redactions is the same as mine, except that
Thurneysen counts F among the MSS. of C (= R³). This
Van Hamel corrects, and Thurneysen would probably himself
adopt the correction after another examination of the text.
But he is not without justification: for R³ is based upon a
lost MS. of R¹, here called *Q, and F is in many respects much
more closely akin to *Q than to L, the MS. adopted by all of
us as typical of R¹.

Van Hamel follows Thurneysen's notation to avoid confusion; but he objects to it on account of the secondary place
which it assigns to the B-group (R²). This redaction is, in
his opinion, of primary importance for the history of the
text, bringing us nearer to the original form than any other.
"B" he considers to be fuller than "A"; and, although he
admits that neither is a copy of the other, he regards "A"
as a mere abstract of the common original, omitting, as
irrelevant, details which from the first were included in the
text, and which "B" preserves.

But on the principle laid down above (p. xxvi), in dealing
with an Irish text, the fuller it is of extraneous detail, the
more likely it is to be *remote* from the original version.

As for Min, appended to the three R² MSS. V, A, R, it is
obviously cognate with "A" (R¹); but it is equally obvious
that it is neither a copy nor an abstract of "A," but an
independent version. Apparently it represents a stage of
the R¹ tradition slightly earlier than that contained in the
extant MSS. of R¹; but it certainly belongs to that group.

What, then, is the relation between these versions? As I
understand it, it is as follows:—

We start with a *Liber Occupationis Hiberniae*, a sort of

quasi-historical romance, with no backing either of history or tradition; an artificial composition, professing to narrate the origin of the Gaedil onward from the Creation of the World (or the Flood), their journeyings, and their settlement in *their* "promised land," Ireland. This production was a slavish copy, we might almost say a parody, of the Biblical story of the Children of Israel. The germ which suggested the idea to the writer was undoubtedly the passage in Orosius (I. 2. 81), wrongly understood as meaning that Ireland was first seen from Brigantia in Spain, where (*ibid.*, § 71) there was a very lofty watch-tower. This suggested a reminiscence of Moses, overlooking the Land of Promise from Mount Pisgah: and the author set himself to work out the parallel, forward and backward. Incidentally Orosius gave trouble to Irish topographers, ancient and modern, by speaking of an Irish river *Scena*, setting them on a hunt for a non-existent *Inber Scēne*. As *se* conventionally represents the sound of *sh* (compare the Vulgate Judges, xii, 6, where the Hebrew word *shibbōleth* is rendered *scibboleth*), we must pronounce this word as *Shena*, and it is then easily recognised as Orosius' version of *Sinann* (genitive *Sinna*) or "Shannon." Further, we must assume that this quasi-Israelite history was written *in Latin*.[23]

Next we must postulate a separate text, compounded out of a number of separate sagas (or rather a number of varieties of one saga), but with a much better claim to enshrine genuine traditional (though not necessarily historical) material. This document still existed as an independent entity in the time of Nennius—or, to be more exact, Nennius had access to a manuscript, possibly of some antiquity, which preserved it, or some of it, in its independent form. It was a brief treatise on the pre-Gaedilic inhabitants of Ireland: and as it contained the expression *dāmh ochtair*, "a troop of eight persons," which Nennius mistook for a proper name, it must have been written in Irish. It does not

---

[23] A clear proof of translation from Latin is presented by some of the place-names, which have been transferred unintelligently into their Irish context in the accusative case. Thus in ¶ 156, to cite but one of many examples, *sech Albaniam . . . sech Ghothiam* must have a Latin original behind them.

appear to have contained the stories of Cessair and the other
antediluvian colonists.

Liber Occupationis soon began to be taken seriously : and
it was inevitable that the small tract just mentioned should
become combined with it, in order to make its historical
record more complete. This changed its character, turning it
into a history of Ireland, rather than a history of the people
then dominant in the country. Nevertheless its title remained
unchanged : it was still *Liber Occupationis*. The interpolation spoilt the logical form of the history : for its readers,
having at last after many vicissitudes reached Ireland, were
now obliged to jump suddenly back to the beginning, both
in time and in space, in order to follow out the second strand
which had thus been interwoven with the narrative. But the
earlier invasions were still of subordinate interest, and for a
time were most likely differentiated by their language from
the main current of the Latin story. If we could be sure
that the opening paragraphs of Min have not been drastically
compressed, the scanty notice there found of the earlier
invasions would very closely resemble the form of this part
of the book when it had reached this stage of the development.

At about the same time, the Cessair narrative (an old
flood-myth mixed up with some *Dindšenchas* material) was
committed to writing, but whether in Latin or in Irish is not
very clear : presently it found a place in front of the interpolation. See further the Introduction to that section.

The history of the text thereafter divided into two streams.
Two schools of history, retaining its framework, each of them
working independently of, and often at variance with, the
other, added new material as they found it.

The next stage was inaugurated by translation from Latin
into Irish. The first translation to be made was undoubtedly
from the text underlying Min. The translator headed his
work, very naturally, "An explanation of *Liber Occupationis*." By now the historical nature of the book was a
fully accepted tradition : it was regarded as a true record of
the past of Ireland and of her people : and in view of its
importance it was considered desirable to make it accessible to
students whose Latin was unequal to a study of the original
text. The associated poems, at this stage not yet incor-

porated with the written text, were of course in Irish from
the first.

A generation or two later, the "A" text, with the
additional material which had accumulated in the interval,
was translated again (R¹); as was also, now for the first time,
the "B" text (R²).

This reconstruction explains all the phenomena completely :

(1) The parallel "Israel" and "Ireland" story.

(2) The short Nennius text, based on an original in Irish,
enumerating the earlier invasions, but ignoring the Milesian
colony.

(3) The mention of a single invasion in the title, though a
large number of invasions are enumerated in the text.

(4) The general similarity of Min and R¹, though the verbal
differences forbid us to regard either as a copy of the other.

(5) The word *miniugud*, "explanation" in the title of Min.

(6) The similarity of framework in R¹ and R², though the
two texts are so profoundly different that they can never have
had a common Irish original.

It may be further suggested that the Latin preface to
Min, where a parallel is drawn between Ireland and Adam's
Paradise, and where there are obvious reminiscences of
Orosius, is actually the preface of the original *Liber
Occupationis,* at least in the form to which it had evolved
at the time when the translation of Min was made. It was
a preface, not an intrinsic part of the text: and subsequent
translators passed it over altogether.

The next phase began when some owner of an R² text, no
longer extant, got hold of a copy of Min. Though R² contains
matter not in Min or R¹, the contrary is also true: and R²
is especially unsatisfactory (from the point of view of a
historian who wants to know everything) in the section containing the Roll of the Kings. I do not agree that this
section, in its earliest form, is an addition to the original text.
I believe that a germ of this record formed an essential part
of the text from the first, and that it developed with the rest.
The postulated scholar sought to remedy the defects of his
version by appending an abbreviated version of Min to his
copy of R². Where Min contained matter already in R², he
left it out, merely writing *ut supra dixi* or the like : this is
enough to show that Min, as we have it, is not independent

                                                            d

of the text to which it is appended. The MS. to which this addition was made we may call √A A R. There is no evidence that either E or D was within its family, or ever possessed this supplementary appendix.

R³ is the pastepot - and - scissors work of a man who anticipated the systematizing labour of Ō Clēirigh. Vexed at the discrepancies between the two traditions, and having a considerable library at his disposal, he took a text of R¹ (*Q) and wrote it out with many interpolations, partly derived from R² (*W), partly from other sources. As we shall see, his MS. of R¹ was imperfect; it had lost the first page, as well as the Partholōn and Nemed sections.

K is also an artificial re-handling of the text. The biblical introduction is, of set purpose, swept away, and the successive invasions are arranged in a more logical order. This redaction is based on R² (D), though it shows some affinities with M; but the compiler *certainly* used a different copy of R², no longer extant, and he took arbitrary liberties with the text. There are many genealogical and other interpolations from sources outside the tradition.

It is my pleasant duty to express my acknowledgements to the Librarians and other officials of the Libraries in which the MSS. are preserved, for unfailing help and courtesy : to Professors Bergin and Eoin Mac Neill, Dr. R. I. Best, the Rev. Paul Grosjean, S.J., Dr. Myles Dillon, and Miss M. Joynt, for permitting me to consult them on various linguistic and other questions that arose during the progress of the work; to Professor R. W. Ditchburn, Trinity College, Dublin, for his unfailing interest and patience in the trouble-some task of photographing illegible passages; to the lamented Provost M. R. James of Eton College, and to the Venerable Archdeacon Seymour, for valuable help in some of the questions on Apocrypha which arose in the criticism of the Biblical prolegomena in Part I; and to the Very Rev. Canon Boylan, LITT.D., for his great kindness in putting at my service a copy of the *Genesis* volume of that magnificent monument of scholarship and of typography, the Vatican edition of the Vulgate text of the Bible.

SECTION I.

From the Creation to the Dispersal of the Nations.

Introduction.

In accordance with the artificial scheme of *Liber Occupationis*, the history of the world from the Creation to the Tower of Babel is first recapitulated. The original form of the text was probably something like this:—

> "In the beginning God made heaven and earth. He gave the bailiffry of Heaven to Lucifer, of earth to Adam. Lucifer sinned and was cast into Hell. He was envious of Adam, for he was assured that Adam would take his place in Heaven. Whereupon he came and tempted Eve to sin, and Adam was driven out of Paradise. The children of Adam sinned thereafter, in that Cain slew Abel. Seth, the third son of Adam, is the ancestor of all the men of the world, for the Flood drowned the whole seed of Adam except Noah and his three sons, Shem, Ham, Japhet. Shem settled in Asia, Ham in Africa, Japhet in Europe. We Gaedil are descended from Japhet."

As we read the text in its present form, and compare the divergent versions, we realise that everything not contained in this bald summary must be a glossarial accretion.

This summary was drawn up before the Vulgate text of the Old Testament had become familiar in Ireland : certainly not later than the eighth century. The Biblical quotations are from an earlier text, as is shown in detail below, in the notes appended to each paragraph. The abbreviator of Min left out the Biblical portion of that version, so that it is lost to us : but it is still possible to recover something of the history of its evolution. We may safely presume that an early intrusion was ¶ 2 (in the form of a bare list of the works of Creation). ¶ 5 entered later ; ¶ 6 was at first shorter than it is now ; and the genealogical matter ¶ 7–10 developed

L.G.—VOL. I.   B

gradually from very small beginnings. The document upon
which two of the interpolations in ¶ 9 are based was early
in existence, but they did not enter the text till a late stage
of its formation.

Besides LF, the extant mss. of R^1, I recognise two important mss., now lost, which have had an influence on the
development of the text. These are *Q, *X. Both of these
were good copies: *X, I am inclined to think, on the whole
the better of the two. *Q began with a highly ornate initial
IN, which occupied a large part of the front page: and the
lettering of the remainder of the page, if not of the folio,
was of extra large size. Some reminiscences of this arrangement, which may be ultimately derived from *Q, appear in
VP. LB also have the large initial IN, and M has got large
letters in its first column: but as will appear presently, these
latter are *not* survivals of the *Q tradition. *Q existed in
a mutilated form down to the time of ∞R^3, and it formed
the chief foundation of his work.

The history of the mutilation is very interesting. It is
evident that $\sqrt{R^2}$ had lost its first folio. One of the owners
of that ms., to repair the deficiency, tore out and appropriated
the first folio of *Q: this made possible the palæographical
influence suggested in the preceding paragraph. By a
chance, this produced continuous sense with the beginning
of the second folio of $\sqrt{R^2}$; though the sense is absurd. Only
in this way can we explain the fact that R^1 and R^2 are
practically identical for the first few paragraphs, and then,
with startling suddenness, fly apart rather than diverge, and
never again have a paragraph in common. Even the verse-
extracts are often set in different contexts. It also explains
the further significant fact that at the point where the texts
part company, a statement is made in R^2, inconsistent with
everything that follows, to the effect that the Flood was a
punishment for the murder of Abel. This statement has
been accidentally produced by the combination of the first
half of a sentence at the bottom of the first folio of *Q with
the second half of a sentence at the top of the second folio
of $\sqrt{R^2}$.

The continuous use of *Q by ∞R^3 begins *immediately*
after this mutilation, proving that *Q was actually the copy

which he used. We shall see presently that ∞ R³, in his
turn, repaired the damage to *Q by tearing out the opening
folios of a translation of the Book of Genesis, and substituting
it for the missing matter. When this act of pillage was
performed, or subsequently, one of the Genesis folios was
torn across: and this accident has made it possible, as is
shown in the proper place, to arrive at some approximation
to an idea of the size of the folios of *Q, and the amount of
literary matter that would go upon each. Now, the first of
these folios must have contained the matter at the beginning,
common to the two redactions R¹ R² (in the present form of
the latter): and it is insufficient to fill one of the ordinary
folios of *Q. We infer, therefore, that much space must have
been expended upon a large initial, and in letters of an extra
large size upon the opening page.

The importation of "Iofer Niger" into ¶ 4, derived from
the Latin Life of St. Juliana, gives us another chronological
hint. If the Old Latin Biblical excerpts suggest an eighth-
century date at latest for the compilation, the name of the
demon suggests a ninth-century date for the beginning of
glossation, the date of the Juliana text being about 800 A.D.
As Iofer Niger exists in L (corrupted), *Q (first folio, transferred to R²) and *X, a MS. which underlies some glossarial
matter in R², he must have been found in √LF *X *Q. This
manuscript, therefore, contained the full text as we have it,
except for such interpolations as were afterwards incorporated. (Though it will afterwards appear that *Q probably
lacked the Partholōn and Nemed sections.) F knows nothing
of Iofer Niger; he must, therefore, have been still glossarial
in √F and passed over by s F.

The history of the gloss in ¶ 1, of the Iofer Niger interpolation in ¶ 4, and of the interpolation ¶ 5, as summarized
in the notes on these passages, is all self-consistent. It
shows that three stems branched off from √LF *X *Q, becoming respectively the parents of L, *X, and F *Q. The
F* Q tradition is slightly the oldest of the three, but the *X
tradition is nearly as old, and in some cases preserves better
readings; it is a pity that we have so little of this MS. F is
a curious text, a mixture of L and *Q; but though very
closely cognate with *Q, it has too much in common with L

to be divorced from it altogether. Though actually a later
MS. than L, it preserves an older stage of the tradition, and
has not travelled so far from it as L has done.

After the extant portion of the original form of R² begins,
the two redactions have nothing in common. This can be
shown by a summary in parallel columns:—

	R¹.	R².
¶ 1.	Genesis I 1.	
2.	List of Works of Creation.	
3.	Lucifer and Adam: revolt of Angels.	Taken over into R² with the first leaf of *Q.
4.	Envy of Lucifer. The Fall.	
5.	Sentence on Adam.	
6.	Cain and Abel.	

	R¹.	R².
7.	Genealogy of Shem: the Flood mentioned.	¶ 11. The Flood.
8.	Dispersal of Nations.	12. Details of the Flood.
9.	Genealogy of Noah.	13. Effects of the Flood.
10.	Genealogy of Magog.	14. The Raven and the Dove.
		15. Noah comes out of the Ark. Dispersal of Nations.
		16. Genealogy of Gãedel Glas.
		17. Chronology.
		18. Nēl goes to Egypt.
		19. A poem on the foregoing history.

It must surely be evident that the brief mention of the
Flood in R¹ is original, while the long and laboured paraphrase
of the Biblical story in R² is imported. The details of the
genealogies are taken from different and mutually contradictory sources. Without doubt, the lost beginning of R²
differed in a like degree from the first six paragraphs of R¹
which were substituted for it: we can have no direct
knowledge of what it may have contained, but we may be
absolutely certain that it emphasized the divine command
on the Sethites to abstain from intermarriage with the
Cainites, and that this command, and the disobedience of it
by the Sethites, came after the R² narrative of the death of
Abel, and was the original antecedent to the Flood narrative—
not improbably as we have it in ¶ 53, which may come, either
from Sex Aetates Mundi, or from R² through *Z.

The redaction R³ is not, like R¹ and R², an independent work. It is essentially a composite, based on the two preceding redactions. The foundation of it is R¹, but it is swelled with large interpolations from R² and from other sources.

The manuscript of R¹ used by ∞ R³ was unquestionably *Q, after it had suffered the loss of its first leaf. For the text of R¹ as it appears in R³ begins, as we have said above, immediately after the lacuna thus caused. To supply the deficiency, ∞ R³ tore the opening leaves out of an Irish translation of the Book of Genesis,[1] thereby killing the translation, of which no other copy survives, and which would have been of enormous linguistic value. This, with its extensive interpolated glosses, occupies ¶¶ 20–85. The relation between the remainder of R³, § I, and the previous redactions is set forth in the following table :—

Paragraph.	Found in MSS.	Source.
86	H	Poem no. V.
87	MH	R². An appended interpolation from Comestor's *Historia Scholastica*.
*88	BMH	R¹. ¶ 7.
*89	BMH	R¹. ¶ 8. Interpolation from *Sex Aetates Mundi*.
90	H	Apparently a different but parallel text.
91	H	*Sex Aetates Mundi*.
*92	BMH	R¹. ¶ 8.
93	H	R². ¶ 15.
*94	BMH	R¹. ¶ 9.
95	H	*Sex Aetates Mundi*, with many interpolations from Isidore, etc.
96	H	Comestor.
97	H	Some other source, not identified.
*98	BMH	R¹. ¶ 9 (end).
*99, 100	BMH	R¹. ¶ 10 much interpolated.

The paragraphs marked with an asterisk, if read continuously (omitting interpolations) will give the text of this part of R¹ as it appeared in *Q.

---

[1] If not of the whole Old Testament, or even the whole Bible.

The Biblical Excerpt.

Reviewing the Biblical excerpt, and its relation to the text as a whole, we naturally ask first if it was prepared *ad hoc* by the compiler of R³, or borrowed by him from some translation previously in existence. To this question there can be but one reasonable answer. Much of the matter in the Biblical chapters was altogether irrelevant to the purpose of ∞ R³ : a short abstract, such as is given by R¹, would have served him as well, or better. The translator expended much trouble over his work; the evidence that he collated the Greek Septuagint with the Vulgate text cannot be set aside; to do this merely as a preface to a historical tract relating to Ireland would involve a heavy expenditure of time, trouble, and valuable parchment. Collation of texts in the Middle Ages, without the easily read printed page, and without alphabetical indexes and other apparatus, would have been a much more formidable task than it is to-day. Certainly the scribes who have transmitted R³ appear to have found much of this preliminary matter wearisome and out of place, as is shown by the reduction of the frequent repetitions of the original (as, for example, I 25, and the list of creatures preserved in the Ark). Another point is the difference in literary style that we feel between the Biblical excerpt and its present context. The translator has certain peculiar mannerisms, to which attention is drawn in the critical notes, and which give him an individuality.

On the other hand, it would be so easy to tear from another MS. the pages required, that we are obliged to accuse ∞ R³ of having committed this crime, to save himself the trouble of otherwise replacing the missing first page of the exemplar before him.

Some examination of the nature of the text which formed the basis of the translator's work now becomes necessary.

For purposes of reference we shall denote the Latin MS. which lay before the translator by the symbol Δ. (New Testament critics have appropriated this symbol to the ninth-century Greco-Latin Codex Sangallensis; but as we shall here have no occasion to refer to that MS., there will be no consequent inconvenience.) Δ was certainly a copy of the Vulgate; from the translation it is possible to restore some of its readings with sufficient assurance to determine its affinities. The chief passages in which Δ deviated from the Standard Text, as constructed in the Vatican Variorum edition, are enumerated below, with a list of the MSS. (not including early printed texts and editions) agreeing with it.[2]

I 2. *erant*: GᶜΛᴴXΠᶜᴰΣᴼBAΦⱽ*ᐧᐧᐧᐧ

I 2. *Domini*: ΛᴴB

I 4. *Deus*: GᶜTMⁱΦᴿᴬ*ZGVPΨM

I 4. *a tenebris*: GᶜΛᴴΠᶜᴰΣᴼBTΦᴿᴬ²ZGVPP²ΨF²MΩM

I 12. *facientem*: ΛᴴΠᶜᴰΩˢ

I 14. *et*: CXΠᶜᴰΣᴼMΦⱽᴾᐧᴬMPΨᴮᴰF²ΩSJM

I 16. omit *ut praeesset*: ΣM

I 18. *a tenebris*: ΛᴴΠᶜᴰΦVP²

I 20. *reptilia*: CΦᴿᴬZG

I 21. *motabilem*: C²ΛL²ᴴΠᴰ*ΣᴼBTMΦᴿᴬZGVΓᴼ²ᐧᴬM PΨᴮᴰFMΩSJM

I 26. omit *que*: CXΠᶜᴰΣᵀᴼMᴼΨF*

II 2. *sexto*: Σᵀ²ΨF*

II 2. *Deus*: O

II 4. *sunt*: ΛL²ᴴX²ΦⱽΨBDF

II 11. *Fison*: CΛᴴXΣᵀᴼMB

III 8. omit *Dei*: X

III 9. ins. *Adam*: CXᐧᴬM

III 11. ins. *Deus*: C*ΛᴴΣᵀᴼMΨF²Ωᴶ

III 20. *Eua*: CΛᴸXΠᴰΣᵀᴼMBTΦᴿᴬZGVPOᐧᴬM²PΨᴰMΩSJM

IV 1. *Euam*: CΛᴸᴴXΠᴰΣᵀᴼMBTΦᴿᴬZGVPᐧᴬMΨᴰMΩSJ

IV 15. *Cain in signum*: ΛᴴΣᴼMBΦᴿᴬZGVPP²ΩS²M

IV 17. ins. *filium nomine*: XΣᵀᴼM

VI 8. *Deo*: ΣᴹTMΦᴿᴬGVPᐧᴹ*ΨM

VII 17. ins. xl *noctibus*: ΛᴴXΣᵀ₂PΨMΩS²M

VIII 7. ins. *non*: ΛᴴX²ΠᶜᒾᴰᒾΣᴼM²BΑ²ΦZ²V²PP*ΨMΩSJM

VIII 17. ins. *-que*: GᶜΛᴴXΣᵀᴼMΩS

XI 20. *Saruch*: XΣᵀᴼ*ΨᴮᴰFMΩS

XI 22. *Nachor*: ΛLᴴXΠᶜΣᴼT²MΦᴿᴬZ²GVPPΨᴮᴰFMΩSJM

XI 26. *Nachor*: ΛLᴴΠᴰ²ΣᴼT²M²ΦᴿᴬZGVPPΨᴮᴰFMΩSJM

XI 26. *Aram*: AKΨᴹΩM

In the above and the following tables, an asterisk denotes a reading abolished by a corrector: these must be reckoned,

---

[2] For details about the manuscripts indicated by the symbols, reference must be made to the Vatican edition; it may be said, however, that the large letters denote families, the small letters individual MSS.

for they presumably belonged to the original tradition of the family to which the MS. belonged. Readings denoted by (¹), (²) are corrections *prima manu* and *secunda manu*. Though they are noted here, they are not taken into account in classifying the MSS. for our present purpose. Some of the above readings may possibly be due to LXX influence. Disregarding, however, this possibility for the moment, we now arrange the Vulgate MSS. in the order of their frequency in the foregoing table, as follows :—

Σ^O 15 + 1*	Φ^R 10	C 7 + 1* (1²)	G^G 4
Λ^H 15	Φ^G 10	H^C 7 (1²)	M 3 (1¹1²)
X 13 (2²)	B 9	Ψ^B 7	O 3 (1²)
Φ^V 12 + 1* (1²)	Ψ^D 9	P 6 + 1* (3²)	A 2 (1²)
Ψ^M 12	Π^D 8 + 1* (2²)	Ψ^F 5 + 2* (4²)	Θ^G 0
Ω^S 11 (2²)	Φ^A 8 + 1* (1²)	T 6 (2²)	Θ^H 0
Σ^M 11 (1²)	Σ^T 8 (2²)	Θ^A 6	G 0
Φ^P 11	Φ^Z 8 (2²)	Θ^M 4 + 2* (1²)	
Ω^M 11	Ω^J 8	A^L 4 (2²)	

The standard text of the Vatican editors is based chiefly upon three important MSS., lettered O, A, G: and it is a logical consequence that in a list of deviations from the Standard Text in any other MS., the number of agreements with these three copies should come at the bottom of the list.

Σ^O, which heads the list, is a Madrid MS., of the eleventh century. Λ^H, which runs it close, is a twelfth-century MS., also at Madrid. The "cousin" of the latter, Λ^L, though derived from a common source, is two centuries earlier, but evidently is much less closely related to Δ. If now we reckon these MSS. by families (counting in the *starred* readings) we shall find, as the average of agreements,

Agreements with the Σ group $\frac{1}{3}$ (16 + 11 + 8) $= \dfrac{35}{3} = 11\frac{2}{3}$

" " Λ group $\frac{1}{2}$ (15 + 4) $= \dfrac{19}{2} = 9\frac{1}{2}$

" " Ω group $\frac{1}{3}$ (11 + 11 + 8) $= \dfrac{30}{3} = 10$

" " Ψ group $\frac{1}{4}$ (13 + 9 + 7 + 7) $= \dfrac{36}{4} = 9$

" " Θ group $\frac{1}{4}$ (6 + 6) $= \dfrac{12}{4} = 3$

This may be a rough-and-ready method of reckoning, but it gives us a definite and apparently satisfactory result. We may leave the Ω group out of account; it consists of three MSS. of French origin, now at Paris, and of the 13-14 century: later, therefore, than any probable date for Δ. The Ψ group is Italian, entirely 12th century—again rather late to have served as the model for the Irish text. The Σ and Λ groups are both Spanish: and we infer that Δ was also a MS. of Spanish origin.

But the translator did not adhere slavishly to the Latin text before him. He had access to, and could use, a copy of the Septuagint; and the influence of this is shown by the following readings:—

I 11. Insert ὁ θεός
I 22. do.
I 26. do.
I 29. τοῖς πετεινοῖς in plural
II 1. τῇ ἕκτῃ
II 8. καὶ ἤκουσαν
II 10, 13. Similarities indicated in the notes.
III 15. καὶ ἔχθραν
III 22. ὁ θεός
IV 8. διέλθωμεν εἰς τὸ πεδίον
IV 9. ὁ θεός
V The ages of the Patriarchs in this chapter.
VII 1. πρὸς Νῶε
VII 3. The insertion of the clean and unclean *birds*.
VII 6. Νῶε · ὁ κατακλυσμός
VII 16. κιβωτόν
VIII 1. καὶ ... ὁ θεός

Some of these, taken by themselves, are not very impressive: but their evidence is cumulative, and the reading in VII 3 is conclusive. The figures in chapter V are less so, for they could have come from Isidore (*Etym.* V. 39): but the unequivocal cases of reference to the Septuagint strengthen the probability of the use of this authority, even where an alternative source is possible.

It is at least a coincidence that this combination of a knowledge of Greek, with some Spanish connexion, meets us again, in the North of Ireland. In the cemetery which contains the few remaining relics of the Monastery of St. Mura at Fahan, Co. Donegal, there is a large slab, bearing beautifully-designed interlacing crosses on each face. On one side there is a pair of human figures, standing with the cross-stem between them, and bearing upon their vesture an Irish inscription which does not here concern us. On the edge there is an inscription in Greek uncials—

ΔΟΞΑ ΚΑΙ ΤΙΜΕ (sic) ΠΑΤΡΙ ΚΑΙ ΥΙΩ ΚΑΙ ΠΝΕΥΜΑΤΙ ΑΓΙΩ
"Glory and Honour to Father and to Son and to Holy Spirit."

This is the first versicle of the "Gloria Patri," in a Spanish form, though in the Greek language. The formula "Glory and Honour," without the second versicle (sicut erat, etc.), was sanctioned by the Council of Toledo, and adopted in the Mozarabic liturgy. Thus we find someone who was at least a superficial Greek scholar, cutting, on an Irish tombstone, a Spanish liturgical formula, in letters resembling those of a Greek uncial MS.: and someone else translating into Irish a Biblical text from a Spanish copy, and able to check his work with a copy of the Septuagint. We have no authority to go further, or to suppose that the translation was actually executed in Fahan. This is not impossible, though the translation could hardly be as old as the slab. But in any case the number of uncial MSS. of the Septuagint available in Ireland can never have been very large.

It is for us a fortunate circumstance that the matter of Genesis XI 10–32 is misplaced in our text, being inserted between the verses VIII 19 and 20. There is no logical reason for this: the cause must have been mechanical, and due to the misplacement of a loose folio.

It follows that the matter which now comes after these verses was contained in a folio which ran from VIII 20 to XI 9. As we do not possess the translation in its original form—there are both omissions and interpolations—a count of words would lead us to wrong conclusions about the size of the folios, or the extent of the matter upon each. But a count of the corresponding words in the Vulgate text will enable us to estimate this with tolerable accuracy. If I have counted aright,

A. Genesis VIII 20–IX 27 in the Vulgate text contains 503 words.
B. „ IX 28–X 31 „ „ „ „ „ 382 „
C. „ X 32–XI 9 „ „ „ „ „ 170 „

B is missing from the translation *as we have it*, but it must have been there originally. Its omission would leave C, the Tower of Babel story, as a small detached narrative, too short for a folio of any reasonable size. It is easy to believe that the LG copyists, who pared away the redundancies of the Flood story, would have "jibbed" at the task of transcribing the tiresome list of incomprehensible names in the "Table of Nations" (Genesis X), which has nothing to do with the Taking of Ireland, and would use up much costly parchment.

A B C together amount to 1,055 words. If the translation of this passage was written upon one folio of vellum, with two columns on each page, there would be the equivalent of about 264 words in each column : or what would fill about 35 out of the 55–60 lines in a column of the *Book of Ballymote*.

I have not counted words back to the beginning of Genesis. But taking a printed edition, not complicated with interspersed references, and omitting the chapter headings, I find that

> Genesis I 1–VIII 19 covers $70\frac{3}{8}$ inches of type.
> Genesis VIII 20–XI 9 „ $22\frac{1}{8}$ „ „ „

The number of words in this printed copy is not evenly distributed : one column in Chapter III, in which the verses are long, contains 252 words, and another, in Chapter V, of exactly the same spacial length, contains 232 words. There is thus a sufficient margin of possible adjustment to permit us to say that the material preceding VIII 19 could have been written on three folios similar to that which we have postulated for VIII 20–XI 9. We infer from this that the matter appropriated by ∞ R³ covered a complete gathering of four folios, or two diplomas (pairs of conjugate folios), and the detached first folio of the next gathering. When a man carries off such a gathering and one extra folio, nothing is more natural for him to do than to slip the loose leaf into the gathering, to prevent it from being lost : and if its proper place is just *after* the last folio of the gathering, he will slip it in just *before* that folio. And this is exactly what he has done, to the confusion of his copyists.

Numbering the five folios of this Biblical MS. 1, 2, 3, 5, 4, in the order in which they ultimately became incorporated in R³, we see that 4 must have ended with the words³ *Hae sunt generationes Sem* (XI 10), which, however, were dropped by the copyists, as they had no meaning in their new context. 5 a began *Sem erat centum annorum* (¶ 69) and ran on to *ueneruntque usque Haran et habitauerunt ibi* (XI 31). This is a little longer than the allowance of 264 words to the column; but the matter of these verses contains many numerals and stereotyped repetitions, which could be much abbreviated : and in any case column β *must* have begun with (XI 32), *Et facti sunt dies Thare.* For we must now notice the further fact, that the lower part of folio 5 was torn away (whether in the original act of theft or by some later accident cannot be ascertained, and is of trifling importance). This tear ran upwards obliquely, from the bottom inner edge to the top outer edge. It carried away from the first column (5 a) parts of all the verses after XI 26, and it left nothing intact in the second column except this one verse, XI 32. The copyists could not, or at least made no attempt to, extract any sense from the remaining fragments of the mutilated lines; and thus it comes about that the misplaced extract from Chapter XI, in ¶ 77, jumps from v. 26 to v. 32, and then stops abruptly. The verso of the folio must have contained, in the first column, a few lines of the story of Abraham hiding his relationship to Sarah in Egypt, and in the second column the end of the story of Lot in Sodom and the beginning of the Battle of the Four Kings with the Five. These fragments were so utterly disconnected with the matter in hand, and with each other, that the copyists left them out.

---

³ Meaning, of course, the Irish translation of these words; and similarly for the other quotations in this paragraph.

This reconstruction of the original form of the Biblical translation is more than a mere curiosity; for as it was possible to attach the Biblical folios to *Q, we may infer that the sizes of the two manuscripts were much about the same. And every scrap of information that we can discover about *Q is of importance, for the history of R^3.

The Chasm in B, M.

B has lost, as already stated, its folio 9, beginning after the words *ocus ro hoslaicit* (Gen. III 7, ¶ 32), and extending to ¶ 138 in § II. This mutilation took place after β and $\sqrt{\beta^1 \beta^2}$ were copied; and a count of words shows that the matter with which they fill this gap would exactly cover a leaf of B. Therefore one folio has been lost, and no more, at this place; a conclusion which accords with the old pagination.

The fragment H almost exactly fills the gap. If the top of the first leaf of this fragment had not been torn away, it would have filled it with suspicious exactness. Suspicious, because it suggests the deduction that the leaves of H were actually torn, from the MS. to which they belonged, by an owner of B, anxious to make his own property complete. They certainly present the appearance of having been pulled out violently.[4]

But the matter in H is considerably longer than what would fill a folio of B, and it contains an extensive passage ignored by the derivatives of B. We infer that there was a lacuna in $\sqrt{B}$, due to the loss of leaves in an ancestral MS., of which s B was unconscious.

When we look up M at this place we find a similar lacuna. It is less extensive; there is some matter common to M and H but unknown to B. Unlike s B, s M was aware of the defect in his exemplar, and he left a half column blank in the hope,

---

[4] It is likely that copies of this lengthy and important text were few, and were much in demand: and that Irish book-collectors were not any more conscientious than the rest of the fraternity. The total disappearance of the copy in *Lebor na Huidri* (ante, p. xxi) was probably the result of someone having been left for a few moments alone with that precious codex.

never to be fulfilled, of finding a more perfect copy from
which to supply the missing matter.

We may represent the relative lengths of the missing
portion in tabular form thus: let a represent the quantity
of matter surviving in M, between the beginning of the lacuna
in B and the beginning of the lacuna in M. Then we have—

  i. A length of a, absent in B, present in M, present in H.
  ii. A length of $5a$, absent in B, absent in M, present in H.
  iii. A length of $2a$, absent in B, present in M, present in H.

The third of these sections is the poem *Athair cáich*, and
a few lines intervening between it and the resumption of B.

The explanation is perfectly simple. B, M, H all derive
from MSS. copied *independently* from an ancestor, $\sqrt{}$BMH.
There can, therefore, be no common ancestor of any two of
these MSS. excluding the third: this is an assured fact of
fundamental importance in the criticism of the MSS. of R³.
The first of the ancestral MSS. to be copied was ∞ H, the
second ∞ M, the third ∞ B. Between the transcribing of
the first and last of these a gathering of four diplomas disappeared from $\sqrt{}$BMH piecemeal. Each folio of $\sqrt{}$BMH
contained matter equal in quantity to a. Here is a diagram
of the gathering—

The whole gathering was intact when ∞ H was copied.
Then the diplomas 4–5, 3–6, as well as folio 2 disappeared;
after which ∞ M was copied. Folio 7 was now loose: it
contained the beginning of *Athair cáich*, which must have
begun at the top of folio 7 *recto* and ended near the end of
folio 8 *verso*. There are 57 quatrains in this poem, so that
the folios of $\sqrt{}$BMH must have been quite small: each page

could not have held more than 15 quatrains. Folio 7, as well as the last diploma 1–8, disappeared before ∞ B was copied.

The impression which a study of the language of the translation leaves is that the latter is not much earlier than R³, with which it is incorporated. Like the O'Clerys and the Four Masters, the translator affects an archaistic style, which he presumably thought was more consistent with the dignity of the text on which he was working. His language, when he is natural, is Middle Irish; his archaisms are Wardour-street revivals rather than survivals. He uses a deponent form for the verb whenever he remembers to do so. He invents forms like *barnimdaigther,* ¶ 24, which he has forgotten in ¶ 25, where we find "dēntar *bar n-imdugad.*" It is more than probable that the MS. which ∞ R³ mutilated was actually the autograph of the translation, and that this was, as we have said, killed by the transaction.

It is clear that the glossators had no idea that they were dealing with a Scriptural text. One of them had to reassure himself that the reference to the Holy Spirit in ¶ 20 is not profane: and another (¶ 30 y²) quotes "Holy Scripture" to corroborate the passage from Holy Scripture upon which he is working!

SECTION I.

First Redaction.

(L 1 *a* 1 : F 1 *a* 1) (*a*)

1. *In principio fecit Deus celum et terram*, .i. [1]Doringne Dīa nem ⁊ talmain ar tūs, ‡ ⁊ nī [2]fil tossach ‡' nā forcend ||[3]' fair-[3]seom [4]fēin ||.

2. [1]Doringne chētus in maiss [2]nem-chruthaig, ⁊ soillsi aingel, ‡ isin [3]cētna [4]Domnuch ||. [5]Doringne [6]firmament ‡ isin Lūan ||. [7]Doringni [8]tal*main* ⁊ muire ‡ [9]sin Mairt ||. [10]Doringni grēin ⁊ ēsca ⁊ [11]renna Nime ‡ [12]sin Cētāin ||. [13]Doringni ēnlaithe ‡ ind āeoir || ⁊ [14]tonnaitecha ‡ in mara || ‡ [15]sin Dardāin ||. [16]Doringni annmanna ‡ in talman || [17]archena, ⁊ Adam do [18]follomnacht foraib, ‡ [19]isind Āine ||. Ro chumsain īarum ‡ Dīa || ‡ [20]issin tSathurn || [21]do foirbthiugud dūla nūa, ‡ ⁊ nī ō [18]follomnacht [22]itir ||.

3. Dobert ‡ [1]īarsain || [2]archinnchecht Nime do [3]Lucifiur, co [4]nōi ngrādaib angel Nime. Dobert [5]archinnchecht talman do Adam ‡ ⁊ do [6]Eua cona claind ||. [7]Imromadar ‡ īarom || Lucifiur (*sic*) [8]conid būi (?) toesech trīn slūaig angel. [9]Rothimmarc (?) in Rī ē co trian in slūaig angel leis i nIfrinn; ⁊ asbert Dīa

---

1. *All variants from* F *unless otherwise stated.* [1] dorindi [2] fuil tosach [3] sium [4] fein *added sec. man* L

2. [1] dorigne cetus [2] n-ecruthaig: *above very faint traces of a gloss* nemfaics(ide) F [3] *om.* [4] -nach [5] dorigne [6] neam .i. firmamaind isan [7] dorigne: *this word is abbreviated to* D *in the following sentences in* L [8] talam ⁊ muir [9] isan F; sin Mairt *om. and ins.* cL [10] dorigne grian ⁊ esga [11] randa [12] isin Cedain F: *om. and ins.* cL [13] dorigne enlaithi [14] tondaitheacha [15] isa Dardain F: *om. and ins.* cL [16] dorigne [17] *at first written* chena, *and the* ar *monogram squeezed in* before *it sec. man.* F

First Redaction

1. *In principio fecit Deus caelum et terram,* i.e., God made Heaven and Earth at the first, [and He Himself hath no beginning nor ending].

2. He made first the formless mass, and the light of angels, [on the first Sunday]. He made Firmament [on the Monday]. He made earth and seas [on the Tuesday]. He made sun and moon and the stars of Heaven [on the Wednesday]. He made birds [of the air] and reptiles [of the sea on the Thursday]. He made beasts [of the earth] in general, and Adam to rule over them, [on the Friday]. Thereafter God rested [on the Saturday] from the accomplishment of a new Creation, [but by no means from its governance].

3. [Thereafter] He gave the bailiffry of Heaven to Lucifer, with the nine orders of the Angels of Heaven. He gave the bailiffry of Earth to Adam [and to Eve, with her progeny]. [Thereafter] Lucifer sinned, so that he was leader of a third of the host of angels. The King confined him with a third of the host of

---

[18] follam- (*bis*)   [19] dia Hainediden, et ro   [20] isan tSatharn*n*
[21] o oipriugad   [22] *ins. sec. man. in small capital letters in* L *marg.*
In the text in *Q: *om* F

3. [1] iarsin   [2] aircinchacht   [3] Luidsifir   [4] nai   [5] aircindacht
[6] Eaba   [7] imroimadar   [8] *obscure in both* L *and* F: *in* F *looks like for* nim cona sluag angel leis .i. na demna   [9] cor hindarbad *and* *om.* co trian sluaig angel

---

(a) For the text of *Q see Second and Third Redactions.

fri muintir Nime : ‡ Dīunsach inti Lucifer ||, [10]*uenite* [11]*ut confundamus consilium eius.*

4. Ro formtig 'trā Lucifer fri Adam, ar derb lais issē no bērtha, līnad Nime tar a ēisi, do. Conid aire sin doluid [2]‡ Iofer Niger || [3]i ndeilb in athrach, [4]co ro aslacht imarbus for ‡ Adam ⁊ || [5]Eua, im [6]thumailt [7]ind ubuill don chrund ergartha. [8]Conid aire sin ro [9]innarbbad Adam a Pardus [10]hi talmain coitchind.

5. [1]Dolluid in Comdiu cucca īarsain, ⁊ atbert fri Adam .i. [2]*Terra es et in* [3]*terram ibis* ‡ .i.   Do thalmain [4]donringned ⁊ [5]hi talmain raga ||.   *In* [6]*sudore uultus tui comedes* [7]*panem tuum* ‡ .i. Nī [8]*fuigbe* sāsam cen[8] sāethar ||. [9]Asbert dana frisin mnāi .i.   *Cum* [10]*dolore et gemitu* [11]*paries filios tuos* [12]*et filias tuas* ‡ .i. [13]bid co ngalar . . . doīulaing (?) tuisema do maccu ||.

L
6. Ro immarbāigestar cland Adaim ‡ īarom || .i. sinser mac (n)Adaim, .i. Cāin miscadach, ro marb a derbrāthair Aibēl [. . tria formud (?)] ⁊ tria saint, lasin (?) enāim chamaill, mar adberat eōlaig . . . . tinnsenadar (?) fingail in domain.

F
Īarsin trā do feallsad clann Adaim for ñail ⁊ dīmus ⁊ imarbus ⁊ fingal, .i. Cāin mac Adaim in sinser, ro marb-sidi a derbrātair .i. Abēl tria saint ⁊ formad, co fid enāma camaill. ‡ Con aire sin dorad Dīa dīlinn tarsin n-uili doman. ||

---

[10] *illegible in* F: *apparently* et dixit Deus *is inserted before* uenite
[11] et

4. [1] iarsin   [2] Iarngir L. *om.* Iofer Niger F   [3] a neilb nathrach [4] coreaslaig   [5] for Eba   [6] thom-   [7] ind ubaill   [8] con de sin [9] hinarbad   [10] isin

angels in his company, in Hell. And God said unto
the Folk of Heaven : [Haughty is this Lucifer], *uenite
ut confundamus consilium eius.*

4. Thereafter Lucifer had envy against Adam, for
he was assured that this would be given him (Adam),
the filling of Heaven in his (Lucifer's) room. Wherefore he [Iofer Niger] came in the form of the serpent,
and persuaded [Adam and] Eve to sin, in the matter
of eating of the apple from the forbidden tree.
Wherefore Adam was expelled from Paradise into
common earth.

5. Thereafter the Lord came to them, and He said unto
Adam, *Terra es et in terram ibis* [*i.e.*, of earth was he
made and into earth shall he go]. *In sudore uultus tui
comedes panem tuum* [*i.e.*, he shall not obtain satisfaction
without labour]. He said further unto the woman : *Cum
dolore et gemitu paries filios tuos et filias tuas* [*i.e.*, it shall
be with . . . insufferable pain that thou shalt bring forth
thy sons].

6. The progeny of Adam
sinned [thereafter], namely,
the elder of the sons of
Adam, Cain the accursed,
who slew his brother Abel
. . . (through his jealousy?)
and through his greed,
with the bone of a camel,
as learned men say. (In
this manner?) began the
kin-murders of the world.

But thereafter the pro-
geny of Adam wrought
treachery, by way of pride,
of haughtiness, of sin, of
kin-murder—Cain son of
Adam, the elder, he slew
his brother Abel through
his greed and his jealousy,
with the shaft of a camel-
bone. [And therefore God
brought a Flood over the
whole earth].

---

5. [1] doluid in Coimdi chuca iarsin ⁊ adbert   [2] tearra   [3] tearaim
[4] dorignid   [5] a   [6] sudoire   [7] panam   [8-8] fuigbed biad
can   [9] adbert dono   [10] doloire   [11] pairras   [12] *om.* et
filias tuas   [13] bid congneid ⁊ galar dofuisema do claindi

7. ¹Seth imorro, in tres mac ²Adaim ³‡ aca mbāi cland ⁊ ‖ is ⁴ūata atiat fir ⁵in domuin uile :

y¹ .i. Nōe mac ⁶Laimīach meic Mathusali meic ⁷Henōc meic ⁸Iared meic Malalel meic ⁹Cainan meic Enos meic ¹⁰Seth meic Adaim :

ūair is ē Nōe in tAdam tānisi, cusa mbertar fir domain ¹¹uile. ¹²Ūair ro bāid in ¹³dīliu sīl Adaim ¹⁴uile, acht Nōe cona trī macaib, .i. Sem, Cham, Iafet, acus a cethri mnaa .i. Cobba ⁊ Olla ⁊ Oliba ⁊ Olībana.

y² ¹⁵Ō dorat īarom Dia dīlind darsin uile ndomuin, nī thērna di dōenib in domuin ōn dīlind acht mad lucht na hairce sin .i. Nōe cona trī maccaib, ⁊ ben Nōe, ⁊ mnaa a mac.¹⁵

Ut dixit poeta,

Slūag nād chlōe cūa-chel . . . .

8. ¹Sem didiu ro gob i nAsia, Cham i nAfraic Iafeth i nEoraip—

Sem rogab i n-Aisia n-ait . . .

Tricha mac ²bātar ac Sem, im ³Arfacsad, im Asur, ⁴⁊ im Persius. Tricha ⁵mac ⁶ac Cam, im Chus ⁷⁊ im Chanan.⁷ A cōic dēc imorro oc Iafeth, im Dannai, im Grēgus, im ⁸Hispāinius, im ⁹Goimarus.

¹⁰No is mōirfeisir ar fichid do macaib badar ic Sem.

---

7. ¹ Seth mac Adaim   ² airigda da bi ac Adam   ³ *this gloss* om. F   ⁴ uad ataid   ⁵ om. in : domain uili   ⁶ Lamiach
⁷ Enog   ⁸ Iareth   ⁹ Cainain   ¹⁰ Seith   ¹¹ uili   ¹² ar do   ¹³ dili
¹⁴ uili   ¹⁵⁻¹⁵ om. F, *and substitute* Imroimadar clann Adaim fri Dia (?)
co tard Dia dile tarsin uile domain co nach terno nech beo eisti acht

7. As for Seth, one of the three sons of Adam [who had progeny], of him are the men of the whole world :

Noe s. Lameeh s. Mathusalem s. Enoch s. Iared s. Malalahel s. Cainan s. Enos s. Seth s. Adam.

For it is Noe who is the second Adam, to whom the men of all the world are traced. For the Flood drowned the whole seed of Adam, except Noe with his three sons, Sem, Ham, Iafeth, and their four wives Coba, Olla, Oliva, Olivana.

Afterwards, when God brought a Flood over the whole world, none of the people of the world escaped from the Flood except it be the people of that ark—Noe with his three sons, and the wife of Noe, and the wives of his sons.

Ut dixit poeta,

Poem no. I.

8. Now Sem settled in Asia, Ham in Africa, Iafeth in Europe—

Poem no. II.

Sem had thirty sons, including Arfaxad, Assur, and Persius. Ham had thirty sons, including Chus and Chanaan. Iafeth had fifteen, including Dannai, Gregus, Hispanius, Gomer.

Or it is twenty-seven sons that Sem had.

---

lucht na hairce .i. Nae cona tri macaib Sem, Cam, Iafeth, cona ceitri mnaib .i. Coba, Olla, Oliba, Olibana, amail asbert in file

8. [1] Sem dana rogab an Aissia, Cam isan Adfraic, Iafeth asa nEoraip [2] badar ic [3] Airfeesat [4] *om.* ┐ [5] *om.* [6] aili co Cam im Cuss [7-7] *om.* [8] Esbainus [9] -mer- [10] *This gloss in* F *only*

Tricha mac mīn monar nglē . . . .

9. ¹Iafeth ‡ trā mac ²Nōe ‖, is ūad ³tūaiscert-leth na Haisia, .i. ⁴Aisia Becc, Armenia, Media, Fir na Scitīa; ⁊ is ⁵ṅad lucht na ⁶Haeorpa uile.

y¹ Grēcus mac Iafeth, is ūad in ⁷Grēg Mōr, ⁊ in ⁷Grēg ⁸Becc, ⁊ ⁷Grēg na Halaxandrach. ⁹Essbāinus mac Iafeth, ō tāit ¹⁰Hispāna. Goimerus mac Iafeth, dā mac laiss, Emoth ⁊ Ibath. Emoth, is ūadh fine thūascirt in domain. Ibath, dā mac leis, .i. ¹¹Bodb ⁊ Baath. Bodb, diar bo mac Dohe.

y² Elinus mac Doi, trī meic leis .i. Armen, Negua, Isacon. Armen ōn, cōic meic leis, Gotus, Cibidus, Uiligotus, Burgantus, ⁊ Longbardus. Negua, trī meic leis, .i. Saxsus, Boarus, Uandalus. Hisicon imorro, in tres ¹²mac Eline, ceitre meic lais, ¹³Romanus, Francus, Britus, Albus.

y³ Is ē in t.Albanus dogab Albin ar tūs cona chlaind, ⁊ is ūadh ainmnigter Albo: cor indarb a brātair tar Muir nIcht, conad ūad Albanaig Leatha Hoidia.

10. ¹Magoth mac Iafiath, is dia chlaind-sin na tūatha tāncatar Ērinn rīa nGāedelaib: .i. ²Parthalōn mac Sera meic Srū meic Esrū meic ³Bimbind meic ⁴Aaithecha meic Magoth meic Iafeth; ⁴⁊ Nemedh mac Aghnumaid meic mPaimp meic Tait meic Sera meic Sriū; ⁊ clanna Nemid, .i. Gaileōin, ⁊ Fir Domnan, ⁊ Fir Bolg, ⁊ Tūatha Dē Danann. Amail isbert in fili,

---

9. ¹ Iafiath   ² Nae   ³ tuait siar-deise na Haisia L tuas-cert-leth na Aisia F   ⁴ Aissia Beg ⁊ Armen ⁊ Fir na Sgeiaithia ⁵ uadh   ⁶ Horpa uili   ⁷ Gree (*ter: in the first the scribe began to write Gree; but discovered his mistake and stopped half-way*) ⁸ beg   ⁹ Hispanus L. *From this point to the bottom of the page (down to and including Poem IV, quatrain 1) L is illegible save for faint traces, sufficiently decipherable to shew that except some ortho-graphical differences the text is identical with F, which is here followed.*

Poem no. III.

9. [With regard to] Iafeth [son of Noe], of him is the northern side of Asia—namely Asia Minor, Armenia, Media, the People of Scythia; and of him are the inhabitants of all Europe.

Greeus s. Iafeth, of him is Grecia Magna, Grecia Parva, and Alexandrian Greece.   Espanus s. Iafeth from whom are the Hispani.   Gomer son of Iafeth had two sons, Emoth and Ibath.   Emoth, of him is the northern people of the world.   Ibath had two sons, Bodb and Baath. Bodb, who had a son Dohe.

Elinus son of Dohe had three sons, Airmen, Negua, Isacon.   As for Airmen, he had five sons, Gutus, Cebidus, Uiligothus, Burgundus, Longbardus.   Negua had three sons, Saxus, Boarus, Uandalus.   Isacon, moreover, one of the three sons of Elenus, he had four sons, Romanus, Francus, Britus, Albanus.

This is that Albanus who first took Albania, with his children, and of him is Alba named : so he drove his brother across the Sea of Icht, and from him are the Albanians of Latium of Italy.

10. Magog son of Iafeth, of his progeny are the peoples who came to Ireland before the Gaedil : to wit Partholon s. Sera s. Sru s. Esru s. Bimbend (*sic*) s. Aithech s. Magog s. Iafeth; and Nemed s. Agnomain s. Pamp s. Tat s. Sera s. Sru; and the progeny of Nemed, the Gaileoin, Fir Domnann, Fir Bolg, and Tuatha De Danann.   As the poet said,

---

F *sometimes uses* ";" *and sometimes* "u;" *to represent final* us: *thus* "Got;", *but* "Uiligotu;". *It has not been thought necessary to preserve this trivial distinction in printing.* [10] Hispania L
[11] *Written* Bod | db, *divided between two lines* F   [12] *om.* mac F; *the word can be detected in* L   [13] *Written* Roman us, *the space large enough to hold an* n
10. [1] *See* ¶ 9 *note* (²)   [2] Partholon L   [3] Bi(?)amin L
[⁴] Fatocht L   [⁴] *om.* ⁊ L

Magog mac an Iafeth . . .

Second Reduction.

(V 1 a 1 : E 1 a 1 : P 1 a 1 : D 3 a 1 *first two folios lost.*)

(The opening paragraphs are numbered to correspond with
R[1], being derived from *Q. a lost MS. of that Redaction;
and are distinguished by a suffixed asterisk.)

1*. [1]*In* [2]*principio fecit Deus celum et terram* .i.
dorighne Dīa [3]Neam ⁊ [4]talmain ar tūs.

2*. ᾽Dorigne [2]cētumus in [3]maiss [4]n-ēcruthaigh, ⁊
soillsi aingeal, ‡ [5]issin cētna Domnuch ||.   [6]Dorigne
firmaimint ‡ [7]is'in' Lūan ||.   [8]Dorigne ta'lmain' ⁊ muir
‡ [9]issin Mairt ||.   [8]'Dorigne' grēin ⁊ [10]ēsca ⁊ 'renda'
Nime ‡ [11]issin Cētāin ||.   Dorigne 'ēnlaithe' ‡ [12]ind
āeoir || ⁊ [13]tondaithechu ‡ na f'airrge' || ‡ Dīa [14]Dardāin
||.   Dorigne anmanda ‡ 'in tal'man || [15]olchena, ⁊ [16]Adam
do [17]follomn'acht' foraib, ‡ [18]issin nĀendidin ||.   R'o
chunsain' ‡ [19]Dīa || īarom ‡ [20]issin [21]tSat'hurn'd || ō
[22]oipriugad a dūla nūa, ‡' ⁊ dorad bendachtain foraib ||,
‡ ⁊ nī ō [23]ollomnacht etir ||.

2 A. y[1] Is 'amlaid [2]dorōna Dīa na dūile : [3].i. araile eo
[4]tossach ⁊ cen crīch, amail [5]aingliu; araile imorro [6]co
tossach ⁊ co crīch, amail anmanda indlightecha ⁊ [7]toirrthe
in [8]talman: araile [9]dana co [10]tosach ⁊ co [11]foreend ⁊ cen
forcend, amail atat na [12]dāine, .i. tossach [13]for a ngenemain
[14]corpdai ⁊ forcend for n-a corpaib-sin, ⁊ cen [15]forcenn for
a n-anmandaib.[15]

1*. [1] *A space left in* E *for an initial monogram, never filled up*
[2] principio fecid VE   [3] nemh E   [4] talamain E

2*. *All variants in these opening paragraphs from* E *unless otherwise stated.*   [1] *ins.* .i. V: doirighne E   [2] cedamus   [3] mais
[4] *sic* VE *but changed by a re-inker to* re cruthaigh, V   [5] isin ced
domh-   [6] dorigni fiormamiint (*doubled* i *due to change of line*)
[7] *words marked* '...' *lost by a tear in the vellum of* V   [8] dorighni (*bis*)
[9] isin mh-   [10] esgai   [11] isin cedaoin   [12] an aoeoir   [13] -aithecha
na fairrghe   [14] -daoin   [15] olcena V   [16] Adamh *om. and sprs.* cE

Poem no. IV.

Second Redaction.

1*. *In principio fecit Deus caelum et terram*, i.e., God made Heaven and Earth at the first.

2*. He made first the formless mass, and the light of Angels, [on the first Sunday]. He made Firmament [on the Monday]. He made earth and sea [on the Tuesday]. He made sun and moon and the stars of Heaven [on the Wednesday]. He made birds [of the air] and [marine] reptiles [on the Thursday]. He made beasts [of the earth] in general, and Adam to rule over them[, on the Friday]. Thereafter [God] rested [on the Saturday] from the accomplishment of His new creation[, and gave them a blessing, but by no means from its governance].

2 A. In this wise God made the creatures: some with beginning and without end, as Angels; some moreover with beginning and with end, as irrational beasts and fruits of the earth; some further with beginning and with termination and without termination, as are men—a beginning to their bodily birth and a termination to their bodies, and no termination to their souls.

---

[17] -amhn-   [18] isind ain-   [19] om.   [20] isin   [21] -arnn
[22] oipriudug V   [23] follamhnacht itir

2A. [1] amhlaid   [2] doroine   [3] om. .i.   [4] tossuch *apparently* V, *but in the handwriting of this MS. it is sometimes difficult to distinguish between* u *and open* a: tosach E   [5] ainghliu   [6] go tosach   [7] toirti an   [8] talmun V   [9] imorro   [10] tosuch V   [11] foircend (*second time abbreviated to* fcend)   [12] daoine   [13] forainngenemain V *for* a ngeinemain E   [14] chorpda   [15-15] -cend: a n-an. *om. and ins.*

y² Is amlaid dana dorōnad ¹⁶in duine sin .i. ¹⁷Adam : a corp⁽ᵃ⁾ do talmain ¹ˣchoitchend . . . .

a chend do ¹⁹tīr Garad, a ²⁰bruindi a tīr Arabia, a ²¹brū a Lodain, a ²²cossa a tīr ²³Agoria :

. . . . a fuil ‡ ⁊ ²⁴a allus ‖ do ²⁵uisci ²⁶in āeoir, a anāl dond āeor, a ²⁷thes do ²ˣtenig, a ²⁹anam do ³⁰thinfiud De.

y³ Isin treas ³¹ūair īar ³²cruthugad Adhaim, ro ³³teipead Eua ³⁴assa tāeb. ³⁵I n-āess trichtaig ro cruthaiged Adam ; ³⁶i n-āess dā bliadan dēc ro ³⁷cruthaiged Eua.

3*.   Dobert ‡ Dīa ‖ ¹aire(h)indeacht Nime do ²Luicifiur, con nāe ³ngrādaib aingel ⁴imbe.   Dobert ‡ ⁵īarsain ‖ ⁶aircindecht talman do ⁷Adam ‡ ⁊ do ˣEua, cona ⁹chlainn ‖. Ro ¹⁰immarbsaigestar ¹¹Lucifuir for ¹²Nim ar ¹³ūail ⁊ ¹⁴dīumus fri Dīa, co ro hindarbadh ¹⁵i cinaigh in ¹⁶dīumsa sin do ¹⁷Neimi, ‡ ¹ˣco triun slūaig aingeal ¹⁹laiss ‖, ²⁰in nlffrinn.   Conid andsin ²¹asbert Dīa fri ²²muintir ²³Nime : ‡ Ro-²⁴dīumsaich ²⁵intī ²⁶Luesifiur (sic) ‖ : ²⁷et dixit, uenite ut ²ˣuideamus ⁊ ²⁹confundamus consilium eius, .i. ³⁰tāit co ro ³¹fēgum ⁊ co ro ³²melachtnaigium comairle ³³indī Lucifiur.   ³⁴Issī cēt breath ruead ³⁵rīam sin.

4*. Ro ¹formtigh ²īarsain Lucifir fri Hadum, derb ³lais issē dobertha ‡ i ffochraic³ do ‖, ⁴līnadh Nime dar a ⁵ēsi.   ⁶Conid aire sin doluidh ⁷‡ Iofer Nigher ‖ ˣi ndeilb nathrach ‡ co curp ⁹sēim ‖, co ro aslacht ¹⁰in imarbus for ¹¹Eua, im ¹²tomailt ¹³ind ¹⁴ubaill don ¹⁵chrund aurgartha, ‡ ⁊ co ro ¹⁶aslaich ¹⁷Eua for Adum ‖ . . .

cE in upper margin   ¹⁶ an   ¹⁷ Adamh   ¹⁸ coitcend   ¹⁹ thir
²⁰ bhruinne   ²¹ bruo   ²² cosa   ²³ -oir-   ²⁴ a luais V
²⁵ usci V uisgi E   ²⁶ ind   ²⁷ tes   ²⁸ tein-   ²⁹ anim V
³⁰ thinfuidh V teinfi-   ³¹ om. V   ³² crutugh-   ³³ teiped Eba
³⁴ asa thaobh   ³⁵ ind aois triochtaige   ³⁶ ind aois   ³⁷ -aigh- here and above

3*. ¹-echt neimhe   ² Lucif.   ³ ngradh-   ⁴ immi   ⁵ iarsin
⁶sic E, airecht V   ⁷ Adham hic et semper E   ⁸ Ebhe   ⁹ cloinn
¹⁰ immarbusaigestar iar sin   ¹¹ Lucifer   ¹² nimh   ¹³ uaill
¹⁴ diom-   ¹⁵ hi cion-   ¹⁶ dimusa   ¹⁷ nimh   ¹⁸ co dtriun
¹⁹ lais   ²⁰ and Ifernn conadh   ²¹ adbert   ²² muindt-   ²³ -mh-
²⁴ dioumsaid   ²⁵ anti   ²⁶ Lucifer   ²⁷ om. et dixit   ²⁸ uidiamus V

In this wise, further, was that man, Adam, made: his body of common earth,

> his head of the land of Garad, his breast of the land of Arabia,
> his belly of Lodain, his legs of the land of Agoria:

his blood [and his sweat] of the water of the air, his breath of the air, his heat of fire, his soul of the breath of God.

In the third hour after the creation of Adam, Eve was drawn out of his side. At the age of a thirty years' space Adam was created, at the age of twelve years Eve was created.

3*. [God] gave the bailiffry of Heaven to Lucifer, with nine orders of Angels about him. [Thereafter] He gave the bailiffry of Earth to Adam [and to Eve with his progeny]. Lucifer made an assault upon Heaven, by reason of pride and haughtiness against God, so that he was expelled, for the crime of that haughtiness, out from Heaven, [with a third of the host of angels in his company], into Hell. So that then God said unto the Folk of Heaven: [Over-haughty is this Lucifer]: *et dixit, Venite ut uideamus et confundamus consilium eius,* i.e., Come and let us see and put to shame the counsel of this Lucifer. That is the first judgement which was ever pronounced.

4*. Thereafter Lucifer had envy against Adam, (for) he was assured that this would be given him [as a reward], to fill Heaven in his room. Wherefore he [Iofer Niger] came in the form of a serpent [with a tenuous body] and persuaded Eve to the sin, in the matter of eating of the apple from the forbidden tree, [and Eve persuaded Adam] . . .

---

uidemus E   29 confundamus   30 taoid   31 fegham   32 melachtem
comairli   33 inti   34 is hi ced breth rugad   35 -mh

4*. 1 foirmtig   2 -sin   3-3 leis ise doberta hi bfochraic   4 lionad
nimhe   5 eisi   6 -adh   7 *initial* I *erased*, E   8 a   9 *ins.*
aieorda: *the text was originally* natrach (sic) aieorda seimh. cE *inserted* co curp seim *interlined, and then, observing that* seim *was already in the text, scratched this word out.*   10 indiumurbus *a correction prima manu of* indium;. *The* "m;" *was scratched out, and in re-written in blacker ink with* v sprs.   11 Ebha   12 -mh-, *the final* t *erased*
13 an   14 -bh-   15 -and argarta   16 Fasl-   17 Ebha

(a) This word should of course be *chorp*: but here and elsewhere I have preferred to let the MSS. speak for themselves without fussy corrections.

5*. Ocus ¹isbert Dīa friu : *De terra* ²*es et in terram ibis;*
‡ .i. Do thalmain ³ataī-siu ⁊ hi talmain ⁴rega ‖. *Et dixit,*
In sudore ⁵*uultus tui comedes* ⁶*panem tuum*; ‡ .i. ⁷Bid a
⁸hallus do gnūisi ⁹domēla do bairgena. ‖ Asbert dana fri
¹⁰Eua : *Cum* ¹¹*dolore et gemitu paries filios tuos* ‡ *et filias*
tuas ‖ : ‡ .i. Bid co ¹²erāit ⁊ ¹³galair tuisēma do ¹⁴maccu
‡' ⁊ t'ingena ‖' ‖.

5ᴀ. Ro thaisbenta na dūile ¹corpta do Adam, (*a*)⁊ nī derna ²fāilte
friu. ³Conid ⁴nire ⁵sain ⁶tarlaicedh ⁷cotlud fair. ⁸Isin cotludh sin
⁹iartain ¹⁰ro ¹¹delbud ¹²Eua, ¹³iar n-a teipe don tsechtmudh .¹⁴asna
¹⁵assa ¹⁶toeb. ¹⁷Conid ¹⁸andsin ¹⁹asbert ²⁰Adum : *Ecce* ²¹*os de*
²²*ossibus meis et* ²³*caro de* ²⁴*carne mea* ‡ .i. ‡' ²⁵is cuma ‖' ²⁶atchim-si
²⁷enāim ²⁸dom ²⁹chnāmaib ⁊ feōil dom ³⁰feōil³¹. ‖ ‡ ³²In ³³chēt-
³⁴ghāire ³⁵dernad ³⁶rīam ³⁷indsin, ³⁸⁊ in ³⁹chēt-fāilte. ³⁸‖

4* *resumed* . . . ¹Iar ²cintaib ³ind ⁴iomarbais, ro
⁵hinnarbad īarsin Adam a ⁶Parrdus ⁷issin talmain
⁸coitchend, ‡ ar nā ⁹toimled ¹⁰tuirthe ¹¹in ¹²Chraind
¹³Bethad ¹⁴i Parrdus; ar dīa ¹⁵toimled, nī ¹⁶fuigbed
¹⁷bāss co brāth, ¹⁸acht ¹⁹slāinte ⁊ ²⁰cenn ²¹fri ²²cotlud ‖.

6*. Ro ¹imarbasaigestar ²īarsain ³clann Adaim .i.
⁴sinnser mac nAdaim .i. ⁵Cāin ⁶misgadhach, do
marbudh a ⁷brāthar .i. ⁸Abēl mac Adaim ⁹tria ¹⁰formud
⁊ ¹¹dīumus. ‡ ¹²Cēt ¹³fingal ¹⁴in domain ¹⁵sin ‖. Do
lecain ¹⁶chamaill ¹⁷dana ro ¹⁸marb Cāin a brāthair.

5*. ¹adbert   ²eis VE   ³ataoisi   ⁴raga   ⁵ultus
⁶painim tuam   ⁷bidh   ⁸hollus   ⁹-meala   ¹⁰Hebha
¹¹doloire - geimitu pairieis filieos   ¹²craid   ¹³galur   ¹⁴maca
  5ᴀ. ¹corpda E   ²failti EP   ³couadh EP   ⁴airi E
⁵sin EP   ⁶tarluic- E: *the word changed by ignorant re-inking to*
tarbiset P   ⁷codl. *hic et semper* EP   ⁸is isin P   ⁹iarom P
¹⁰do P   ¹¹dealb- EP   ¹²Ebha *hic et semper* EP   ¹³ar P: theipedh E
¹⁴assna E, esna P   ¹⁵asa EP   ¹⁶thaobh E taobh P   ¹⁷-adh P
¹⁸ansin P: *the re-inker has missed the stroke over the* n   ¹⁹adbert E
aspert P   ²⁰Adh- *hic et semper* E   ²¹oss V   ²²oisibus E
²⁴caireo E   ²⁴carni V cairne EP   ²⁵om. is cuma E   ²⁶adeimsi E
doeimsi P   ²⁷-mh E: enaim dom *dittographed* V   ²⁸domh E
doma P   ²⁹en-EP, -mh P   ³⁰feoil E feoilsi P   ³¹ins. fein E
³²an P   ³³ced EP   ³¹choibche V caibhgi E   ³⁵ins. ⁊ an
cet failti P: dodorondad (*sic*) E. doronnad P   ³⁶riamh E   ³⁷inisin
V andsin P   ³⁸ ³⁸ om. P   ³⁹ced-failti E

5*. And God said unto them: *De terra es et in terram ibis*, [*i.e.*, Of earth thou art and into earth shalt thou go]. *Et dixit, In sudore uultus tui comedes panem tuum*, [*i.e.*, It shall be in the sweat of thy face that thou shalt eat thy loaves]. He said further unto Eve, *Cum dolore et gemitu paries filios tuos* [*et filias tuas, i.e.*, It shall be with torment and sickness that thou shalt bring forth thy sons and thy daughters].

5A. The corporeal creation was displayed to Adam, and he accepted them not. Wherefore a sleep was cast upon him. In that sleep thereafter was Eve fashioned, after being drawn from the seventh rib out of his side. And then said Adam: *Ecce os de ossibus meis, et caro de carne mea* [*i.e.* (*b*) it is as it were that (?) I see a bone of my bones and flesh of my flesh. That is the first laugh which was ever uttered, and the first welcome].

4*. . . . After incurring the guilt of the transgression, Adam was then expelled out of Paradise into the common earth, [lest he should eat the fruits of the Tree of Life in Paradise; for were he to eat, he would never die, but have health and ease of mind(*c*) (?)].

6*. Thereafter the progeny of Adam committed transgression, to wit, the elder of the sons of Adam, Cain the accursed, by the slaying of his brother Abel son of Adam in his envy and haughtiness. [That was the first kin-murder of the world]. With the cheek-

---

4*. ¹ EP *are punctuated so as to append the first four words to the preceding* ¶: a E   ² centaibh P   ³ and E an P   ⁴ imarb- P -uis P   ⁵ innarbad V hiondarbad E   ⁶ Pardus E Parrthus P ⁷ isin EP   ⁸ -cend EP   ⁹ -mhl- EP : -dh P   ¹⁰ tor- E toirthi P ¹¹ an EP   ¹² chroinn E cr- P   ¹³ irgairti pui i Parrtus P   ¹⁴ a Pardus air E   ¹⁵ dtoimh- E toimledh P   ¹⁶ fuig- E -bedh P ¹⁷ bas EP   ¹⁸ ach P   ¹⁹ -uti EP   ²⁰ cend EP   ²¹ fria P ²² codl- EP

6* ¹ imarbaighes dais E imarb*aigh*sistair P   ² -sin E *om.* P ³ cland E clanna P   ⁴ sindser E sinser P   ⁵ Cadin *changed sec. man. to* Caim E Caidin P   ⁶ miscadac P   ⁷ bh- E   ⁸ Aibel E ⁹ tri P   ¹⁰ -ad E, at P   ¹¹ dio- E, diu- P   ¹² ced EP   ¹³ -ce- P ¹⁴ an P   ¹⁵ sain V *om.* E   ¹⁶ camh- P (E *here illegible*)   ¹⁷ *om.* P

(*a*) Here P becomes legible.
(*b*) *Is cuma* is meaningless: see the note on this ¶.
(*c*) See the note on this ¶.

‡ [19]No mar [20]atberat araile, fō [21]intamail [22]marbtha na [32]n-idhbart, [24]issī a [25]glacc ro [26]īad immo [27]brāigid. ||

Here ends the matter on the leaf derived from. *Q: the original text of R[2], as we have it, begins at this point.

11. . . . [1]conid desin [2]tuc Dīa [3]dīliu [4]dar in domain [5]imaille, [6]connach tērna beō dīb acht [7]Nōe [8]cona [9]mnāi, ‡ .i. a [10]siur [11]fodesin ||, ⁊ [12]cona [13]thrīb macaib, ‡ ⁊ bātar [14]iat-sidhe fir a trī n-ingen, || [15]⁊ cona [16]thrīb ingenaib, ‡ ⁊ [17]bādar [18]iat-side mnā na [19]trī mac ||.

12. Ocus ba hē [1]fochond a [2]sāertha sech cāch, ar [3]nīr chumasesat cairdes fri [4]clainn [5]Cāin; ⁊ [6]dīa [7]līnad [8]in [9]domain [10]doridissi. Cethracha [11]lāithe don [12]dīlind [13]ic sīlind. Sē cēt bliadan [14]āess [15]Nāe [16]in tan dochuaid [17]ina [18]airce, ‡ in tan [19]tarnaic [20]do Nōe cumtach ⁊ [21]ecor na hairci īar [22]forcedal Dē ‡' .i. [23]dēda do [24]inglan, [25]trēda [26]imorro ‡'' nō [27]sechta ||'' do glan, [28]dāig [29]idparta dēis [30]na [31]dīlind ||' ||. Luid [32]dana [33]Nāe cona [34]macaib ‡ ⁊ cona ingenaib || ⁊ cona [35]sēitchib [36]ina [37]airce[(a)], hi [38]sechtmad dēc [39]ēsca [40]Mai. ‡ For [41]nōn [40]Mai lotar isin [42]n-airce. || Dā cubat dēg din . . . ñas na [43]slēibtib [44]atā [45]airdiu.

[18] marp P   [19] *om.* no . . araile P   [20] adberad E   [21] innamh- P
[22] *morta with* b *sprs.* V -bhth- P   [23] n-idhbartai P   [24] no asi P
[25] ghlac P   [26] hiadh ima P   [27] bradaid E br-aid P
11. [1] conadh P   [2] tug E   [3] dili EP   [4] tars EP   [5] *om.* P
[6] E *illegible:* conach tucad beo (*changed by re-inker to* bed) diph P
[7] Naoi E Naei P   [8] -nai P   [9] mnaoi E   [10] *s not dotted* P
[11] badesin E fodeisin (*changed by re-inker to* -siu) P   [12] a (*om.* con) P
[13] tri mic P   [14] iadside E iad sidie P   [15] *om.* ⁊ P   [16] tri
hinngenaiph P   [17] batar E   [18] iadsidie P   [19] dtri E
12. [1] *ins.* so P: fochand E foēui (*changed by re-inker to* focui) P
[2] saortha E saorthai P   [3] -ad cairdes E: ni ro cumusca a geairdus P
[4] cloind E   [5] Caidin P   [6] do P   [7] lion- EP   [8] an P
[9] domuin V   [10] -dhisi P   [11] -thi P   [12] dilinn E: dilin (*changed*

bone of a camel Cain slew his brother. [Or, as others say, after the likeness of the slaying of the sacrifices, it was his grasp which he closed around his neck] . . .

---

11. . . . so that it was on that account that God brought a Flood over the world altogether, so that none thereof escaped alive except Noe and his wife, [his own sister], and his three sons, [who were the husbands of his three daughters], and his three daughters, [who were the wives of the three sons].

12. Now this was the reason for their deliverance to the exclusion of all others, for that they mingled no friendship with the progeny of Cain; and for their replenishing of the earth again. Forty days was the Flood a-raining. Six hundred years was the age of Noe when he went into his ark, [when there came to Noe the construction and ordering of the ark in accordance with the teaching of God: pairs of the unclean, triple pairs (or sevens) of the clean, for the purpose of sacrifice after the Flood]. So Noe went with his sons [and with his daughters] and with their wives, into his ark, on the seventeenth day of the moon of May. [On the nones of May they went into the Ark.] Twelve cubits [was the water] above the highest mountains.

---

by re-inker to dilui) P   [13] hic E ag P   [14] aois EP   [15] Naoi E .ix. (*sic*) P   [16] an P   [17] *om.* -a P   [18] aire P   [19] tairnig E tra tairnic P   [20] *om.* E, do .ix. P: cumdadach E, cumhdach P   [21] ecor E egor P: hairce V   [22] bf- P foirc- E   [23] -da *erased* P   [24] ning- V   [25] treada E tredha P   [26] *om.* P   [27] secht EP   [28] -gh P   [29] iodbar- E idhh- P   [30] *om.* na E   [31] -end EP   [32] dono P   [33] Naoi E Naei P   [34] macaibh . . . ingenuiph P   [35] -eibh P   [36] *om.* -a P   [37] aire P   [38] secht P   [39] esgu EP   [40] Maoi E (*bis*)   [41] noin P   [42] *om.* n- E: airc EP   [43] sleibi V sleibht*ibh* E sleipti P   [44] ita E   [45] hairdi E a hairdi P

(a) E inserts a full stop here, and begins a new sentence with the following Hi.

Dēcc [46]cubait don airce [47]fo [48]usce, [49]⁊ fiche ōs [50]usce : [51]⁊ is aire [52]is a dēcc fo [53]usce, [54].i. dā-dēg don [55]dīlin ōs [56]in [57]tslēib as [58]airdi, ar dāig na [59]hairci, ar is dēcc cubat dī fo [60]usce : [49] ⁊ nīr bo furāil [61]dā cubait [62]dana do usce [63]etir druim na [64]hairci ⁊ mullaige na [65]slīab.   [66]Conid aire sin [67]itā [68]dā cubait dēcc [69]ind airdi [70]na huisci ōs [71]cech [72]slēib [73]airdd.

13. Ro [1]bāidh [2]in [3]dīliu [4]na huile [5]dāine ⁊ [6]anmanna [7]archena, acht lucht na [8]haircce, ‡ ⁊ [9]Enōg, fil [10]hi Parrdus do [11]chathugud [12]ria [13]Hainnticrist, ⁊ [14]Findtan mac [15]Bochra.   [16]Issē [17]adfēda na [18]scēla-sa do cāch, īar ndīliun. ||

14. Hi [1]cind [2]cōicad lāithe ar cēt [3]rogabsat na [4]husce [5]sercadh.   Secht [6]lāithe [7]fichet ⁊ secht [8]mīss [9]dind [10]airce ō [11]thuinn do [12]thuind, [13]co ndesidh for [14]slēib Armenia.   Ro [15]sergsat na [16]husce [17]cosin . . . . [18]dechmud [19]mīss [20]atchessa mullaige na [14]slīab.   Hi [21]cind secht lā cethrachat īar sin ro [22]oslaic Nōe senister na [23]haircce ⁊ [24]fāitte [25]in fīach [26]immach ; ⁊ nī [27]thānic [28]i frithissi.   Ro [29]lēic in [30]colum [31]īar na [32]bārach, ⁊ [33]tānic [34]ar [35]cūlu, ar nī fuair airm [36]ind anadh. [37]Fōidis [38]Nōe [39]doriss [40]hi [41]cind secht [42]lāithi, ⁊ [43]doluid la [44]fescor, ⁊ [45]gessca [46]ola-chrainn cona [47]dhuillib ina

---

[46] cubaid E   [47] fon uus fo us *(tangled in re-inking)* E   [48] uisqe P
[49-49] *om.* V   [50] uisqe P   [51] om. - P   [52] as P   [53] uisqe P   [57] ⁊ for .i. P
[55] -inn P   [56] an P   [57] -eiph P   [58] airde P   [59] -ce P
[60] uisqe P   [61] *ins.* dana E coic *for* da EP   [62] *om.* dana do usce E :
dono do uisce P   [63] itir E   [64] -ce P   [65] sliabh P   [66] -adh E -ad P
[67] iata E. it P   [68] .u. for .ii. E : cupait P   [69] in airde P   [70] an us- E
ind us- P   [71] gach EP   [72] sleiph P   [73] aird EP
13. [1] baid E   [2] an P   [3] dili E dile P   [4] ina P   [5] daoine E
[6] -nnai P   [7] -cena E   [8] -ci E -ce P   [9] Encog E Enogh P   [10] a E
[11] cath- P   [12] fri E   [13] haner V haiuntier E ain xp̄ P   [14] Fint. E
-nnt- P   [15] Bocra P   [16] ise EP   [17] atfed E -eta P   [18] scel;a E
secai so P

Ten cubits was the ark under water, and twenty above water: and this is why it was ten under water—the Flood had twelve above the highest mountain, for the sake of the ark, for it (the ark) had ten cubits under water. So that two cubits of water would not be excessive between the keel of the ark and the tops of the mountains. Therefore the waters were twelve cubits in depth above every lofty mountain.

13. The Flood drowned all the men and beasts together, except the people of the ark, [and Enoch, who is in Paradise to fight against Antichrist, and Fintan son of Bochra. He it is who should relate these stories to all men, after the Flood].

14. At the end of a hundred and fifty days the waters began to dry up. Twenty-seven days and seven months was the ark (moving) from wave to wave, till it settled on a mountain of Armenia. The waters dried up until the <tenth month : on the first day of the> tenth month the tops of the mountains were seen. At the end of forty-seven days thereafter, Noe opened a window of the ark, and he sent the raven forth; and it came not back again. He let the dove out on the morrow, and it came back, for it found no place where it should stay. Noah sent it forth

---

14. ¹ cinn E geinn P   ² chaogad E .lª. P   ³ -a *changed to* -ad cE -bhsat P   ⁴ huis- E -scedha P   ⁵ serg- E serec- P   ⁶ -thi P ⁷ -at P   ⁸ mis EP   ⁹ don EP   ¹⁰ aire P   ¹¹ tuinn EP ¹² tuinn E thuinn P   ¹³ con-deis- E -deisigh P   ¹⁴ sliabh P (*bis*) ¹⁵ sergtsat V *apparently* -gsat *changed to* -gsad cE -gsat P   ¹⁶ huis- EP ¹⁷ gusan E   ¹⁸ deem. E   ¹⁹ mis EP   ²⁰ adcesai E atceassa P ²¹ cinn P   ²² fosgail Naoi seinistir E, fosloig Naei feinister P ²³ hairci E hairce P   ²⁴ faiti EP   ²⁵ an P   ²⁶ amach EP ²⁷ tainic EP   ²⁸ for cula a bfritisi E, i frithisi P   ²⁹ leig E leice P ³⁰ colaim E   ³¹ ar P   ³² marach P   ³³ tain- EP   ³⁴ for E ³⁵ cula EP : fuair E   ³⁶ an an E, ar n-anfad P   ³⁷ faidis E ³⁸ Nai E   ³⁹ doridisi P   ⁴⁰ a E   ⁴¹ ge- EP   ⁴² -the E   ⁴³ -dh P ⁴⁴ fesgor E feascc- P   ⁴⁵ gesga E gescai P   ⁴⁶ alo-er P   ⁴⁷ duill- P

⁴⁸bēolu. Ocus ro ⁴⁹fāid ⁵⁰hi cind secht ⁵¹lā doridissi, ⁊ nī ⁵²tānic ⁵³ar ⁵⁴cūlu.

15. Ro ¹rāid Dīa fri ²Nōe ³tiachtain ⁴assin ⁵n-airce, ⁶hi sechtmad ⁷lā fichet ⁸ēscai ⁹Mai, ‡ for ¹⁰pridnōin ⁹Mai, ‖ isin ¹¹cētna bliadain ar sē cētaib ¹²āisse ¹³Nōe.

y¹ ¹⁴Tossach na ¹⁵hāeisse ¹⁶tānaiste ¹⁷in domain. ¹⁸Co ¹⁹gen ²⁰Abraim ro ²¹saich .i. dā bliadain ²²nōchat ar dib ²³cētaib īar ²⁴fīrinde na ²⁵nEbraide, īarsin ²⁶Septin imorro is dā bliadain cethrachat ar ²⁷ocht ccētaib.

²⁸Dorōne ²⁹Nōe īarsin altoir do ³⁰chumtach do ³¹Dīa ‡ .i. in ³²cētna ³³altōir īar ³⁴ndīlind ‖. ³⁵Cōica ar ³⁶trī cētaib bliadan ³⁷bāi ²⁹Nōe ³⁸i mbeth'aid īar ³⁹nd'ilind : ⁴⁰ocus ⁴¹ro ⁴²rand ⁴³Nōe ⁴⁴in domun ⁴⁵hi ⁴⁶trib rand'aib ⁴⁷itir' a ⁴⁸maccu.

y² ⁴⁹Anmand mac ⁵⁰Nōe, .i. ⁵¹Sem. ⁵²Cam, Iafet. ⁵³Anmand 'a' mban iarum. Olla, ⁵⁴Olībana, Oliua : *de quibus dicitur* ⁵⁵*hoc carmen*

Slūag nād chlōe cūa-chel . . .

Cam trā, ⁵⁶ro gab-side in ⁵⁷nAffraicc ⊓ ⁵⁸deisscert-leth na ⁵⁹Haissia. ⁶⁰Sem for ⁶¹medōn ⁶²Aissia, ō sruth Eofrait co tracht airthir ⁶³in ⁶⁴bethad. Is ō ⁶⁵Iafeth

---

⁴⁴ -la E -lau P   ⁴⁹ faoidh E faidh P   ⁵⁰ a gcenn E hi cinn ⁵¹ la *yc* V *sprs*: doridisi E, -dhisi P   ⁵² tainice P   ⁵³ for E ⁵⁴ gcnla P
15. ¹raidh P   ² Naoi E Nai P   ³ teacht P   ⁴ assind E as in P   ⁵ aire EP *(om.* n-)   ⁶ *om.* hi P   ⁷ *om.* la VE   ⁸ esgai E escca P   ⁹ Maoi E *(bis)*   ¹⁰ prittnoin P   ¹¹ cedna E   ¹² aois EP ¹³ Naoi E .ix. P   ¹⁴ tossuch V tosach EP   ¹⁵ haoisi EP   ¹⁶ tanuste P ¹⁷ an E   ¹⁸ go E   ¹⁹ gein EP   ²⁰ Apraim P   ²¹ soich P ²² nochad E   ²³ -aiph P   ²⁴ bf- EP   ²⁵ nEabr- E nEpr- P ²⁶ Seibtin E   ²⁷ dcccc. P   ²⁸ -oine E   ²⁹ Naoi E Nai P *(bis)* ³⁰ cumdach E qmhdach P   ³¹ Dhia P   ³² cedna E   ³³ h-alt- P   ³⁴ -inn E ³⁵ caoga P   ³⁶ *written* tri .ccc. E   ³⁷ baoi E   ³⁸ ina E: *words*

again at the end of seven days, and it came with the evening, having a twig of an olive-tree with its leaves in its beak. And he sent it forth again at the end of seven days, and it came not back.

15. God said unto Noe to come out of the Ark, on the twenty-seventh day of the moon of May, [on the day before the nones of May,] in the six hundred and first year of the age of Noe.

The beginning of the second age of the world. To the birth of Abram it reached, two hundred ninety and two years according to the Hebrew verity, but according to the Septuagint it is eight hundred forty and two years.

Thereafter Noe caused an altar to be builded to God [, the first altar that was made after the Flood]. Three hundred and fifty years was Noe alive after the Flood: and Noe divided the world into three parts among his sons.

The names of the sons of Noe: Sem, Ham, Iafeth. The names of their wives thereafter: Olla, Olivana, Oliva(*a*): *de quibus dicitur hoc carmen:*

Poem no. I.

As for Ham, he settled in Africa and the south side of Asia. Sem over the middle of Asia, from the river of Euphrates to the eastern border of the world. Of

---

and letters marked thus '. . . .' torn away V   [39] -inn E   [40] occus P [41] do E   [42] rann EP   [43] Naoi E   [44] an P   [45] a E   [46] trip P [47] etir P   [48] -ca E   [49] -nda E -udai P   [50] Naoi EP: *ins dana* E [51] Seimh E   [52] Camh E Camm P   [53] -nn EP   [54] Oilibai Oilibana E: Oliua Olibanu P   [55] hocc cairm- P   [56] -bhsidhe P [57] Affraicc E -aic P: (*om.* n-)   [58] deise- E dq P   [59] Haisia EP [60] Seimh EP   [61] -medhon EP   [62] Aissai E Aisia P   [63] om. in E; an P   [64] betha EP   [65] Iathfedh E Iafeith P

(*a*) EP give the names of these women in the correct order: Olibana was the wife of Iafeth.

trā tūaiscert-leth na [66]Haissia, ⁊ lucht na Heorpa uile : ⁊ dīa [67]clainn [68]duinde [69]in n-ar [70]nGāidelaib.

16. [1]Gāidel Glass ar sen-athair, mac-[2]side Niūil meic [3]Fēniusa Farrsaidh meic [4]Eogein meic [5]Glūnřind meic [6]Lāmřind meic [7]Etheoir meic [8]Thōe meic [9]Boidb meic [10]Sem meic Mair meic [11]Aurthacht meic Abuith meic Ara meic [12]Iarra meic Srū meic [13]Esrū meic Baaith meic [14]Rifaith [15]Scut, [16]ō tāit [17]Scuit. Ocus [18]issē [19]Rifath [20]Scot [21]tucastar [22]Scotic ōn Tur, ar ba [23]sē in sesed prīm-[24]thaisech ro [25]bāi i [26]ccumtach [27]in [28]Tuir Nemrōith.

Is follus de sin nach [29]raibe [30]Fēnius [31]hi cumtach in Tuir, mar [32]atberat na [33]senchaide cen [34]comšīniudh [35]chomhaimseraid. Is aire [36]so ōn, ar [37]issē [38]Fōenu Farsaid in [39]seised fer dēc do [40]šīl [41]Riafaid [42]tuc [43]Scotic ōn [44]Tur.

17. Dā bliadain [1]sescat ō [2]scāiliud [3]in Tuir co [4]flaith Nin meic [5]Peil. Ceithre bliadna dēc ar [6]trib fichtib ar ocht cētaib ō thūs [7]flatha Nin co [8]deirid flatha Tutanes, [9]rīg [10]in domain. [11]Fria lind-[12]side ro toglad [13]Trōe [14]din thogail [15]dēdenaig. Secht mbliadna īarsin thogail sin, co [16]tuc [17]Aenias ‡ mac [18]Anaciss ‖ ‡ [19]Lauinia ‖ [20]ingen [21]Latin meic Puin : [22]conid trī bliadna cethrachat ar nōi cētaib ō [23]scāiliud in Tuir co [24]tuc

---

[66] Haisia EP   [67] cloinn E   [68] -nne EP   [69] nar (om. i) P
[70] -eal- E nGaidheal- P

16. [1] ins. .i. EP; Gaoid- E   [2] -dhe VP   [3] Feiniusa Fars- EP
[4] Ebir E Eimhir P   [5] Gluin- EP, -nn E   [6] Lamhř- E Laimhf- P
[7] Eothoir E Ei- P   [8] Taoi EP   [9] Bridliph P   [10] Seim E
[11] Urthacht E Aurtachtt P   [12] Iara EP   [13] Essru E   [14] Rifbaidth
(d expuncted) E   [15] Scot E Sgot P   [16] odtait P   [17] Sguit P
[18] ise E ase P   [19] -aith E   [20] Sgot P   [21] ins. tucc (an incorporated gloss on tucastar) V : tugustar EP   [22] Scotig E Sgoitic P   [23] se in seised E, he an seisedh P   [24] -tuis- V -thoiss- E primh-tois- P   [25] bui EP   [26] cumdach P   [27] an P   [28] Tur (with subscript i added sec. man.) P   [29] roibe E raiphe P   [30] Foenius E Feinius P   [31] i ccumt-

Iafeth is the north side of Asia, and the people of all Europe: and of his progeny are we who are Gaedil.

16. Gaidel Glas our ancestor, he was s. Nel s. Feinius Farsaid s. Eogan s. Glunfhind s. Lamfhind s. Etheor s. Thoe s. Bodb s. Sem s. Mar s. Aurthacht s. Aboth s. Ara s. Iara s. Sru s. Esru s. Baath s. Rifath Scot, from whom are the Scots. Now it is Rifath Scot who brought the Scotic Language from the Tower, for he was one of the six principal chieftains who were at the building of the Tower of Nemrod.

From that, it is clear that Feinius was not at the building of the Tower, as the historians say who have not harmonized the synchronism. This is why we say so, for Feinius was the sixteenth in descent from Rifath, who brought Scotic from the Tower.

17. Sixty-two years from the dispersal of the Tower to the princedom of Ninus son of Belus. Eight hundred seventy and four years from the beginning of the princedom of Ninus to the end of the princedom of Tutanes, king of the world. Toward his time was Troy taken for the last time. There were seven years after that capture, till Aeneas [son of Anchises] took [Lavinia] daughter of Latinus s.

E hi cumdach P   ³²adberad E (the d *yc* E) adberait P   ³³uide E aidhe VP   ³⁴chomsiniud E -sinedh P   ³⁵comaimsiraid E comhaimsire P ³⁶seo E   ³⁷ise EP   ³⁸Foenius E Feinus (with *subscript* i *added sec. man.*) P   ³⁹seissed E seisedh P   ⁴⁰siol P   ⁴¹-aith E: *ins.* Sguit P   ⁴²tuce E   ⁴³-icc E, Sgoitic P   ⁴⁴Tor P

17. ¹-ccat E -lxx- *second* x *expuncted* P   ²sgaoil- P   ³an P ⁴dtuce Aenias *written here and expuncted* P   ⁵Pheil E   ⁶tri EP ⁷flaitusai P   ⁸derid V deired E -edh P   ⁹ri EP   ¹⁰an P ¹¹*ins.* ⁊ P   ¹²-dhe VP   ¹³Troie V Trai P   ¹⁴din tog- E don toce- P ¹⁵-aigh E deighean- P   ¹⁶tuce E dtuce P   ¹⁷Aneas E Acinas P The glosses following this word are *gg* in VP, 55 in E.   ¹⁸Anachis E Aineis P   ¹⁹Lauina EP   ²⁰ingin E   ²¹Lathin P   ²²conadh P ²³sgaoil- P: in Tuir *yc* V   ²⁴tuce Aeneas ingin E: dtuce Aeinas P

Aeniass ingen [25]Latin, ⁊ [25]Latin [26]doróne [27]a cuir [28]friss.

[29]Is follus as sin conach cert-[30]tiaghait [31]lucht [32]ind [33]Auraicepta, [34]combad hē [35]Laitin in [36]seissed prīm-[38]thóiseeh [39]ind Tuir, ⁊ a [40]fot [41]anñass [42]etorru [43]cethracha bliadan, o [44]scāiliud in Tuir co [45]tānic [46]Foenius Farsaidh [47]atūaidh asin [48]Scithia cona [49]scoil, do [50]iarraidh na [51]mbērla : ar do-[52]rumenatar [53]fosgebtais [54]and, ar bīth [55]as ass ro [56]scāilit. [57]Dā bliadain īar [58]tiachtain do [59]Fēnius atūaid [60]corice Nin.

18. Is [1]ē Nēl mac [2]Feniusa Farsaid [3]asrubrumar forcongart [4]Forand [5]Cineris rī [6]Eigipti [7]ar imad a [9]fesa ⁊ a [10]eōlais ⁊ a [11]foghluma : ⁊ [12]dobert [13]Forand [14]ferann do, ⁊ [15]dobreath a [16]ingen [17].i. [18]Scota a hainm.

[19]Ocus asberat araile [20]comadh aire [21]adbertha "Scota" [22]fria, ar ba [23]"Scot" ainm a fir, ⁊ [24]"Scuit" ainm na [25]tūaithe dia [26]rabe [27]in fer; *unde dicitur* [28]"Scotus" ⁊ [28]"Scota."

19. [1]Conidh [2]do sin [3]asberar [4]so [5]sīss—

---

[25] Laitin P (bis)   [26] *ins.* fein E: doroine P   [27] acuir *written as one word* VP, *but om.* a E   [28] fris P   [29] iss E   [30] -aid E   [31] luicht E : luꝑ *changed by re-inker to* ais (*the* l *can still be traced faintly*) P   [32] na P   [33] auraicepta E nuraicp P   [34] comadh P   [35] Latin E   [36] insseiss- E .uii. mad P   [38] -tois- P   [39] in E an P   [40] fot E fod P   [41] -as P   [42] -orrai P   [43] .lx. E   [44] sgaoil- P   [45] dtanic P   [46] Feinius P   [47] -aid assin E   [48] Sgeithia P   [49] sgoil P   [50] iaraidh V   [51] -lae E -lai P   [52] -att *changed to* -atar V ruimnetar P   [53] -dais P   [54] ann EP : ar *dittographed owing to change of column* V   [55] is E   [56] sgaoilsit P   [57] .u. V   [58] tichtain (*om.* do) E   [59] Foen- E Feinius P   [60] -ricce P

Faunus: so that there are nine hundred forty and three years from the dispersal of the Tower till Aeneas took the daughter of Latinus, and Latinus made his treaties with him.

From that it is clear that the authors of the *Auraicept* do not reach a correct conclusion, that Latinus was one of the six chief leaders of the Tower, seeing that the length downward between them is forty years, from the dispersal of the Tower till Feinius Farsaid came from the north, out of Scythia with his School, to seek for the languages : for they thought that they would find them there[a] inasmuch as it was from thence that they were dispersed. There were two years after the coming of Feinius from the north until Ninus.

18. It is the aforesaid Nel son of Feinius Farsaid whom Pharao Cincris King of Egypt invited, for the greatness of his skill, his knowledge, and his learning : and Pharao granted him an estate, and his daughter, Scota her name, was bestowed.

Some say that the reason why she was called "Scota" was that "Scot" was her husband's name, and "Scots" the name of the people from whom he came; *unde dicitur* "Scotus" and "Scota."

19. So that the following is said of those matters—

---

18. [1] he E   [2] Foen- E Fein- P   [3] asrubramar E asrubartamar P [4] -nn E   [5] Cinciris P   [6] Egipt EP   [7] ar immed E ar imat P [9] fessa E feassai *re-inked to* feuisai P   [10] eolusa E   [11] -lumma E -gh- P [12] dober V tuc P   [13] -ainn E -ann P   [14] ferand E feron (*changed by re-inker to* ferch-*)* P   [15] dobertha *yc*E dobreth P   [16] ingin E   [17] *om.* .i. E: *ins.* do P   [18] Sgotai P   [19] *om.* ⁊ E   [20] combad E   [21] asbertha E atbertha P   [22] frie E *punctuated* fria arba. Sgot *by re-inker* P [23] Sgot P   [24] Sguit P   [25] -thi P   [26] raibe E raibhi P   [27] an P [28] -tt- E (*bis*): Sgota P
19. [1] Conid E conadh P   [2] de E   [3] asbert P   [4] *om.* so E [5] *om.* siss EP

(a) i.e. at the Tower.

Athair cāich, Coimsid Nime . . .

Third Redaction.

(B 8 *a* 1 : M 264 *a* 1 : H 103 *a* 1 :
from ¶ 32 : β 32 . 13 : β¹ 32 . 22 : β² 6 . 28.)

I.

*The beginning of the Third Redaction is a translation
into Irish of the first eleven chapters of the Book of Genesis.
For the history of this translation, and of its connexion with
the text, see* ante, *p. 6. In the following pages the Biblical
text is printed in larger type (the verses being numbered):*

BOOK OF GENESIS

CHAPTER I.

20. (1) *In ¹principio creauit Deus celum et terram*
.i. ro ²thuissimh Dīa ³Neamh ⁊ ⁴talumh ⁵ar tūs.

y¹   ⁊ nī ⁶fuil tossach fair-⁷simh ⁸feisin, na foirceand.

y²   Is amhlaidh ⁹dorighni Dīa na ¹⁰dūili : aroili dīb co
¹¹tosach ⁊ cen chrīch, amhail aingliu ; ¹²araili dībh ¹³cu
¹⁴tossach ⁊ co ¹⁵forcend, amhail ¹⁶anmanda indlighthe ⁊
¹⁷toirrthe in talman ; ¹⁸araile dībh imorro co ¹⁹tossach ⁊ co
²⁰foircend ⁊ ²¹cen ²²foircend, amail ²³atait dāine, .i. ²⁴tossach
for a ²⁵ngeinemain ²⁶corpardha ⁊ ²⁷forcend for a ²⁸corpthaib,
⁊ ²⁹gan ³⁰forcenn for a n-anmandaibh.

y³   Isin Domnach ³¹dorighni Dīa in mais ³²n-adhbul-
mhōir ³³nemhcruthaigh ‡ .i. ³⁴adbhur na ndūl ³⁵corparda
‡′ .i. ³⁶tene ⁊ ³⁷āeor, ³⁸talam ⁊ usce ′, ∥ ‡ hi .xu. kallann
³⁹April dono do reir Ebraide ⁊ ⁴⁰Latinda, ∥ ‡′ cen co tucadh

---

20. *Variants from* M *unless otherwise stated. It may be said here,
once for all, that the lenition of* b, d, g, m, *is almost invariably left
unmarked in this MS.* ¹ princcipio ² thuisim ³ *tus.* .i. in tAthair
Neamda ⁴ talam ⁵ *om.* ar tus : *ins.* isin tosach .i. isin Mac ⁶ fuil
tosach ⁷ -seam ⁸ na foirceand feisin B ⁹ doroinde ¹⁰ duile
aroile ¹¹ tosach ¹² -oile ¹³ co ¹⁴ tosach ¹⁵ foirceand M ;

Poem no. V.

Third Redaction.

at the end of each chapter is a restoration of the text of the Latin MS. from which it was translated, with textual notes. The numerous glosses and interpolations are printed in smaller type, and all necessary annotations are given in the commentary at the end of this section of the entire work.

BOOK OF GENESIS

Chapter I.

20. (1) *In principio creauit Deus caelum et terram* i.e., God created Heaven and Earth at the first.

And He hath no beginning Himself, nor ending.

In this wise God made the creatures: some of them with beginning and without end, as Angels; some of them with beginning and with termination, as irrational beasts and fruits of the earth; some of them moreover with beginning and with termination and without termination, as are men—a beginning to their bodily birth and a termination to their bodies, and without termination to their souls.

On the Sunday God made the immense formless mass, [the materials of the corporeal creatures, fire and air, earth and water, upon the fifteenth of the kalends of April according to Hebrews and Latins, although no sun

---

a dot over e *erased* B   [16] -nna aindligthecha   [17] toirthi   [18] -oile
[19] tosach [20] -ceand [21] cean [22] -ceand [23] itait na daine [24] tosach
[25] -eam- [26] chorparda [27] foirceand [28] *sic* M, corp B [29] cen
[30] foirceand [31] doridne [32] -bal-moir [33] -aich [34] -bar [35] *sic* M;
corpdha *changed by late corrector to* corpdhada B   [26] tened   [37] aeoir
[38] usqi ┐ talam [39] Aibril [40] Laitinda

grīan ⁴¹for rith co se ‖′; is and ⁴²dorighni Dīa ⁴³tindscetal denma na ndūl. Isin Lūan, ‡ hi .xiiii. kallann ⁴⁴April, ‖ dorighni Dīa Neam. ⁴⁵Isand Mairt, ⁴⁶‡ hi .xiii. kallann ⁴⁷April, ‖ ⁴⁸dorighni Dīa in talam, ⁊ ⁴⁹tug muir ina ⁵⁰timceall. Isin ⁵¹Cētāin, ‡ hi .xii. kallann ⁵²April, ‖ ⁵³dorigni Dīa grīan ⁊ ēsca ⁊ ⁵⁴rēltanda ⁊ ⁵⁵renda nimhe. Isin Dardāin, ‡ .i. in .xi. kallann ⁵⁶April ‖, dorigni Dīa na hanmanda ⁵⁷muiridhi ⁊ ⁵⁸eathaidi in ⁵⁹āeoir. ⁶⁰Isan Āine imorro ‡ ⁶¹.i. hi .x. kallann ⁶²April, ‖ ⁶³dorigni Dīa Adham ⁊ na huili anmanda talmaidi. Ro ⁶⁴cumsain Dia imorro ⁶⁵isan ⁶⁶tSatharrnd ‡ .i. hi .ix. kallann ⁶⁷April ‖, .i. ⁶⁸ō ⁶⁹oipriugadh dūla nūa.

(2) Iar tuismeadh trā ⁷⁰nime ⁊ talman, is amhlaidh ⁷¹bāi in talam, ⁊ sē dimain cen ⁷²torrti, ⁊ sē ⁷³fāss ⁷⁴falum cen ⁷⁵aitreabhaidhe. Ocus no bīdis ‡ in tan sin ‖ ⁷⁶dorchata ⁷⁷dlūithi for ⁷⁸dreich na ⁷⁹hāibhisi—

.i. ⁸⁰adbur ⁸¹coitchend na ndūl—

⁊ ⁸²no fortairctha ⁸³Spīrut in ⁸⁴Comdedh for na ⁸⁵huiscib.

Ni ⁸⁶locdacht ⁸⁷trā rāiter ⁸⁸sund don ⁸⁹Spīrut Nāem, acht ⁹⁰dearrscaithi ⁊ miadhamlacht de, seacha dūilibh.

(3) Ocus ro rāidh Dīa ‡ .i. in tAthair Nemdha ‖, Dēntar ⁹¹in tsoillsi. Ocus ⁹²dorignedh in tsoillsi. (4) Ro therba ⁊ ro ⁹³deiligh Dīa in ⁹⁴soillsi [s²M] ōna ⁹⁵dorchadaibh. (5) Ocus dorad ainm "Lāe" don tsoillsi, ⁊ tuc ainm na ⁹⁶"Haidhchi" do na ⁹⁷dorchaib. Ocus dorōnadh amlaidh sin ⁹⁸feascoir ⁊ ⁹⁹maiden .i. in ¹⁰⁰cēt lā.

---

⁴¹ frith *stroke of abbreviation over f added see. man.* B   ⁴² doroinde ⁴³ -eadal   ⁴⁴ Aibril   ⁴⁵ isin   ⁴⁶ *ins.* dono   ⁴⁷ Aipril   ⁴⁸ doridne ⁴⁹ tuc   ⁵⁰ thimchell   ⁵¹ chedain am. hi   ⁵² Aip-   ⁵³ dorinde   ⁵⁴ retlanda ⁵⁵ reanda   ⁵⁶ Aip-   ⁵⁷ -ide   ⁵⁸ -ide   ⁵⁹ *a point over the* e M   ⁶⁰ isind ⁶¹ *om.* .i.   ⁶² Aip-   ⁶³ doroinde   ⁶⁴ chumson   ⁶⁵ isin   ⁶⁶ -arnn ⁶⁷ Aib-   ⁶⁸ *om.* o   ⁶⁹ oibreadugad   ⁷⁰ nimi   ⁷¹ *ins.* ro   ⁷² toirchi ⁷³ fas   ⁷⁴ -am   ⁷⁵ -ebaide   ⁷⁶ -ada   ⁷⁷ *the* l *written in rasura as*

was set upon its course as yet]; it is then that God made
a beginning of fashioning the creatures. On the Monday,
[on the fourteenth of the kalends of April,] God made
Heaven. On the Tuesday, [on the thirteenth of the
kalends of April,] God made the earth, and brought Sea
around it. On the Wednesday, [on the twelfth of the
kalends of April,] God made sun and moon and stars and
heavenly bodies. On the Thursday, [on the eleventh of
the kalends of April] God made the marine beasts and
the birds of the air. On the Friday, moreover, [on the
tenth of the kalends of April,] God made Adam and all
the terrestrial beasts. Moreover God ceased on the
Saturday, [the ninth of the kalends of April,] from the
work of a new creation.

(2) Now, after the creation of Heaven and Earth, thus
was the earth; fallow without fruit, bare and empty
without indweller. And thick darknesses were at
that time over the face of the abyss—

the common material of the creatures—

And the Spirit of the Lord was borne over the
waters.

No wickedness is spoken here of the Holy Spirit, but
excellence and honour of Him, beyond the creatures.

(3) and God [the Heavenly Father] said: Let the
Light be made. And the light was made. (4) God
separated and divided the light from the darknesses.
(5) And He gave the name 'Day' to the light, and
the name 'Night' to the darknesses. And thus were
made evening and morning, the first day.

---

is also the eich of dreich B [78] dreikh [79] -beisi [80] -bar. A dot
written over the b, afterwards scratched out, and later re-inscrted, B
[81] cheand [82] no forehairthen [83] -rud [84] Choimdead [85] hus-
[86] lochtach [87] thra [88] sunn [89] -rit Naeim [90] dears- [91] inn
preceded by an erasure that would hold about 4 letters. [92] doridnead
[93] delidh [94] thoillsi [95] dorchaib [96] -dche [97] sic M -eaib B
[98] -scor [99] maidean an .i. with in written sec. man. above the .i. M
[100] om. cet B

21. (6) Ro rāidh ¹dana : Dēntar ²in fĭrmaimint a meadhōn na n-usci, ³ꞁ fodlad na n-usci³ ō na ⁴huiscib. (7) Ocus ⁵dorigni Dīa ⁶in firmaimint, ꞁ ro fogail na usci ro ⁷bātar fō Firmaimint ō na ⁸huiscibh ro ⁹bātar ōs Firmaimint : ꞁ ¹⁰doirigneadh amlaidh sin. (8) Ocus ¹¹tug ¹²Dīa ainm ' Nimhe' ¹³do Firmaimint, ꞁ ¹⁴dorighnedh ¹⁵feascoir ꞁ ¹⁶maiden, .i. ¹⁷in lāā tānaise.

22. (9) Ro rāidh imorro Dīa : ¹Tinōilter na ²husci atait fō Nimh ³i n-ōen inadh, ⁴ꞁ artraigeadh ⁵in tirim : ꞁ dorigneadh amlaidh sin. (10) Ocus ⁶is ē ainm ⁷tug Dīa don ⁸tirim, .i. ⁹Talam : acus ro ¹⁰gairmeastar Dīa ¹¹comthinōla na ¹²n-uisci, ¹³Muiridhi. Ocus ¹⁴atconnaire Dīa cor bo maith. (11) Ocus ¹⁵atbert Dīa : ¹⁶Clandaigeadh ¹⁷an talam fēr n-uraide, ꞁ fēr dogēna sīl ; ꞁ clannaigeadh¹⁷ ¹⁸crand toradh-¹⁹tairetheach, dodhēna toradh do rēir a ²⁰ceineōil, ꞁ a mbia a sīl and fēin for ²¹talmuin. (12) Ocus ro lēig ²²in talum fēr n-uraide trīd, ꞁ fēr dognīdh ²³sīl do ²⁴rēir a ²⁵ceineōil ; ꞁ ro ²⁶lēc ²⁷crand dognīd torad, ꞁ no ²⁸thechtadh ²⁹gach sīl do rēir a ³⁰carnaili. Ocus ³¹adconnaire Dīa sin, cor bho maith. (13) Ocus ³²dorighnedh ³³fescoir ꞁ ³⁴maiten, .i. ³⁵in tres lāā.

23. (14) Ro rāidh ¹imorro Dīa : Dēntar ²lēspairedha solus-³thaitneamacha ⁴i firmaimint ⁵indimhi, [s¹M] ꞁ ⁶deilighead ⁷lā ꞁ ⁸aidhchi : ꞁ ⁹bīt i ¹⁰comartaibh ꞁ i ¹¹n-aimsiribh, i ¹²l-lāithedhaibh ꞁ i ¹³mbliadhnaibh, (15) co ro ¹⁴taitneat i ¹⁵firmaimint ¹⁶ind nimi, ꞁ co ro

---

21. ¹ dono   ² annirmaimint   ³⁻³ om. B.   ⁴ husc-   ⁵ -gne
⁶ annirmaimint   ⁷ badar   ⁸ husc-   ⁹ badar   ¹⁰ doridnead   ¹¹ tue
¹² Di B   ¹³ donirmaimint   ¹⁴ -gnead   ¹⁵ -cor   ¹⁶ -dean   ¹⁷ om. in
    22. ¹ -tear   ² us-   ³ an en   ⁴ ꞁ ar- dittographed owing to change of column B   ⁵ an   ⁶ as   ⁷ tue   ⁸ talmain B   ⁹ tirim (tirim acus written tir imacus) B : acus here also in M   ¹⁰ -estair   ¹¹ coimthinola (a g written and erased after the second o)   ¹² n-usci
¹³ muirige   ¹⁴ adchonnaire   ¹⁵ adb-   ¹⁶ clannaigead   ¹⁷⁻¹⁷ om. B

21. (6) Further He said: Let the firmament be
made in the midst of the waters, and let it divide the
waters from the waters. (7) And God made the
firmament, and divided the waters that were beneath
Firmament from the waters that were above
Firmament: and thus was it done. (8) And God gave
the name of 'Heaven' to Firmament, and evening and
morning were made, the second day.

22. (9) Moreover God said: Let the waters that
are under Heaven be collected into one place, and let
the Dry appear: and so was it done. (10) And this
is the name which God gave to the Dry, 'Earth':
and God called the assemblages of the waters, 'Seas.'
And God saw that it was good. (11) And God said:
Let the earth bring forth green grass, and grass that
shall make seed; and let it bring forth the fruit-
bearing tree that shall make fruit according to its
kind, and that shall have its seed within itself upon
earth. (12) And the earth put forth green grass, and
grass that maketh seed according to its kind, and it
put forth the tree that maketh fruit, and that hath
every seed according to its species. And God saw
that to be good. (13) And evening and morning were
made, the third day.

23. (14) Moreover God said: Let brightly shining
lights be made in the firmament of Heaven, and let
them divide Day and Night: and let them be for signs
and for times, for days and for years, (15) that they
may shine in the firmament of Heaven, and

---

[18] crann   [19] thairceach   [20] a chel no a cenel   [21] -main   [22] an talam
[23] *ins.* a   [24] rel   [25] cheinel   [26] leig   [27] crann   [28] -eacht-
[29] gan B   [30] ernaile   [31] -chonn   [32] -gnead   [33] feascor : feascoir .i.
deireadh láe *written in top marg. in* 18th *cent. hand* B   [34] maidean
[35] an treas la
   23. [1] Dia imorro   [2] -eada   [3] -tait-   [4] a fir-   [5] inime
[6] deligthear   [7] lae   [8] -dche   [9] bid   [10] -arthaib   [11] -sir-, *the* i
*yc*B   [12] -ead-   [13] mbliadain   [14] thaitnead   [15] -mam-   [16] indimi

[17]soillsiget in [18]talam. Ocus [19]dorignedh amlaidh sin.
(16) Ocus doroindi [20]Dīa dā [21]lēaspaire [22]solus-mōra :
dorighni am in lēspaire is mō ‡ .i. in [23]grēin ‖ co
[24]ropdanaiged don lō, ⁊ in [25]lēspaire is lughu isin
[26]n-aidhci ‡ .i. [27]ind ēsca ‖. Ocus [28]dorigni rētlanda,
(17) ⁊ ro [29]suigidh iat [30]i firnaimint [31]indimi, co ro
[32]taitnidis for talmain, (18) [33]⁊ co ro aptainigdis [34]do
lō ⁊ [34]do aidhchi, ⁊ co [35]ndeilightis [36]in [37]soillsi ō na
dorchaibh. Ocus [38]atconnaic Dīa [39]sin, [40]cor bo maith.
(19) Ocus [41]dorignedh [42]fescoir ⁊ [43]maitin, [44].i. in
[45]cetramadh lāā.

24. (20) Ro rāidh [1]dana Dīa : [2]Turgbhat na [3]huisci
[4]tondaitechu na hanma [5]beoaigheas, ⁊ [6]folūaimneachu
fo irmaimint [7]indimi. Ocus [8]dorigned amlaidh sin.
(21) Ocus ro [9]thuissim Dīa [10]bleidhmila mōra ‡
muiridi ‖, ⁊ [11]ind uili n-annand mbeōthach ⁊ [12]so-cums-
caightheach ro [13]turgbatar na husci i n-a [14]n-ernailibh.
Ocus ro [15]tuissimh Dīa [16]in uili [17]folūaimneachu do
[18]rēr a [19]ceneōil, ⁊ [20]adconairc Dīa [21]cor bo maith sin.
(22) Ocus ro [22]bennai[ge]stear Dīa dōibh, ⁊ ro rāidh :
Foirbridh ⁊ [23]barnimdaighter ⁊ līnaidh usci in mhara,
⁊ [24]imdaighthear na heōin for talmain. (23) Ocus
[25]dorigned amlaidh sin [26]maiten ⁊ [27]fescoir, [28].i. in
[29]cūicedh lā.

25. (24) Ro rāidh [1]dono Dīa, ‡ .i. [2]in Tuismeadh ‖ :
[3]Turgbadh in [4]talmun (sic) na hanmanda [5]examla īar
n-a [6]cenēl imchubhaidh, .i. iuminti ⁊ [7]tondaitechu, ⁊

[17] s-ged   [18] sic M, tal- B   [19] doridnead   [20] om. Dia   [21] lesbairi
[22] solusda mora   [23] grian   [24] rapdanaided   [25] -airi   [26] -chi
[27] int   [28] doridni   [29] suigig   [30] a   [31] indime   [32] thaitnidis
[33] ⁊ (obscured by a blot) con apdanigis   [34] don (bis)   [35] -gdis
[36] om.   [37] soll-   [38] adchondaire   [39] om.   [40] apparently go mbo
changed sec. man. to gor bo M   [41] -ead   [42] -cor   [43] -ten   [44] om. .i.
[45] ceathrumad la
24. [1] Dia dono   [2] turcbad   [3] husci   [4] tonnaichu   [5] -ges

may illuminate the earth. And thus was it done.
(16) And God made two bright and great lights : He
made the greater light [the sun] that it might rule over
the day, and the lesser light in the night [the moon].
And He made stars, (17) and set them in the firmament
of Heaven, that they might shine upon the earth,
(18) and that they might rule over day and over
night, and might divide the light from the darknesses.
And God saw that to be good. (19) And evening and
morning were made, the fourth day.

24. (20) God said further : Let the waters bring
forth reptiles of the life that quickeneth, and birds
under the firmament of Heaven. And so was it done.
(21) And God created great [sea]-monsters, and
every living and mobile beast which the waters brought
forth in their species. And God created all the birds
according to their kind, and God saw that to be good.
(22) And God blessed them, and said : Increase and
be ye multiplied, and fill the water of the sea, and let
the birds be multiplied upon the land. (23) And thus
were morning and evening made, the fifth day.

25. (24) Further God [the Creator] said : Let the
earth bring forth the different animals after their
fitting kind, cattle and reptiles, and the beasts of

---

⁶ -echu   ⁷ -ime   ⁸ doridnead *changed by late corrector to* dorignead
in marg. M   ⁹ tuisim   ¹⁰ -ili   ¹¹ inn   ¹² -caith-   ¹³ thurebadar
¹⁴ hern- B   ¹⁵ *written* τ'puii *(an abbreviation which would more
naturally suggest* tursimh) B, čuin M.   ¹⁶ inn   ¹⁷ -each   ¹⁸ reir
¹⁹ cheniuil   ²⁰ -chond-   ²¹ sin cor bo maith   ²² beandachais
²³ -gth-   ²⁴ -gther   ²⁵ dorignidh B doridnead M   ²⁶ maiden   ²⁷ -cor
²⁸ *om.* .i.   ²⁹ -ead
     25. ¹ Dia dono   ² *om. in* B : t;m. M. *So lower down in the* ¶.
th;im.   ³ turebad   ⁴ -muin   ⁵ ecs-   ⁶ -eol   ⁷ -aithechu

ˢbīasda in ⁹talmun iar n-a n-earnailib imchuibhdibh;
⁊ ¹⁰doridned amlaidh sin.   (26) Ocus do rāidh Dīa :
¹¹Dēnum ¹²in ¹³Duini ¹⁴for n-īmāigin ⁊ for ¹⁵cosmhailus
fodēn, ⁊ remhapdanaighed do īascaib in mara, ⁊ do
¹⁶folūaimneaibh indimi, ⁊ do ¹⁷bhīastaibh in uili
¹⁸talman.   (27) Ocus ro ¹⁹thuissim Dīa in Duini ²⁰fō
īmāigin fodēn—

> Is amlaidh trā dorigni Dīa in duine, .i. a ²¹corp do
> ²²talmain ‡', ²³.i. a ²⁴chend a tīr Garad, a ucht ⁊ a bruindi
> a tīr ²⁵Arabia, a brū a ²⁶Lodain, a ²⁷cossa a tīr Agoiria, ‖' a
> fuil do usci ‡ in ²ˢāer ‖. a anāl do āeor, a ²⁹teas do ³⁰teinidh,
> a ³¹anam do ³²tinfedh Dē.   Is amlaidh sin ³³atāt na ³⁴ceithre
> dūili ³⁵i ngach duini.

—ro thuisim ³⁶ēm fear ⁊ mnaī fo īmāigin Dē.   Ro
thuisim ³⁷iat (28) ⁊ ro ³⁸bennach dōibh ⁊ ro rāid :
Forbrid ⁊ dēntar bar n-imdugadh, ⁊ līnaidh in
³⁹talmuin, ⁊ fomāmaigid dūibh hī, ⁊ ⁴⁰tigernaigid do
īascaibh in mara ⁊ do ⁴¹eathaitibh inime ⁊ do na huilibh
anmandaibh ⁴²for talmain.   (29) Ocus ⁴³ro rāidh
Dīa : Doradus dāibh co follus in uili ⁴⁴īear ⁴⁵tairgis
sīl for talmain, ⁊ na huili ⁴⁶crondu ⁴⁷techtait indtibh
fodēn | sīlni a ⁴⁸ceineōil |⁽ᵃ⁾ ⁴⁹comchubhaid, ardāigh co
ᶜ⁰mbēadh sin dāibh a mbiadh ⁊ a n-aileamain : (30) ⁊ do
uilibh anmandaibh in talman, ⁊ do uilibh ⁵¹eathaitibh
in ⁵²nimi, ⁊ do na huilibh ⁵³da īil ⁵⁴cumscugadh i
talmain, ⁊ is ⁵⁵inntibh atā ⁵⁶ainim beoighes, co ro
ᶜ'techat co tomultus.   Ocus ⁵⁸dorigned amlaidh sin.
(31) Ocus ⁵⁹adchondaire Dīa na huili ⁶⁰dorigni, ‡ ⁊
ᶜ¹do bhadar ‖, ⁶²comdar maithi co ⁶³hadhbul.   Ocus
ᶜ⁴dorighnedh ⁶⁵fescoir ⁊ ⁶⁶maiten, in seiseadh lā.

ˢ -sta   ⁹ -man   ¹⁰ dorigni B   ¹¹ denaid   ¹² *om.* in   ¹³ duine
¹⁴ foim maigin *(second word in rasura)* B fornimaigin M   ¹⁵ cosmailis
¹⁶ foluaimneachaib innimi   ¹⁷ pinstaib   ¹ˢ thal-   ¹⁹ tusim Dia in
Dui*ne*   ²⁰ foi maigin B   ²¹ chorp   ²² thal-   ²³ ⁊ *for* .i.
²⁴ cheand   ²⁵ Araibia   ²⁶ Lotain   ²⁷ chosa   ²⁸ aeoir   ²⁹ theas
³⁰ thenid   ³¹ ainm B anim M   ³² thinfead   ³³ itat   ³⁴ -thri   ³⁵ in
each duine   ³⁶ aen īear B   ³⁷ *ins.* imorro : iad   ³ˢ beandach

the earth after their fitting species; and so was it done.   (25) [*This verse missing.*]   (26) And God said: Let us make the Man under our own image and likeness, and let him have dominion over the fishes of the sea, and over the birds of Heaven, and over the beasts of the whole earth.   (27) And God created the Man under His own image—

Now in this wise did God make the Man: his body of earth [his head of the land of Garad, his breast and bosom of the land of Arabia, his belly of Lodain, his legs of the land of Agoiria], his blood of [the] water [of the air], his breath of air, his heat of fire, his soul of the breath of God. Thus it is that the four elements are in every man.

In truth He made man and woman under the image of God.   He created them (28) and blessed them and said: Increase, and let your multiplication be accomplished, and fill the earth, and subdue it unto yourselves, and lord it over the fishes of the sea and the birds of the Heaven and all the beasts upon the earth.   (29) And God said: See, I have given you all the grass that bringeth forth seed upon the earth, and all the trees that have the seed of their proper kind within themselves, that they may be for food and sustenance unto you: (30) and unto all the beasts of the earth, and unto all the birds of Heaven, and unto all that have motion upon the earth, and that have within them the soul that quickeneth, that they may have them for nourishment.   And thus was it done.   (31) And God saw all things that He had made [and that were], that they were wondrous good: and evening and morning were made, the sixth day.

---

[39] talam   [40] tigernaidhi B   [41] -dib   [42] *ins.* fuilet   [43] *om.* ro B   [44] fer   [45] -rceas   [46] chrunnu   [47] -taid intib fodein silne   [48] chen-   [49] comcubhaib B   [50] mbeith   [51] -dib   [52] nime   [53] do fil   [54] -gud   [55] intib   [56] ainm beoaiges   [57] thechtad   [58] -ghnidh B doridnead M   [59] oteonaire B   [60] dorigne   [61] ro badar   [62] comdartha B   [63] -dbal   [64] -ridned   [65] -cor   [66] -den.

(a) These 3 words *s²* M

E

20. (1)*(a)* In principio ¹creauit Deus caelum et terram.
(2) ²[Terra autem erat inanis et uacua] et ³tenebrae ⁴*erant*
super faciem abyssi: et Spiritus ⁵*Domini* ferebatur super
aquas.   (3) Dixitque Deus: Fiat lux.   Et facta est lux.
(4) ⁶[Et uidit Deus lucem quod esset bona,] et ⁷diuisit ⁸*Deus*
lucem ⁹*a tenebris*.   (5) Appellauitque lucem 'Diem,' et
tenebras 'Noctem.'   Factumque est ¹⁰<ita> uespere et mane,
dies ¹¹primus.

21. (6) Dixit quoque ¹[Deus]: Fiat firmamentum in
medio aquarum, et diuidat aquas ab aquis.   (7) Et fecit Deus
firmamentum, diuisitque aquas quae erant sub ²firmamento
³*ab aquis* quae erant super firmamentum: et factum est ita.
(8) Vocauitque Deus firmamentum 'Caelum,' et factum est
uespere et mane, dies secundus.

22. (9) Dixit uero Deus: Congregentur aquae quae sub
caelo sunt in locum unum, et appareat arida: factumque est
ita.   (10) Et uocauit Deus aridam, Terram; congregationesque
aquarum appellauit Maria.   Et uidit Deus quod esset bonum.
(11) Et ait ¹<Deus>: Germinet terra herbam uirentem et
²facientem semen, et lignum pomiferum faciens fructum iuxta
³genus suum, cuius semen in semetipso sit super terram.
⁴[Et factum est ita].   (12) Et protulit terra herbam uirentem
et ⁵*facientem* semen iuxta genus suum, lignumque faciens
fructum et habens unumquodque sementem secundum
speciem suam.   Et uidit Deus quod esset bonum.   (13) Factumque est uespere et mane, dies tertius.

23. (14) Dixit autem Deus: Fiant ¹luminaria in firmamento caeli, ²*et* dividant diem ac noctem, et sint in signa,
et tempora, ³[et] dies, et annos, (15) ut luceant in firmamento
caeli, et inluminent terram.   Et factum est ita.   (16) Fecitque
Deus duo magna luminaria: luminare maius ut praeesset
diei, et luminare minus ⁴[ut praeesset] nocti: et ⁵<fecit>
stellas, (17) et posuit eas in firmamento caeli, ut lucerent
super terram, (18) et praeessent diei ac nocti, et diuiderent

---

(a) *Italics* in the Latin text denote readings differing from that followed in
the Vatican *variorum* edition of the Vulgate (here called ST = Standard Text).
[Square] brackets mark words in the Latin not represented in the Irish translation.   <Angled> brackets denote words presupposed by the Irish translation,
but not represented in any of the MSS. of the Vulgate used in the Vatican edition.

lucem ⁶*a tenebris*. Et uidit Deus quod esset bonum. (19) Et factum est uespere et mane, dies quartus.

24. (20) Dixit etiam Deus: Produceant aquae ¹*reptilia* animae uiuentis, et ²*uolatilia* ³[super terram] sub firmamento caeli: <Et factum est ita>. (21) Creauitque Deus cete grandia ⁴<marina>, et omnem animam uiuentem atque ⁵*motabilem* quam produxerunt aquae in species suas. Et ⁶<creauit Deus> ⁷omnia *uolatilia* secundum genus suum, et uidit Deus quod esset bonum. (22) Benedixitque eis ⁸<Deus>, dicens: Crescite et multiplicamini, et replete aquas maris, auesque multiplicentur super terram. (23) Et factum est ⁹<ita> uespere et mane, dies quintus.

25. (24) Dixit quoque Deus: Producat terra ¹*animalia diuersa* in genere suo, iumenta et reptilia, et bestias terrae secundum species suas; factumque est ita. (25) ²[*This verse missing.*] (26) Et ait ³<Deus>: Faciamus hominem ad imaginem et similtudinem nostram, et praesit piscibus maris, et uolatilibus caeli, et bestiis universae⁴[que] terrae ⁵[omnique reptili quod mouetur in terra]. (27) Et creauit Deus hominem ad imaginem suam. ⁶Ad imaginem Dei creauit [illum] masculum et feminam. Creauit eos, (28) Benedixitque illis ⁷[Deus] et ait: Crescite et multiplicamini, et replete terram, et subicite eam, et dominamini piscibus maris et uolatilibus caeli et uniuersis animantibus ⁸[quae mouentur] super terram. (29) Dixitque Deus ⁹Ecce, dedi uobis omnem herbam adferentem semen super terram, et uniuersa ligna quae habent in semetipsis sementem generis sui, ut sint uobis ¹⁰in escam: (30) et cunctis animantibus terrae ¹¹*omnisque uolucribus* caeli, et universis quae mouentur in terra, et in quibus est anima uiuens, ut habeant ad uescendum. Et factum est ita. (31) Viditque Deus cuncta quae fecit, et erant ualde bona: et factum est uespere et mane, dies sextus.

NOTES ON THE BIBLICAL TEXT, CHAPTER I.

The following abbreviations are used in these notes:—

Heb.—The original Hebrew text.

LXX.—The Greek rendering, commonly called the Septuagint.

OL.—The Old Latin version or versions.

Vulg.—The Vulgate.

ST—The Standard text, as set forth in the Vatican *variorum* edition
    of the Vulgate. (For the *apparatus criticus* of the Latin
    text, reference must be made to this comprehensive work.)
Δ—The MS. of the Vulgate used by the Irish translator.
Tr.—The Irish translator, or his translation.
R³, sR³—The Third Redaction of LG; a Scribe of the Third
    Redaction.

¶ 20. [1]*creauit*, not *fecit*, as in R¹ R², showing at the outset
that we have now to deal with a Vulgate text. [2]The bracketed
words are paraphrased only in the text of Tr.: possibly by
sR³, who inserted some of the long interpolation just preceding, in order to complete its incorporation with the text.
It may be worth noting, as a coincidence, that the *sense* of
the paraphrase resembles the possible alternative reading of
the well-known syntactic ambiguity at the beginning of Heb.
(on which see any standard commentary, such as Driver's or
Skinner's). These opening words can be, and probably ought
to be, translated "In the beginning of God's creating . . .
the earth was without form . . ." To this version the sense
of the Irish text approximates. [3]The plural *dorchata*,
corresponding to the Latin *tenebrae*, is an illustration of
Tr.'s almost slavish literalness. On the other hand, he never
hesitates to strengthen his rendering by inserting synonyms
or adjectives (as here *dluithi*). [4]*Erant*, rejected in ST, but
contained in many MSS. *Nobidis* shows that it was found
in Δ. *In tan sin* corresponds to nothing in any MS., and is
presumably an incorporated gloss. [5]*Dei* in ST, *Domini* in
two MSS. only. [6]Either Tr. or sR³ has committed haplography. Possibly Tr.'s eye wandered unconsciously from
et uidit to *et diuisit*. [7]One of the commonest mannerisms
of Tr. is to render one Latin word by two synonyms, as here,
ro therba ⁊ ro deilig. [8]*Deus* rejected by ST, but supported
by a few MSS. as well as Heb. and LXX. [9]*Ac tenebras* ST:
but numerous MSS. have *a tenebris*. [10]No authority for
amlaid sin in any version or MS. [11]"One day" in all
versions and MSS.: "the first day" in Tr.

¶ 21. [1]*Deus* omitted, probably by a scribal error induced
by *dana* following. [2]Under the influence of the Latin text
Tr. has dropped the article before *firmamentum* in the later
verses of this ¶, as in the earlier redactions. [3]*Ab his* in ST.
Only one MS. (which also has the rare reading *Domini*,
¶ 20 note[5]) has *ab aquis*. The point is not of much critical

importance, as Irish idiom would almost require the repetition of the substantive.

¶ 22. ¹*Deus* not in any Vulg. MS. It is, however, found in LXX (καὶ εἶπεν ὁ θεός). ²No authority for the repetition of *fer* in Tr., but it is practically required by Irish idiom. ³*A chel no a cenel*, the variant reading in B, recalls the LXX κατὰ γένος καὶ καθ᾽ ὁμοιότητα. ⁴The bracketed words probably dropped by sR³. ⁵*Adferentem* in ST *facientem* in OL, also found in a few Vulg. MSS.

¶ 23. ¹*Lispaireda solus-taitnemacha* is a good illustration of the tendency to verbosity which Tr. displays, for all his literalness. ²*Ut* in ST, but there is considerable support for *et*. ³No authority for the omission of *et*. ⁴*Ut praeesset* omitted by one Vulg. MS. only. ⁵No authority for *fecit* here. ⁶*Ac tenebras* in ST. Two MSS. have *a tenebras*, and several *a tenebris*. One has *ac tenebris*.

¶ 24. ¹*Reptile* in ST : *reptilia* in a few MSS. and some quotations. The plural also in LXX. ²*Volatile* in ST. Vulg. follows Heb. idiom in using a neuter singular collectively, and there is no Latin authority for the plural here. LXX, however, has the plural πετεινά. ³Haplography by sR³ : probably ꝑcalm̄ lost before ꝑmaim̄. ⁴No authority for *marina*, presupposed by the Irish *muiridi*. The latter is probably a gloss. ⁵*Mutabilem* in ST, but *motabilem* has much support. ⁶No authority for these words. ⁷As before, the plural is used for singular collective. ⁸*Deus* not in Vulg., but LXX has ὁ θεός. ⁹Note (¹⁰) in ¶ 20 applies here also.

¶ 25. ¹*Animam uiuentem* in ST : nothing like rendering in Tr. in any version or MS.: possibly Tr. misread *uiuentem* as *diuersam*. ²As verse (25) is almost literally identical with (24), it could easily have been passed over by a careless or lazy scribe. ³*Deus* not in Vulg., but LXX has ὁ θεός. ⁴There is some MS. authority for the omission of *que*. ⁵This sentence lost, presumably on account of the repetition *terrae . . . terra*, or its Irish equivalent. ⁶The punctuation of the Latin text presupposed by Tr. is different from that usually followed. ⁷No authority for the omission of *Deus*, or ⁸of *quae mouentur*. ⁹*Co follus* or *is follus* is Tr.'s bad but invariable rendering for *ecce*. ¹⁰*In escam* rendered by *a mbiad ⁊ a n-ailemain:* a good illustration of Tr.'s fondness for piling up synonyms. ¹¹*Omnique uolueri* in ST. No authority for the plural in Vulg., but LXX has πᾶσι τοῖς πετεινοῖς.

CHAPTER II.

26. (1) Ro ¹toirbthighid didu na ²Nimi ⁊ in ³talam ⁊ ⁴a n-uili cumdach.   (2) Ocus ro ⁵comhslānaighstear Dīa isin ⁶seisead lō in uili gnīm dorōindi; ⁊ ro cumsain Dīa isin ⁷tsechtmadh lō ōn uili gnīm issed ōn ro ⁸forbhthighthestar.   (3) Ocus ro ⁹bennachas Dīa in seachtmadh lāā ⁊ ro ¹⁰nāemastar hē, nair ro ¹¹cumsain ann ōn uili gnīm ro ¹²tuissimh.

27. (4) Is iad so trā ¹tuismeadha in Nimi ⁊ in talman, in tan do ²tuismit imalle, isin lō ³a ndearnai ⁴an Coimdi Dīa ⁴Neam ⁊ ⁵talum, (5) resīu na thurebad in talam ⁶uili ⁷fualascaigh in ⁸feraind, ⁊ resīu ⁹ro clandaighedh in talam fēr in ¹⁰feraind; ūair ¹¹nuchu dearna Dīa fearthain for talmain, ⁊ nī ¹²ro bī and in tan sin ¹³duini ro ¹⁴oipredaigheadh in talam.   (6) Acht na freasgabad ōn talmuin ¹⁵topar, ro ¹⁶fliuchadh ⁊ ro bocadh ¹⁷uili dreach in talman.   (7) Ro ¹⁸crutaigh dono Dīa ¹⁹duini ²⁰do criaidh in talmun coitchind, ⁊ ro ²¹thinfeastar Dīa tinfeadh beathadh i n-a gnūis, ⁊ ²²dorignedh in ²³duine, i n-anmain na ²⁴beōaigheadh.

In tan ²⁵dorōnad duine ⁊ nach ²⁶raibi ainm fair, con-debhairt Dīa re ²⁷cheatra hainglibh dul d'iarraidh anma dō.   Ocus dochuaidh Michel dochum in airthir, ⁊ ²⁸adcon-dairee rētlaind .i. ²⁹Anatoile a ainm, ⁊ ³⁰dorat leis cēt litir ³¹in n-anma sin.   Ocus ³²docuaidh Raphel ³³fodhess, ⁊ atconnaic rētlaind ³⁴ann .i. ³⁵Dissis a hainm, ⁊ ³⁶dorat a cēt litir³⁶.   Ocus dochuaidh ³⁷Gaibriel ³⁸fotūaidh, ⁊ ³⁹atconnaic in ⁴⁰rētlaind ⁴¹dianadh hainm Arethos, ⁊ ⁴²dorat

---

26. ¹ -tigid   ² Nime   ³ talman   ⁴ in uili MSS.   ⁵ chomslan-aigestair   ⁶ sesed   ⁷ seachtmad . . . ised   ⁸ orbtigeastair   ⁹ bennachastair   ¹⁰ -astair   ¹¹ cumsan and   ¹² thusim
27. ¹ t;meada indime   ² thuismit M t;im M   ³ om. a ndearnai B   ⁴⁻⁴ in Coimdiu .i. Dia nemda   ⁵ taiam ⁊ resiu na thurgbad M: talam na turebadh resiu B   ⁶ uile   ⁷ -caich   ⁸feraind   ⁹ ⁊ instead of ro (resiu ⁊ cland. in rasura) B   ¹⁰ feraind   ¹¹ nocho   ¹² roibi

CHAPTER II.

26. (1) So the Heavens and the earth and all their adornment were completed. (2) And God finished upon the sixth day all the work which He did; and God rested upon the seventh day from every work which He accomplished. (3) And God blessed the seventh day and hallowed it, for He rested in it from every work which He created.

27. (4) Now these are the generations of the Heaven and the earth, when they were created together, in the day when the Lord God made Heaven and earth, (5) before the earth was raising up all the plants of the field, and before the earth was producing the grass of the field; for God made not rain upon the earth, and there was not there, at that time, a man who should till the earth. (6) But from the earth would rise a spring, to moisten and to soften all the face of the earth. (7) So God created a man out of the clay of the common earth, and God breathed the breath of life into his face, and the Man was made, a soul that was quickened.

When Man was made and as he had no name, God said to four angels to go in search of a name for him. Michael went to the east, and saw a star, *Anatole* its name, and he brought with him the first letter of that name. Raphael went southward, and saw a star there, *Dusis* its name, and he brought its first letter. Gabriel went northward, and saw the star called *Arctos*, and brought with him the first letter of the name. Uriel went westward, and saw a star

[13] duine [14] aitrebad [15] tobar [16] ḟliuchad [17] om. nili : drech [18] chruthaich [19] duine [20] don eriaid in talman choitchind [21] -tair [22] doridnead [23] dune [24] mbeoaiged [25] dorondad dune [26] roibe [27] ceithri [28] atcondaire [29] Anathole a hainm [30] dorad (bis) [31] an anma (bis) [32] dochuaid [33] -deas ┐ adchonnaire [34] om. ann [35] Dessis [36] ins. les [37] Gabriel [38] fothuaid [39] adcondaire [40] retla [41] dianaid ainm [42] dorad les

leis cēt litir [31]in n-anma sin. Doehuaidh [43]dana Uriel sīar, ⁊ [44]adconnaic [45]rētlaind isin [46]fuinedh [47]diana hainm Mesimbria, ⁊ [48]tug leis in cēt litir. Ocus [49]adbert Dīa: Legh, a [50]Uriel, na litri-sea. Ro rāidh [51]Uiriel: Adham. Ocus adbert Dīa: Bīdh amlaidh[52].

28. (8) Ro [1]chlonasdar imorro Dīa Parrthus na [2]Toili ‡ .i. [3]locc na n-airirdacht ‖ ōn [4]tossach, ⁊ is and ro suighidh in duine ro [5]cruthaigistar, ‡ .i. Adham ‖. (9) Ocus ro [6]thairg Dīa ⁊ ro tusim [7]don n-ūir in [8]uili crand socraidh ālaind ō [9]feghadh, ⁊ in uili crand [10]āilgin co [11]tomultus. Ro suidhigh [12]dana Dīa Crand Bheathadh [13]a meadhon [14]Parrthuis, ⁊ [15]Crand [16]Feassa Maithusa ⁊ Uilc. (10) Ocus no [17]thēigeadh sruth [18]sechtair [19]a Parrtus, co [20]ceitri cennaib fair, do [21]moethugadh ⁊ do [22]bocgucadh Parrduis, ⁊ in [23]talman [24]uili co [25]coitcend.

y[1] Is [26]iat so imorro [27]anmanda na [28]ceitri [29]cend sin, ⁊ na [30]ceitri sruth [31]filit ‡ [32]sel ‖ [33]seachtar eistibh, fo [34]ceitri airdibh in [35]domuin; .i. [36]Fisson ⁊ Geon, [37]Tigris ⁊ [38]Eofraiteis.

(11) Fisson imorro, ‡ [39]risinabar sruth nGaind, sair [40]gach [41]ndīriuch [42]tēidside ‖—is ē in sruth sin [43]timchellus uili [44]talmain [45]Euilath .i. inadh sin [46]a ngeinidar ōr [47]lōgmur lān-ālaind; (12) ⁊ is andsin fogabar [48]boellium, ⁊ in [49]leg lōgmar [50]eli [51]dianadh ainm onichinus.

.i. cloch gabhus [52]inti delba na [53]mblāth. [54]Boellium [55]imorro .i. [56]leg [57]lōgmar [58]lān-solusta, issī fogebh in

---

[43] dono   [44] atcondaire   [45] ins. in   [46] fuinead   [47] dianad and om. hainm   [48] tuc les   [49] -beart   [50] Uiriel   [51] Urel   [52] ins. ol se
28 [1] clandustair   [2] Tole   [3] log   [4] tosach   [5] cruthaigestair
[6] thaire   [7] do nuir   [8] uile crand sochraid   [9] fegad   [10] ailgen
[11] -alt-   [12] Dia dono   [13] i   [14] -d: [15] -ann   [16] fesa
[17] -ged   [18] seach-   [19] om. a Parrtus   [20] -thrib cend-   [21] maeth-
[22] bogugad   [23] tal- B, taiman corrected prima manu to talman M
[24] uile   [25] -cheand   [26] iad   [27] anmand   [28] -thri   [29] crand

in the sunset called *Mesembria*, and brought with him the
first letter.   God said : Uriel, read these letters.   Uriel
said : Adam.   And God said : So be it.

28. (8) Moreover God planted a Paradise of
Pleasure [*i.e.* the place of delights] from the
beginning, and it is there that He set the man whom
He had created[, Adam].   (9) And God prepared and
created of the clay every tree pleasant and fair to
see, and every tree sweet to taste.   Also God set the
Tree of Life in the midst of Paradise, and the Tree
of Knowledge of Good and of Evil.   (10) And a river
would go past out of Paradise having four branches,
to moisten and to soften Paradise, and the whole earth
in general.

Now these are the names of those four branches, and of
the four streams which are [a space] beyond, out of them,
through the four quarters of the earth ; Phison and Geon,
Tigris and Euphrates.

(11) As for Phison, [which is called the river of
Ganges, eastward straight it goeth].   It is that stream
which surroundeth all the land of Euilath, that place
where gold is generated, precious and most beautiful :
(12) and there is found bdellium, and the other
precious stone which is called onyx,

a stone which receiveth within itself the figures of flowers.
Bdellium, moreover, is a precious, most brilliant stone,

---

cend, *the former word stroked through and expuncted* B   [30] cethri
[31] -lead   [32] *om.* sel   [33] sechtair   [34] cheithri h-   [35] -main
[36] Fison *hic et semper*   [37] *ins.* ꜖   [38] Eofraites   [39] frisin-   [40] each
[41] -rech   [42] teitside   [43] -chillis   [44] thalmuin   [45] Euibath B
[46] angenend   [47] -mar   [48] bo eill-   [49] leag   [50] ele   [51] -naid
[52] innti   [53] *carelessly written so as to look like* niblath B
[54] bo ellium   [55] *om.* imorro   [56] leag   [57] *initial* l *in rasura*
extending back to g *of preceding word* B   [58] lan-solusda isi

[59]mairgreit isin [60]ucht ; ꞁ in baili [61]a faghaibh hī, nī thēit sciei, acht anadh [62]isin inat sin.

(13) Geon imorro, ‡ frisinabar Nilus, ‖ in sruth [63]tānaisse ‡ ꞁ [64]fothūaidh [65]thēitsidhe ‖ ꞁ is ē in sruth sin [66]timcellus ꞁ [67]tacmaigheas uili talmuin [68]na Heitheoibi. (14) In [69]tres sruth imorro .i. Tigris [70]‡ sīar [71]tēit-sidhe [72]gach [73]ndīriuch ‖ fri tīrib [74]Asardha. In [75]ceatramad sruth imorro .i. [76]Eufraiteis, ‡ [77]fodhess [78]gach [79]ndīriuch [80]thēidside, co roith[80] trē lār [81]mBabilōini. ‖

Tobar Parrduis, būan a blad . . .

29. (15) [1]Rug īarom Dīa leis in [2]duine ‡ .i. Adham, ‖ ‡' īar n-a [3]dhēnum ꞁ īar n-a cruthugad[3], ‖' ꞁ ro suigidh hē i [4]Parrthus na Toili, ardāigh co [5]n-oiprigeadh ‡ .i. co n-aireadh ꞁ co mbenadh, [6]gan allus [6]gan [7]torrsi ‖, ꜗ co [8]coimētadh, ‡ .i. co ro [9]selbadh [10]Parrthus [11]gan sārugadh [12]timna [13]ꞁ aithni Dē ‖. (16) Ocus ro [14]athain Dīa do ar rāidis ris : Tombail ꞁ caith [15]a [16]thorudh gach craind fil i [17]Parrthus, (17) Nī ro [18]chaithea do [19]toradh Craind Feassa Maithusa ꞁ Uile imorro, uair [20]cibedh lā a caithfea nī do thoradh in [21]craind sin, [22]atbēla ō bhās.

y[1] Cair ro bo [23]chindti [24]demin [25]bāss dō, ōn lō ro chaithfeadh : is airi ro rāidhidh [26]so.

y[2] Is airi ro [27]thoirmise Dīa toradh in chraind sin do [28]chaiteam, co [29]feasad Adham a bheith fo cumachta ꞁ fo smacht in [30]Coimdhedh.

---

[59]-ret   [60]usi*n* B (*a misreading of* uꝑ)   [61]i fagaib   [62]isa ninat sin
[63]-usti   [64]bo-   [65]theid-   [66]-chillis   [67]tacmainges uili talmain
[68]na Theoipe B   [69]treas   [70]*ins.* ꞁ   [71]theid   [72]cach
[73]-rech   [74]-rrda   [75]ceathrumad   [76]Eofraites   [77]fa B fo M : deas M   [78]cach   [79]-reach   [80-80]*om.* B : thre   [81]mBaibiloine.
29. [1]ruc   [2]dune   [3-3]denam . . . chru-   [4]-dus   [5]-ged

which findeth the pearl in its bosom : the place where it [the stone] findeth it [the pearl] it goeth no further, but abideth in that place.

(13) As for Geon, [the which is called Nilus], the second river, [northward it goeth] and it is that river which surroundeth and encompasseth the whole land of Ethiopia. (14) As for the third river, Tigris, [westward it goeth straight] toward the Assyrian regions. The fourth river, Eufrates, [southward it goeth straight, so that it floweth through the middle of Babylonia.]

Poem no. VI.

29. (15) Thereafter God took with Him the man [Adam, after he was fashioned and created] and set him in the Paradise of Pleasure, that he might till it [*i.e.* that he might plough and reap, without sweat and without weariness,] and keep it, [*i.e.* that he might possess Paradise without transgressing the covenant and commandment of God]. (16) And God commanded, having said to him : Partake and eat of the fruit of every tree that is in Paradise, (17) howbeit thou shalt not eat aught of the fruit of the Tree of Knowledge of Good and of Evil, for whatsoever day thou eatest aught of the fruit of that tree, thou shalt die the death.

For sure and certain was death for him, from the day in which he should eat : for that reason said He this.

The reason why God forbade the eating of the fruit of that tree, was that Adam might know that he was under the power and authority of the Lord.

30. (18) Ro rāidh Dīa ¹dana : Nī maith duine do
beith ²āenar.   Dēnun desidhe dō ³fortachtaighidh bus
⁴cosmail fris.   (19) Ō ᵈro cruthaighidh didu uili
anmand in talman do criaidh, ⁊ uili ⁶folūaimhnigh in
Nimi, tug Dīa ⁷leis iad co Hadhamh, co ⁸feghadh ⁊
co ⁹fessad ceti anmand ō ¹⁰ngairfidh Adham ¹¹iat. Ūair
is ē ainm ¹²fil for ¹³gach ¹⁴anmand, in t-ainm ō ra ghair
Adham hē ¹⁵anusin.   (20) Ocus ro ¹⁶gairmeastair
Adhamh ō ¹⁷n-anmandaibh ¹⁸fēin na huili anmanda
¹⁹sin, ⁊ ²⁰uile folūaimnechu Nime, ⁊ ²¹huili bhīasta in
talman.   ²²Nuchu n-agbadh Adhamh imorro in tan sin
fortachtaigh dā chosmail ²³fēin.   (21) ²⁴Ronfuid didhu
Dīa sūan ²⁵sadhal sīr-codulta in Adam, ⁊ o ro ²⁶chodail
Adhamh, ²⁷ro thōgaib Dīa ²⁸ōen asna ²⁹dā asnaibh, ⁊
ro līn o feōil a inadh.

Is ³⁰aire ro aslaigh Dia cotludh for Adamh, comad as
³¹aiti tuigsi na neichi spīradallta ⁊ ³²fiss na todochaide;
³³ar ro līn Dīa hē ō ³⁴spīrud ēagna ⁊ ³⁵fāistini ³⁶fōchētōir
isin ³⁷cotludh sin.

(22) Ocus ro ³⁸cumdaig Dīa in t-asna dorad a
Hadhamh, co mbo ³⁹bean ētrocht ⁴⁰lān-ālainn ⁴¹lān-
dēnmach, ⁊ dorad leis co Hadham.   (23) Ocus ro rāidh
Adamh : is follus ⁴²conid ī enāim dom ⁴³enāmaibh ⁴⁴⁊
⁴⁵conidh feōil dom ⁴⁶feōil-sea ⁑ is ī seo cēt ⁴⁷fāitsini
dorighni Adamh ‖ : ⁊ bidh ⁴⁸de a sloind-seo *uirago*, ñair
is do fir ⁴⁹dorōnadh.

Is ī ⁵⁰so cēt coibhti ⁊ cēt ⁵¹fāistini dorigni Adamh, amail
indistear isin ⁵²scriptuir dīadha .i. *Ecce* ⁵³*os de* ⁵⁴*ossibus
meis, et caro de carne* ⁵⁵*mea.*

---

30. ¹ dono   ² aenur   ³ fortachtaidi   ⁴ chosmail   ⁵ ra chruthaid
⁶ foluaimneach inime tuc   ⁷ les   ⁸ fedad   ⁹ feasad   ¹⁰ ngairfead
¹¹ iad   ¹² fuil   ¹³ each   ¹⁴ anmanna B   ¹⁵ and-   ¹⁶ -ist-
¹⁷ *om.* n-   ¹⁸ fen   ¹⁹ *om.* sin   ²⁰ uili foluaimneacha   ²¹ uili piasta
²² nocho   ²³ fen   ²⁴ ro find (*sic*) B   ²⁵ sadail sam-chotalta
²⁶ chotail   ²⁷ oen do thocaib (*sic*)   ²⁸ aen : in *written in marg. in
late hand before* oen, *and then scratched out.* B   ²⁹ dia   ³⁰ airi ro

30. (18) God said further: It is not good for a man to be alone. Let us therefore make for him an helper that shall be like unto him. (19) Now when every animal of the earth was formed of clay, and every bird of the Heaven, God brought them with Him to Adam, to see and know by what name Adam would call them. For this is the name that every animal hath, the name by which Adam called it at that time. (20) And Adam called all those animals by their own names, and all the birds of Heaven, and all the beasts of the Earth. But Adam could not at that time find an helper like to himself. (21) So God sent a quiet sleep of lasting slumber upon Adam, and as Adam slept, God took one of his ribs, and filled its place with flesh.

This is why God enticed a sleep upon Adam, for it [sleep] is the chosen teacher of spiritual matters and of knowledge of the future: for God filled him forthwith with a spirit of wisdom and of prophecy in that sleep.

(22) And God fashioned the rib which He took out of Adam, so that it was a bright woman, perfect in comeliness and in shape, and He brought her with Him to Adam. (23) And Adam said: Lo, this is bone of my bones and flesh of my flesh [this is the first prophecy which Adam made]; and therefore let her name be *uirago*, seeing that it was of man that she was made.

This is the first bride-gift and the first prophecy which Adam made, as it is related in the Holy Scripture, *Ecce os de ossibus meis, et caro de carne mea.*

Toslaic   [31] aidi tuicsi na neichid spiritalta   [32] fis na togochaidi
[33] aro   [34] -rait   [35] -tine   [36] -doir   [37] -tlad: *a dot with no significance over the t,* B   [38] -daid   [39] ben edrocht   [40] -aind
[41] -tenm- B   [42] con i B, conid (*om. following* i) M   [43] chnamaib
[44] *om.* ⁊ B   [45] conad   [46] Teoil-sea so cet B: *om.* sea M   [47] Taitsine
dorigne   [48] he   [49] doronnad   [50] seo cet choibchi   [51] Taitsine
dorigne   [52] scribtuir   [53] oss B   [54] osibus M   [55] *om.* mea.

(24) Is airi sin ⁵⁶fuicfis in duine ⁵⁷a athair ⁊ a māthair,
⊣ lenfas da sētigh, ⊣ ⁵⁸beidid dīas an āen cholaind,
⁑ arāi grādha, no ar ⁵⁹tusmidh cloindi ‖.   (25) Is
amlaid imorro baī ⁶⁰ccachtar de na ⁶¹dēissi sin, ⊣ ⁶²siat
⁶³nochta, .i. Adamh ⊣ a ⁶⁴sēitigh : ⊣ nīr bo ⁶⁵nār leo.

26. (1) Igitur perfecti sunt caeli et terra et omnis ornatus
eorum.   (2) Compleuitque Deus die ¹ *sexto* opus ²<omne>
[suum] quod fecerat; et requieuit ³<Deus> die septimo ab
universo opere ⁴<id> quod patrarat.   (3) Et benedixit <Deus>
diei septimo et sanctificauit illum, quia in ipso cessauerat ab
omni opere [suo] quod ereauit [Deus ut faceret].

27. (4) Istae ¹*sunt* generationes caeli et terrae, quando
²<simul> creata sunt, in die quo feeit ³Dominus Deus caelum
et terram.   (5) ⁴Antequam oreretur in terra omne uirgultum
agri, et ⁵*antequam* germinaret <terra> omnem herbam : non
enim pluerat ⁶*Deus* super terram, et homo non erat qui
operaret terram.   (6) Sed fons ascendebat e terra, ⁷inrigans
uniuersam superficiem terrae.   (7) Formauit igitur [Domi-
nus] Deus de limo terrae ⁸<uulgaris>, et inspirauit in faciem
eius spiraculum uitae, et factus est homo, in animam uiuentem.

28. (8) Plantauerat autem ¹[Dominus] Deus Paradisum
Voluptatis a principio, in quo posuit hominem quem forma-
uerat.   (9) Produxitque [Dominus] Deus de humo omne
lignum pulchrum uisu, et <omne lignum> ad uescendum
suaue.   Lignum etiam Vitae ²<posuit Deus> in medio
Paradisi, Lignumque Scientiae Boni et Mali.   (10) Et
fluuius egrediebatur de ³*Paradiso* ad inrigandum Paradisum
[qui inde diuiditur in] quattuor capita.   (11) ⁴[Nomen uni]

(24) Wherefore shall the man leave his father and his mother, and shall attach himself to his wife, and they shall be two persons in one flesh [for the sake of love, and for begetting of progeny.]. (25) Now in this wise were both of those twain, naked, to wit Adam and his wife: and they counted it no shame.

---

⁵Fison : ipse est qui circuit omnem terram Euilath, ubi nascitur aurum.   [(12) et aurum terrae illius] optimum [est] : ibi inuenitur ⁶bdellium et lapis onychinus.   (13) [Et nomen] fluuio secundo, Geon: ipse est qui circuit omnem terram Aethiopiae.   (14) [Nomen uero] fluminis tertii Tigris : ipse uadit contra Assyrios.   Fluuius autem quartus, [ipsa est] Eufrates.

29. (15) Tulit ergo [Dominus] Deus hominem, et posuit eum in Paradiso Voluptatis, ut operaretur et custodiret illum. (16) Praecepitque ei ¹<Deus> dicens : Ex omni ligno Paradisi comede, (17) de Ligno autem Scientiae Boni et Mali ne comedas; in quocumque die comediris ex eo, ²morte morieris.

30. (18) Dixit quoque [Dominus] Deus : Non est bonum esse hominem solum.   Faciamus ei ¹<igitur> adiutorem similem sui.   (19) Formatis igitur [Dominus] Deus de humo cunctis animantibus terrae, et uniuersis uolatilibus caeli, adduxit ea ad Adam ut uideret quid uocaret ea.   Omne enim quod ²<tunc> uocauit Adam animae uiuentis ipsum est nomen eius.   (20) Appellauitque Adam nominibus suis cuncta animantia, et uniuersa uolatilia caeli, et omnes bestias terrae. Adam vero ³<tum> non inueniebatur adiutor similis eius. (21) Inmisit ergo [Dominus] Deus ⁴soporem in Adam; cumque obdormisset tulit unam de costis eius, et repleuit

---

⁶⁰ cecht-   ⁶¹ desi   ⁶² siad   ⁶³ nocht   ⁶⁴ set·   ⁶⁵ nair

carnem pro ea. (22) Et aedificauit [Dominus] Deus costam quam tulerat de Adam in mulierem, et adduxit eam ad Adam. (23) Dixitque Adam: *Ecce* os ex ossibus meis, et caro de carne mea; haec uocabitur Virago, quoniam de uiro *facta* est. (24) Quamobrem relinquet homo patrem suum et matrem, et adhaerebit uxori suae, et erunt duo in carne uno. (25) Erant autem uterque nudi, Adam scilicet et uxor eius, et non erubescebant.

Notes on the Biblical Text, Chapter II.

¶ 26. ¹Septimo ST sexto OL. LXX, one Vulg. MS. *prima manu* and one *secunda manu*. ²No authority for *omne*. ³*Deus* found in one MS. only: no other authority. ⁴No authority for the emphatic form *issed ōn*.

¶ 27. ¹*Sunt* not in ST, but has fair support. ²No original for *imalle* in any MS. ³*Dominus* rendered here, but not later: see notes on this ¶. In the Latin MSS., *Deus* is occasionally omitted in the combination *Dominus Deus*, but not *Dominus*. ⁴The order of words in ST and all MSS. and Versions is *Et omne uirgultum agri antequam oreretur in terra, omnemque herbam regionis priusquam germinaret.* ⁵*Priusquam*, ST. One MS. has *antequam*, which corresponds more closely to the Irish repetition *resīu . . . resīu*. But we can hardly lay any critical stress upon this. ⁶*Dominus Deus* in ST and MSS.: see note (³). ⁷*Inrigans* is represented in Tr. by two Irish words, *ro fliuchad ⁊ ro bocad*. This mannerism is so constant in Tr. that it is hardly necessary to call further attention to it. ⁸*Coitchend*, which has no original in the Versions or MSS., is most likely an incorporated gloss.

¶ 28. ¹See note (³) in preceding ¶: no further note need be taken of this point. ²No authority for these words. ³*De loco uoluptatis* ST and all Vulg. MSS.: ἐξ Ἐδέμ LXX. No authority for *de Paradiso*. [4]This part of Tr. has suffered to such an extent from the intrusions of scribes and glossators that the Latin original cannot be restored with certainty. [5]Spelt *Phison* in ST, but several MSS. have the spelling with F. [6]The Irish *boellium* is the pardonable blunder of a copyist. The verbosity of the rendering of *et lapis onychinus* may be original, but is more probably a scribal modification, meant to make these hard words clearer.

¶ 29. [1]One MS. has *Dominus* here: κύριος ὁ θεός LXX, *Dominus Deus* O.L. [2]Literally rendered, *atbēla ō bās*.

¶ 30. [1]*Deside* in Tr.: no authority in Versions or MSS. [2]*Annsin*: no authority in Latin Vers., but conceivably Tr. looked up the Greek and misread ἐάν as ἔνθα. The rendering of this verse is less literal than usual. *Animae uiuentis* is treated simply as *animal*, and *omne* is transferred from the "names" to the "animals." [3]*In tan sin:* no authority in Versions or MSS. [4]Note the intrusive adjectives in Tr. here and after *ben* in the following verse. These may be due to the original Tr., but are more probably interpolated. See ¶ 31 note ([1]). [5]*Is follus*, as already said, represents an original *ecce*. *Ecce* also appears in the Latin quotation in the gloss, and it must have been familiar from some earlier version which also influenced R[2] (¶ 5 A). It is not found in any Vulg. MS. ST has *hoc nunc*, LXX τοῦτο νῦν. [6]*Sumpta* in ST and all authorities.

CHAPTER III.

31. (1) Ro bāi ‡ in tan sin ‖ nathair ba 'celgachu
‡ ⁊ b'²amaindsiu ⁊ ba tñaichliu' ‖ ō uilib ³anmandaibh
in ⁴talmun ⁵dorōinde Dīa.

y¹ Ro ⁶formthigh Lucifear fri Hadhamh, dearbh leis is
ē dobert[h]a in Ncam tar a ⁷ēis, dia līnadh : ⁸conidh airi
sin dochuaidh ⁹a ndeilb ¹⁰naithreach, co ro ¹¹faslaigh
¹²imurbus for ¹³Eua, im thoradh in ¹⁴craind crgartha do
thomailt; co ro ¹⁵faslaigh Eua for Adamh.

y² Is ī sco cēt ¹⁶cheist ⁊ cēt ¹⁷imcomarc ¹⁸dorigni dīabul
isin domun. *Cur precepit* etc.

Ocus ‡ is ī in athair sin ‖ ro rāidh ¹⁹risin mnaī : Cid
dīa ²⁰forcongair Dīa duibsi ²¹gen nī do ²²chaitheamh do
uili ²³crand ²⁴Parrthuis? (2) Ro ²⁵reagair in bhean
²⁶don nathraigh : ²⁷Caithmit ‡ ⁊ ²⁸no sāstar ‖ do thoradh
na crand ²⁹atat i ³⁰Parrthus; (3) ro ³¹forchongair Dīa
³²dūin imorro na ro ³³chaithmis do thoradh in ³⁴craind
atā ³⁵a meadōn ³⁶Parrthuis, ⁊ na ³⁷ro taidlimmis hē,
³⁸na ³⁹ro aiplium o thircur. (4) Ro rāidh imorro ⁴⁰in
nathair ⁴¹frisin mnaī : ⁴²Nuchu n-eipiltaisi etir ō bhās.
(5) Do-⁴³fuicfind Dīa imorro ⁴⁴secip lā chaithfithi-si do
⁴⁵toradh in craind sin, co ⁴⁶n-oslaicfiter bar ruisc ‡ .i.
⁴⁷im uile ‖ .i. co mbeithi amail aingliu i tuicthi maith
⁊ olc.

32. (6) ¹Atconnairc didu in bean cor bo maith in
crand re ²tomultus ⁊ re ³chaithium, ⁊ ⁴cor bo socraidh

---

31. ¹⁻¹cealgachu ⁊ fa hanmaindi ⁊ fa hamaindsiu ⁊ ba tuaithli
² anaimsiu B   ³ *a dot over the d without significance* M   ⁴ -man
⁵ *ins.* do neoch; dorindi   ⁶ foirmdig   ⁷ esi   ⁸ conad   ⁹ i
¹⁰ nathrach   ¹¹ faslaich   ¹² imarbuss   ¹³ Eba   ¹⁴ chraind
¹⁵ faslaid Eba   ¹⁶ chest M qist B   ¹⁷ -meh-   ¹⁸ -gue   ¹⁹ frisin
²⁰ ro forch-   ²¹ cen   ²² chaithim   ²³ chrand   ²⁴ -duis fesin :
a bhaili *here written in marg. in late hand* B   ²⁵ frecair   ²⁶ da

CHAPTER III.

31. (1) [At that time] there was a serpent, the wiliest[, the craftiest, and the subtlest] of all the beasts of the earth which God made.

Lucifer was envious against Adam : he was assured that the Heaven would be given to him in his [own] room, to fill it.   Wherefore he went in the form of a serpent, and enticed sin upon Eve, in the matter of eating of the forbidden tree; so Eve made enticement upon Adam.

This is the first question and the first enquiry which a devil made in the world.   *Cur praecepit* etc.

And [it is that serpent which] said unto the woman : For what reason hath God forbidden you to eat aught of every tree of Paradise?   (2) The woman answered the serpent : We eat of [and are sated with] the fruit of the trees that are in Paradise; (3) but God hath commanded us not to eat of the fruit of the tree that is in the midst of Paradise, nor even to touch it, lest we die by a chance.   (4) But the serpent said unto the woman : Ye shall not at all die the death.   (5) But God knoweth that in whatsoever day ye shall eat of the fruit of that tree, that your eyes shall be opened [concerning evil]—that is, that ye shall be as angels, in good and evil fortune.

32. (6) So the woman saw that the tree was good for eating and for partaking, and that it was pleasant

---

nathair   [27] *an inserted* i *sprs. above* m *in late hand* B caithmimait M
[28] nar B   [29] itait   [30] -dus   [31] For-   [32] -ud   [33] caithis B
[34] chraind   [35] i medon   [36] -dais   [37] ra thaidlimais   [38] *ins.* ⁊
[39] ra aibleam M: thirchur B   [40] an athair   [41] forsin   [42] nocho
n-ebeltaisi itir   [43] fuicind   [44] seichip   [45] thorad in chraind   [46] -ther
[47] in n-ule
    32. [1] atchondaire M   [2] thomaltos M   [3] -eam M   [4] ro bo

so-airfiteach ō roscaibh ⁊ ō ⁵feghadh : ⁊ dorad ‡ in bean
‖ nī do thoradh in ⁶craind dīa ⁷indsaigi, ⁊ ro
⁸chaitheastair, ⁊ ⁹dorat da fir ‡ .i. ¹⁰Adamh ‖ ⁊ ro
¹¹chaiteastair.   (7) Ocus ro ¹²hoslaicit (a) | ruisc ‡
¹²meanman ⁊ ¹⁴aigenta ‖ na ¹⁵deisi sin ‡ ¹⁶fri ¹⁷fios
⁊ ¹⁸eōlas in ¹⁹pecaich, ²⁰na ²¹dearnsiat ²²gos in ²³n-ūair
sin ‖; ⁊ ō ²⁴ro tuicsedar a mbeith ²⁵nochta, ro ²⁶fuigsitar
²⁷duillinna na ²⁸fidhei ⁊ ²⁹dorinsetar ³⁰fūathrōga dōibh
‡ ³¹do na ³²duillinnaibh ‖.   (8) Ocus adchualadar-somh
³³‡ .i. Adamh ⁊ Eua imorro ‖ guth ³⁴an Choimhdia ‡
.i. Dē ‖ ³⁵a n-imthigidh ‡ a ³⁶ndealbh ³⁷aingil ‖ ³⁸a
bPairrthuis, ³⁹a bhfoghra gaoithi dearmhairi ⁴⁰īar
meodhōn lāi.   Ro ⁴¹folaigh ⁴²hē ⁊ a ⁴³setigh ⁴⁴a |
⁴⁵medhōn (b) chrainn Pairrthuis.

33. (9) ¹Agas ro ²gairmeastair Dīa Adhamh ³‡ ō
guth aingleagda ‖ ⁊ ro rāidh⁴ : A ⁵Adamh, cāit ataī?
(10) Ro ⁶frecair ⁷imorro ⁸Adhamh ⁊ ⁹ro rāidh :
¹⁰Adchualadhus do ¹¹ghuth ¹²a bPairrthais, ⁊
¹³romghabh ¹⁴eagla, ¹⁵ōr bham ¹⁶nocht, ⁊ ro ¹⁷foilgios
mē.   (11) Ro rāidh Dīa : Cia ¹⁸ro inndios ¹⁹dhuit do
bheith ²⁰nocht acht Mē fēin?   ²¹In ro ²²chaithis ²³torad

sochraid M   ⁵ fegad M   ⁶ chraind M   ⁷ hindsaigid M   ⁸ -ist- M
⁹ dorad M   ¹⁰ dAdam M   ¹¹ -thist- M   ¹² hoslaicid a M
¹³ menman Mβ²   ¹⁴ aicinta M aigennta β¹ -nntadh β²   ¹⁵ desin M
¹⁶ fria β¹²   ¹⁷ fis M   ⁔⁸ eolus β⁰²   ¹⁹ -aid M phecaidh β¹² (-ea- β²)
²⁰ nach β²   ²¹ dearnsad M dernsat β¹ ndern siad β²   ²² cus an M gus an β²
²³ om. n- Mβ¹²   ²¹ ra thuicistair M ro tuigset ar β¹ ro tuigsat ar β²
²⁵ nocht M nochtadh β¹²   ²⁶ fuigseadar M fuigsiodar β¹²   ²⁷ duillinda
M duillionnadh β¹²   ²⁸ fice M fidheidh β¹²   ²⁹ -rindsedar M rinnsetar β¹²
³⁰ fuathrogadh β¹² (-gh- β²)   ³¹ don na β¹²   ³² -eannaib M -enn- β¹²
³³ om. this gloss β¹²   ³¹ in Choimded M in Choimhdia and om. .i. Dē β¹²
³⁵ na imthiged M .i. deanam thigidh β¹ ag denamh chucadh β²
³⁶ ndeilh M deailbh β²   ³⁷ src M aingeal β aingila β¹ aingilia β²
³⁸ a Parrdus M om. β¹²   ³⁹ i fogur gaithi M, a bhfoghradh (g β²)
gaoithe dermhaire β¹²   ⁴⁰ iar meadon M iar mhedhoin (d β¹) β¹²

and agreeable to eyes and to sight : and [the woman]
took of the fruit of the tree to herself and she did
eat, and gave to her husband [Adam] and he did eat.
(7) And the eyes [of mind and understanding] of those
twain were opened [to a knowledge and perception of
sin, that they had not committed until that hour] ;
and as they realized that they were naked, they sewed
the leaves of the fig-tree and made them aprons [of
the leaves].   (8) And they [Adam and Eve] heard
the voice of the Lord [God] a-walking [in the form
of an angel] in Paradise in the sound of a violent
wind, after midday.   He and his wife hid them in the
midst of the tree-growth of Paradise.

33. (9) And God called Adam [making use of an
angelic voice], and said : Adam, where art thou?
(10) Howbeit Adam answered and said : I heard Thy
voice in Paradise, and fear laid hold on me, for I was
naked, and I hid me.   (11) God said : Who told thee
that thou wast naked, other than Myself?   Hast thou
eaten fruit of the Tree which I forbade thee?
(12) And Adam said : The woman whom Thou gavest

41 falaid M folaidh β12   42 Adhamh β1 Adamh β2   43 šeitigh β12
44 ins. iad β12   45 i meadon chraind Parrduis M a medoin (dh β2)
chrainn (cr- β2) Pharrthais β12 : m(e)duin H (throughout H, the lenition
of b, d, g, and m is rarely indicated)
33. 1 ⁊ M Oeus β2   2 -mist- M -mest- β12   3 this gloss in M only :
there does not appear to be sufficient room for it in H   4 ins. fris MH
5 Adaim M   6 freagair M fregair β12   7 om. imorro β12   8 Adam
H a Adhamh β   9 ra raid H   10 -adus M -asadh β12   11 guth-su M
12 i Parrdus M om. β12   13 romgob M gab H ro in ghabh β roghabh β1
doghabh β2   14 egla H   15 oir for ar hic et semper H, ar M,
oram β12   16 anocht β2   17 foilg- M -ghas β12   18 ro indis MH
(ra for ro hic et semper H) dinnis β12   19 duit M β1 duid H   20 nocht.
Acht (sic) M nochtadh as β12   21 ni ro M nior β nuar β1 mar a β2
22 chaithios β -es β12   23 torrad M β

(a) Text as printed from this point follows β, as a folio has been lost from B.
(b) H here begins.   Owing to the torn condition of the first leaf of H, only
words that are here underdotted remain in the opening lines.

[24]in [25]chrainn [26]do ro tairmioscios iomut?   (12) [27]Agas
do [28]rāidh Adhamh :   [29]In bhean [30]doraitaisi damhsa
[21]in [32]āentaidh dorad [33]domh [34]do [35]chrann [36]�011 ro
[37]chaithius.   (13) Ocus ro rāidh Dīa frisin [38]mnaī :
[39]Cia dīa ndernais anī so?   Is [40]ead ro [41]freagraistair
[42]in bhean[43] : In [44]nathair nimhe ro [45]mheallastair mē,
�011 [46]ro [47]chaithius.

34. (14) [1]Ocus ro rāidh in [2]Coimhdhi ris in
[3]nathair : Ūair [4]dorighni[s]-siu in nī [5]so, [6]isat
mallachta [7]eidir [8]uilibh anmandaibh ꓘ [9]bīastaibh in
[10]talamh.[(a)]   Bidh [11]ar do [12]bhruinni [13]imtigfea, ꓘ bidh
talamh [14]caithfea ō [15]uilibh [16]lāethibh do [17]bheathadh.
(15) Ocus [18]snighidhfetsa [19]nāimhdenus [20]edrut ꓘ in
[21]mnaī, ꓘ [22]eadar [23]do sīl ꓘ [24]sīol na mnā[23] : [25]tñairgfidh
[26]in bhen do [27]chenn, ꓘ [28]intledaighfesu dīsi [29]i leith a
cosaibh.   (16) Ro rāidh [30]dana don [31]mnaoi : [32]Imdaigh-

---

[24] an H β[12]   [25] -nd MH crann β[2]   [26] om. do: ro thairmise
umut M : do ro thoirmisgis iomum β[12]   [27] ocus ro M : om. ꓘ; ra H
[28] radh β[12]   [29] ins. fos β[12] : an ben da- H an bhean β[2]   [30] rad-
aisiu M -radaisidh β[1] -radaisi β[2]: dhamhsa β[12]   [31] im M
[32] oentaid H aon- β[12]   [33] dam MH damh β[12]   [31] don MH
do don β[12]   [35] crand H   [36] ins. in torad M   [37] chaithis
M -thes β[12]   [38] mnaoi β[2]   [39] cid dia ndearnais inni seo MH : anni β[12]
[40] edh β[12]   [41] raid M; fregair β[12]   [42] an ben, An athair H in bheinn
β in bhen β[12]   [43] ins. oga freagra M   [44] nathar β[12]: om. nimhe MH
[45] mellastair MH mheall β[12]   [46] om. ro β[1]   [47] chaithis torad in chraind
M : chaithes β[12].

34. [1] om. ꓘ M   [2] an for in M: Coimdiu fris in MH Choimdhe β[12]
(mh β[2])   [3] athraid M athair H nathar β[12]   [4] doridnis (om. siu) M
dorignis H rinnisigh β[1] rinnighsidh β[2]   [5] seo M   [6] ꓘ isad mallachta M

me as companion gave me of a tree, and I ate. (13) And God said unto the woman : Wherefore hast thou done this thing?   What the woman answered was : The serpent deceived me, and I did eat.

34. (14) And the Lord said unto the serpent : In that thou hast done this thing, thou art accursed among all the animals and beasts of the earth.   It shall be upon thy breast that thou shalt go : it shall be earth that thou shalt eat, for all the days of thy life.   (15) And I shall set enmity between thee and the woman, and between thy seed and the seed of the woman : the woman shall stamp upon thy head, and thou shalt lurk aside from her, hiding from feet. (16) Moreover He said unto the woman : I shall

isath β^{012} -chtadh β^1 -cht β^2 [7] itir MH idir β^{12} [8] uile anamaibh β^{12} [9] piastaib M biastaib H   [10] talman M   [11] air β^2 [12] bruindi H -nne β^1 -ne β^2 [13] -mth- MH imtigfedh β^{12} [14] chaithfea MH caithfedh β^{12} [15] uile β^1 [16] laithib M laoithibh β^{12} (-oth- β^1) [17]-eth- β^{12} [18] suigid feadsa M suighfedsadh β^{12} [19] -deanus M -denas β^1 [20] eadrud M edrud H   [21] mhnai β^1 [22] itir M idir β^1 edra β^2 [23-23] bhur siol β^{12} [24] sil MH   [25] tuairefid MH -argfad β^{12} [26] an ben H : an *also* β^2 [27] cheann M chend H cenn β^2 [28] intlaed- faigfea-su M -fe-su H : dissi β : indleadaigh fesu disi β^{12} (fes a β^2) [29] i leath o chosaib M illeth o cossaib H i leit a cosuib β^2 [30] dono Dia MH dan dia don mhnai β^{12} [31] mnai M mnai *om. y sprs.* c H [32] -feadsa M -fetsa H iomadfadsa β^{12}

(a) The β MSS. treat *talamh* as indeclinable.

fcadh-sa [33]t'athaisi, ⁊ [34]bidh [35]i ngalair ⁊ i [36]ngoirtius
tuismeadha do [37]chompiortha ⁊ do [38]chlanna ‡ .i.
[39]iomad [40]galar mīsda [41]dhuit ‖ ⁊ [42]bidh fo [43]chumhachta
(a)[44]tir [45]bia, ⁊ [46]biadh a [47]thighernus [48]ort. (17) Ro
rāidh [49]imorro Dīa [50]go Hadhamh : [51]Uair [52]atchuala-
dhus guth ⁊ aslach do [53]sētchi, ⁊ [54]an ūair ro [55]chaithis
don [56]chroinn ro [57]thoirmiosciusa [58]ionnut, is [59]mallachda
in talamh [60]id'gnīmh : ⁊ [61]bidh a sāethraibh ⁊ a
snīmhaibh [62]chaithfea biadh [63]ō'n uilibh [64]lāethibh do
[c5]bhethadh. (18) Ocus [66]clannaighfidh [67]in talamh dit
spīne [68]gēra ⁊ [69]drisi [70]deilgneacha, (19) ⁊ [71]bidh in
allus do ghnūisi ‡ [72]⁊ i foghnamh do [73]chuirp ⁊ do
[74]cholla ‖ [75]caithfea [76]luibhi ⁊ [77]toirrthi [78]in [79]talamh,
⁊ [80]notsāsfar ō [81]bhiadhaibh : [82]cen cor athadchuir fon
[83]talmain d'indearna Dīa thū. Uair is do lūaithread
⁊ do[83] thalmain [84]dorōnadh, ⁊ is [85]fae [86]ragha.

35. (20) Ocus ro [1]ghairmeastair [2]Adhamh [3]ainm a
[4]sētchi .i. [5]Eua, [6]īar sin nī ro bhaī, [7]gor bho māthair

[33]thathaisi M tataisi β^1 daithaisi β^2 [34]biadh β^1 biaidh β^2
[35]ingalar M β^{12} angalar H   [36]ngoirtes thuis- H -ort- β^2:
tuismedh (ed β^1) do chomhphrechadh β^{12} [37]coimpearta M
-perta H   [38]clanda M clannadh (ch. β^1) β^{12} [39]imad galair MH
[40]ghalar miostadh β^{12} [41]duid MH   [42]biadh β^1 biaidh β^2
[44]cumachta M cumhachtadh β^{12} (comh- β^2)   [44]tfir β^{12} [45]om. bia β^{12}
[46]biaid MH biaigh β^1 biaidh β^2 [47]-earn- M tig- β^2 -as β^1 [48]fort MH
[49]om. imorro Dia β^{12} [50]eo MH   [51]oir β^{12} [52]adchualadus M
adchualaidais (ais sprs yc) H -asadh β^{12} [53]seitchi H šeitche β^{12}
[54]om. an MH   [55]chaithios β : do for preceding ro H   [56]chrund
MH chrann β^1 crann β^2 [57]thairmis-ciusa M -eusa H -casadh β^{12}
[58]ummut M umut H iomad β^{12} [59]-chta M -chtha H -achtadh β^1 -acht β^2
[60]ad H it β : nim β nimh β^{12} [61]bid a saetraib H biodh a sethraibh β^{12}
[62]caithfi H caitfedh β^{12} [63]o uilib MH on uile β^2 [64]laithib MH

multiply thy shames, and it shall be in sickness and
in distress that thou shalt bring forth thy offspring
and thy progeny [i.e. thou shalt have many monthly
sicknesses]. And under the power of a man shalt thou
be, and his lordship shall be over thee. (17) Moreover
God said to Adam: In that thou hast hearkened to
the voice and incitement of thy wife, and in that thou
hast eaten of the tree that I forbade thee, cursed is
the earth in thy deed. It shall be in labours and in
tribulations that thou shalt eat food, for all the days
of thy life. (18) And the earth shall bring forth for
thee sharp thorns, and spiny brushwood, (19) and it
shall be in the sweat of thy face [and in the servitude
of thy body and of thy frame] thou shalt eat of the
plants and fruits of the earth and shalt be satisfied
with victuals, till He shall have laid thee again
under(b) the earth from which God made thee. For
it is of dust and of earth that he was made, and
under it shall he go.

35. (20) And Adam called the name of his wife Eua,
by reason of the fact that she was mother of all living

---

[65] beathad M [66] clandaigfead M clanaigñ H [67] an H β¹ [68] geradh β¹² [69] drise M -sedh β¹ -sa β² [70] delglecha M -necha H -nechadh β¹² [71] biadh β¹²: an *for* in H [72] ⁊ a fodnum H ag fognamh β¹² [73] choirp β¹ [74] colla β² [75] chaithfea M chaithñ H -feadh β¹² [76] luibi H luibhibh β¹² [77] toirthi MH toraibh β¹² [78] an H na talmhan β¹² [79] talman M [80] notsastar M nodsastar H notfasfar β¹² [81] bi- β² [82] cein MH gen go rathadhchuir β¹² (*in* β² radh *corr. to* rath) [83-83] *om.* β⁰¹² [84] -unad M [85] fai H [86] radha β²

35. [1] gairmistair M -m;t- H -ester β¹² [2] a Adhamh β¹² (Aadh. β²) [3] ainim β¹² [4] seitchi MH (se- M) seitche β¹² [5] Eabha β¹² [6] iarsani H [7] corbo MH gor ba β¹²

(a) From this point the text of H is continuous till the end of the column.
(b) Following the reading of M.

na [8]n-uili [9]mbeō ‡ .i. na udāine ||. (21) [10]Doroighni [11]dana Dīa do [12]Adhamh [13]⁊ da [14]sēithigh [15]tonochu ⁊ inaru [16]croichnidhi (*sic*)[17], ⁊ ro [18]ēit iat.

36. (22) Ocus ro rāidh Dīa : Is follus [1]dorōnadh Adhamh [2]amail [3]āen ñaine, go fios [4]maithiosa ⁊ uile [5]aigi—

[6]Mar [7]bhadh ed [8]adberadh Dīa : Ni [9]uair Adhamh [10]an nī rob āil [11]leis .i. bheith [12]amail [13]ōen [14]ñaine. Ro [15]malairt [16]imorro ⁊ ro [17]seachmhaill in [18]maithius ⁊ in [19]glaine mbunaid i ndernad hē.

[20]Dīchuiremh trā [21]anoissa [22]a [23]bPairthas, [24]na [25]ro chaithea nī [26]do [27]Chrann [28]na [29]Beathadh, ⁊ [30]nara beō hē trē [31]bhithadh. (23) Ro [32]dhīchuir imorro Dīa Adhamh [33]a Parrthus na Toile, ⁊ ro [34]suidhigh hē isin [35]talmhuin coitchenn dīa [36]ndernadh [37]e. (24) Ocus ro [38]ordaigh Dīa [39]Hirufīn [40]a bhfiaghnuisi [41]Phairrtuis, ⁊ [42]cloidheamh teinntighi [43]i n-a lāimh, do [44]choimhed Parrthais ⁊ [45]slighidh Crainn [46]na [47]Beathadh.

---

[5] nuile M β¹²   [9] beo H in bheo β dhuine i *and om. gloss* β¹² [10] doroindi M daroigni H dorighnedh β¹²   [11] dono MH *om.* β¹² [13] Adamh β¹   [15] is β¹²   [14] setig M seitchi H seitche β¹² [15] donacha imaru β donacha ionnara β¹²   [16] croicind M croicend *changed by corrector to* -eand H craicnedh β¹²   [17] *ins.* endatha H [18] eid iad H.

36. [1] dorondad M -ronn- H : dAdam H   [2] ainim aon uaine β¹²   [3] oen uaindi co fis M aen uainni co fis H   [4] maithiusa M maithusa H -sa β¹ [5] aici MH aigi β¹²   [6] *ins.* .i. MH   [7] bad M bud ead H badh β¹² [8] -ered M -eiread H adbh- β²   [9] fuair H   [10] in ni MH β¹² indi ro bail β   [11] ris β¹²   [12] amhuil β¹   [13] eon M aen H aon β¹ [14] uaindi M uainne H   [15]- lart M mhal- β¹   [16] *om.* β² [17] seachmall M sechmall H sechmhail β¹²   [18] maithus H maithiosa β mhaithesadh β¹²

[i.e. of mankind].   (21) Moreover God made for Adam and for his wife tunics and mantles of hides, and clothed them.

36. (22) And God said : Lo, Adam hath been made as one of us, having a knowledge of good and of evil—

As though what God would say was : Adam obtained not the thing which he desired, to be as one of us.   But he changed and neglected the goodness and the original purity in which he was made.

So let us drive him now forth from Paradise, lest he should eat aught of the Tree of Life, and lest he should be alive for ever.   (23) Wherefore God drave Adam forth from the Paradise of Pleasure, and set him in the common earth of which he was made. (24) And God ordained a Seraph in the forefront of Paradise, with a fiery sword in his hand, to guard Paradise and the way of the Tree of Life.

---

[19] glaini H ghlainni mbuncadh indearnad M ghloine in buined inderna β^{12} (buinedh β^2)   [20] -eam M -em H, diochuradh *and om.* tra β^{12} [21] anosa M anossa H anosadh β^{12} [22] *ins.* Adam MH   [23] Parrdus M Parrtus H Parrtas β^{12} [24] no β^2 [25] ra chaithi H chaithedh β^{12} [26] don β [27] chrunn M crund H chrainn β [28] *om.* na MH [29] bethadh β^{12} [30] nar ba M   [31] bithu MH e tre bhiadhadh β^{12} [32] dhiochuir *and om.* imorro β^{12} [33] a Parrdus na Tole M Toili H Pharrthas natolia β^{12} [34] suigid M fuigid H suigh β^{12} [35] talam choitchind MH (-inn H); talamh β^{12} [36] -earn- M nderna β^1 ndernada β^2 [37] *om.* e MH   [38] ordaid M -aidh β^1 [39] *om.* β^{12} [40] hi fiadnaisi M hi fiadnaissi H -fiadhnuise β^{12} [41] -d; M -th; H Pharrthais (-art β^2) β^{12} [42] claidem M claidim H -emh β^{12} tendtigi M tentigi H -ighe β^{12} [43] i laimh aingil β^{12} [44] choinet Parrduis M Pharrthus H *om.* Parrth. ⁊ β^{12} [45] sligheadh H slighe β^{12}: Chraind M Craind H Chrainn β^{12} (Cr. β^2)   [46] *om.* na MH.   [47] bhethadh β^1 betad β^2

31. (1) Sed et serpens erat ¹callidior cunctis animantibus terrae quae fecerat [Dominus] Deus; qui dixit ad mulierem: Cur praecepit Deus uobis ut non comederitis de omni ligno Paradisi? (2) Cui respondit mulier: De fructu lignorum quae sunt in Paradiso uescemur, (3) de fructu uero ligni quod est in medio Paradisi praecepit nobis Deus ne comederemus, et ne tangeremus illud, ne ²forte moriamur. (4) Dixit autem serpens ad mulierem: Nequaquam morte moriemini, (5) scit enim Deus quod in quocunque die comederitis ex eo, aperientur oculi uestri, et eritis sicut ³*angeli*, scientes bonum et malum.

32. (6) Vidit igitur mulier quod bonum esset lignum ad uescendum, et ¹pulchrum oculis, aspectuque delectabile; et tulit de fructu illius et comedit, deditque uiro suo qui comedit. (7) Et aperti sunt oculi amborum, cumque cognouissent esse se nudos, consuerunt folia ficus et fecerunt sibi perizomata. (8) Et ²*audiuerunt* vocem Domini ³[Dei] deambulantis in Paradiso ⁴[ad auram] post meridiem. Abscondit se et uxor eius ⁵[a facie Domini Dei] in medio ligni Paradisi.

33. (9) Vocauitque [Dominus] Deus Adam et dixit: ¹<Adam> ubi es? (10) ²*Respondit uero Adam dicens*: Vocem tuam audiui in Paradiso et timui, eo quod nudus essem, et abscondi me. (11) [Cui] dixit ³<Deus>: Quis [enim] indicauit tibi quod nudus esses ⁴nisi *egomet*? Ex ligno de quo tibi praeceperam ne comederes comedisti? (12) Dixitque Adam: Mulier quam dedisti sociam mihi dedit mihi de ligno, et comedi. (13) Et dixit [Dominus] Deus ad mulierem: Quare hoc fecisti? ⁵*Hoc est quod respondit* mulier: Serpens decepit me, et comedi.

34. (14) Et ait Dominus ¹[Deus] ad serpentem: Quia fecisti hoc, maledictus es inter omnia animantia et bestias terrae. Super pectus tuum gradieris, et terram comedis cunctis diebus uitae tuae. (15) ²[Et] inimicitias ponam inter te et mulierem, et ³[inter] semen tuum et semen illius. Ipsa conteret caput tuum, ⁴et insidiaberis calcaneo eius. (16) Mulieri quoque dixit: Multiplicabo aerumnas tuas et

⁵conceptus tuos : in dolore paries filios, et sub uiri potestate
eris, et ipse dominabitur tui.   (17) Ad Adam vero dixit
⁶[Deus] : Quia audisti ⁷uocem [et temptationem] uxoris tuae,
et comedisti de ligno ex quo praeceperam tibi ne comederes,
maledicta terra in opere tuo : in laboribus comedes ⁸e[sc]am
cunctis diebus uitae tuae.   (18) Spinas et tribulos germinabit
tibi, et comedes herbas terrae, (19) in sudore uultus tui
uesceris ⁹pane, donee reuertaris in terram de qua ¹⁰*fecit te
Deus*, quia puluis es, et in puluerem reuerteris.

35. (20) Et uocauit Adam nomen uxoris suae ¹*Eua*, eo
quod mater esset cunctorum uiuentium.   (21) Fecit quoque
[Dominus] Deus Adam et uxori eius tunicas pellicias, et
induit eos.

36. (22) ¹Et ait ²<Deus> : Ecce Adam factus est quasi
unus ex nobis, sciens bonum et malum : nunc ergo, ne ³[forte
mittat manum suam et] sumat etiam de Ligno Vitae, et
comedat et uiuat in aeternum, <emittamus eum de Paradiso>.
(23) Emisit ⁵<ergo> eum [Dominus] Deus de Paradiso
Voluptatis ⁶*et posuit eum in* terra de qua *factus* est.
(24) ⁷[Eiecitque Adam] et collocauit <Deus> ante Paradisum
[Voluptatis] Cherubin, et flammeum gladium ⁸[atque uer-
satilem] ad custodiendam uiam Ligni Vitae.

Notes on the Biblical Text, Chapter III.

¶ 31. ¹On the adjectives qualifying this word in Tr. and
on the representation of the simple word *qui* by *is i in athair
sin*, see the notes on this ¶.   ²*O thircur*, which means ''from
a chance, accident,'' and in a good sense ''from a windfall,''
suggests that the translator did not completely understand
the Latin *forte*. I am indebted to Miss M. Joynt for some
references to passages containing this word.   ³*Dii* in ST and
all MSS. θεοί LXX. The rendering ''angels'' is a piece of

Jewish exegesis, possibly conveyed to Tr. by some commentary. Skinner quotes Abraham ibn Ezra, † c. 1167.

¶ 32. [1]Tr. has missed the elegant chiasmus of the Latin. [2]*Cum audissent* in ST and Vulg. MSS. Tr. here follows LXX in making the clause independent (as in Heb.): καὶ ἤκουσαν τὴν φωνὴν κ.τ.λ. [3]By exception, *Domini* is here translated. Only one Vulg. MS. omits *Dei*. [4]*Ad auram* has been curiously misunderstood by Tr. [5]These words must have been lost from the Irish text at an early date by some carelessness, which in this case it is impossible to explain.

¶ 33. [1]LXX and a few Vulg. MSS. insert *Adam* here. [2]Nearer to LXX (καὶ εἶπεν αὐτῷ) than to Vulg. (*qui ait*). *Adam* may or may not be here an intrusive gloss. [3]*Deus* rejected by ST, but found in several MSS. and ancient quotations. [4]In Vulg., *quod nudus esses, nisi quod ex ligno*, etc. (so in LXX, τὶς ἀνήγγειλέν σοι ... εἰ μὴ κ.τ.λ.) This must have been the reading in Δ, but *quod* must have been written in such a way that Tr. misread it as a contraction for *egomet*, thus producing the nonsense *acht Mē fēin*, which, naturally, has given some trouble to his copyists. He then began a new sentence with *Ex ligno*, thus accidentally falling into accord with the Hebrew punctuation. [5]Slightly closer to LXX (καὶ εἶπεν ἡ γυνή) than to Vulg. (*quae respondit*).

¶ 34. [1]Only two MSS. omit *Deus*. [2]No authority in Vulg. for inserting *et*, but LXX has καί. It also has (like Tr.) ἔχθραν in the singular, unlike Vulg., in which *inimicitiam* has very slender authority. [3]No authority for repetition of *inter* in Vulg., but found in LXX. This point is of no critical importance, however, as the repetition is practically required by Irish idiom. [4]As suggested in the notes to this ¶, Tr. does not seem to have completely understood this passage: his rendering is rather free. [5]Tr. seems to have regarded *conceptus tuos* as linked to the following words, governed by *paries* rather than by *multiplicabo*, and to have supplied in imagination *et* before *filios*. [6]No authority for *Deus* here. [7]⁊ *aslach* is possibly another instance of Tr.'s fondness for duplication, but it may also be an intrusive gloss. ⁸*cam* in Vulg., *αὐτήν* in LXX. Apparently Tr. took *cam* for a contraction of *escam*. ⁹A gloss has ousted the original translation of this simple word. ¹⁰*Sumptus eo*, Vulg. For a similar translation compare II. 23.

¶ 35. ¹*Hauam* in ST, but there is plenty of authority for *Eua*, as well as some for *Acua, Acuam*, and *Euam*.

¶ 36. ¹This ¶ has suffered considerably in translation or transmission. ²No Latin authority for *Deus*, but LXX has *κύριος ὁ θεός.* ³The equivalent of these words was lost early, presumably because two consecutive sentences began with *na ro*. ⁴There is an effective rhetorical aposiopesis in the text here, in all versions from Heb. downwards. But Tr., assuming that something had dropped from the text, has made an attempt at filling the gap! ⁵No authority for *imorro*, but LXX and a few Vulg. MSS. have *καί, et*. ⁶*Ut operaretur terram de qua sumptus est* in ST. Tr. has here gone altogether off the rails. We have already seen reason to suspect (¶ 33 note (⁴) above) that the handwriting of Δ was not perfectly clear to him, and it is conceivable that *ut operaretur* was so written as to be read carelessly as *et posuit eum in*. Once more we see *sumptus* translated as though it were *factus* (cf. II 23, III 19). ⁷Possibly Tr. or one of his copyists thought these words superfluous after *ro dhíchuir*, just before. ⁸*I n-a láimh* appears to be a gloss that has ousted the Latin *atque uersatilem*.

CHAPTER IV.

37. ¹Is follus ²as so, ³inn airt ⁴ro bhadar ⁵a bPairrthus ⁶corptar ⁷ōea.

(1) Ro ⁸etargnaigh imorro ⁹Adhamh⁶ ¹⁰Eua a ¹¹seitigh.⁽ᵃ⁾ Ro ¹²choimpir sī, ⁊ ro ¹³thuisimh Cāin ¹⁴dō.

Chāin ¹⁴, ¹⁵*poseissio* no ¹⁶*lamentacio* ¹⁷*interpretatur*, .i. is ē ¹⁸mīnughadh ⁊ cīall fil isin ¹⁹bhfocail sin, ²⁰.i. Cāin .i. ²¹scalbh : ⁊ ²²is do ²³foillsighadh na ²⁴cēilli sin ro rāidh Adhamh ²⁵Caneithi .i.—

ro ²⁶sealbhus duine trē ²⁷Dīa. **(2)** ²⁸Ocus ro ²⁹thuissimh ³⁰dana Eua ³¹dorighissi mac ³²eile, .i. Abēl. Is ³³amhlaidh ³⁴imorro ³⁵bhaoi ³⁶Abēil, ³⁷na ³⁸āoeghairi caoirach ³⁹hē, ⁊ Cāin .i. ⁴⁰tīrfreacuirti ēiside. **(3)** ⁴¹Dorighnidh imorro īar ⁴²lāithedaibh ⁴³imdaibh ⁴⁴con n-edhbradh Cāin ⁴⁵māini do ⁴⁶thortibh in ⁴⁷talamh do Dhīa : **(4)** ⁴⁸dorighni dono ⁴⁹Abēl ⁵⁰iodhbartha do ⁵¹phrīomhgheinibh ⁵²derrscaidhthechaibh a ⁵³treōit do Dhīa. Ocus ro ⁵⁴fēgastair ⁵⁵in ⁵⁶Coimhdhia ⁵⁷co ⁵⁸Habēl ⁊ ⁵⁹go maoinibh, **(5)** nī ro ⁶⁰fēgastar ⁶¹imorro ⁶²go Cāin ⁶³no ⁶⁴go ⁶⁵maoinibh.

Is as ro ⁶⁶thuigestar Cāin ⁶⁷gor tholtnachset maoini Abēl do Dhīa, ⁶⁸nī ro ⁶⁹toltnaighsetar ⁷⁰imorro ⁷¹a maoini fēin,

---

37. ¹ as β¹² ² aso M ais so β ³ inairet M indaired H as follus as so ar (air β²) a ndibirt β¹² ⁴ ra badar H ⁵ i Parrdus M a Parrthus H i Pharthas β¹² ⁶⁻⁶ gur torrehadh (torrchad β²) i dergnaidh Adhamh ⁊ β¹² ⁷ occa H ⁸ etargnaid M eadargnaid H ⁹ Adam H ¹⁰ *ins.* agus: Eabha β¹² ¹¹ a setig M, a seitig H, *om.* a seitigh ro choimpir si β¹² (*but not* β) ¹² comper M ¹³ tuismedh β¹² ¹⁴⁻¹⁴ do Cain M a (fa β²) chialluighes (ci- β²) β¹² ¹⁵ posesio M possesio β¹² ¹⁶ -tio M β² ¹⁷ *om.* β¹² (*b*) ¹⁸ mineagud M ciall ⁊ miniughadh β¹² ¹⁹ focol M bhfocal β¹² ²⁰ is M β *om.* β¹² ²¹ selb M seilbh β¹² ²² *om.* β¹² ²³ foillseagad M sealbhughadh β¹² ²⁴ -le β¹² ²⁵ canei β canai me β¹² ²⁶ selbus M -as β¹² ²⁷ Dhia β¹² ²⁸ agas β¹² ²⁹ tusim M (*the* im *sprs.* s M): toismidh β¹² ³⁰ *om.* M ³¹ doridise M *om.* β¹² ³² aile .i. Aibel M ³³ amhladh β¹² ³⁴ *om.* β¹² (*this word almost invariably om. by the* β MSS.) ³⁵ bai M bhi β¹² ³⁶ Aibel M Abel β¹² ³⁷ *om.* na β ³⁸ aegairi chaerach M aoidhire β¹ aoidhre β²: caoraeh β¹² ³⁹ *om.* β¹² ⁴⁰ tirfreenaire frechuirthig esige (*a* d *sprs over the* g) M: tir-freacuirthe eisidhe β¹² ⁴¹ -ridned M

CHAPTER IV.

37. It is evident from this that so long as they were in Paradise, they were virgins.

(1) Now Adam knew Eua his wife. She conceived and brought forth Cain to him.

Cain, *possessio* or *lamentatio interpretatur,* i.e. this is the explanation and meaning which is in that word, "Cain"; i.e. "possession." And to set forth that meaning Adam said "Caneithi," i.e.

I have acquired a man through God. (2) And Eua brought forth again another son, Abel. Thus was Abel, a shepherd of sheep, and Cain, an husbandman was he. (3) It came to pass, moreover, after many days, that Cain would offer gifts of the fruits of the earth to God : (4) but Abel made offerings of the choice firstlings of his flock to God. And the Lord looked upon Abel and upon his gifts, (5) but He looked not upon Cain and upon his gifts.

Thus did Cain understand that the gifts of Abel were acceptable to God, but that his own gifts were not accept-

-nedh *and om.* imorro β^{12} [42] laitheadaib M laidhidaibh β laidhidegh β^{12} (-eg β^2)   [43] iomdh- β^{12} [44] conedbrad (the d y sbs c) M go n-iodhbaradh *and om.* Cain β^{12} [45] maine M maoine β^{12} [46] thoirthaib M thoraibh β^{12} [47] talman M   [48] doridni M do (*om.* righni dono) β^{12} [49] Aibel M Abeal β^1 [50] edbarta M -barthadh β^{12} (-arr- β^1) [51] primgenib M priomhghinibh β^{12} [52] dearrscaitheachaibh M derscaidh-thechaibh β^{12} [53] threoit M -oid β^{12} [54] *a very faint dot over the* f M [55] an β^{12} [56] Coimdi M   [57] go β^{12} [58] Haibel M   [59] co a mainib M da m. β^{12} [60] Tegastair M   [61] *om.* β^{12} [62] *om.* M, do β^{12}.   [63] na M [64] da β^{12} [65] mainib M mhaoin- β^{12} [66] thuigistair M   [67] cor tholtnaigsead maine M gur tholtnach siad maoiuibh β^{12} [68] nior ro β^{12} [69] tholtnaigsedar M toltnach siad β^{12} [70] *om.* β^{12} [71] a ye M :

(a) Here a lacuna in H begins.

(b) Not *om.* in β, but a corrector who thought it ought to be there but did not notice it inserted it in marg. It is written as an abbreviation (an i and a p crossed) and probably was so written in B, in such a way that it could easily be overlooked.

[72]ar [73]ticeth [74]teine do [75]Nimh [76]for [77]eadhbartaib Abēl, [78]nī [79]tigedh imorro [76]for [80]iodhbairtaibh [81]Cāin.

Ocus ro [82]fergaidh Cāin [83]go [84]dearmhāir, ⁊ [85]dorochair a [86]ghnūis ‡ a [87]t-toirsi ⁊ [88]in dubha ||.

38. (6) [1]Ocus ro rāidh [2]in [3]Coimhdhia [4]go Cāin : [5]Cidh ar [6]ar [7]feargaighais, ⁊ [5]cidh ara [8]torchair do ghnūis [9]‡ i t-toirrsi ||?   (7) [10]Cidh ōn, ar Dīa, nach [11]fuidbheasu a [12]comāin madh maith [13]doghneis? [14]Madh ole [15]dono [13]dogneis, bidh [16]fogus a [17]indeochadh [18]fort.   (8) Ocus [19]adubhairt Cāin [20]co [21]Habēl, go a bhrāthair : Tīagham amach isin [22]bhfearann.   [23]Iar [24]tochtain [25]dāibh [26]isin [27]bhferonn ro [28]comhēirigh Cāin [29]an aghaidh [30]Aibeōil [31]a bhrāthar, ⁊ ro [32]mairb hē—

y[1] [33].i. isin [34]cathraigh [35]danadh ainm Damascus.

y[2] [36]Abēl dono, cēd marb in domain, ⁊ rob ē Aibēl [37]in cēt [38]mairtir(a) ro [39]bāi arīam, ⁊ [40]ba(b) toltanach ro adaimh a martra[40].   .....

(9) (c)Ocus ro rāidh Dīa [41]go Cāin : [42]Cāit a [43]bhfuil [44]Abēl do bhrāthair? Ro [45]fregair Cāin : Nī [46]feidar; cidh ōn, ‡ [47]ar Cāin ||, in [48]missi [49]is [50]coimhēdaigh dom' bhrāthair[50]?

---

maine M mhaoine β[12]   [72]⁊ β[12]   [73]teigead (ge in rasura) M tigedh β[12]   [74]tene M   [75]neimh β[12]   [76]fo M (bis) [77]iobarrthaibh β[1] iodhbarthaibh β[2]   [78]ins. ⁊ M   [79]thiced M [80]idbartaib M iodhbarraibh β[12]   [81]Chain β   [82]feargaidead M fergadh β[12]   [82]co M   [84]dermhar β[12]   [85]ro chuir β[12] (om. do-) [86]gnuisi M   [87]toirrsi M ttuirsedh β[12]   [88]andubha β[12]
38. [1]This word spelt agus, agas indifferently β[12]   [2]an β[12] [3]Coimdi M -mbdlia β[2]   [4]co M   [5]cia β[12] (bis)   [6]om. β[12] [7]fergaidis y sprs. s M fergais β[12]   [8]ttor- β[2]   [9]an interrogation-mark ins. here β[2]: i toirrsi M attuirsed β[2]   [10]cēd M cia β[12] [11]-bhesa β[12]   [12]chomain M -aoin β[12]   [13]dognes M doghnidhis β[12] (bis) [14]ma β[12]   [15]om. M β[12]   [16]fecus M   [17]ineochad β[12] [18]om. M fert β[12]   [19]adurbairt M   [20]go β[12]   [21]Haibel co M: om. go β[12] [22]ferann M bhfer- β[12]   [23]om. β[12]   [24]tiachtain M   [25]ins. imorro,

able—in that fire would come from Heaven upon the offerings of Abel, but would not come upon the offerings of Cain.

and Cain was exceeding wroth, and his countenance fell ⁖ in distress and in gloom. ‖

38. (6) And the Lord said unto Cain : Wherefore wast thou wroth, and wherefore hath thy countenance fallen [in distress]?   (7) How now, said God, shalt thou not obtain its equivalent if thou doest well?   But if it be evil that thou doest, vengeance for it shall be nigh unto thee.   (8) And Cain said unto Abel his brother : Let us go out into the field.   After they had gone into the field, Cain rose up against Abel his brother and slew him,

In the city which is called Damascus.

Now Abel was the first dead man of the world, and he was the first martyr that ever was; and with good will he made confession in martyrdom.

(9) And God said unto Cain : Where is Abel thy brother?   Cain answered : I know not.   How now, [said Cain], is it I who am custodian for my brother?

---

doib M : doibh β¹² ²⁶ *ins.* amach M ²⁷ fearann M bfer- β² -ann β¹² ²⁸ choimerig M coimh- β¹ -rghe β¹² ²⁹ in M ³⁰ Abel β¹² ³¹ a brathair β *om.* β¹² ³² *ins.* iad a da laim fo bragait cor ba M : marb M; mharbh e β¹² ² ³³ *om.* .i. M ³⁴ chathraid M chathraigh β² ³⁵ dianad M darab ainim β¹² ³⁶ *sic* M : *om.* cet marb . . . Aibel β. Abel (din *sic, bracketed in both* MSS.) an ched mairbh ┐ marthar bha [ba β²] ariamh ┐ ba [badh β²] toltanach [toil- β²] ro H-Adhamh a mhartra [martra β²] β¹² ³⁷ an β ³⁸ mairtir M ³⁹ bhaoi ariamh β ⁴⁰⁻⁴⁹ do tholtanaich ┐ ro adaim a martra M ⁴¹ co M ⁴² cia hait β¹² ⁴³ fuil M bfuil β¹² ⁴⁴ do derbhrathair [dh β²] Abel β¹² ⁴⁵ frecair M fregair β¹² ⁴⁶ feadar M fedair β¹ ⁴⁷ *om.* ar Cain : an β¹² ⁴⁸ misi M β¹² ⁴⁹ bhas β¹ bus β² ⁵⁰⁻⁵⁰ comhedaid do β¹²

(a) s² M.   (b) H here resumes.   (c) s¹ M.

y³ Is ī ⁵¹so ⁵²in ⁵³dara ⁵⁴cēd bhrēg, .i. ⁵⁵an ⁵⁶dīabhul ar
⁵⁷ttūs, ⁵⁸Cāin īartain.

(10) Ocus ro rāidh Dīa ⁵⁹go Cāin : ⁶⁰Cid doroinnais⁶⁰?
⁶¹Nūallaigh �7 ⁶²ēigidh ⁶³chugum don ⁶⁴talmhunn guth �7
foghar ⁶⁵fola do ⁶⁶brāthar.

   y⁴ Trī ⁶⁶nūalla ⁶⁷ro saghat dochum Dē ⁶⁸gan ⁶⁹fuireach :
.i. ⁷⁰nūall fola ⁷¹finnghaili, ⁷²amhuil ⁷³nūaill fola ⁷⁴Abēil īar
n-a dortadh ⁷⁵do Chāin, ⁷⁶da bhrāthair ; �7 ⁷⁷nūall ⁷⁸pheacaidh
⁷⁹indirigh, amhuil ⁸⁰nuall ⁸¹pheacadh na ⁸²Sodamdha : �7
⁸³nūall �7 gair na mbocht īar mbreith ⁸⁴ūaithibh a
n-⁸⁵ionmhais �7 ⁸⁶īar n-a ⁸⁷slat.

39. (11) ¹Biadh-sa ²dono �7 tū ³mallachdha for
⁴talmhain ‡ �7 ⁵budh ⁶mallachta dono ⁷in talamh ‖ ⁸ro
foslaic a bēal �7 ⁹ro ghabh fuil do ¹⁰brāthar ‡ ¹¹īar n-a
¹²dortadh ‖ ¹³dot lāimh.

   y¹ ¹⁴Ūair āirmid na staraigeda dīada co rob do fid
chnāma camaill ro marb Cāin a brāthair og ingairi chāerach.

(12) ¹⁵Agus ¹⁶in tan ¹⁷oibridfeasu ¹⁸in ¹⁹talamh sin, ni⁽ᵃ⁾

⁵¹ sco M   ⁵² an β¹²   ⁵³ daradh breg β¹   ⁵⁴ cet breath (sic) M   ⁵⁵ om. an M
⁵⁶ diabal MH β¹²   ⁵⁷ tus MH β¹²   ⁵⁸ ins. �7 M   ⁵⁹ co M
⁶⁰⁻⁶⁰ doronnais pecad �7 gnim n-adbal M cia doroinnis β¹²   ⁶¹ nuallaid
MH   ⁶² egid M eigid H eighidh β¹²   ⁶³ chucum M chugam β¹²
⁶⁴ talmain M talamh β¹²   ⁶⁵ foladh β¹²   ⁶⁶ bhrathair β : bh- also β¹²
⁶⁶ nuala M nuaillaidh β¹²   ⁶⁷ do H : saiged M, sagaid H   ⁶⁸ cen M
⁶⁹ fuireach M fhuirech β¹²   ⁷⁰ nuaill β¹²   ⁷¹ fingaile M fingaili H
fionghaile β¹²   ⁷² amail MH   ⁷³ nuall fola MH n. foladh β¹
⁷⁴ Aibel M Abel β¹   ⁷⁵ dha β¹²   ⁷⁶ dia H, om. da bhr. β¹²   ⁷⁷ nuaill β¹²
⁷⁸ peeaid MH pecaidh β¹²   ⁷⁹ om. M   ⁸⁰ nuaill β¹²   ⁸¹ peeaid M
pecadh β¹²   ⁸² Sodoma H Sodomaitibh β¹²   ⁸³ nuaill β¹

This is one of the first two lies—the devil first and Cain afterwards.

(10) And God said unto Cain : What hast thou done? The voice and cry of thy brother's blood maketh complaint and call unto me from the earth.

There are three cries which made their way to God without delay : the cry of the blood of kin-murder, as the cry of the blood of Abel after it was shed by Cain his brother : the cry of iniquitous sin, as the cry of the sin of the Sodomites : and the cry and lamentation of the poor, when their goods have been taken from them and when they have been slaughtered.

39. (11) Thou also shalt be accursed upon the earth [and the earth also shall be accursed] which hath opened her mouth and received the blood of thy brother [after it had been shed] at thy hand.

For the sacred historians consider that it was with a shank of a camel-bone that Cain slew his brother, as he tended sheep.

(12) And when thou shalt till the earth, she shall not

---

84 uadhadh β^{12} 85 indmais MH ioumhus β^{12} 86 ar β^1 om. β^2
87 slad M β^{12}

39. 1 biasu MH   2 om. dono ⁊ tu β^{12}: om. ⁊ H, but ye
3 -chta M -uighe β^{12} 4 tall- β^2 -mhuin β^{12} 5 bid M bu β^{12} 6 -chda
M mallach dana β, mallaighthe β^1 -uighe β^2: om. dono β^{12} 7 an H
8 ro (ra H): slnig (sl- M) Abel MH : fosglaic a beul β^{12} 9 rogob M
ragab H   10 bhrathair β (bh- also β^{12})   11 ar M β^1 12 dhor- β^1
13 dod H β^{12} 14 y^1 in M only   15 ocus M   16 an M β^{12}
17 oibrigfeadfa-su M oibrigfessu H oipd oibrid feasu β^1 cuspd oibrid
corr. in marg. to oipd β^2 18 an H   19 talmain M

(a) H is preserved continuously from this point to the next lacuna.

²⁰thibradh a ²¹toirtha dhuit : ꓿ ²²biasu ²³faelnedach ꓿
²⁴teitheach ‡ a ²⁵hinud i n-inud ‖ for ²⁶talnhain.
(13) Ocus ro ráidh Cáin ²⁷go Día : Is mō ꓿ is ²⁸fuilliu
²⁹m'indirghi ³⁰inās mar ³¹dlighim loghadh.

y² ³²Dearchāiniudh ³³dono ³⁴dorighni Cáin ³⁵sund ³⁶in
tan ³⁷ro rāid na brīathra-sa : Nī ³⁸gheabha-sa a ³⁹Dō, ꓿ nī
⁴⁰thibrea ⁴¹damh loghadh ⁴²ce dagncor ⁴³aithrighi. Ocus
⁴⁴egnach Dē dō-⁴⁵som sin.

(14) Is follus, ar Cáin, ⁴⁶dichraighsiu misi ⁴⁷andiu ō
⁴⁸dhreach in ⁴⁹talamh, ꓿ ⁵⁰namfoilgeabhthar ōd' ghnūis.
⁵¹Bam ⁵²teichtheach ⁵³faelnedach-sa for ⁵⁴talnhuin, ꓿
⁵⁵muirfidh ꓿ ⁵⁶nīmhcheagela ⁵⁷neach mē. (15) Agas ro
rāidh Día ⁵⁸go Cáin : Nī ⁵⁹ba ⁶⁰hamhlaidh sin ⁶¹dogh-
cntar, acht ⁶²pīanfaithair a ⁶³secht ⁶⁴cudruima ⁶⁵gach
aon ⁶⁶do ⁶⁷mhuirfeas Cáin—

y³   .i. Nī hē ⁶⁸leighios ⁶⁹peacaidh ⁷⁰fogheabha bās ⁷¹oband
amhuil ⁷²saili, acht ⁷³mera ⁷⁴go ⁷⁵fada ⁷⁶gorab ⁷⁷mōidi do
⁷⁸phīan ꓿ do ⁷⁹dīoghail.

Ro ⁸⁰suidhidh Día Cáin ⁸¹i ⁸²comhartha ⁸³conach
marbhadh ⁸⁴nach ⁸⁵duine hē.

y⁴   .i. ⁸⁶cnoce ina ⁸⁷ēadan ⁸⁸‡ ꓿ cnoc ceachtar a dā grūad
꓿ cnoc for each cois ꓿ for each lāim ‖⁸⁸. ꓿ a bheith ⁸⁹ghan
⁹⁰ulcha, ⁹¹no a bheith ⁹²teiththeach.

²⁰ thibra MH -bhr- β tiubhradh β¹² ²¹ thoirthi MH thoradh β¹² ²² biadhsa
β¹² ²³ -neadach M faoil- β¹ ²⁴ techech M teithibh β¹² ²⁵ a hinad
aninad M anin *with* ad *above* H hionad, ionad β¹² ²⁶ -an β¹ ²⁷ co MH
²⁸ fuilli MH ²⁹ minudirgi H in innirge β¹ inncirge β² ³⁰ na H
³¹ dhl- β¹² ³² der- MH -nead M -nid H -aoinedh β¹² ³³ *om.* β¹²
³⁴ -dne M -gni H dorinigh β¹² ³⁵ sunn β¹² ³⁶ antan H β¹ ³⁷ so β¹²: *om.* ro
raid na briathra-sa β⁰¹²: na briathra-sa *in* M *only* ³⁸ geba-su MH gheabadh
(*om.* -sa) β¹² ³⁹ Dhe β¹ ⁴⁰ tibra M thibri H thibredh β¹ thiubhredh
β² ⁴¹ dhamh β¹²: logad dam MH ⁴² ge dogncor M ge do ner H
ced agnair β¹² ⁴³ -ide M -igi H -ighthe β¹² ⁴⁴ ecnach MH
⁴⁵ dosam sin H do san am sin β⁰¹² ⁴⁶ dichuirid-siu M diacuirisi H
diachragh *and om.* -siu β¹² ⁴⁷ aniug MH aniu β¹² ⁴⁸ dreich MH
-ech β¹² ⁴⁹ -lmau M an tal- H ⁵⁰ nomfoilgebthar MH -gebhar β¹²
(gh- β²) ⁵¹ bain β¹² ⁵² teicheach M -teach H teichthech β¹²
(-teith β²) ⁵³ -nead- M faoil- β¹² ⁵⁴ -lmain M ⁵⁵ murf. H muirbhfedh β¹²

yield her fruits unto thee: and thou shalt be a wanderer and a fugitive [from place to place] upon the earth. (13) And Cain said unto God: Greater and huger is my iniquity than that I deserve forgiveness.

It was despair that Cain expressed there when he said these words: Thou, O God, shalt not receive, and shalt not give me forgiveness, though I should work repentance. That was a blasphemy of God on his part.

(14) Lo, said Cain, Thou hast driven me today from the face of the earth, and I shall be hidden from Thy face. I shall be a fugitive and a wanderer upon the earth, and anyone shall slay me, and shall not spare me. (15) And God said unto Cain: Not thus shall it be done: but everyone who shall slay Cain shall be punished sevenfold.

i.e. Sudden death is not the remedy for sin that thou shalt obtain as thou thinkest: but thou shalt live long, so that thy punishment may be the greater.

God set Cain in a sign, so that no man should slay him—

a lump upon his forehead [and a lump (on) each of his cheeks, and a lump on each foot and on each hand] and his being beardless, and being a fugitive.

---

[56] nimcoicela MH (-gela H) -chealgadh β^{12} [57] nech MH β^{12} [58] co MH [59] bu β^2 [60] -ladh β^{12} [61] do-dhentar β^{12} [62] -faidear M -faigter H -fuighther β^{12} [63] seacht M ṡ- β^{12} [64] enduma MH chodrumadh β^{12} (cod- β^2) [65] cach oen M cach aen H: gac β^1 [66] om. do MH   [67] muirfes MH marbhas tú β^{12} (mh- β^2)   [68] -ges M -g; H   [69] pecaid MH pecadh β^{12} [70] fogeba MH fogheabhadh β^{12} [71] opand M obann H β^2 [72] ṡaile M ṡaili H saoile β^{12} [73] mairradh β maredh β^{12} (mair- β^1) [74] co MH   [75] fata M fadadh β^{12} [76] corob M corop H gurab β^{12} [77] moide M β^{12} [78] pian M   [79] digal MH dh- β^{12} [80] ṡnigid MH (ṡ- M) suighe β^{12} [81] hi H   [82] -thadh β^{12} [83] connach H gonach β^{12} [84] om. nach β^{12} [85] duine nduine β [86] cnoc M cnoc ionna β^{12} [87] hedan H etan M edan β [88-88] in M only   [89] cen M can H gan β^{12} [90] ulchain M ulchadh β^{12} [91] ꞁ M   [92] teitheadach M teichteach H (the eb yc), teitheach β^2

40. (16) ¹Ro scibh Cáin ²imorro o ³freagnarcus in ⁴Coimhdhedh, ⁊ ro ⁵aitreabhaidh, ⁶is sē ⁷teitheach ⁸dāsachtach, i riud ⁹airtheraigh ¹⁰an feroinn dar ainm¹⁰ ¹¹Eden—

.i. ¹²ferand sin fil ¹³inn airthear na ¹⁴Haissia.

(17) Ro ¹⁵etairgnaidh Cáin a ¹⁶sēitigh ⊣ ro ¹⁷coimparastar ¹⁸sī ¹⁹mac .i. ²⁰Enōch, ⊣ ro ²¹cumhdaigh-sium ²²cathraigh, ⊣ ²³tug ²⁴ainm dī ō ²⁵ainm a ²⁶mic²⁷, .i. Enōch. (18) Ro ²⁸thusim ²⁹imorro Enōch ³⁰Iaradh, ³¹⊣ ³²ro thuisimh ³³Iaradh ³⁴Mauiabel. ³⁵Ro thuisimh ³⁶Mauiabel Matusael. ³⁷Ro ³⁸tusimh ³⁹Matusael Laimhīach ‡ ⁴⁰diamus .i. ōn dā mnāi ‖.

41. (19) ¹Dorad ²imorro ³in ⁴Lambīach ⁵sin dā ⁶sēitigh, ⁷Adda ⊣ ⁸Sella a ⁹n-anmanda-sidhe. (20) ¹⁰Agas ¹¹ro thusimh Adda ¹²Iabal; is ¹³ēisidhe ¹⁴ba hathair ‡ ¹⁵⊣ ¹⁶ba ¹⁷taoisech ‖ ¹⁸na n-āgairi ⊣ nanī ¹⁹no aitreabhdais ¦⁽ᵃ⁾ a ²⁰bpuiblibh ‡ ¹⁵⊣ ²¹a bhfāissaighibh ‖. (21) Iubal imorro ²²ainm a ²³bhrāthar; is ēsidhe ²⁴ro bha athair ‡ ⊣ ²⁵rob aireach ‖ ²⁶nanī ro ²⁷chlechtaitis cruit ⊣ ²⁸orgain. (22) Ro ²⁹tusmestair ³⁰dana ³¹Sealla ³²mac ³³don ³⁴Laimhīach ³⁵cēadhna .i. ³⁶Tupalcān ³⁷a

---

40. ¹ ra scib H   ² *om*. β¹²   ³ freacnarcus MH (free-H) fergnarcus β²   ⁴ Coimdead M an Choimdead H Choimhdbe β¹²   ⁵ aitreb MH (-eab M)   ⁶ ⊣ M ise H *om*. is β¹² re *for* se β²   ⁷ teichtheach H   ⁸ dhasachtach [*blank space that would hold four letters*] fuind β : dh. i bhfuinn β¹²   ⁹ iartharaid M iartharaig H airerthaigh β¹²   ¹⁰⁻¹⁰ *om*. β¹² : in (an H) fearaind (f. M fer- H) MH : dianaid M dianad H   ¹¹ Etan M Eadon no Eden H Edin β¹ Eoin β²   ¹² *om*. ferand sin fil β¹² : fearann M fuil H   ¹³ an iarthar M an oirrther H   ¹⁴ Haisia M Asia (*om*. na) β¹²   ¹⁵ eadarguaid (edar- H) MH : edar- β¹²   ¹⁶ setig M seidid H   ¹⁷ choimpristair MH -peir- β¹²   ¹⁸ *om*. si MH   ¹⁹ inac β²   ²⁰ Eanoch β¹ Eanoe β²   ²¹ cumdaigsim H chum- β¹² -siom β¹²   ²² cathraid M   ²³ tuc MH   ²⁴ ainim β¹²   ²⁵ anmuin MH ainmuin β ainim β¹²   ²⁶ mhic β¹²   ²⁷ *ins*. primgenid M   ²⁸ tuisim M ra thuis. H thuisiumh β¹²   ²⁹ *om*. β¹²   ³⁰ *ins*. mac .i. M : Iarad M Iaareth H Iaret β¹²   ³¹ *om*. ⊣ M   ³² M ra tuisim H *om*. β¹²   ³³ *ins*. imorro MH : Iareth Manuel H Iaree β¹ Iaret β²   ³⁴ *ins*. mac .i. M; Manibel M   ³⁵ ro (*not* ra) thuisim H *om*. β¹²   ³⁶ Maubel mac .i. Maithiusael M; Manuel Mathasael H Manabel Matusaoil β²   ³⁷ ra H : *om*. ro tusimh, *ins*. ⊣ β¹²   ³⁸ thusim M

40. (16) Then Cain departed from the presence of the Lord, and dwelt, a wild fugitive, in the eastern border of the land called Eden—

The land which is in the east of Asia.

(17) Cain knew his wife, and she conceived a son, Enoch; and he founded a city and gave it a name from the name of his son, Enoch. (18) And Enoch begat Irad, and Irad begat Maviahel, Maviahel begat Mathusahel. Mathusahel begat Lamech [the bigamist, i.e. (so called) from the two wives].

41. (19) Now that Lamech took two wives, Ada and Sella their names. (20) And Ada bore Iabel; he it is who was father [and chief] of shepherds and of those who used to dwell in tents [and in desert places]. (21) Iubal, moreover, was the name of his brother: he it is who was father [and leader] of those who would handle harps and organs. (22) And Sella bore a son to the same Lamech, Tubalcain his name. He,

thuisim H   ³⁹ Mathasael mac .i. Laimiach M Mathusael Laimiach H om. Matusael β²   ⁴⁰ this g. in M only.

41. ¹ darad H   ² om. β¹²   ³ an H om. β¹²   ⁴ Laimiach MH Lamiach β¹² (-iac β¹)   ⁵ hi siu .i. β⁰¹²   ⁶ seitig M seitid H ⁷ ins. .i. MH   ⁸ Sealla H β¹²   ⁹ -and-side MH (-sidi H) om. a naumauda β¹²   ¹⁰ ocus M   ¹¹ ra H thuisim Ada (foll. by full stop) H: thuisiumh β¹ -iomh β²   ¹² ins. mac do Laimiach .i. M   ¹³ eside M cissidi H esidhe β¹² ¹⁴ bu hathar β¹²   ¹⁵ probably .i. to be read for ꝛ (bis) all MSS.   ¹⁶ bu β² ¹⁷ taiseach M toissich H   ¹⁸ do, with na sprs. ys M: na naegairi H nagari β¹² haegairib M   ¹⁹ ra aitreabadais H -trebd- M noch aitreabhas β¹² ²⁰ puiblib M   ²¹ i fásaidib M a bfasaibh β¹²   ²² ainim β¹²   ²³ brathar M brathair β⁰²   ²⁴ rob athair M ro ba β¹   ²⁵ ro badh β²   ²⁶ looks like nam in β¹, but may be given benefit of doubt: certainly nam β²   ²⁷ clechtaidis M lechtatis β leachtadaois β¹²   ²⁸ organ M   ²⁹ thuismedar β¹²   ³⁰ dono M om. β¹²   ³¹ Sella M   ³² mac dittographed β¹   ³³ do β⁰¹²   ³⁴ -ech β¹ ³⁵ cetna M cedna β¹²   ³⁶ Tubalchain M Tubalcon β¹²   ³⁷ -dhe β om. a

(a) H lacuna begins.

ainm-side. [38]Rob ēside [39]imorro [40]an [41]chēd [42]cheard
[43]⁊ [40]an [44]cēad gabha ⁊ [45]in chēad [46]sāer. Ocus [47]rug
[45]Sella inghen īarsin, .i. [49]Nema siur [50]Tubalcāin.

[51]Ba hī [52]sin in [53]chēad druineach ⁊ is ī ro [54]chēad-chum
ēdach re cāch ar [55]ttūs.

42. (23) [1]Agas ro rāidh [2]Laimhīach re [3]sēitchibh .i.
re [4]Hada ⁊ re [5]Sella : [6]A sēitchi Laimhīach[6], [7]ēistidh
mo [8]guth[9], oighidh ⁊ [10]tuigidh mo [11]bhrīathair. [12]Cair
ro [13]mharbhus [14]fer amuigh [15]aniu, ⁊ is [16]inund fodhēn
ro [17]chreachnaideas [18]annsin. [19]Uairistar [20]form, ⁊
[21]tri [22]formad ro [23]mhairbhus in [24]māeth-ōglach [25]sein.

[26]⁊ [27]ba gnīomh comhāidhmhi lesiumh sin, [28]ūair is tria
[29]dhīomus - [30]in dōcbhāil ro rāidh.

(24) [31]In tī [32]trāā [33]muirfeas Cāin, [34]indechfaidhair
in [35]tseachtoll īair : [31]in tī [32]imorro [33]mhuirfes
[34]Laimhīach, [35]pīanfaidhair hē a [36]secht [37]cudrama fa
seachtmhoghait.

43. (25) Ro [1]etargnaidh [2]dana Adhamh [3]dorighisi
‡ .i. |[(a)] [4]Eua ||. ⁊ [5]ro [6]thusimb sī mac dō, [7]⁊ do ro

---

ainm-side β¹² ³⁸ ro ba hisidhe β² ³⁹ om. imorro M β¹² ⁴⁰ in M β² (bis)
⁴¹ cet M (ter) ced β² ⁴² cerd β² goba . . . cherd . . . sáer M ⁴³ om. ⁊
β¹² ⁴⁴ ched-ghabhadh β¹² (gabh- β²) ⁴⁵ an β¹² ⁴⁶ saor β¹² ⁴⁷ ruc M
⁴⁸ Sealla β¹ Seall β² ⁴⁹ Neama β¹ ⁵⁰ Thubalchain M ⁵¹ fa M
⁵² sidhe β¹² ⁵³ ched ruinech M ced dr. β² ⁵⁴ chet M ced cumedach
β⁰¹² ⁵⁵ tus M β¹²
42. ¹ ocus M β² ² Lamiac β¹ Laimiach M β² ³ heitchib M ⁴ Hadda M
β¹² ⁵ Scalla β¹² ⁶⁻⁶ da seitig Laimiach (attached to preceding) M om. β¹²
⁷ estig M ⁸ ghuth β¹² ⁹ ins. ol se M ¹⁰ tuicid M tugadh β²,
an attempt made afterwards to insert an i before the g ¹¹ briathra M
-thar β¹ ¹² om. β¹² ¹³ mbhairbhus β² ¹⁴ fear M ¹⁵ aniug M
¹⁶ inand M ann β¹² ¹⁷ chrechtnaideas M cheachtnaighius β cechtnaighes
β¹² ¹⁸ om. β¹ ¹⁹ oir (uair β⁰) is tar (tair β²) form (f. β⁰) β⁰¹²
²⁰ formad M ²¹ tria M ²² for- β² ²³ marbas M mharbhas β¹²

moreover, was the first wright, the first smith, and the first carpenter. And Sella bore a daughter thereafter, Noemma, sister of Tubalcain.

She was the first weaver, and the first who fashioned raiment for everyone in the beginning.

42. (23) And Lamech said to his wives, Ada and Sella : Ye wives of Lamech, hear my voice, heed and understand my word. For I have slain a man without, today, and it is the very same thing that I wounded (him) there. He injured me, and through jealousy I slew that tender youth.

And he thought it a deed for boasting, for it was through his haughtiness and in vainglory that he spoke.

(24) He then who shall slay Cain, it shall be revenged upon him sevenfold : but he who shall slay Lamech, shall be punished seventy and seven times the equivalent.

43. (25) Then Adam knew again <his wife>, [to wit Eua] and she bore a son to him, and Adam called that

[24] maoth- β^{12} *(In β^2 owing to change of page dittographed thus:* in maethog | an maethoglach) [25] sen M sin β^{12} [26] .i. β^0 [27] fa gnim comaidme lesim in gnim sin M go maidhmi leasiumh β^{12} [28] oir β^2 [29] dimus M -mas β^1 [30] ind tocbail M in docbal β^2 [31] an β^{12} *(bis)* [32] thra M *om.* β^{12} [33] murfeas M ro mharbhas β^{12} [34] indeachfaidear M -faigher β^1 -faisgar (s *expuncted*) β^2 [35] seacht ollfair M secht oll fair β techt ollfair β^{12} [32] *om.* β^{12} [33] muirfeas M muirbhthas β^{12} [34] Lamiac β^1 [35] -dear M dher β^{12} [36] seacht M secht β^{12} [37] cutruma fo seachtmogat M cudrumadh (cad- β^1) fo seachtmhoghadh (s- β^1) β^{12}

43. [1] eadar- M cadargnadh β^2 [2] dono M dion β^1 dionn β^2 [3] -disi M dorighsi β [4] Eabha β^{12} [5] *om.* ro β^2 [6] thuisim M tuisiomh β^{12} [7] *om.* β^{12} *(not β)*; *om.* do ro M, -easd- M Adam M

(a) s^2 M.

gairmeastair Adhaimh in mac sin[7] .i. [8]Seth : ⁊ [9]is edh
ro rāidh : [10]Dorat [11]Dīa [12]dhamh, ‡ air Adhamh ‖
[13]"ar" .i. sīol [14]sāmh [15]saineamhail aile, tar [16]a ēisi
[17]Abeōil ro mhairbh Cāin.   (26) [18]Ro ghenair |[(a)] mac do
[19]Seith .i. Enos [20]a ainm-side.   Is [21]ē an tEnos sin ro
[22]thionnsgain ar [23]ttūs ariam in [24]gairm ⁊ [25]atach anma
[26]an Coimhdhia.[(b)]

β.

43a. Mac dh'Enos Cáin-
can.   Mac do-sidēn Male-
leth.   Mac do-sidēn Iáreth.
Mac do-sēn Enoc.   Mac
do-sidēn Matasaliam.   Mac
do-sēn Laimhiach.   Mac
do sidhēn Nōe.

β[12].

Ghein Enos Canaan.   Gein
Canaan Malaleel.   [1]G h e i n
Malaleel Iaret.   Gein Iaret
Enoc.   [2]Gein Enoc Matusalem.
[2]Gein Matusalem Lamiac, ⁊
mac dosin Nōe.

---

37. (1) Adam vero cognouit [1]Euam uxorem suam, quae
concepit et peperit Cain, [dicens] Possedi hominem per
Deum.   (2) Rursusque peperit [2]*filium alium,* Abel : fuit
autem Abel pastor ouium, et Cain agricola.   (3) Factum est
autem post multos dies ut offerret Cain de fructibus terrae
munera [3]*Deo,* (4) Abel quoque obtulit <Deo> de primogenitis
gregis sui, et de adipibus eorum.   Et respexit Dominus ad
Abel et ad munera eius, (5) ad Cain uero et ad munera eius
non respexit.   Iratusque est Cain uehementer et concidit
uultus eius.

38. (6) Dixitque Dominus ad Cain : Quare mestus es, et
cur concidit facies tua?   (7) [1]Nonne si bene egeris recipies?
Sin autem male, statim in foribus peccatum aderit ; [sed
sub te erit appetitus eius, et tu dominaberis illius].

---

[8] Set β[2]   [9] is seadh ro raidh β ro radh (*om.* is edh) β[12]   [10] tug β[12]
[11] *om.* Dïa M   [12] dam ar M *om.* dhamh . . . ar .i. β[12]   [13] *om.* ar M
[14] saimh β[2]   [15] seanamhuil eile β[12]   [16] *om.* a M β[12] : eis β[12]
[17] Aibeoil ro marb M Abel do mharbhadh (*om.* Cain) β[12]   [18] ⁊ ro

son Seth; and thus he spake : God hath given me [said Adam] "ar" that is, other gentle excellent seed, in the room of Abel, whom Cain slew. (26) A son was born to Seth, Enos his name. It is that Enos who began at the very first to call upon and to invoke the name of the Lord.

β.	β¹².
43a. A son to Enos, Cainan. A son to him, Malalehel. A son to him, Iared. A son to him, Enoch. A son to him, Mathusalam. A son to him, Lamech. A son to him, Noe.	Enos begat Cainan. Cainan begat Malalehel. Malalehel begat Iared. Iared begat Enoch. Enoch begat Mathusalam. Mathusalam begat Lamech, and Noe was son to him.

---

(8) Dixitque Cain ad Abel fratrem suum : Egrediamur ²*in agrum*. Cumque essent in agro, consurrexit Cain aduersus Abel fratrem suum et interfecit eum. (9) Et ait ³*Deus* ad Cain : Vbi est Abel frater tuus? Qui respondit : Nescio; num custos fratris mei sum? (10) Dixitque ⁴<Deus> ad ⁵*Cain* : Quid fecisti? Vox sanguinis fratris tui clamat ad me de terra.

39. (11) Nunc igitur maledictus eris super terram, quae aperuit os suum et suscepit sanguinem fratris tui de manu tua. (12) <Et> cum operatus fueris eam, non dabit tibi fructus suos : nagus et profugus eris super terram. (13) Dixitque Cain ad *Deum* : Maior est iniquitas mea quam ut ueniam merear. (14) Ecce eicis me hodie a facie terrae et a facie tua abscondar. [Et] ero nagus et profugus in terra, omnis ¹[igitur qui inuenerit me] occidet me.

---

geinther β¹²   ¹⁹ Seth M β¹²   ²⁰ *om.* a ainm-side *ins.* ⁊ β¹²   ²¹ he in M ²² thinscain M thion sguin β¹²   ²³ tus riam M : -amh β¹ mgh- β² ²⁵ atath M aatach β¹²   ²⁶ in Choimdead M, on Choimhdhia β¹² **43a.** ¹ gein β²   ² gen β² (*bis*)

(*a*) *s*¹ M.
(*b*) B lacuna begins. The ¶ here numbered 43a attempts, on the part of the late copies, to supply connecting matter between the two sides of the gap.

(15) Dixitque ei *Deus*: Nequaquam ita fiet, sed omnis qui occiderit Cain septuplum punietur. Posuit[que] *Deus* Cain ²<in> signum, ut non eum interficeret omnis ³[qui inuenisset eum].

40. (16) Egressusque Cain a facie Domini habitauit in terra, profugus, ad orientalem plagam Eden.   (17) Cognouit autem Cain uxorem suam, quae concepit ¹[et peperit] ²<filium nomine> Enoch: et aedificauit ciuitatem, uocauitque nomen eius ex nomine filii sui Enoch.   (18) Porro Enoch genuit Irad, et Irad genuit Mauiahel, et Mauiahel genuit Mathusahel, et Mathusahel genuit Lamech.

41. (19) Qui accepit uxores duas, nomen uni ¹Ada, et nomen alteri Sella.   (20) Genuitque Ada Iabel, qui fuit pater habitantum in tentoriis atque pastorum: (21) et nomen fratris eius Iubal, ipse fuit pater canentium cithara et organo. (22) Sella quoque genuit ²Tubalcain, qui fuit malleator et faber in cuncta opera aeris et ferri. ³Soror vero Tubalcain Noemma.

42. (23) Dixitque Lamech uxoribus suis ¹Adae et Sellae: Audite uocem meam, uxores Lamech, auscultate sermonem meum, quoniam occidi uirum in uulnus meum, et adulescentulum in liuorem meum.   (24) Septuplum ultio dabitur de Cain, de Lamech uero septuagies septies.

43. (25) Cognouit quoque adhuc Adam ¹[uxorem suam], et peperit filium, uocauitque ²nomen eius Seth, dicens: Posuit mihi semen aliud pro Abel, quem occidit Cain.   (26) Sed et Seth natus est filius, quem uocauit Enos: isti coepit inuocare nomen Domini.

NOTES ON THE BIBLICAL TEXT, CHAPTER IV.

¶ 37. *Hauam* in ST, but as before *Euam* has much support. ²*Fratrem eius* in ST and all Versions and MSS. ³*Domino* in ST and all Versions and MSS.

¶ 38. ¹This verse, of which the best commentators can make but little, is baldly paraphrased by Tr., who has omitted the unintelligible last clause altogether. ²The Irish is closer to LXX (διέλθωμεν εἰς τὸ πεδίον). The original is lost from the Massoretic Hebrew text, but must be supplied (the English Revised Version makeshift "and Cain told Abel his brother" is inadmissible). ³Dominus in ST, but ὁ θεός in LXX. ⁴Deus omitted in Vulg., but ὁ θεός in LXX. One Vulg. MS. has Dominus. ⁵Eum ST and all MSS. No equivalent in LXX.

¶ 39. ¹, ³These two similar passages are necessary to the sense, and presumably were in the original text of Tr. It is a curious coincidence that they should both have disappeared. ²In omitted by ST, but there is authority for it, as for in Cain signum and in signum Cain.

¶ 40. ¹⁊ ro thuisim was probably in the text originally, but dropped out early. ²Filium nomine found in four MSS., but ST omits.

¶ 41. ¹This name is spelt with one d in all Versions and MSS. ²The interpolated mac don Lāimhiach cēadna doubtless was originally a gloss explaining the personality of Tupaleān (Tubalcain). There is no authority behind the statement in Tr. that he was the first craftsman in his trades. ³There is no authority for the verbose Irish ocus rug Sella ingen īar sin.

¶ 42. ¹Tr. here follows Vulg. against other Versions in transferring the names of the wives from the beginning of the song (where the poetical structure requires them) to the prose introductory matter. The translation of the song is corrupt, and as it stands is partly unintelligible. See the notes to this ¶.

¶ 43. ¹A scitig has been extruded from the text by the gloss .i. Eua. ²The speaker was certainly Eve, not Adam. The latter name, for which there is no authority whatever, is doubtless an interpolation.

CHAPTER V.

44. (1) As ¹ē so thrā leabar ‡⁽ᵃ⁾ .i. in Genis, no canōin pedarlaigi ‖ tuismeada Adaim. Isin lō in ra ²thuisim Dīa in duine fo chosmailis fodēin, (2) ro thuisim fear ⁊ mnāi, ⁊ ro beandach dōib, ⁊ tuc in n-ainm as *Adam* ‡⁽ᵃ⁾ .i. duni ‖ dōib isin lō in ro thuismit.

y¹ Āirmit eōlaig na sdairi dīada nā ro beannaig Dīa do Adam ō daridni in pecad.

y² I cind sē n-ūair co leith do lō doridni Adam ⁊ Eba in pecad, .i. torad Chraind na hAithni do ch⁽ᵇ⁾aithem, trē aslach na nathrach.

(3) Tricha bliadan ar cēt ro bo slān do Adam in tan rucad Seth dō (4) ⁊ doridned lāitheada Adaim īar tuismed ³Seth dō .i. ocht cēt bliadan, ⁊ ro thuisim maccu ⁊ ingena. (5) Ocus ⁴doridnead ⁵uile sāegal ⁶Adaim .i. ⁷tricha ar ⁸nōib cētaib bliadan, ⁊ adbath Adam ⁹īar sin.

y³ ¹⁰Ocus ro hadnaiced sin chathraid dīanad ainm Sabrōn, co roibi a chorp sa baili sin co tānic in dīli tar in domun : cor scarsad tonna na dīlenn a chorp ⁊ a cheand re chēle, co rucsad leo na tonna in cenn o Sabrōn co Golgotha, cor thoiris an Golgotha co chrochad Crīst. Co rob trē chend Adaim tarla cend na croichi : co ndeachaid fuil in Choimdead fo agaid Adaim, conad mar sin do baistead Adam ar tūs, do rēir eōlach na sdairi dīada¹⁰.

45. (6) Cūic bliadna ar cēt imorro ¹fa slān do Seth in tan rucad ²Enos dō. (7) Seacht ³mbliadna ar cūic cētaib īar tuismead Enos fa hē sāegal ⁴Seth, ⁊ ro

CHAPTER V.

44. (1) Now this is the book [of Genesis, or of the Old Testament canon] of the creation of Adam. In the day in which God created Man under His own likeness (2) He created man and woman, and blessed them, and gave them the name from *Adam* [i.e. *man*] in the day wherein they were created.

y¹ Those skilled in sacred history consider that God gave no blessing to Adam after he committed the sin.

y² At the end of six hours and a half of the day did Adam and Eve commit the sin, namely the eating of the Tree of Knowledge, by the incitement of the serpent.

(3) An hundred and thirty years had Adam complete when Seth was born to him, (4) and the days of Adam after the birth of Seth to him were made eight hundred years, and he begat sons and daughters. (5) And all the life of Adam was made nine hundred and thirty years, and Adam died thereafter.

And he was buried in the city which is called Hebron, so that his body was in that place till the Flood came over the world : and the waves of the Flood sundered his body and his head each from the other, and the waves carried the head with them from Hebron to Golgotha. It abode in Golgotha till the Crucifixion of Christ. And it was through the head of Adam that the end of the Cross came : and the blood of the Lord fell over the face of Adam, and thus was Adam baptized for the first time, according to men skilled in sacred history.

45. (6) An hundred and five years were complete for Seth, when Enos was born to him. (7) Five hundred and seven years was the life of Seth after

---

⁴ -ned H   ⁵ uili H   ⁶ Adam M   ⁷ *spelt* triK *in* M   ⁸ nae M
⁹ iartain H   ¹⁰⁻¹⁰ *in* M *only*
45. ¹ ba H   ² Enoss H   ³ bliadna *ye* H   ⁴ Seith H

(*a*) These glosses interlined.   (*b*) H resumes.

L.G.—VOL. I.   H

thuisim ⁵maccu ⁊ ingena.   (8) Dā bliadain dēc ar sē
⁶chētaib ⁷fa hē uili ⁸sāegail Seth, ⁊ adbath Seth īar sin.

46. (9) Nōcha ar chēd bliadan ‡ .i. deich mbliadan
ar ¹nāe ²fichtib bliadan ‖ is ead fa slān do Enos ³in tan
rucad Cainen dō.   (10) Īar tuismed imorro⁽ᵃ⁾ ⁴Chainen
dō, fa beō hē fri rē chūic mbliadan ⁵dēc ar secht cētaib,
⁊ ro thuisim maccu ⊣ ingena.   (11) Ocus ⁶doridnead
uili lāitheada Enos .i. cūic bliadna ar nāi cētaib, ⊣
adbath īarsin.

47. (12) Seachtmoga ar chēt bliadan ¹‡ .i. deich
mbliadan ⊣ ocht fichit bliadan ‖ is ed ²fa slān do
³Chainean ⁴in tan ro thuisim Malalel.   (13) Ceathracha
ar seacht cētaib bliadan imorro is ed ⁵fa beō Cainen
īar ⁶tuismed Malalel ⁷dō, ⊣ ro ⁸thuismistair maccu ⊣
ingena.   (14) Ocus ⁹dorignit uili ¹⁰lāitheada ¹¹Chainean
.i. deich mbliadan ar nāi cētaib bliadan, ⊣ adbath
¹²īarsin.

48. (15) ¹Cūic bliadna ²sescad ar chēd is ed ³fa slān
do Malalel ⁴in tan ro thuisim ⁵Iareth.   (16) Tricha ar
seacht cētaib bliadan imorro ba beō hē īar ⁶tuismed
Iareth, ⊣ ro thuisim maccu ⊣ ingena.   (17) Ocus
⁷doridnit uili lāitheada Malalel ⁸cūic bliadna nōchat
ar ocht cētaib, ⊣ adbath ⁹īarsin.

49. (18) Dā bliadain seascad ar chēd ¹fa slān do
²Iareth ³in tan ro thuisim ⁵Enōc.   (19) Ocht cēd bliadan

---

⁵ macu *hic et semper* H   ⁶ chedaib M   ⁷ ba H   ⁸ saegal Seith H
46. ¹ nai H   ² *sic* H, fichit M   ³ an tan rugad H   ⁴ Chainein,
do bo beo H   ⁵ deg H   ⁶ dorigned uili laitheda Enóss H
47. ¹ *ins.* dono H   ² ba H   ²·nēṅ H   ⁴ an H   ⁵ ba H
⁶ tus (*om.* -med) H   ⁷ *om.* dō H   ⁸ thuisimstair H   ⁹ dorigned H

the birth of Enos, and he begat sons and daughters.
(8) Six hundred and twelve years was the whole of
the life of Seth, and Seth died thereafter.

46. (9) An hundred and ninety years, [that is, nine
score and ten years] were complete to Enos when
Cainan was born to him.   (10) Now after the birth
of Cainan to him, he was alive for a space of seven
hundred and fifteen years, and begat sons and
daughters.   (11) And all the days of Enos were made
nine hundred and five years, and he died thereafter.

47. (12) An hundred and seventy years [that is,
eight score and ten years] were complete for Cainan
when he begat Malalehel.   (13) Seven hundred and
forty years moreover was Cainan alive after Malalehel
was born to him, and he begat sons and daughters.
(14) And all the days of Cainan were made nine
hundred and ten years, and he died thereafter.

48. (15) An hundred sixty and five years were
complete for Malalehel when he begat Iared.
(16) Seven hundred and thirty years was he alive,
moreover, after the birth of Iared, and he begat sons
and daughters.   (17) And all the days of Malalehel
were made eight hundred ninety and five years, and he
died thereafter.

49. (18) An hundred sixty and two years were
complete for Iared when he begat Enoch.   (19) Eight

---

10 laitheda H   11 -nén H   12 Cainén iartain H
   48. 1 Cuig H   2 lxx. H   3 ba H   4 an H   5 Iaareth H
6 -edh H *hic et semper*   7 dorignid uili laithedha H   8 *ins. .i.;*
cuig H   9 Malalel iartain H.
   49. 1 ba H   2 Iaareth H   3 an tan ra thuisim Enoch H

(a) H preserved continuously from here.

imorro ro baī ⁴ina beathaig īar tuismed ⁵Enōc, ꝶ ro
thuisim maccu ꝶ ingena.   (20) Ocus ⁶doridnead uili
lāitheada ⁷Iareth .i. dā bliadain sescad ar nāi cētaib, ꝶ
adbath ⁷Iareth īarsin.

50. (21) Cūic bliadna sescad ar chēt ¹fa slān do
²Enōc ³in tan ro thuisim ⁴Mathasalem.   (22) Ocus is
do ⁵rēr Dē ro imthig Enōc : dā chēd bliadan imorro
dō ⁶i mbeathaid choitchind chāich īar tuismed
⁷Mathusalam, ꝶ ro thuisim maccu ꝶ ingena.   (23) Ocus
⁸dorignaid uili ⁹lāitheada Enōc .i. cōic bliadna sescat
ar trī cētaib, (24) ꝶ ¹⁰ro imthig ¹¹do rēr ¹²thoile Dē,

ꝶ ¹³fa ¹⁴in inadaib diamraib ¹⁵dīthrubdaib, ō beathaid
choitchind chāich, no aitrebad ¹⁶in fer ¹⁷sin cēin,

no co ¹⁸ruc Dīa leis hē,¹⁹

ꝶ²⁰ ro co śuigid hē ²¹i Parrdus ūasal Adaim.   Ocus is ē
²²in t-Enōc sin, ²³.i. mac ²⁴Iareth, ro airic na dēce
²⁵n-anmand airegda Ebraidi, ō ro ²⁶cēt-gairmead Dīa ar
tūs(a), o anmandaib ēcsamlaib na nEabraide.

51. (25) ¹Ro thuisim dono Mathasalem Laimiach,
isin sechtmad bliadain ochtmogat ar ched a aisi.
(26) Da bliadain ar ochtmogaid ar secht cetaib fa beo
Mathasalem iar tuismed Laimiach do, ꝶ ro thuisim
maccu ꝶ ingena.   (27) Ocus doridnit uili laitheda
²Mathasaelim, .i. noi mbliadna ceathrachad ar noe
cedaib, ꝶ fuair bas iartain.

⁴aua beathaid H   ⁵Enóch H (bis)   ⁶dorigned a uili laitheda H
⁷Iaareth H (bis)
50. ¹ba H   ²Enoch H   ³an H   ⁴Mathasailem H
⁵reir Dia ra himig Euóch H   ⁶a mbethaid H   ⁷Mathasailem H
⁸dognidh H   ⁹laitheda H   ¹⁰ra imid   ¹¹do reir H
¹²thoili H   ¹³bá H   ¹⁴om. iu H   ¹⁵dithrubaib H   ¹⁶an H

hundred years, moreover, was he in his life after the
birth of Enoch, and he begat sons and daughters.
(20) And all the days of Iared were made nine
hundred sixty and two years, and Iared died thereafter.

50. (21) An hundred sixty and five years were
complete for Enoch when he begat Mathusalam.
(22) And it is in God's way that Enoch walked : two
hundred years had he in the common life of every
man after the birth of Mathusalam, and he begat sons
and daughters.   (23) And all the days of Enoch were
made three hundred sixty and five years, (24) and he
walked according to the will of God,

> And it was in waste and desert places, away from the
> common life of every man, that that man was living for a
> season,

till God took him with Himself,

> and set him in the noble Paradise of Adam. Now this is
> that Enoch son of Iared, who invented the ten excellent
> Hebrew names, by which God was first called, out of the
> different names of the Hebrews.

51. (25) Now Mathusalam begat Lamech, in the
hundred eighty and seventh year of his age.
(26) Seven hundred eighty and two years was
Mathusalam alive after the birth of Lamech to him,
and he begat sons and daughters.   (27) And all the
days of Mathusalam were made nine hundred forty
and nine years, and he died thereafter.

---

[17] sain H   [18] rug H   [19] *ins.* a Parrdhus H   [20] cur šuigid H
[21] a H   [22] an H   [23] *om.* .i. H   [24] Iaareth H   [25] n-anmanda
aireada Eabraidi H   [26] -meadh H

51. [1] The marks of prolongation are here omitted in accordance
with p. xxvi   [2] Written Mathasaeli in √M. Not understanding this,
sM wrote Mathasael-i

(*a*) H lacuna begins.

52. (28) Ro thuisim imorro Laimiach Noe, isin dara bliadain ar ochtmogat ar chet a aisi.

Is hē dono eitercheart ⁊ mīnugad cīallaidi in anma, ¹.i. Nōe, .i. *requies* .i. cumsanad.

(29) Uair is ed ro raid Laimiach iar tuismed Nae : Bid he in mac-sa ²coimdidnaphas ⁊ saerfas sind o gnimaib ⁊ o gnimaib ar lam isin talmain mallachtnaich mirathmair, ro eascain Dia,

ar pecad Adaim ⁊ Eua ⁊ Cāin chlāin, chosnomaich, chelgaig, cona chloind.

(30) Coic bliadna nochad ar coic cetaib ba he saegal Laimiach iar tuismed Noe do, ⁊ ro thuisim maccu ⁊ ingena.   (31) Ocus dorignit uile laitheada Laimiach .i. seacht mbliadna sechtmogat ar ³secht cetaib, ⁊ fuair bas iarsin⁽ᵃ⁾ . . . .

----

44. (1) Hic est liber generationis Adam. In die qua creauit Deus hominem ad similitudinem ¹*suam*, (2) masculum et feminam creauit eos, et benedixit illos, et uocauit nomen eorum "Adam," in die qua creati sunt.   (3) Vixit autem Adam centum triginta annis et genuit ²[ad similitudinem et imaginem suam, uocauitque nomen eius] Seth : (4) et facti sunt dies Adam postquam genuit Seth octingenti anni, genuitque filios et filias.   (5) Et factum est omne tempus quod vixit Adam, anni nonaginti triginta, et mortuus est.

45-49. It is unnecessary to transcribe the Latin of these formal paragraphs, but some important details with regard to the ages of the Patriarchs are set forth in the notes at the end of the chapter.

----

52. ¹ is *for* .i. M   ² coimdid naphas M   ³ sē M

(a) M lacuna begins.

52. (28) Moreover Lamech begat Noe, in the hundred eighty and second year of his age.

This is the interpretation, and the significant sense of the name Noe; *requies*, or "rest."

(29) For thus did Lamech speak after the birth of Noe : this boy shall be he who shall comfort and deliver us from labours, from the labours of our hands in the accursed ill-fated earth, which God cursed,

for the sin of Adam and Eve, and Cain, the iniquitous, contentious, and deceiving, with his progeny.

(30) Five hundred ninety and five years was the life of Lamech after the birth of Noe to him, and he begat sons and daughters.   (31) And all the days of Lamech were made seven hundred seventy and seven years, and he died thereafter . . . .

---

50. (21) ¹Porro Enoch uixit sexaginta quinque annis et genuit Mathusalam.   (22) Et ambulauit Enoch cum Deo postquam genuit Mathusalam *ducentis* annis, et genuit filios et filias.   (23) Et facti sunt dies Enoch trecenti sexaginta quinque anni, (24) ambulauitque cum Deo [et non apparuit] quia tulit eum Deus.

51. (This paragraph partakes of the formal nature of most of the chapter.)

52. (28) Vixit autem Lamech centum octoginta duobus annis, et genuit [filium (29) uocauitque nomen eius] Noe, dicens : Iste consolabitur nos ab operibus et laboribus manuum nostrarum in terra, cui maledixit Dominus.   (30) Vixitque Lamech postquam genuit Noe quingentos nonaginta quinque annos, et genuit filios et filias (31) et facti sunt omnes dies Lamech septingenti septuaginta septem anni, et mortuus est² . . .

Notes on the Biblical Text, Chapter V.

¶ 44. ¹The punctuation, doubtless by accident, follows the OL. But there is no authority for the substitution of *suam* for *Dei*. ²This passage was perhaps dropped from Tr. owing to an eye-confusion induced by the similar passage in the preceding verse.

¶ 45–49. In the ages of the Patriarchs Tr. follows the authority of LXX (and Isidore) as against Vulg. This is shown in the following table. (A = age of each patriarch at birth of firstborn, B = years lived after firstborn, C = total age.)

	Septuagint.			Vulgate.			Irish Translation.		
	A	B	C	A	B	C	A	B	C
Seth ...	205	707	912	105	807	912	105	507	612
Enos ...	190	715	905	90	815	905	190	715	905
Kenan ...	170	740	910	70	840	910	170	740	910
Mahalalel	165	730	895	65	830	895	165	730	895
Jared ...	162	800	962	162	800	962	162	800	962
Enoch ...	165	200	365	65	300	365	165	200	365
Methu-selah	167	802	969	187	782	969	187	782	945 (sic)
Lamech	188	565	753	182	595	777	182	595	677 (sic)

In the Irish text .xl. has been miswritten for .lx. in the age of Methuselah, and in the age of Lamech a "c" has been omitted. The 677 years of Lamech's age is a mere copyist's mistake which has here been corrected in the text, .dc. having been written instead of .dcc. The reduction of the age of Seth by 300 years has no authority.

¶ 50. ¹This paragraph has been much worked over by the interpolation and assimilation of details from the apocrypha of Enoch. It has almost parted company with the Latin original.

¶ 52. ¹There is here a hint that Tr. is for the moment becoming weary of his work. He does not show his usual care in finding different words for *operibus et laboribus*: contrast verses 4, 5 of this chapter, where he has duly observed the difference of *dies* and *tempus* (*láitheada, sáegal*). The rendering (or more probably the transmission) of the paragraph is rather too free for any certain establishment of the Latin text. ²It is uncertain whether *iarsin*, the last word before the lacuna, belongs to v. 31 (where the Latin does not call for it) or begins the lost v. 32, which enumerated the sons of Noah.

Chapter VI.

53. . . . (*a*)Ro forcongair Dīa] for chlannaib Se[th na
ro chummasedais cairde]s fri clannaib Cain, ⁊ na ra [clann-
aigdis friu ⁊ na tuedais] mna dib. Arai sin tra, odchond-
[cadar clanna Seth iad, tucsat ingena] airedha clainn Cain.
Tangadar tar [in forcital, ⁊ ro clannaigset] friu tar sarugad
nDe. Conad airi sin [ro geinsit fomoraig ⁊] lupraganaig
⁊ cach egosc dodea[lbda torothorda ra bai] for dainib an
domuin ria ndilind.

A[tberat araile nach dib-sidi] iarricht imorro; is do śil
Chaim.

54. (3) Ocus ra [raid Dia : Ni anfaid nios] fada
mo Spirad isin duine ‡ .i. ana ¹[¹⁷. . . . .] duine ||,
conaid coland ‡ .i. ar a ro-med d[¹⁵ . . . . || ⁊]
forbabtar laithedha in duini i cind fichet [bliadan ar
cet. (4) Do badar] imorro for talmain ar tan sin
giganteis, ‡ .i. cora[id o macaib] mileata ⁊ ó
hingenaib colacha Cain ||.

55. (5) Ot[chondairc Dia] imorro—

techt tar timna dóib ‡ a feirg, a feill, a f[¹⁰. . . .]rad, a
n-úaill, a n-ecrabad ||, ra chindustair na hui[li daini] do
dibadh ⁊ do dilgend.

—Conad iarom ra raid Dia : (7) [Sgrios]fed, ar Se,
an duini ra thuisim o dreich an talman, ‡ [ˢconid tucad]
dono dilgenn for uilib annandaib an talman, ⁊ for
enaib an aeoir || uair tanig aithrechus dam a ndenma.
(8) Fuair Náe imorro airmidin ⁊ onoir a fiadnaisi De—

---

54. ¹ The small number prefixed to this and such similar lacunae as
cannot be certainly filled up indicates the approximate number of
characters that have been lost: the number of lost *letters* may have

Chapter VI.

53. . . . God forbade the descendants of Seth to mingle friendship with those of Cain, or to beget children by them, or to take wives from them.   In spite of that, however, when the descendants of Seth saw them, they took the beautiful daughters of the descendants of Cain.   They transgressed the commandment, and had children by them in despite of God.   Wherefore there were born giants and dwarfs and every unshapely monstrous being that was among the people of the world before the Flood.

> Others say however that it is not of them that they were found: it is of the seed of Ham.

54. (3) And God said: My Spirit shall not remain longer in man [i.e. in . . . . . man] for he is flesh [i.e. for the exceeding greatness of his (sins? . . .)] : and the days of man shall be brought to a close at the end of an hundred and twenty years.   (4) Now there were *gigantes* upon the earth at that time, [i.e. champions of the warlike sons and the fleshly daughters of Cain.]

55. (5) Now when God saw—

that they were transgressing the covenant [in wrath, in treachery, in . . . ., in pride, in impiety], He determined to annihilate and to destroy all men.

Wherefore God said: (7) I shall root out, said He, Man, whom I have created, from the face of the earth, [(so there was brought) destruction upon all the beasts of the earth and upon the birds of the air] for repentance for having made them hath come on Me. (8) But Noe found favour and honour before God.

---

been greater, for allowance must be made for possible compendia, contractions, and suspensions.

(a) A few letters of the previous line left (. . . sadt . a . . .), which will not fit in with anything.

Air is e Náe aenfer firen forbthe frith do chlannaib
sainemla Seith, na ra cumaise fri clannaib claena Cain.

56. (11) Ra truaillned ⁊ ra línad tra an talam o ulc
‡ ⁊ indirgi na ndaini ‖; (12) ⁊ ód chondaire Dia ani
sin (13) ra raid fri Náe: Tanig, ar Se, crich ⁊ forba
na huili cholla am fiadnaissi. Millfed ⁊ malartfad uili
aitrebaidi an talman, ‡ otá min co mór ‖.

57. ‡ Ra raid Dia dono fri Náe ‖ (14) Dena-sa, ar
Se, duit feisin aire lethain luchtmair lan-fáirsing, o
crandaib snaigthi slemnaigthi—

y¹ nach dernad ⁊ nach dingentar long bus samail di ar
med, ar daingne, ar disli, ar deig-dénum.
y² Ocus is amlaid dorindead ⁊ ceitri slesa furri.

Déna-sa dono inti aideda imda ecsamla, ⁊ slemnaig-
fedsa in airce ar medón ⁊ dia n-echtair o bidamain.

y³ (a) Is é imorro aigned fil isin bidamain, nach milleadh
cruimi na gaetha na uisce na tes ngreine, na cranda do
curter inti.

(15) Ocus dena-su tri cet cubad hi fad na hairci, ⁊
caoga cubad in a ¹leithedh, ⁊ tricha cubad ina hairdi.
(16) Ocus déna seinistir isa n-airce, ⁊ aen chubad ana
tigi.

y³ (b) Atiad a hadbair, .i. glae iuda ⁊ ²bidamain ⁊ cré,
‡ .i. úir thiri Siría ‖. Bui Dia Anarlaoite ra chumaisc na
hadbair sin tré na cheli, tré forgeall Dé fair: brathair do
Eibifenius do saer na hairci. Uair do mac do [¹⁰. . . .] ³nus
iad araen. Aitreb a comuir cach cineil [ainmide i]uti,
Nir cuiread aen ⁴tairrngi uma na iaraind inti. [Is re

---

57. ¹ *The final d is a little doubtful*   ² *The scribe began to*

For this Noe is the one righteous perfect man who was found, of the excellent children of Seth, who had not mingled with the iniquitous children of Cain.

56. (11) Now the earth was corrupted and filled with evil [and with the iniquity of men], (12) and when God saw that, (13) He said unto Noe : The end and termination of all flesh hath come before Me. I shall destroy and confound all the inhabitants of the earth [both small and great].

57. [Moreover God said to Noe :] (14) Make thou, said He, for thyself a broad capacious roomy ark of timbers chipped and smoothed—

so that never was made nor shall be made a ship like unto it in size, in firmness, in trustworthiness, and in good crafts-manship.

And thus was it made, with four sides to it.

Make also within it many various chambers, and let the ark be smooth inside and out with pitch.

Now this is the nature that pitch possesses, that no worms, nor winds, nor water, nor sun-heat destroys the timbers that have been placed in it.

(15) And make three hundred cubits in the length of the ark, and fifty cubits in its breadth, and thirty cubits in its height. (16) And make a window in the ark, and one cubit in its thickness.

These are its materials, glue and pitch and clay, [that is, mould of the land of Syria]. It was Dia Anarlaoite who mixed these materials together, by the revelation of God. He was brother to Epiphenius, the wright of the ark, for they were the two sons of (—)nus. There was a dwelling in preparation for every sort of

---

write eré here, but realised and corrected his mistake after writing the r
² *The first half of this* n *torn away*   ⁴ *the* g *sprs.* c II

bida]main do chomdluthugad a clar ré cheili. Secht
la [amain] sul do fer tosach na dilenn, ⁊ is amlaid bai Náe
cona [macai]b, ⁊ a leth-gluini dessa fúithib, ⁊ siad ag
edarguidi Dé im [f]oirithin d'fadbail.

Da raid Dia co Náe : Dena-su imorro [d]orus na hairci
ara slis, ⁊ dena cendacuili inti co feicib deiligtecha
eaturru.

58. (17) Daber-sa co follus ‡ ar Dia ‖ uisci na
dilenn for talmain, do marbad hina huili cholla hi
fuil 'spirad bethad fo nim, ⁊ biaid forba ⁊ crich for na
huilib itát a talmain.   (18) Ocus doden caradrad rit,
⁊ raga-su ²isa n-airce ⁊ do seidig ‡ .i. Coba ingen
Laimiach, do siur-sin ‖, ⁊ do micc ⁊ seitchi do mac
imailli ritsiu, ‡ ⁊ is úaid do geinsid diblinaib ‖.
(19) Ocus bera leat isa n-airc caraid cacha hanmanda
in ecoisc chechtarda fil for talmain, ardáig a mbethad
do choiméd ‡ ⁊ silta uaithib iar ndilinn ‖.   (21) Bera
dono let isi n-áircc biad cubaid comadais ‡ do cach
anmanda, *et reliqua*, dligtheach ⁊ indligthech ‖, ⁊ bid
biad duidse ⁊ doib-sim sin do chaithim.   (22) Daroini
tra Náe na huili neithi ro forchongair Dia dó.

---

54. ¹(3) Dixitque Deus : Non permanebit Spiritus meus in
homine ²*diutius,* quia caro est, ³eruntque dies illius centum
uiginti annorum.   (4) Gigantes autem erant super terram in
diebus illis⁴ . . .

---

58. ¹ *the* a sbs.   ² *first written* ifa *and afterwards corrected.*

animal within it. Not a nail of bronze or of iron was put into it: with pitch was its timber secured together. There were only seven days before the first of the Flood poured down, and thus were Noe and his sons, with their right knees bent under them, interceding with God to obtain succour.

God said unto Noe : Make, moreover, the door of the ark in its side, and make chambers within it, with separating roof-beams between them.

58. (17) Lo [said God] I shall bring the water of the Flood over the earth, to slay altogether flesh in which is a spirit of life beneath the heaven, and there shall be termination and end upon all that are in the earth. (18) And I shall make a compact with thee : and thou shalt go into the ark, thou and thy wife [Coba, daughter of Lamech, thy sister] and thy sons and the wives of thy sons together with thee [and of thee were they born on both sides]. (19) And thou shalt take with thee into the ark a pair of every animal, in each shape that is on the earth, in order to preserve their life [and for seeding from them after the Flood]. (21) Thou shalt take also with thee into ark food, meet and fitting [for every animal, *et reliqua*, lawful and unlawful] and it shall be food for thee and for them, to eat thereof. (22) So Noe did all the things which God commanded him.

---

55. (5) Videns autem Deus[1] . . . . (7) Delebo, inquit, hominem quem creaui a facie terrae, [2]ab homine usque ad animantia, a reptili usque ad uolucres caeli, paenitet enim me fecisse eos. (8) Noe vero inuenit gratiam coram [3]Deo
. . . . .

56. . . . . [1](11) Corrupta est autem terra [coram Deo] et
repleta est iniquitate.   (12) Cumque uidisset Deus [2]. . . .
(13) Dixit ad Noe: Finis uniuersae carnis uenit coram me
[3]. . . . Ego disperdam eos cum terra.

57. (14) [1]Fac tibi aream de lignis leuigatis.   Mansiunculas
in area facies, et bitumine linies intrinsecus et extrinsecus.
(15) Et sic facies eam: trecentorum cubitorum erit longitudo
areae, quinquaginta cubitorum latitudo, et triginta cubitorum
altitudo illius.   (16) Fenestram in area facies, et in <uno>
cubito consummabis summitatem.   Ostium autem areae pones
ex latere deorsum: cenacula et tristega facies in ea.

58. (17) Ego ergo adducam diluuii aquas super terram,
ut interficiam omnem carnem in qua spiritus uitae est
subter caelum, uniuersa quae in terra sunt consumentur.
(18) Ponamque foedus meum tecum, et ingredieris aream, tu
et filii tui, uxor tua et uxores filiorum tuorum tecum (19) et
ex cunctis animantibus uniuersae carnis bina induces in
aream [1]. . . . (20) . . . . ut possint uiuere.   (21) Tolles
igitur tecum ex omnibus escis quae mandi possunt, et com-
portabis apud te, et erunt tam tibi quam illis in cibum.
(22) Fecit ergo Noe omnia quae praeceperat illi Deus.

Notes on the Biblical Text, Chapter VI.

¶ 54. [1]Verses 1, 2, lost. [2]*In aeternum*, Vulg. [3]This obscure
and probably corrupt passage, usually (though not always)
taken by commentators to indicate a limitation of the life of
the human individual, is understood by Tr. in the alternative
sense—a term upon the duration of the human race.   [4]The
remainder of this verse dropped out.

¶ 55. [1]Remainder of this verse and verse 6 dropped out.
[2](*Conid tucad*) *dilgenn* is obviously a marginal comment
which has entered the text, and probably necessitated some

subsequent modification of the context to modify the nonsense which it produced. ³*Domino* in ST., but *Deo* has some support.

¶ 56. ¹Verses 9, 10 omitted or lost.   ², ³These passages possibly discarded by Tr. or by a copyist because they repeat matter set forth immediately before.

¶ 57. ¹This ¶ has been rendered with tolerable literalness; only in one place does Tr. stray from the text—where he renders the corrupt and unintelligible *in cubito consummabis summitatem* as though it meant that the walls of the ark should be a cubit thick. This is also the theory of the author of the poem no. V : but the text cannot bear this meaning. The rendering of *tristega*, "storey," by *feice*, "roof-beam," is noteworthy. The paragraph is so farced with glosses that it is difficult to keep on the track of the biblical narrative.

¶ 58. ¹The long passage here omitted enumerated the birds, cattle, reptiles, etc. It must have been in Tr. originally, for it is presupposed by the *et reliqua* of the gloss following. Probably some impatient scribe dropped them as being irrelevant to the main purpose of the present text.

CHAPTER VII.

59. (1) Ocus da raid Día ré Náe : Imthig-siu isin airce ⁊ do muintir uili mailli rit, ar as tú aen-t̄irén fuaras isin chinead-sa. (2) Béra leat dono isin airce na sechta ⁊ na sechta ona huilib anmandaib glanaib, .i. mascul ⁊ femen. Bera lett dono a dó ⁊ a dó ona hanmumnaib inglanaib, .i. mascul ⁊ femen. (3) Bera dono let na sechta ⁊ na sechta o ethaidib glanaib inimi[a] .i. mascul ⁊ femen. Bera dono let na deda ⁊ na ¹deada do na foluaimnechaib inglanaib .i. mascul ⁊ femen. (4) Daber-sa dono, ar Día re ²Nae, a forba an sechtmad laithi oniu, fleochad silteach saidbir for talmain, ri re cethrachat laa ⁊ cethrachat aidchi. Ocus dilegfad ⁊ dicurfet o dreich an talman in uili fó-thairisim dorignus. (5) Darone tra Nae na huili ra athin Día dó.

60. (6) Sé cet bliadan dono ba slán do Náe an tan tanig an dile tar in talmain, (7) ⁊ dochuaid Náe, cona macaib ⁊ cona seitchib imailli ris, isa n-airce for uisci na dilenn, (8) ⁊ rug leis na huili anmanna glana ⁊ inglana (9) amail ro forchongair Día dó.

61. (10) O ra comlanaiged tra secht laithi na sechtmaini, ra iltóndaid ⁊ ra imdaig uisci na dilenn for talmain (11) ⁊ ra brisit uili thopur na haibeisi mori—

ra brucht ⁊ ro sceustar an talam súas ina huili thoipri diamra díchelta ra badar and.

Ra foslaigid dono cámt̄ithisi ‡ ⁊ seinistir ‖ nimi anúas (12) ⁊ ra silsedar andsin cetha trena troim-¹t̄leachaid for talmain fri ré ²cetracha laa ⁊ cethracha aidchi :

---

59. ¹ *the* ⁊ *sbs.*   ² *sprs.* c H
61. ¹ *The first* a *yc* H   ² *thus written in full, not* -chat

CHAPTER VII.

59. (1) And God said unto Noe : Go into the ark, and all thy people with thee, for thou art the only righteous man that I have found in this generation. (2) Thou shalt take with thee into the ark sets of seven of all the clean animals, male and female. Thou shalt take with thee sets of two of the unclean animals, male and female. (3) Thou shalt take with thee moreover sets of seven of the clean birds of heaven, male and female. Thou shalt take with thee sets of two of the unclean fowls, male and female. (4) I shall bring, said God unto Noe, the end upon the seventh day from today, a strong showering deluge upon the earth, for the space of forty days and forty nights. And I shall extinguish and remove from the face of the earth every substance which I have made. (5) So Noe did all that God commanded him.

60. (6) Now six hundred years were complete for Noe when the Flood came over the earth, (7) and Noe, with his sons and with their wives along with him, went into the ark upon the waters of the Flood, (8) and he took with him all the animals clean and unclean (9) as God commanded him.

61. (10) Now when the seven days of the week were completed, the waters of the Flood swelled mightily and increased upon the earth, (11) and every spring of the great deep burst open—

the earth opened up and vomited altogether the hidden secret springs that were in it.

Moreover the sluices [and windows] of heaven were opened from above, (12) and then strong heavy-wetting showers poured upon the earth for a space of forty days and forty nights :

(a) First written *glaiab inmi* and then corrected.

⁊ caoga ar cet laa imorro ra bai can tragadh.   I seachtmad
³loo deg an mís tanusti ‡ .i. an mís Mai ‖, ra thinscain an
dili fertain : isin ló sin ‡ .i. hi sechtmad decc in mis
tanaisi ‖, luid Náe a muintir ochtair isa n-aire.

(13) In airtical dono ‡ .i. a tosach ‖ an lái in ra
thinoilit na huili anmanda tria chetugad ⁊ cumachta
Dé dochum na hairci dia hinotacht, ‡ is andsin sanradh
do linadh ‖ ra laineeradh in aire druim-lethan domain.

Bá gnim saethair suad-lama, o chlarud chaem-cumachta.

62. (15) Iar ndul trá do Náe ina airce cona muintir
ochtair, ⁊ iar ¹tinol na n-uili ²anmidi ⁊ na n-uili anmand
n-ilarda n-examla inti (16) cos na huilib neichib
taiscithib ra athin Dia do Náe, ra íad Día dia n-echtair
an aire (17) ⁊ doradad for talmain fri re cethrachat laa
⁊ cethrachat aidchi.   Ocus ra imdaigid na huisci ⁊ ro
thogbadar na huisci súas an airdi o talmain in airec
(18) úas tondaib na dilenn.

Ocus ra bai an airec ar snam a hinad a n-inad.

63. (19) Ra forbair ⁊ ra imtaid an t-uisci for
talmain (20) co ruacht coic cubaid deg úas cach sleib
is airdiu ra bai ¹fo n-uili nim.   (21) Ocus tucad dilcend
⁊ comarba [*lege* commarbad] coitcend for na huilib
dainib (22) ⁊ for na huili a raibi spirad bethad for
talmain—

ar a n-íumus ⁊ ar a n-anumuloid do Dia.

(23) Ba marthanach imorro Náe a aenur, ⁊ cach áen
ra bai amaille ris isin airec; (24) ⁊ ra bai an diuli for
dreich an talmain ri ré ²caoga ar cet laa,

can esbaid can digbáil forri.

---

³ *first written* loog; *the* de *y sprs.* c H
   62. ¹ *Doubtful mark here ins.* c H   ² anmidi ⁊ *y sprs.* c H

and it was an hundred and fifty days without drying up.
On the seventeenth day of the second month [the month
of May] the Flood began to pour: on that day [i.e. on the
seventeenth of the second month,] Noe, his company of
eight persons, went into the ark.

(13) In the article, [that is, in the beginning] of the
day, in which all the animals assembled, by the
command and power of God, to the ark to enter it,
[it is then exactly that it was filled] the broad-keeled
deep ark was fully ordered.

It was the product of the labour of skilled craftsmen, with
boarding of beauty and strength.

62. (15) Now after Noe went into his ark, with his
company of eight persons, and when all the creatures
and all the manifold various beasts were assembled
within it, (16) with all the things in store, which God
had commanded Noe, God shut the ark from the
outside, (17) and there was a downpour upon the earth
for a space of forty days and forty nights. And the
waters increased, and the waters bore the ark aloft
from off the earth (18) upon the waves of the Flood.

And the ark was swimming from place to place.

63. (19) The water increased and augmented upon
the earth (20) till it reached fifteen cubits above every
highest hill that was under the whole heaven. (21) And
destruction and a general common death was brought
upon all men, (22) and upon all that had a spirit of
life upon the earth,

for their haughtiness and lack of humility toward God.

(23) But Noe alone endured, and all that were with
him in the ark; (24) and the Flood was over the face
of the earth for a space of an hundred and fifty days,

without diminution or decreasing.

---

63. ¹ fo *yc* H   ² *written* .l.a.

59. (1) Dixitque *Deus* ad [1]*Noe* : Ingredere, tu et omnis domus tua, aream; te enim uidi iustum [eoram me] in generatione hoc. (2) Ex omnibus animantibus mundis tolles septena septena, masculum et feminam. De animantibus uero non mundis, duo duo, masculum et feminam. (3) [Sed et] de uolatilibus caeli <mundis, tolles> septena septena, masculum et feminam. <De uolueribus non mundis tolles duo duo, masculum et feminam>, [3][ut saluetur semen super faciem uniuersae terrae]. (4) Adhuc enim ego pluam super terram quadraginta diebus et quadraginta noctibus, et delebo omnem substantiam quam feci de superficie terrae. (5) Fecit ergo Noe omnia quae mandauerat ei *Deus*.

60. (6) Eratque [1]<Noe> sescentorum annorum quando [2]diluuii aquae inundauerunt super terram, (7) et ingressus est Noe et filii eius [3]*et uxores eorum* eum eo in aream [4]propter aquas diluuii. (8) De animantibus quoque mundis et immundis . . . . . (9) sicut praeceperat Deus [5]*eo*.

61. (10) Cumque transissent septem dies aquae diluuii inundauerunt super terram (11) [1]. . . . <et> rupti sunt omnes fortes abyssi magnae et [2]cataractae caeli apertae sunt (12) et facta est pluuia super terram quadraginta diebus et quadraginta noctibus. (13) In articulo diei illius ingressus [3]. . . .

62. (15, 16) *These verses paraphrased only* . . . . sicut praeceperat ei Deus, [et] inclusit [1]*arcam Deus* deforis. (17) Factumque est diluuium quadraginta diebus [2]<et quadraginta noctibus> super terram. Et multiplicatae sunt aquae, et eleuauerunt aream in sublimine a terrae. (18) . . . . super aquas <diluuii>.

63. (19) Et aquae praeualuerunt nimis super terram . . . . (20) quindecim cubitis altior fuit aqua super montes [1]*sub uniuerso caelo*. (21) [2]. . . . uniuersi homines (22) et cuncta in quibus spiraculum uitae est in terra mortua sunt. (23) . . . . remansit autem solus Noe et qui cum eo erant in area. (24) Obtinueruntque aquae terras centum quinquaginta diebus.

NOTES ON THE BIBLICAL TEXT, CHAPTER VII.

¶ 59. [1]*ad eum* (in some MSS. *ad illum*) Vulg. : but πρὸς Νῶε in LXX. There is no authority in any of the Versions or

MSS. for the emphasis laid upon Noah being the *one* just man of his generation. ²The distinction between unclean and clean birds is lost not only from Vulg., but even from the current text of Heb. It is, however, preserved in LXX, which is clearly the authority here followed by Tr.: καὶ ἀπὸ τῶν πετεινῶν τοῦ οὐρανοῦ τῶν καθαρῶν ἑπτὰ ἑπτά, ἄρσεν καὶ θῆλυ ; καὶ ἀπὸ [πάντων] τῶν πετεινῶν τῶν μὴ καθαρῶν δύο δύο, ἄρσεν καὶ θῆλυ. The word πάντων, not rendered by Tr., is absent from some important MSS. ³The equivalent of these words were dropped out from "ןH and were reinstated in the margin, most likely by the copyist himself on discovering his mistake. They have crept back into the text in the wrong place (gloss after vi. 19).

¶ 60. ¹Νῶε in LXX, not in Vulg. ²*An dile* is closer to ὁ καταλυκσμός (LXX) than to *diluuii aquae* (Vulg.): contrast *aquas diluuii* in the following verse (in LXX, τὸ ὕδωρ τοῦ κατακλυσμοῦ), duly rendered *uisci na dilenn* by Tr. ³The abbreviation of the verbal exuberance of the original text is probably due to weary scribes; compare the abbreviation of the repeated catalogue of the animals in v. 8. ⁴*Propter aquas = for uisci:* has Tr. misread *super* for *propter*? ⁵*Noe,* Vulg.

¶ 61. ¹A passage omitted here, presumably because it merely repeats what has gone before. ²*Cataractae* (LXX καταράκται) which may here be translated "sluices," represents the Heb. 'ĕrubōth, literally "windows" (so in English Auth. and Revised versions). A glossator seems to have discovered this meaning from some source of information, and to have interlined .i. *seinistir*. When this ꝅ became *g*, the .i. as usual slipped into ꝛ. ³From this point to the beginning of ¶ 62 the passage has been written in an abridged or paraphrased form, and deserts the Latin original.

¶ 62. ¹Τὴν κιβωτόν in LXX: but *arcam* not in any Vulg. MS. ²Not in ST, but found in numerous Vulg. MSS., and also in LXX.

¶ 63. ¹*Sub uniuerso caelo* is out of place; it belongs to the clause at the end of v. 19, which is here omitted. Two clauses have here been abbreviated and combined into one. ²Here, and also in v. 23, a long catalogue of the creatures which perished is again omitted.

CHAPTER VIII.

64. (1) Ra ¹chuimnig imorro Dia ‡ ⁊ ra airchis ‖
ani Naei ⁊ na n-uili ammandaib ⁊ na n-uili úmenti ra
badar amailli fri Nae ina aire. Ocus dorad Dia gáeth
‡ do sugad na n-uisci ‖ ⁊ ²ro digbaid na huisci.
(2) Ocus ra hiadaid topur na haibéisi ⁊ camfithisi nime,
⁊ ra thairmiscid na fleochadha do nim.   (3) Ocus ra
thathcursedar na huisci don talmain is na hinadaib
as a tancadar, ⁊ ra digbaid na huisce a cind caoga ar
cet laithi.   (4) Seacht laithi sechtmogad ⁊ secht mís
don airce o thuind do thuind, corgab airisim a sleib
Armeinia.   (5) Ra sergaid na huisci cosin deccmad
mís. Isin cet ló don deccmad mís adces mullaidi na
sliab.

65. (6) I cind cethracha laa iarsin ra ¹foslaic Náe
seinistir na hairece ⁊ rusléig an fiach amach, (7) ⁊ ní
thanig doridisi.   (8) ‡ An sechtmad lá iar sin ‖ do
leig-sin an colam amach—

   ⁊ ra dún an aire andiaid an choluim ar omun na ngaeth—

(9) Ocus tanic an colum ²ar culu, air ni fuair baili a
tairisfed—

   ⁊ do thairind ar an aire, o nach fuair foslaicthi hi, ⁊ gabais
glés dá gulbuin forsan clár—

⁊ do sin Náe a laim amach ar cend an choluim ⁊ tuc
leis asdeach hé isa n-aire.   (10) Ra léig dono dorigisi
a cind secht laa amach an colum, (11) ⁊ tanig a fescur
‡ an lai cetna ‖ ⁊ gesca olacraind cona duillennaib
úraidi ina belaib.

   Ocus do béndach Náe eisim de sin ⁊ ra mallach an fiach,

CHAPTER VIII.

64. (1) But God was mindful of [and had compassion upon] the said Noe, and all the animals and all the cattle that were with Noe in his ark.   And God sent a wind [to suck up the water], and the water decreased.   (2) And the well-spring of the deep and the sluices of Heaven were closed, and the showers from Heaven were withheld.   (3) And the waters were restored to the earth into the places whence they had come, and the waters decreased at the end of an hundred and fifty days.   (4) Seventy and seven days and seven months was the ark from wave to wave, till it took rest in a mountain of Armenia.   (5) The waters were drying up till the tenth month.   Upon the first day of the tenth month the tops of the mountains appeared.

65. (6) At the end of forty days thereafter Noe opened the window of the ark and let out the raven (7) and it came not again.   (8) [On the seventh day thereafter] he let out the dove—

and closed the ark after the dove, for fear of the winds—

(9) And the dove came back, for it found no place where it should stand,

and descended upon the ark, as it found it not opened, and made a working with its beak upon the board—

and Noe stretched his hand forth for the dove and brought it with him into the ark.   (10) Then he let the dove out again at the end of the seven days, (11) and it came in the evening [of the same day] with a twig of an olive-tree having its fresh leaves in its beak.

And Noe blessed it, and cursed the raven; and for that,

---

65. ¹s *y sprs. c* H   ²r *y sprs. c* H

⁊ tue ³Dia de sin a dath-sain forsan ⁊iach ⁊ taitnem an
⁴⁊iaich fair-sim ar anumlacht in ⁵⁊iaich.

Ra thuig Náe cor digbaid na huisci. (12) Ocus aráidh
ra ernaid secht laa aili an tan ra leig ⁶amach an colum
an tres feacht, ⁊ ni thanig dorigisi,

uair ni rangadar a les.

66. (13) An cet la don cet bliadain ‡ iar ¹ndilind ‖
ar sugad na n-uisci, do ²scail Náe dorus na hairci, ⁊
do dech sé an doman ana thimchell. (14) Isin sechtmad
laa fichit don cet mí tanig Dia do labairt fris, (15) ⁊
is ed ra raid Dia co Náé : (16) Eirig asa n-aire, ar Se,
⁊ do seidid ⁊ do ³mic ⁊ seitchi do mac, (17) ⁊ beir lat na
huili ⁴anmanna filed isa n-aire ⁊ incheimnig for
talmain. Forbrid ⁊ ⁵dobarnimdaighther for talmain.
(18) Dachuaid diu Nae asa n-aire—

hi sechtmad fichit ‡ ésca Mai imorro ‖ an mís tanaisi :

.i. an mís Mai atharrach isin cet bliadain.

Sé cet bliadan do bo slan do Náe an tan sin. Sé bliadna
caoga ⁊ se cet ⁊ mili bliadan o cruthugad Adaim co sin, *ut
dixit,*

Cēt aimser in bethad bind . . .

Dachuaid imorro seidig Náe, ⁊ dochuadar a mic ⁊
⁶dochuadar seitchi a mac (19) ⁊ na huili ainimidi
rabadar isa n-aire eisti.

Isin sechtmad fichit an mís cetna atharraig tanic eisti,
an ⁷Aine imorro a laithi sechtmaine. Conad se deg ⁊

---

³Dia *y sprs. c* H   ⁴⁊ *y sprs. c* H   ⁵*second* i *y sbs. c* H
⁶amach *y sbs. c* H

God gave the colour of the former to the raven, and the sheen of the raven to the other, for the insubordination of the raven.

Noe understood that the waters were decreased. (12) Howbeit, he waited other seven days and then let out the dove for the third time, and it came not again—

for there was no need.

66. (13) On the first day of the first year [after the Flood], upon the sucking-up of the waters, Noe loosened the door of the ark and looked on the earth round about him. (14) On the twenty-seventh day of the first month God came to speak with him, (15) and thus God spake unto Noe : (16) Rise from out the ark, said He, thou and thy wife and thy sons and the wives of thy sons, (17) and take with thee all the beasts that are in the ark, and step forth upon the earth. Increase and be ye multiplied upon the earth. (18) So Noe went out of the ark,

in the twenty-seventh day [of the moon of May] of the second month :

that is, the secondary month of May in the first year.

Six hundred years were complete for Noe at that time. One thousand six hundred fifty and six years from the creation of Adam till then, *ut dixit,*

Poem no. VII.

—and further the wife of Noe went, and his sons and the wives of his sons (19) and all the beasts that were in the ark went out of it.

On the twenty-seventh day of the same secondary month, he came out of it : as regards the day of the week, on

---

66. ¹d *y sprs. c* H   ²l *yc* H   ³i *y sbs. c* H   ⁴ *written* aña
⁵ *written* do bar nim daighther   ⁶the u *sprs. s* H   ⁷ *written* Aen mi H

bliadain deiside ra bai Náe isa n-airec. An sechtmad deg
don mis cetna, ‡ .i. in mís Mai ‖, ra thinscain an dili
fertain : an dechmad uathad ésca ‡ in mís tanaisi ‖ an mí
doluid Náe isa n-aire, ⁊ a muintir ochtair, cos na huilib
anmandaib ⁊ anmigib rug leis inti : .i. cupla do cach
fiadach neoch do beth re sílad .i. ceitri lanumna do dainib,
⁊ ceitri lanumna deg do énaib, ⁊ secht lánumnu do chinelaib
eisc, ⁊ lanomain do cach cinel egsamail o sin amach bai isa
n-aire. Dia Haini didine arai laithi sechtmaini dochnaid
Náe isa n-aire, ⁊ Dia Mairt dolodar aisti iartain, *ut dicitur*,

Dia Haine docúas inti . . .

67. O thucad dana an dili tar an doman, ra baided na
huili dainé (*sic*) acht Náe cona tri macaib ⁊ cona ceitri
mnáib, amail ra raidsimar romaind. Ar is é Náe an tAdam
tanaisti, cosa mberar fir domain ; ⁊ Énóce an tAdam saér
(*sic*) : Crist imorro an tAdam deidenach, trés ar sáerad síl
an trir remraite do raidsimar romaind, an a tuc hé féin a
croich césta tar cend an trir sin dá n-eissi, ⁊ dorad an
mbroid a Hiffern dar sacrad lucht na coic n-aimsir ar aen
sligi.

68. Sé cet bliadan do ba slán do Náe an tan tanig an dili
tar an doman : caoga ⁊ tri cet bliadan ra bai Nae a mbethaid
iar ndilinn : conad caoga ⁊ noi cet bliadan sin uili. Uair is
e Náe an ceatramad duine do síl ¹Adaim as[s]ia saegal
indisis cánoin, .i. Adam ⁊ Iareth ⁊ Mathasailem ⁊ Náe.
Tricha ⁊ noi cet bliadan saegal Adaim. Dá bliadain sescat
⁊ noi cet saegal Iareth. Noi mbliadna sescat ⁊ noi cet
saegal Mathasailem. Caoga ⁊ noi cet bliadan saegal Náe :
amail adbearar andso—

Ceatra as [s]ia saegal slán . . . .

_____

68. ¹ y *sprs. s* H

Friday. So that thence Noe was a year and sixteen <days> in the ark. On the seventeenth day of the same month, [that is, the month of May], the Flood began to shower: on the tenth of the moon [of the second month] of the month, Noe went into the ark with his company of eight persons, and with all the animals and beasts that he took with him into it. These were, a couple of every wild creature, whatsoever should be for seeding; to wit four human pairs, fourteen pairs of birds, seven pairs of species of fish and a pair of every different kind from that onwards, that were in the ark. As regards the day of the week, it was a Friday that Noe went into the ark, and Tuesday they came out of it afterwards, *ut dicitur*,

Poem no. VIII.

67. Now when the Flood was brought over the world, all men were drowned save Noe and his three sons and their four wives, as we have said above. For Noe is the second Adam, to whom the men of the world are traced: and Enoch is the innocent (?) Adam: but Christ is the last Adam, by whom the seed of the aforesaid three, already mentioned, were saved, when He gave Himself on the cross of suffering instead of those three, after their time, and brought the harrowing over Hell by which the people of the five Ages all at once were saved.

68. Six hundred years were complete for Noe when the Flood came over the world: three hundred and fifty years was Noe in life after the Flood: so all that makes nine hundred and fifty years. For Noe is one of the four men of the seed of Adam, of whom the Canon telleth that had longest life—namely Adam, Iared, Mathusalam, and Noe. Nine hundred and thirty years was the life of Adam. Nine hundred sixty and two years the life of Iared. Nine hundred sixty and nine years the life of Mathusalam. Nine hundred and fifty years the life of Noe: as is said here—

Poem no. IX.

64. (1) Recordatus est autem Deus Noe, cunctorumque animantium et omnium iumentorum quae erant eum eo in area.   ¹<Et> adduxit ²<Deus> spiritum super terram, et inminutae sunt aquae.   (2) Et clausi sunt ³fontes abyssi et cataractae caeli, et prohibitae sunt pluuiae de caeli. (3) ⁴Reuersaeque aquae de terra euntes et redeuntes, et ceperunt minui post centum quinquaginta dies, (4) Requic-uitque area mense ⁵septime uicesima septima die mensis super ⁶montem Armeniae.   (5) At uero aquae ibant et decrescebant usque ad decimum mensem.   Decimo enim mense prima die mensis apparuerunt cacumina montium.

65. (6) Cumque transissent quadraginta dies, aperiens Noe fenestram areae [quam fecerat] dimisit coruum, (7) qui . . . ¹<non> reuertebatur . . .   (8) Emisit quoque columbam . . . (9) quae cum non inuenisset ubi requiesceret [pes eius], reuersa est . . . extenditque manum et adpraehensam intulit in aream.   (10) Expectatis autem ultra septem diebus [aliis] rursum dimisit columbam [ex area] (11) at illa uenit [ad eum] ad uesperam, portans ramum oliuae uirentibus foliis in ore suo.   Intellexit ergo Noe quod cessassent aquae [super terram].   (12) Expectauitque nihilominus septem alios dies, et emisit columbam, quae non est reuersa ultra ²[ad eum].

66. (13) ¹[Igitur sescentesimo] primo anno, [primo mense], primo die [mensis] <post> inminutae sunt aquae [super terram], et aperiens Noe tectum areae aspexit ². . . . (14) Mense ³primo septima et uicesima die mensis ⁴. . . . (15) locutus est autem Deus ad Noe, dicens : (16) Egredere de area, tu et uxor tua, filii tui et uxores filiorum tuorum [tecum] : (17) cuncta ⁵<que> animantia quae sunt apud te . . . educ tecum, et ingredimini super terram.   Crescite et multiplicamini super terram.   (18) ⁶Egressus est ergo Noe et filii eius, uxor illius et uxores filiorum eius cum eo, (19) sed et omnia animantia . . . .

Notes on the Biblical Text, Chapter VIII.

¶ 64. ¹*Et* in only two Vulg. mss., but καί in LXX.   ²*Deus* not in any Vulg. ms., but ὁ θεός in LXX.   ³Plural in Vulg.

and LXX, but singular in Tr. [4]The rendering of this verse seems a little closer to LXX : καὶ ενεδίδου τὸ ὕδωρ πορευόμενον ἀπὸ τῆς γῆς· ενεδίδου τὸ ὕδωρ καὶ ἠλαττονοῦτο κ.τ.λ. [5]These numbers have become corrupted : evidently .uii lá .xx. has degenerated into .uii. lxx. [6]Plural in Vulg. and LXX, but sing. in Tr.

¶ 65. [1]*Non* not in ST, but in numerous MSS. (in nearly half, however ins. *sec. man.*). Also in LXX. [2]The biblical text has suffered severely by glossarial encroachment and substitution in this paragraph.

¶ 66. [1]Tr. in its present form corrupt and imperfect. *Iar ndilind* must be removed as glossarial : perhaps *ar sugad* has somehow developed out of *ar sē cētaib*. Confusion of a scribe's eye has caused the loss of *primo mense*. [2]The words filling this gap have no biblical warrant : they are a gloss, which has ousted the original text. [3]*Don cēt mī* is a mistake : all Versions agree on "the *second* month." [4]Here again a gloss has expelled the original sentence. [5]*-que* not in ST, but in several MSS. : also καί in LXX. [6]This verse is interrupted by a chronological interpolation in the middle of a sentence. The mention of Noah's wife before his sons is in accordance with LXX : but it may be a mere translator's inadvertence.

¶ 67, 68. These paragraphs are interpolations, and are no part of the Biblical Text.

CHAPTER XI.

69. (10) Ced bliadan ba slan do Sem an tan ra thuisim Arifaxad, a cind dá bliadain iar ndilinn. (11) Cuig cet bliadan imorro bai iar tuismedh Arafaxad, ┐ ra thuisim macu ┐ ingena.

70. (12) Cúig bliadna trichat ba slán do Airifaxad an tan ra thuisim Saile. (13) Tri bliadna ar tri cetaib bá beó Arafaxad iar tuismedh Saili dó, ┐ ra thuisim macu ┐ ingena.

71. (14) Tricha bliadan do bo slan do Saili an tan ra thuisim Eber. (15) Tri bliadna ar ceithri cetaib imorro bá beo hé iar tusmedh Eber dó, ┐ ra thuisimh macu ┐ ingena.

72. (16) Ceitri bliadna trichad imorro bá slan do Eber an tan ra thusim Faillech. (17) Ocus tricha ar cet bliadan bá beo he iar tusmedh Faillech do, ┐ da thusim macu ┐ ingena.

73. (18) Tricha bliadna ba slan do Faillech an tan thusim Réú. (19) Noi mbliadna ar dib cetaib imorro ba beo he iar thusmedh Réu dó, ┐ ro tuisim macu ┐ ingena.

74. (20) Cuig bliadna trichat ba slan do Réú an tan ra thuisim Sarúch dó. (21) Cetheora bliadna ar dib cetaib imorro bá beó hé an tan ‡(a) no iar || ra tusmedh Sarúch do, ┐ ra tuisim macu ┐ ingena.

75. (22) Tricha bliadna imorro ba slan do Saruch an tan ra thusim Náchor. (23) Da cet bliadan imorro bá beó hé an tan ra tusmedh Nachór dó, ┐ ra tuisim macu ┐ ingena.

(a) This gloss interlined above.

CHAPTER XI.

69. (10) Sem had an hundred years complete when he begat Arfaxad, at the end of two years after the Flood. (11) Five hundred years was he, further, after the birth of Arfaxad, and he begat sons and daughters.

70. (12) Thirty-five years were complete for Arfaxad when he begat Sale. (13) Three hundred and three years was Arfaxad alive after the birth of Sale to him, and he begat sons and daughters.

71. (14) Thirty years were complete for Sale when he begat Eber. (15) Four hundred and three years was he alive further, after the birth of Eber to him, and he begat sons and daughters.

72. (16) Thirty-four years moreover were complete for Eber when he begat Faleg. (17) An hundred and thirty years was he alive after the birth of Faleg to him, and he begat sons and daughters.

73. (18) Thirty years were complete for Faleg when he begat Reu. (19) Two hundred and nine years moreover was he alive after the birth of Reu to him, and he begat sons and daughters.

74. (20) Thirty-five years were complete for Reu when he begat Saruch. (21) Two hundred and four years moreover was he alive when [or, after] Saruch was born to him, and he begat sons and daughters.

75. (22) Thirty years moreover were complete for Saruch when he begat Nachor. (23) Two hundred years moreover was he alive when Nachor was born to him, and he begat sons and daughters.

76. (24) Noi mbliadna fichit dono ba slan do Nachór an tan ra thuisim Taré. (25) Noi bliadna deg imorro ar cét ba beo hé iar tusmedh Tharé dó, ⁊ ra tuisim macu ⁊ ingena iartain.

77. (26) Sechtmoga bliadan ba slan do Tharre an tan ra thusim Abram ⁊ Nachór ⁊ Aram. (32) Acus ba hé uili saegail Tharre coic bliadna ar dib cetaib, ⁊ adbath a Carrán a tir Chandán iartain.

Ocus is é an tAbram sin cendadart an tres aimser an domain : da bliadain ar nochat ar noi cetaib ó dilinn co gein Abraim a tír Chailldiorum.

NOTES ON THE BIBLICAL TEXT, CHAPTER XI.

On the displacement of this passage see p. 11 *ff*. It is not necessary to print the Latin original here : Tr. adheres to Vulg., and ignores LXX, which inserts an additional generation (Καινάν. between Arfaxad and Sale), and has several differences in the numerical statements of the ages. The only deviations in Tr. from ST are the age of Eber (130 instead of 430) and of Reu (35 before son's birth, 204 after as against Vulg. 32–207). There is some very slight

---

CHAPTER VIII (resumed).

78. (20) Ra chumdaig Náe altoir don Choimdid ‡ iar ndilinn ‖ ⁊ doroini idbarta toltanacha forthi do Dia ona huilib cethraib ‡ ⁊ óna huilib énaib ‖ ⁊ eathaidib glanaib—

⁊ is i sin cet ¹altoir ra cumdaiged ²sa domain.

---

78. ¹ *y sprs. s* H   ² *scribe wrote* ⁊ *and then wrote* s *with a sbs. over it*

76. (24) Twenty nine years were complete for Nachor when he begat Thare. (25) An hundred and nineteen years moreover was he alive after the birth of Thare to him, and he begat sons and daughters thereafter.

77. (26) Seventy years were complete for Thare when he begat Abram and Nachor and Aram. (32) And all the life of Thare was two hundred and five years, and he died in Haran in the land of Canaan thereafter.

And that Abram is the head-rest of the Third Age of the world: nine hundred ninety and two years from the Flood to the birth of Abram in the land of the Chaldeans.

---

support for the Irish figures, but most likely they originated in copyists' errors: it is easy to confuse xxxii with xxxu and ccciiii with ccuii. In H, our only MS. for this portion, the word *cuig* in the Reu passage is written in full, so that the error, if it be an error, goes back to "/H. The spellings Saruch (ver. 20) Nachor (vers. 22, 26) Aram (v. 26) as against the ST Sarug, Nahor, Aran, are to be noted.

---

78. (20) Noe built an altar unto the Lord [after the Flood] and made acceptable offerings upon it unto God, of all the clean four-footed beasts [and of all birds] and clean fowls.

That was the first altar that was built in the world.

(21) Ocus bá so-airigthi ailgen lá Dia an edbairt sin;
ocus adbert Dia fri Náe, Nocha mallachab ‡ .i. nocha
tibar dilind || don doman doridisi ardaig na ndaine,
ar is aibrisc a n-aicned ⁊ is tairberta trascartha
airiugad ⁊ imragad in cridi dáennae dochum uile do
dénum.   Nocha muirbeb dono o so ³amach in n-uili
n-anmain mbi amail doronus.   (22) Acht beidit ó na
huilib láthib don talmuin .i. earrach ⁊ samrad ⁊ fodmar
⁴[⁊ gemred cen cumsanad].

---

78. (20) Aedificauit autem Noe altare Domino, et tollens
de cunctis pecoribus et noluribus mundis obtulit holocausta
super altare.   (21) Odoratusque est *Deus* odorem suauitatis
et ait ad eum : Nequaquam ultra maledicam terrae propter
homines, sensus enim et cogitatio humani cordis in malum
prona sunt [ab adulescentia sua].   Non igitur ultra percutiam
omnem animantem sicut feci.   (22) Cunctis diebus terrae,

CHAPTER IX.

79. (1) Ra bendach Dia Nae cona macaib, ⁊ adbert
friu: Foirbr[id ⁊ dobar]nimdaigther ⁊ linaid an
talmain. (2) ⁊ bid far smacht ⁊ far [n-uamain for
uil]ib anmundaib an talman, ⁊ for uilib énaib an aeoir
[archena—

⁊ ro] thidnaicc doib uili domain,

iascc an mara (3) ⁊ cach an[mide der]scaigther ⁊ a
ïuil betha : ⁊ caithfigthisi na huili sin amail uile úraidi,

---

³ am *sprs.* c H   ⁴ *these words torn away*

(21) And God considered that offering to be worthy
of acceptation and pleasant.   And God said unto Noe :
I shall not curse [i.e. I shall not bring a Flood upon]
the world again by reason of men, for fragile is their
nature, and the perception and imagination of the
human heart are given over and subdued to work
wickedness.   I shall not slay, moreover, from hence-
forth every living soul as I have done.   (22) But all
the days of the earth there shall be spring and summer
and autumn and winter without cessation.

[sementis et messis], frigus et aestus, aestas et hiemps, [nox
et dies], non requiescent.

Note on the Biblical Text, Chapter VIII.

¶ 78. This paragraph represents the text of ST with
tolerable literalness : but whether with intention or not, the
strong anthropomorphism of verse 21 is softened.

Chapter IX.

79. (1) God blessed Noe and his sons, and said unto
them : Increase and be ye multiplied and fill the earth
(2) and your authority and terror shall be over all
the beasts of the earth and all the birds of the air
together—

and He gave the whole world to them,

fish of the sea (3) and every beast that moveth and
that hath life in itself : and ye shall eat of those all,

(4) cénmótha aen ni namá, .i. can feoil cona fuil do chaithem.   (5) Ár sirfeadsa ꞇ toibeochad bar fuili-si cna huilib phiastaib ꞇ ona huilib dainib, ꞇ sirfead anmain cach duine o cach áen muirfes hé.   (6) Ar cach áen doirtfes in fuil ndaena, doirtfigter a fuil aris : fó imaigin ꞇ cosmailus De dorigned an duine. (7) Sibsi imorro, ar Dia fri Náe cona macaib, forbrig ꞏ dobarnimdaigter ꞇ linaid an talmain.

80. (8) Asbert dono Dia fri Nae cona macaib, (9) Ordaigfedsa ꞇ biaid mo charadradh imailli frib ꞇ for bar claind do bar n-eissi (10) ꞇ fris na huilib tangadar asin airc.   (11) ꞇ ni thibar dilinn tar an Domun doridisi,

cénmothá an tan dofas crich coitchend chaich i l-loo bratha.

(13) Dabér imorro comartha mo charadraig daib isin <n>em, ꞇ cein adcifigter an comartha sin o nim (15) ni bia crich na comarba coitcend for na dainib. Is e so in comartha, .i. mo boga ina sduaig isin nim.

Conad do sin ata an sduag nime .i. a tabairt do chomartha caradraig do chlannaib Nae iar ndilinn, .i. co mbia Dia an áentaid friu, aireid ¹adcistear an sduag nime.   Is follus imorro asso cona roibhibh an sduag nime ria ndilind,

ꞇ nocha bia coic bliadna dég ria mbrath.

(19) O na tri macaib-si tra Náe, .i. Sém, ꞇ Cám ꞇ Iaféth, ra silsad ꞇ ro thuismit an t-uili chinead dáena iar ndilinn.

80. ¹ second a sbs.

as of every green thing, (4) except only one thing : ye
shall not eat of flesh with the blood thereof. (5) For
I shall demand and require your blood of all beasts
and of all men, and I shall demand the life of every
man from every one who shall slay him. (6) For
everyone that shall shed man's blood, his blood shall
be shed in turn : under the image and likeness of God
was man made. (7) But ye, said God to Noe and his
sons, increase and be ye multiplied and fill the earth.

80. (8) Moreover God said unto Noe and his sons,
(9) I shall ordain, and there shall be, My friendship
with you and upon your progeny after you (10) and
with all that came out of the Ark. (11) And I shall
not bring a Flood over the world again,

except when the common end of every man shall come
about in the Day of Judgement.

(13) Moreover, I shall put a sign of My friendship to
you in the Heaven, and so long as that sign shall be
seen from Heaven (15) there shall be no end nor
common death upon men. This is the sign, My bow
arching in the Heaven.

Therefore for that purpose is the rainbow, given for a sign
of friendship to the progeny of Noe after the Flood, that
God shall be united with them so long as the rainbow is
seen. Howbeit it is clear from this that the rainbow did
not exist before the Flood,

and that it shall not have being for fifteen years before the
Judgement.

(19) From those three sons of Noe, Sem, Ham, and
Iafeth, was the whole human race after the Flood
begotten and born.

81. (20) Ra thindscain dono Náe tirfrecar do denum, ⁊ ra clannastar finemain. (21) Ocus luid fechtus Náe in a diaid sin i n-a theipernácuili do ól fina. Rangab 'meisci, ⁊ do thuit a chodlad fair, ⁊ do rochair a edach de, co mbai nocht ina theiparnacal. (22) Iar sin doluid Cám .i. athair Chandain, anadóchum, ⁊ adchondairc bullu innara a athar iar n-a nochtad, co ndernaid gairi uime. Luid amach iarsin ⁊ adfed dia braitrib, ⁘ .i. do Iaféd ⁊ do Sém ‖ amail ra bai a n-athair ⁊ sé nocht. (23) Dalodur imorro Sém ⁊ Iáfeth isin tebernacuili, ⁊ is amlaid imorro dochuadar ⁊ a culu rempu, árdáig co nach faichtis feli a n-athar : ⁊ doradsad a édach ²thairis ⁊ ra fagsad ana codlad hé, ⁊ lodar uad iarsin. (24) An tan imorro ra eirig Nae as a chodlad, do faillsiged dó gnimartha na mac sin : conad andsin ra mallach a athair Cám, ⁊ is ed ra ráid : (25) Is mallachda ⁊ is coirpthi, ⁊ biaid Cám coma mogh moghad dá braithrib. (26) Ocus isbert Nae : Ra bendacha an Coimdi ani an Sém, ⁊ bid Cam a fognam dó ; (27) Ocus ra lethnaidi Dia Iáfeth, ⁊ aitrebad a teibarnácuilib Sem, ⁊ bid Cam ag fognam do Iafeth.

Conad hé Cam cet duine ra mallaigedh iar ndilinn,

conad iarsin ra geinidar lupracanaig ⁊ fomoraig ⁊ gaburchind ⁊ cach egasg do-delba archena fil for dainib—

Iarsin tucad gid dilgend ar Chandandaib, ⁊ tucad a ferand do macaib Israel a comartha na mallacht cedna sin. Uair ro bo do síl Chaim Candandai, ⁊ is tresin mallachtain cedna dilgend clann Dardain ⁊ Ioiph, cor marb cach a cheli dib.

—conad hé sin bunad na torathar.

---

81. ¹c sprs. s H   ²is sprs. s **H**

81. (20) Now Noe began to work husbandry, and planted a vineyard. (21) And on a time, after those things, Noe went into his tent to drink wine. Drunkenness seized hold on him, and his sleep fell on him, and his raiment slipped down from him, so that he was naked in his tent. (22) Thereafter came Ham father of Canaan, in to him, and saw the shameful members of his father which had become uncovered, and he made a mock of him. Then he went out; and he tells his brethren [Iafeth and Sem] how that their father was naked. (23) So Sem and Iafeth came into the tent; and in this manner they went, with their backs forward, that they should not see the nakedness of their father: and they put his raiment over him and left him asleep, and came again away from him. (24) Now when Noe arose from his sleep, the doings of those sons were revealed to him: and then his father cursed Ham, and thus he spake: (25) Cursed and corrupt is Ham, and he shall be as it were a slave of slaves for his brethren. (26) And Noe said: Let the Lord bless the aforesaid Sem, and let Ham be in service to him; (27) and let God enlarge Iafeth, and let him dwell in the tents of Sem, and let Ham be in service to Iafeth.

So that this Ham is the first man who was cursed after the Flood:

and thereafter there were born dwarfs and giants and horse-heads and every unshapely form in general that there is among men—

Thereafter there was brought [as it were](a) destruction upon the Canaanites, and their land was given to the sons of Israel, in token of those same curses. For the Canaanites were of the seed of Ham, and it is through that same curse that there was the destruction of the children of Dardan and Ioph, so that each of them slew his fellow.

—so that that was the origin of the monsters.

(a) See the note on this paragraph.

79. (1) Benedixitque Deus Noe et filiis eius, et dixit ad eos : Crescite et multiplicamini et implete terram (2) et terror uester ac tremor sit super cuncta animalia terrae et super omnes uolucres caeli [1]. . . . . (3) Et omne quod mouetur et uiuit erit uobis in cibum quasi holera uiuentia . . . . (4) excepto quod carnem cum sanguine non comedetis.   (5) Sanguinem enim animarum uestrarum requiram de manu cunctarum bestiarum et de manu hominis, de manu uiri [et fratris eius] requiram animam hominis, (6) Quicumque effuderit humanum sanguinem, fundetur sanguis illius : ad imaginem quippe Dei factus est homo.   (7) Vos autem crescite et multiplicamini et . . . . . implete terram.

80. (8) Haec quoque dixit Deus ad Noe et ad filios eius cum eo, (9) [Ecce] ego statuam pactum meum uobiscum et cum semine uestro post uos (10) et . . . cunctis quae egressa sunt de area . . . . (11) . . . . nequaquam . . . . erit deinceps diluuium dissipans terram . . . . (12) . . . . hoc signum foederis . . . . (13) ponam in nubibus . . . . (19) [1]Tres . . . . filii Noe, ab his disseminatum est omne humanum genus . . . .

81. (20) Coepitque Noe uir agricola excercere terram et plantauit uineam.   (21) [1]. . . . . . . inebriatus est, et nudatus est in tabernaculo suo.   (22) Quod cum uidisset Ham pater Chanaan, uerenda scilicet patris sui esse nuda . . . . . nuntiauit duobus fratribus suis foras.   (23) At uero Sem et Iafeth . . . . incidentes retrorsum . . . patris sui uirilia non uiderant.   (24) Evigilans autem Noe ex uino. cum didicisset quae fecera<n>t fili<i> su<i> . . . (25) ait : Maledictus [2]Cham, servus seruorum erit fratribus suis.   (26) Dixitque <Noe> : Benedictus Dominus <Deus> Sem, sit Cham servus eius. (27) Dilatet Deus Iafeth, et habitet in tabernaculis Sem, sitque Cham seruus eius.

NOTES ON THE BIBLICAL TEXT, CHAPTER IX.

¶ 79. [1]This part of the verse has probably been lost owing to confusion caused by the repetition of the equivalents of *mouentur . . . mouetur*. A glossator, observing the omission of the reference to fishes, inserted it in *oratio obliqua*, which betrays the intrusion.

¶ 80. [1]As in previous passages, glossarial interpolations borrowed from *Sex Aetates Mundi* have here ousted the biblical lemmata ; and though the framework of the Latin original is preserved, the words of the text cannot be completely recovered.

¶ 81. The remarks on the preceding paragraph are applicable here, if anything, to yet greater extent. [2]There is slight support in the MSS. of both LXX and Vulg., for the substitution of *Cham* for Chanaan (or Chandan): but (*a*) such an obvious, if inaccurate, change could have been made at any stage independently, and (*b*) it must have been made in the II tradition subsequently to the incorporation of the interpolated passages.

The following notes, which should follow ¶ 85 (pp. 142-3), are printed here for typographical convenience:—

82. (32) Haec familiae Noe iuxta populos et nationes suas: ab his divisae sunt gentes in terra post diluuium.

83. (1) Erat autem terra labii unius et sermonum eorundem . . . . .

84. (2) . . . . . (3) Dixitque alter ad proximum suum: Venite faciamus lateres, et coquamus eos igni. Habuerantque lateres pro saxis et bitumen pro cemento. (4) Et dixerunt: Venite faciamus nobis ciuitatem et turrem cuius culmen pertingat ad caelum, et celebremus nomen nostrum, antequam diuidamur in uniuersas terras.

85. (5) Descendit autem *Deus* ut uideret ciuitatem et turrem quam aedificabant filii Adam: (6) Et dixit Deus, Ecce, unus est populus et unum labium omnibus: coeperuntque hoc facere, nec desistent a cogitationibus suis donec eas opere compleant. (7) [Venite igitur] descendamus et confundamus ibi linguam eorum, ut non audiat unusquisque uocem proximi sui. (8) Atque ita diuisit eos Dominus ex illo loco in uniuersas terras, et cessauerunt aedificare ciuitatem (9) Ed ideirco uocatum est nomen eius Babel, quia ibi confusum est labium uniuersae terrae, et inde dispersit eos *Deus* super faciem cunctarum regionum.

¶ 82. This, the only surviving portion of the "Table of Nations," is very freely paraphrased in Tr.

The rendering of Chapter XI, 1-9, is useless for critical purposes: the story has been practically re-written; inflated (after the manner of the later romances) with eumbrous accumulations of adjectives; and rendered partly unintelligible, especially in verses 4 and 6, by intrusive glosses.

CHAPTER X.

(*Vers.* 1–31 *desunt.*)

82. (32) Ra silsad imorro clanna Nae, ⁊ ro imdaigsead for talmain amail adbert Dia friú : ⁊ ra roinnsed ⁊ ra fogailsead an talmain eturru iar ndilinn.

CHAPTER XI.

83. (1) Is amlaid imorro bai an talam an tan sin, ⁊ áen berla inand ag na huilib dainib ra batar fair,

⁊ Goirthigern a ainm, .i. an berla Ebraidhi,

no cor scailed na berlada ag an Tur.   Is amlaid so adcaemnacair sin dia ndernad gnim n-ingnad(*a*) n-indligteach isin domun an tan sin dorisi.

84. [¹⁷. . . . .] difulning fir an domain an tan sin [¹⁵. . . . .] btha amor thoraid in talmain toir c[⁹. . . . . . .]htuig a rabadar.   (3) Ocus adbert cach dib ri araile [⁹. . . . . .] co tirmaigem an criaid ro-ruaid, ro-rigin [⁵. . . . . .]id, taidlig, tesaidi, curab caidigter cairrgi cruaide, [⁵. . . . . .] garba.   Dentar dono lind an bidamain blaith bith[⁴. . . .]in : ara n-ael n-alaind n-aendatha.   (4) Ocus dono ráidsed beos : [⁴. . . . . .] ⁊ dentar lind cathair chaem-¹cumdaigthi ⁊ dun daingen [bi]th-²foduigthe.   Dentar lind dono tor ro-mór, ro-remar, rigda, ro-ard, ro-fada, co ria ‡ co feici fir ‖ nime ‡ no uas aeor ard uasnadach ‖ cleithi cendmullaig an tuir sin.   Ocus dono mortar ⁊ medaigter ar n-ainm anós ar irdarcus, riasiu ronscailter ⁊ ronscapthar hi crichaib ciana comaigthi.   Ocus dorigned uili leosam an gnim sin.

---

84. ¹cum *sprs. s* H   ² *the* MS. *reads* bith-foghlaidhi, *which cannot be right.*

(*a*) Not clearly written : ngnᴀᴅ apparently covering over something else (indecipherable) that had been written in error.

CHAPTER X.

82. (32) So the children of Noe increased and multiplied upon the earth as God said unto them : and they divided and parted the earth between them after the Flood.

CHAPTER XI.

83. (1) Now the earth was in this wise at that time, all men that were upon it having one and the same language,

and Gorthigern was its name, i.e. the Hebrew language,

until the languages were separated at the Tower. That came to pass in this manner, when a wonderful lawless deed was done in the world at that time once again.

84. [An] intolerable [famine ? ? seized the] men of the world at that time [and there could not be fo]und a trough (?) of the fruit of the [. . . . .] earth in the east where they were. (3) And each said to the other [go to,] that we may dry the very red, very stiff . . . bright heated clay, that it may be as solid as hard . . . . rough rocks. Let there also be made by us the smooth ever-[stiff?] pitch : for their beautiful lime of uniform colour. (4) Moreover they said further : . . . . and let there be made by us a fair-erected castle, and a strong everlastingly founded fortress. Let there be also made by us a very great, wide, royal, lofty, tall, tower, that the ridgepole of the summit of that tower may reach [that men may see] the heavens, [or above the high upper air]. And thus let our name be magnified and enlarged from on high in glory, before we be divided and scattered through lands distant and strange. And this deed was wholly done by them.

85. (5) Ra thainustar imorro Dia do [fech]ad na catrach ⁊ an tuir ro cunndaigsed maic Adaim—

.i. maic an duini thruaid thalmaidi phecaid ⁊ oiltua sin isin ¹scribtuir diada .i. maic Adaim do rád dib.

(6) Ocus adbert Dia : Is follus ataid na huili dáini conad aen phopul iad, conad aen berla fuil acu : ²‡ - nocha n-uil ‖ ⁊ nocha n-anfad ona ³n-imraitib ra thinscansadar, nocha chomlánaiged iad ²‡ o gnimaib ‖. (7) Comfuiscem iarom ⁊ bruigem a mberla blaith, builid, binn, conna ra thuigi neach dib guth araili. (8) Ra mescaid dono, rá medraid, rá meraigid an lucht sin ré hilar na mberla ⁴n-anaich<ne> n-examail : ⁊ is amlaid sin ra ansadar óna gnimuib ra thinscansadar dono do denum. (9) Ocus is airi sin ra gairmead ainm an inaid sin Babel, .i. cumasc : ar is and ra cumuscid uili berla an talman, .i. na da berla sechtmogat, o tri macaib Náe. Ra scáil Dia na cineada sin isin n-uili talmain.

Here the Extract from the Book of Genesis ends.

86. Ra raind Náe an doman a tri itir a macaib, .i. Sém an Aissia, Cam an Afraice, Iafeth an Eóraip. Ocus adbath each fer dib ana rand bodeisin : .i. marb tra Sém a mullaig Sleibi Radruip do thes ngreine, marb Iafeth a mullach Sleibi Formeinia, adbath (*a*)Cam a mulla (*sic*) Sleibi Rafán. Conad ar an fath sin adrubrad an duan-sa,

(*b*)*Athair cáich, Coimsid Nime* . . . . .

87. ¹Ar sin ²trā ³ro ⁴feallsat clanda Adaim for ūaill ⁊ for ⁵dīmos ⁊ for imarbus ⁊ for fingail, .i. Cāin mac Adaim ⁶in sindser ro ⁷marb-sidēn a ⁸dearbrāthair .i. Abēl, tria

---

85. ¹ *The scribe began to repeat* isin, *but finding his mistake before he wrote the* n *he scratched out the* i's, *and adapted the* s *as the initial of the following word* ²⁻² *probably the disjecta membra of a gloss,* ⁊ nocha n-uil[liu] ō gnīmaib, *"and there is none greater by reason of*

85. (5) Now God descended to see the city and the tower which the sons of Adam were building—

i.e. the sons of the wretched, earthy, man of sin: that is a reproach in the divine scripture, to call them 'sons of Adam.'

(6) And God said: Lo, all men are as it were one people, and they have one language; and they will not cease from the purposes which they have begun, till they have fulfilled them. (7) Let us therefore confuse and crush their smooth, gentle, tuneful speech, that none of them may understand the voice of another. (8) So that people was confused, maddened, and caused to err, with the multitude of the different unknown languages: and thus they left off from their deeds which they had begun to do. (9) Wherefore the name of that place was called "Babel," i.e. "confusion": for there all the languages of the world were confused, to wit the seventy-two languages, from the three sons of Noe. God scattered those nations into the whole earth.

---

86. Noe divided the world into three parts among his sons: Sem in Asia, Ham in Africa, Iafeth in Europe. And each of them died in his own division. Sem died on the summit of Sliab Radruip of the heat of the sun, Iafeth died on the summit of Sliab Armenia, Ham died on the summit of Sliab Rafan. So that the following song was said of that matter—

Poem no. V.

87. Thereafter the children of Adam played false, in pride, in haughtiness, in sin, and in kin-murder: Cain son of Adam, the elder, he slew his brother Abel through his

---

deeds." *The second i of gnimaib sbs. and blotted.* [3] h-im. MS.
[4] *bracketed letters not in* MS.
87. (*variae lectiones from* H, *text from* M) [1] iar [2] thra [3] ra (*ut semper*) [4] feallsad [5] dimus [6] an seindser [7] marbsigein [8] derb-

(*a*) Cain MS.   (*b*) M here resumes.

⁹saint ⁊ tria ¹⁰formot, do ⁱⁱid chnāma ¹¹chamaill; conad airi sin ¹²dorad Dīa ¹³dīlind ¹⁴tars in n-uili doman.

¹⁵Ocus nīr gein mac a cind a bliadna ō athair ¹⁶acht Adam namā, ūair is fīr nar ¹⁷slān acht āen bliadain ¹⁸Adaim, ¹⁹madab imslān, in ūair ²⁰ro ²¹compread Cāin.

88. Seth mac ¹Adam imorro, ²in treas mac ³aireada ⁴ro bai ⁵ac Adam, ⁶⁊ is ūad ⁷atāt fir domain uili, ‡ .i. Nāe mac Laimīach meic ⁸Mathasalem meic Enōc meic Iareth meic Malaleth meic Cainen meic ⁹Enos meic ¹⁶Seth meic Adaim. ||⁽ᵃ⁾ ¹¹Is hē thrā Nae ¹²in ¹³tAdam ¹⁴tānusti, ¹⁵cosa ¹⁶mberar fir ¹⁷domain uili. ¹⁸Ūair ro ¹⁹bāid ²⁰in ²¹dīli ²²sīl ²³Adaim, ²⁴acht ²⁵Nāe cona trī macaib .i. ²⁶Sem, ²⁷Cam, ²⁸Iathfed, ⁊ a ²⁹ceithri mnā ³⁰.i. Coba ³¹⊣ Olla ³²⊣ ³³Oliua ⊣ ³⁴Olīuana.

³⁵Imroimadair ³⁶‡ dosfaidead || ³⁷clanna ³⁸Adaim, ³⁹co tard ⁴⁰Dīa ⁴¹dīlind ⁴²tarsin ⁴³uili ⁴⁴doman, ⁴⁵conach tērno ⁴⁶nech beō ⁴⁷eisti acht lucht na ⁴⁸hairci .i. ⁴⁹Nāe ⁵⁰cona ⁵¹trī macaib .i. Sem, ⁵²Cam, Iathfed cona ⁵³ceithri mnāib .i. Coba ⊣ Olla ⁵⁴⊣ Oliba ⊣ Olīuana,⁵³

⁵⁵amail asbert⁵⁶—

   Slūag nād chlōe cūa-chel . . . . .

---

⁹ saint   ¹⁰ formad   ¹¹ camuill   ¹² darad   ¹³ an dile
¹⁴ tarsa nuili   ¹⁵ *om.* ⊣   ¹⁶ ach o Adam   ¹⁷ slan   ¹⁸ Adhaim
¹⁹ madob imlan an   ²⁰ do   ²¹ -pred
    88. ¹ Adaim and *om.* imorro H   ² an tres H   ³ aireda H
⁴ *om.* ro H   ⁵ ag H   ⁶ *om.* ⊣ H   ⁷ ataid H   ⁸ -sail- H
⁹ Enois H   ¹⁰ Seith H   ¹¹ orú is é Nae H oir is e an (in β²) Noe
sin β⁰¹²   ¹² an H   ¹³ tAdhamh β¹²   ¹⁴ tanaisti H tanasti β
tainaiste β¹²   ¹⁵ gusa β⁰¹²   ¹⁶ mairedh β¹ mared β²   ¹⁷ *ins.* an
and om. uili β⁰¹²: uili *also om.* H: domh- β¹²   ¹⁸ oir β¹²: do H   ¹⁹ bhaith
β bhaidh β¹²   ²⁰ an H β   ²¹ diliudh β¹²   ²² siol β⁰¹²
²³ nAdhaimh uili β Adhamh nile β¹²   ²⁴ ach H   ²⁵ Noe gona tri
macaibh β: Naoi gona thri macaibh β¹²   ²⁶ Semh β   ²⁷ Caim β
²⁸ *ins.* ⊣ β¹²: Iafeth H β Iaphet β¹²   ²⁹ ceitri H geeithre mnaibh β¹

envy and jealousy, with a shaft of a camel-bone. Wherefore God brought a Flood over the whole earth.

Now never was son born of father at the end of a year save [from] Adam only: for it is true that one year of Adam was not complete, if indeed it was quite complete, when Cain was conceived.

88. As for Seth, son of Adam, one of the three eminent sons which Adam had, from him are the men of the whole earth. [Noe s. Lamech s. Mathusalam s. Enoch s. Iared s. Malalehel s. Cainan s. Enos s. Seth s. Adam]. Now Noe is the second Adam, to whom are traced the men of the whole earth. For the Flood drowned the seed of Adam save Noe and his three sons, Sem, Ham, Iafeth, and their four wives Coba, Olla, Oliva, Olivana.

The progeny of Adam sinned [fell]; so God brought a Flood over the whole earth, so that not one escaped from it alive except the people of the ark, to wit Noe and his three sons, Sem, Ham, Iafeth, with their four wives Coba, Olla, Oliva, and Olivana.

As one said—

Poem no. I.

---

eceitre mnaibh β^2 [30] *om.* .i. β^2 [31] *om.* ⁊ β^{12} [32] *om.* ⁊ β^{12} [33] Oliu M Oliva β^1 *om.* β^2 [34] Olibana M Olivana β^1 [35] *this y om.* H: im ro imair β imromhair β^{12} [36] *om.* β^{012} [37] *ins.* a suidiu β: clann β^{02} clainn β^1 [38] Adhaimh β Adhamh β^{12} [39] co darat β co tarat β^{12} [40] *om.* β^{12} [41] an dillinn β in diliu β^{12} [42] tarsan β^{012} [43] uile β^{012} [44] dhomainn β domhainn β^1 domhaann β^2 [45] gonach β^{12} [46] *om.* M neach β^{12} [47] *om.* β^{012} [48] haireedh β^{12} [49] Noe β^{012} [50-50] a chlann ⁊ a mnaibh do reir an file β^{12} [51] thri β^0 [52] Cham ⁊ Iafeth β^0 [53-53] ceathra mnaibh .i. Cobha Olla Oliua Oliuana [54] ⁊ Oliba *om.* M *and sprs. but miswritten* ⁊ Olibana   [55] amail adbert an fili H amail asbeart an filidh β

(a) Text of B here resumes, but is still preserved in the transcripts only.

89. Ō ¹Adam ²co dīlind ³in chēt āis. ⁴Is ē seo ⁵am ⁶in līn ⁷bliadan fil innti ⁸cheadus,⁴ .i. sē ⁹bliadna ¹⁰cāecad ¹¹ar sē ¹²chēdaib ¹³ar ¹⁴mīle, ¹⁵amail asbert ¹⁶in file—¹⁵

Cēt aimsir in bethad bind . . . .

¹⁷Is ¹⁸iad ¹⁹seo ²⁰airich ²¹na cēt āisi sin ²²cona ²³sāeglaib, īar Seth ²⁴cheadas²²—

²⁵Adam	deccexxx bl.	²⁷Cainen	deccex bl.
²⁶Seth	dexii bl.	²⁸Malaleth	deccc bl.
Enos	decccu bl.	²⁹Iareth	deccelxu bl.
	³⁰Enoc	ccelxu bl.	
	³¹Mathasalem	deccelxix bl.	
	³²Laimiach	³³declxxuii bl.	

³⁴Sem ³⁵dono rogob i nAisia, Cam ³⁶i nAfraic, ³⁷Iathfed ³⁸a nEoraip, ³⁹amail asbert in fili,

Sēm rogab i n-Aisia n-ait . . . .

90. Ra thuismid ⁊ ra chlannaigsed tra na tri meic-sin Nae, .i. Sem, Cam, Iafeth, cineada ⁊ clanda imda ilarda examla, .i. da chinel sechtmogat ‡ .i. da chined dēg ar tri fichtib ‖. Is amlaid seo imorro ra tusmid ⁊ ra seailit na cinela sin, .i. secht cinela fichit dib o Sēm, tricha imorro o Cham, a enig dēg o Iafeth, conad da chinēl sechtmogat sin uili. Ocus conad dá berla sechtmogat tucad doib iar tairmesc an Tuir Nemruaid; conad a cind dece mbliadain iarsin do tebustair Feinius Farrsaid berla na nGaeidel as na dib sechtmogat, co rustaisealb dia dalta, .i. do mac Adnomuin, .i. do Gaeidel.

No comad a cind dece mbliadan iar scailead don scoil for cach leth dorébi Feinius Farsaid(a) ‡ .i. in sai ‖ berla na nGaeidel as na dib berlaib sechtmogat, ⊣ dorad iarsin do Niul, dia mac bodeisin.

Darad-sidi do Gaeidil Glas mac Niuil ⊣ dia macaib-sein bodeisin, conad uada-sidi ainmnigter in berla sin.

---

89. ¹Adbamh β⁰¹² ²go dilioun β go dilinn β¹² ³an ched ais H in ced aois β ced aois an domhuin β¹² (-ain β²) ⁴⁻⁴om. β¹² as H ⁵om. am H β ⁶an H om. β ⁷bliadhna β ⁸ceadus β inti *and om.* cheadus H ⁹-dhna β⁰¹² ¹⁰caogad β⁰¹² ¹¹re β¹² ¹²chead β ched β¹² ¹³air β² ¹⁴mili H mhili β mhile β¹ ¹⁵⁻¹⁵om. β¹²: amhuil β ¹⁶inso H in fili β¹ ¹⁷ins. ⊣ H β⁰¹²: as β⁰¹² ¹⁸iat β ¹⁹so H β¹² ²⁰airid H airigh β athrachadh β¹² ²¹na cet aissi H na baoisi β na haoise β¹² ²²⁻²²marlle ris an rae do mhair siad β¹² ²³saeghlaib H

89. From Adam to the Flood is the First Age. This is the tally of years that are in it first, one thousand six hundred fifty and six years, as the poet said,

Poem no. VII.

These are the leaders of that First Age, with their lives, after Seth first of all—

Adam	930 years	Cainan	910 years
Seth	612 „	Malalehel	800 „
Enos	905 „	Iared	965 „
		Enoch	365 years
		Mathusalam	969 „
		Lamech	777 „

So Seth settled in Asia, Ham in Africa, Iafeth in Europe, as the poet said,

Poem no. II.

90. Now those three sons of Noe, Sem, Ham, Iafeth, begat and fathered many numerous and various nations and progenies, to wit, seventy-two peoples [i.e. three score and twelve peoples]. Now thus were these peoples born and scattered: twenty-seven of them from Sem, thirty from Ham, fifteen from Iafeth, which makes in all seventy-two peoples. And there were seventy-two languages given to them after the confusion of Nemrod's Tower: so that in the end of ten years after that, Feinius Farsaid extracted the speech of the Gaedil out of the seventy-two languages, and set it forth to his fosterling, the son of Agnomain, Gaedil.

Or perhaps it was at the end of ten years after the scattering of the school on every side that Feinius Farsaid [the sage] extracted the speech of the Gaedil out of the seventy-two languages, and gave it afterwards to Nel, his own son.

He gave it to Gaedil Glas son of Nel, and to *his* sons; so that from them is the language named.

---

saoghlaibh β   [24] chedus H cheatas   [25] Adhamh β[012]   [26] Set β[12]
[27] Cainan β Canaan β[12]   [28] Malalel β Malaleal β[12]   [29] Iarat β[12]   [30] deeelxu
β[012]   [31] Mathasailem H Methusalem β[12]   [32] Lamhiach β Lamiac β[12]
[33] deelxuii M deelxxuiii β[12]   [34] *ins.* do Naoi ⁊ a thriar mac .i. β[12]
[35] *om.* dono: dogab imorro an Aissia H: dana roghabh in nAissia β gab
Sem an Asia Cam an Aifric ⁊ Iafeth (Iaphet β²) Enrop β[12]   [36] a nAfraice
H in nAfraic β   [37] Iafeth H   [38] in nEoraip β   [39] amail inso
H amhail asbert infili β *om.* β[12]

(a) interlined.

91. Ra imdaig tra uimir na cinel sin [sech n-uimir na mberla; ar] ataid isa nAffraice il-chinela [im oen-berla, cen (?)] atharrach tengad accu. Is ed fodera sa(n), na rab[atar] ach da chinel sechtmogat thall acon Tur, an tan ra sg[ailed na] berladha : ꝛ cé ra himdaigead na cinela, na ro im[daiged (?) i] n-airim chinel n-examail iad, acht a leigi*ud* a fo-tasg*or* na cinel [ba] nesa doib. Conad lia na cinela iar tothacht an[date na berlae, cian] cob lia iar n-uimir.

92. [1]Conad ō na trī macaib sin Nāe ro [2]geneadar [3]na dā [4]chenel [5]sechtmogat īar [6]n-dīlind, [7]cona dib [8]berlaib sechtmogat [9]tucad dōib [9]īarsin, ac [10]tairmesc [11]in Tuir [12]Nemrūaid. [13]Conad i cind [14]dece [15]mbliadan [16]īarsin ro [17]thebistair [18]Feinius Farrsaich [19]bērla na [20]nGāedeal [21]as na [22]dīb bērlaib [23]sechtmogat.[1]

[24]Tricha [1]⁜ no .uii.xx ‖ mac [25]badar [26]ag [27]Sem, [28]um [29]Airifacsad, [28]um [30]Assur, [28]um [31]Peirsius.

[32]Ocus is [33]dia [34]sīl-sidi na [35]Hebraidi. [36]Is iad so na [37]eōic [38]meic [39]ō ra sīlad aigi, .i. [40]Alam, [41]Assur, [42]Airifacsad, [43]Luid, is Aram: ꝛ cia [44]ainmnigter [45]eōic meic [46]ag Sem, ni [47]tabar a [48]n-āirim [49]acht [50]cincad dā mac dīb.

[51]Tricha [52]mac imorro badar oc Cham, im [53]Chuss, im [54]Mesram, im [55]Futh im [56]Chandán,

Ocus [57]cia [58]ainmnigter [59]tricha mac [60]oc Cam, ni [61]tabar a n-āirem [62]acht cinead [63]dā mac dīb.

92. [1-1] *om.* H : conadh o thri macaib-siden Noe β (*these words om.* β[12]   [2] gheinseadar β[012] (g- β², -edar β¹ -edair β²)   [3] *om.* na β[12] [4] cheineil β[012] (-el β[12])   [5] deag is tri fithchiod β[012] (deg . . fitheit β[12]) [6] -inn β[012]   [7] ins. o chlannaib Naoi β[12] : conadh da bhearla β, gonadh da bherladh β[12]   [8] tugadh doibh β[012]   [9] iarsoin β[012] (-soin β¹ iair- β²)   [10] toirmeasg β toirmiosg β[12]   [11] an β²   [12] Neamhruaidh β Nemrodh β[12] (-mh- β²)   [13] conadh a ccend β - a gcenn β[12]   [14] deich β[12]   [15] bliadhna β[012]   [16] -soin β   [17] teipestair β[012] (-ar β²) [18] Fionnus Farsaigh β[12] F. Fairsaidh β   [19] berladh β[12]   [20] nGaoidheal β[012] (-dhel β[12])   [21] *ins.* ꝛ β¹   [22] di bherlaibh β da bherladh β[12] [23] sechtmhodh β[12]   [24] *text from here printed as in* H : *interlined* ꝗ *in* H only   [25] ins. ro M do β[12] : bhadair β bhadar β[12]   [26] ac M a β[12] [27] *ins.* mac Nae β[12]   [28] im M β (*bis*)   [29] Airifaxat β Arfaexsat β[12] [30] Asur M   [31] Persius M β[012]   [32] nair M : *om.* is β[62]   [33] da sil-side M [34] siol-sen β; siol (*om.* sen) β[12]   [35] Heabraidi M Heabhraidhe β[012]

91. Now the number of those peoples increased beyond the numbers of the languages; for there are in Africa many peoples having one language, and no change of tongue. This is the reason thereof, that there were only seventy-two peoples yonder at the Tower, when the languages were separated: and though the peoples were multiplied, they were not multiplied in the computation of different peoples, but were left as a subordinate company of the peoples nearest to them. So that the nations are greater in substance than the languages, though they are not greater in number.

92. So that it is from those three sons of Noe that the seventy-two peoples were born after the Flood, with their seventy-two languages that were given to them thereafter, at the confusion of Nemrod's Tower. And it was at the end of ten years thereafter that Feinius Farsaid extracted the language of the Gaedil out of the seventy-two languages.

Sem had thirty [or twenty seven] sons, including Arfaxad, Assur, Persius—

and it is of his seed that the Hebrews come. These are the five sons from whom he had descendants, Elam, Assur, Arfaxad, Lud, and Aram: and though five sons of Sem are named, I do not give in enumeration the descent of more than two of them.

Ham had thirty sons, including Chus, Mesraim, Fut, Chanaan,

and though thirty sons of Ham are named, I do not give in enumeration the descent of more than two of them.

(-aidh β^{12}) [36] no comad iad so M no gomadh iat so β ר is iad so β^{12} [37] cuig β coig β^{12} [38] maic β^{12} [39] oir sioladh aige β da (do β^2) cloinn ar bhfagham (air bhfh- β^2) sliocht β^{12}: aici M [40] Alamh β^{12} [41] Asur M [42] Arafaxat M Arifaxat β Arfacsad β^{12} [43] Luidi Saram MH Ludi Sarain β Ludi Saram β^{12} [44] ghth- β^{12} -thear M [45] coig β na coig β^{12} [46] ac M aig Semh β sin Seim β^{12} [47] tabhair β^{012} [48] airem M aireamh β airenh β^{12} [49] ach H [50] cinneamh en dá mhac dibh β ceinemh in da mhac dhiobh β^{12} [51] Triothchad (Triochad β^2) mac bhadh ag Cam mhac Naoi um Cus um Esrom um Futh um Canaan β^{12} [52] mac aile oc Cam M mac eile o Cham β [53] Chus M Cus β [54] Esram H Easrom β [55] Futh β [58] Cannain β [57] gia β [56] -gthear M -ghthear β -ghther an β^{12} [59] triotchad β^1 triothchadh β^2 [60] ag Cam β sin *and om.* oc Cam β^{12} [61] tabhair β tabhar β^1 toabhar β^2 [63] diobh acht cinneadh da mac β^{012} (dhiobh, cinedh, mhac β^{12}) [63] *ins.* a H

A ⁶⁴cūig dēg ⁶⁵imorro ⁶⁶ag Iafeth.

M

⁶⁷im ⁶⁸Danai, ⁶⁹im ⁷⁰Grēgus, ⁶⁵im ⁷¹Espanus ⁶⁹ im ⁷²Goimerus : ⁷³no ⁷⁴is ⁷⁵morseser ar fichit do macaib badar aici ⁊ .i. oc Sem ||.

no ⁷⁶cumad iad so anmanda ⁷⁷na mac sin Iathfeth, .i. ⁷⁸Gomer, ⁷⁸Magoc, Magia, Iaban, Tubal, ⁷⁹Masoth, ⁸⁰Tirus, ⁸¹Maisechda.

H

⁊ ni tabar a n-āirim ach cinedh tri mac dib. Ni hamlaid ra badar na meic aili can geinemhain uaidhib: acht ri ro geinir uaidib ni ar bu dingmala ainm ceincoil da tabairt forro.

Is ⁸²amlaid ⁸³sin ⁸⁴imorro ⁸⁵do ⁸⁶silsad na ⁸⁷cinela sin, ⁸⁸.i. a ⁸⁹secht fichit fichit dīb ō Sem, ⁹⁰tricha imorro ō Cham. ⁹¹cūic ⁹²cenela dēg o ⁹³Iafeth,⁸⁸ ⁹⁴ut dicitur

Tricha mac mīn, monar ngle . . . . .

93. Iathféth dono mac Náe, ¹is úad tuaiscert-leth na Haissia ⁊ lucht na Heorpa uili. Sém imorro for medon Aissia, ó Sruth Éofrait co tracht airthir an betha. Cam dono ragab-sidi an Affraice, ⁊ deiscert-leth na Haissia.

94. ¹Iáfed ²dono³, is iad a ⁴chlann-sidi ⁵lenfamaid ⁶anossa. ⁷Is ⁸ñad ⁹tūaiscert-¹⁰leath ¹¹na ¹²Haissia ¹³uili, .i. ¹⁴Aissia Beg ¹⁵⁊ ¹⁶Airmein ¹⁷⁊ fir na Sceithia

⁶⁴ cuic dec M   ⁶⁵ om. β   ⁶⁶ oc Iathfed M ag Iaphet β ⁶⁷ in β um β¹²   ⁶⁸ -nn- β⁰¹²   ⁶⁹ um β¹² (ter)   ⁷⁰ Greagus β¹² ⁷¹ Easp- β⁰¹²   ⁷² Gomerus β Gomerius β¹ Gomeretis β²   ⁷³⁻⁷³ o seisear dhiobh (dhiobh β²) mar ata β¹²   ⁷⁴ om. is β   ⁷⁵ morseisiur air fichit do mhacaibh bhadar ag Semh β   ⁷⁶ gomadh β, possibly cumad iad so cert anmanda in M: the writing here partly effaced by a blot badly rubbed out, and there is room for a letter or two more than is printed in the text   ⁷⁷ mac Iafeth   ⁷⁸ Maghach (Magach β¹ -och β²) Madia Iuban β¹²   ⁷⁹ Massoth β¹² Massoc β   ⁸⁰ Tiras β⁰¹² ⁸¹ Maisecdha β Maisectadh β¹²   ⁸² amhladh β amhlaidh β¹²   ⁸³ seo

Iafeth had fifteen,

including Danai, Gregus, Espanus, Gomerus: or [Sem] had twenty-seven sons.

Or perhaps these are the names of the sons of Iafeth—Gomer, Magog, Madai, Iavan, Tubal, Mosoch, Tiras, Maisechda.

And I do not give in enumeration the descent of more than three of them. It is not the case that the other sons had no descendants: but none were born from them worthy of being called "a people."

Thus it is that those peoples were descended, twenty-seven from Sem, thirty from Ham, fifteen from Iafeth, *ut dicitur*

Poem no. III.

93. Iafeth son of Noe, of him is the northern side of Asia and the people of all Europe. Sem over the middle of Asia, from the river Euphrates to the eastern region of the world. Ham settled in Africa and on the southern side of Asia.

94. As for Iafeth, it is his progeny which we shall follow now. From him is the northern side of all Asia, namely Asia Minor, and Armenia, and the people of

M β so β¹² [81] om. β¹² [85] ro M β⁰¹² [86] silad M sioladh β⁰¹² (ś β²) [87] cenela M cineala β cinedhaibh β¹ cinethchaibh β² [88-88] om. β¹² [89] seacht xxit diobh o Seimh triocha β¹² [90] ins. ꞁ M [91] ins. ꞁ M: a cuig deg β [92] cinela H [93] Iathfed M [94] amail asbert in teolach seo M amail isbert an filidh β do reir an fhile β¹²

93. [1] sprs. s H

94. [1] Iathfed M Iaphet β¹² [2] tra M β om. β¹² [3] ins. mac Nae M mhac Naoi β¹² mac Nai mac Laimhiach β [4] cland-sen M chlan β¹: om. side β⁰¹² [5] lean- β -aoid β¹² [6] om. M β⁰¹² [7] ins. ꞁ β [8] uadh β naidh β¹² [9] tnaitsciort β¹² (-th- β²) [10] leithi M [11] na dittographed β¹ [12] Haisia M β⁰¹² [13] om. M β⁰¹² [14] Aisia M Aissia β¹² [15] .i. for ꞁ β¹² [16] Airmen M Armein β¹² [17-17] om. β

[18]7 is [19]ūad [20]an Grēg Beg 7 an Grēg Mōr [17]7 Grēg na [21]Halax*andria*.[18] [22]Ocus is ūad [20]lucht na Heorpa [23]uili.

[24]Ocus dono is dīa cloind cach gabāil dogab Ērinn, cenmothā Cessair namā.[22] [24]

95. (A) Do chlannaib Iafed andso bodesta. Iafeth dono mac Nác 7 Oliuana a bean, ro thechtsad ocht maccu, .i. Gomer, Magóg, Maigia, Iabal ‡ no Eónae ‖ ‡ .i. an seindser ‖, Tubal, Masoch, Tirus, Maisegda.

(B) Gomer imorro, is uada ataid Galladagdai, 7 is inann iadside 7 Gailli. Ainm aili dóib Gailligregi.

> Cid dia n-abur Gailligregi ré síl Gomeir meic Iafeth? Ninsa.
> Gailli iad do bunad adbeir Asuidhir, 7 dorad rigi an feraind dianad ainm Bétania don Gregdo-sidi irandus dia thir ar chongnam fris. Ra ansad aigi an agaid a braithrech; 7 is airi sin adberar Gailligregi riu, ar a mbeith itir Greg 7 Gaillia do bunad, 7 ni heir comad mac do Goimer Gregus.

(C) Teasallus mac Greguis ra cumdaig an catraig diana ainm Tesalónica, 7 is inti ro follannaigsed a flaithus. Is uad ainmnigter in Tesaill iar firind, 7 o <a> athair ainmnigter an Greg.

(D) Ceitri meic la Goimeir, .i. Ripad Scot o taid Senit; 7 dob eiscin Ibath mac Goimeir, senathar Feiniusa Farrsaid ‡ .i. Feinius Farrsaid mac Baaith meic Ibaith meic Goimeir meic Iafeth ‖.

> Cid dia n-abar Greg Sceithegda re Gaeidealaib, ar ní do síl Neimid meic Adnomain iad do bunad? Is do lucht na Sceithia dóib, uair is do síl Feiniusa Farrsaid doib cá raibi flaithus na Sceithia. Acht ceana ni raibi rigi na Sceithia aigi acht a flaithus, 7 ar a mbeith do chlaunaib Goimer adberar Greg re Gaeidelaib; 7 as decair lind a (a)scartain ré Goimér da reir sin.

(E) Na tri meic aili Goimeir, .i. Asceinex, otaid Reigine, Erifam o taid Páplagoine, Togarm o tait Frigia 7 Ilia.

---

[18] [18] *om.* M   [19] uaidh β[1] uatha β[2]   [20-20] *om.* β[12]   [21] -dreach β
[22-22] *om.* β   [23] uile β[12]   [24-24] *om.* M β[12]

Scythia; and from him are Graecia Parva, and Graecia Magna, and Alexandrian Greece. Of him also are the people of all Europe.

Moreover it is of his progeny that is every Taking which took Ireland, save only Cessair.

95. (A) Of the children of Iafeth here now. Iafeth son of Noe and Olivana his wife, they had eight sons, Gomer, Magog, Madai, Iabal or Iavan, [the eldest], Tubal, Mosoch, Thiras, Maisegda.

(B) As for Gomer, of him are the Galladagdae [= Galatae], and they are the same as the Galli. Another name for them is Gallograeci.

> Why is the seed of Gomer son of Iafeth called "Gallograeci"? They were fundamentally Galli, says Isidorus: and the ruler of the land called Bithynia gave to the Greeks a portion of his land for giving him help. They stayed with him to oppose his brethren; and for that reason they are called Gallograeci, because they were fundamentally in part Greeks, in part Galli; and it will not arise that Gregus was a son of Gomer.

(C) Thessalus son of Gregus built the city called Thessalonica, and therein he ruled his kingdom. From him is Thessaly named authentically, and Greece is named from his father.

(D) Gomer had four sons, Rifath Scot from whom are the Scots; now he was Ibath son of Gomer, the grandfather of Feinius Farsaid [Feinius Farsaid s. Baath s. Ibath s. Gomer s. Iafeth].

> Why are the Gaedil called Greeks of Scythia, seeing that fundamentally they are not of the seed of Nemed son of Agnomain? They are of the people of Scythia, for they are of the seed of Feinius Farrsaid, who had the princedom of Scythia. However, he had not the kingdom of Scythia, but its princedom: and as they are of the progeny of Gomer, the Gaedil are called Greeks. We find it hard to disconnect them from Gomer on that account.

(E) The three other sons of Gomer were Aschenez, of whom are the Rhegini, Rifath of whom are the Paphlagonians, Thogorma of whom are Phrygia and Ilia.

(a) MS. -thair, clumsily corrected sec. man.

(F) Maigia no Meda mac Iafed, *a quo* Meda; ⁊ ragabsa l
ochtar o Meadaib rigi an domain.

(G) Ionán mac Iafeth, is uaidib-séin ataid Iondaid, ⁊ is
uad rasgeinseadar Eoldaid.   Ocus ainm aili do, Greg mac
Iafeth. [Is uad] ainmnigter an cuiged berla na Gregi, .i.
an berla Eol[da, ⁊ is ua]d ainmnigter Gregaig iar firind.
Uair is co Gregus mac [Iafeth ber]ar genelach Alaxandair
meic Philip rig Greg, ⁊ is uad Gregaig [⁴. . . .]cain. Ocus
is uad adberar an Muir Eonda.

(H) Coig meic aigi-sidi, .i. Elisa, Tairsis, Seithim,
Dodáinim, Gregus.   Elissa *a quo* Eigila, .i. geinilach
Sicimórum.   Tairsis, is uad Tairsis ⁊ Cillegda.   Seithim
a quo Ioif mac Saduiru, amail adbeir leabar Augustin o
Chathair De, ⁊ uada Ceitheagdai.   Is uaidib-sein ainm-
nigther cathair na Cipricai, .i. Ceithunt.

(I) Dodainim, is uadha-sidi Rodai.   Is uaidib-sein ra
foglad indseda Mara Toirrian, cona cinelaib examlaib, .i.
Inis Roid, ⁊ Inis Coirbdith, ⁊ Inis Sicil, ⁊ Inis Creid, ⁊ Inis
Ceithiria, ⁊ Inis Rodain, ⁊ oiléna cirimda ele, incóch na ra
thuirmsemar súnd, árdaig mi-chuimni.   Gregus *a quo*
Gregaig.

(K) Tubal, is uada atáid Iberdaid ⁻ Espandai; ‡ no
comad mac d'Iaféd Easpanus o táid Espandai ‖, ⁊
Celtiberdai, ⁻ Édaldai. Uair Eiperus, do sil Tubail do
chinel Iafeth, a quo Eipiritarum, ⁊ ór gein Ianus rí na
Heiperda.   Is é cet ri da gab Románchu. ⁻ is úad ainmnigter mí Ienuair, ⁊ is úad Coirinti.

(L) Massoch, is uada ataid Capadusdai.(*a*)   Tiruss, is
uada ataid Tragdai.   Maissegda, dibaid-sein.

(M) Magóg, is uada ataid fir na Sceithia ⁊ na Gaith, .i.
Gaidil.   Cuig meic lá Magóg, .i. Baath, ⁊ Ibath, ⁻ Barachan,
⁻ Emoth, ⁊ Aithechta.   Baath dono, mac dó-sein Feinius
Farrsaid, athair na Sceithegda.   Feinius Farrsaid dono,

(*a*) *Capaddai* written and ᵹ changed clumsily to ꝺ : (= dus), *see. man.*

(F) Madai or Meda, son of Iafeth, *a quo* the Medes; and eight men of the Medes took the kingship of the world.

(G) Ionan son of Iafeth, from them (*sic*) are the Ionians, and from him were the Aeolians born.   He has another name, Gregus son of Iafeth.   From him is named one of the five languages of the Greeks, the Aeolic, and from him the Greeks are named authentically.   For the genealogy of Alexander son of Philip, king of Greece, is traced to Gregus son of Iafeth and from him are the . . . (?) Greeks.   Also, the Ionian Sea is named after him.

(H) He had five sons, Elissa, Tharsis, Cetthim, Dodanim, Gregus.   Elissa *a quo* Aetolia, the pedigree-stem of the Siculi.   Tharsis, from him are Tarsus and the Cilicians.   Cetthim, *a quo* is Iuppiter son of Saturn, as the book of Augustine *De Ciuitate Dei* saith, and of whom are the Citii.   From them is named the city of the Cyprii, namely Citium.

(I) Dodanim, from him are the Rhodii.   By these people the islands of the Torrian Sea, with their various inhabitants, were appropriated, to wit Rhodes, and Carpathos, and Sicily, and Crete, and Cytherea, and the Balearic Islands, and very many other islands which we have not enumerated here, owing to failure of memory.   Gregus, *a quo* the Greeks.

(K) Tubal, from him are the Iberi and the Hispani [or perhaps Easpanus was a son to Iafeth, and from him are the Hispani] and the Celtiberi and the Itali.   For [it is] Eperus, of the seed of Tubal of the race of Iafeth, *a quo* the Epirotae, and from whom sprang Ianus, king of the Epirotae.   He is the first king who took over the Romans.   From him is named the month of January, and from him are the Quirites.

(L) Mosoch, of him are the Cappadoces.   Thiras, of him are the Thraces.   Maisegda is missing.

(M) Magog, of him are the men of Scythia and the Goths, that is, the Gaedil.   Magog had five sons, Baath, Ibath, Barachan, Emoth, Aithechta.   As for Baath, his son was Feinius Farrsaid, father of the Scythians.   As for Feinius

mac Baaith meic Magóg meic Iafeth. Adberaid araile
imorro is Feinius Farrsaid mac Baaith meic Ibáith meic
Goimeir meic Iafeth.

(N) Ibath dono, an mac aili do Magóg, mac dosaidi
Alainius.   Tri meic aigi-sidi, .i. Airmein, Negua, Isieón.
Coic meic ag Armón (sic), .i. Gotus, Uiligotus, Cebitus,
Brugandus (sic), Longbardus.   Negúa dono, ceitre(a) meic
lais, .i. Uandalus, Saxus, Bogardus, Longbardus.   Isicon
imorro, an tres mac Elainius, ceitri meic lais, .i. Frangeus,
Romanus, Albanus a quo Albania an Aisia Big, ⁊
Albanactus mac Britan meic Siluius meic Ascain meic
Aeniasa meic Anicis a quo Alba Iartair : ⁊ Britus, o raiter
Indsi Bretan.

(O) Is andsin do randad an doman a tri randaib, .i.
Eóraip ⁊ Afraice ⁊ Assia. Secht mbliadna dece ré scailead
na mberlad tanig an ced fer do šil Iáfeth is an Eóraip, .i.
Alainius mac Ibaith meic Magog meic Iafeth meic Náe.
Alainius, is uada atáid Frainge ⁊ Romanaig ; ⁊ is amlaid
thanig a tri meic laiss, .i. Airmein, Neagua, Issicon : conad
a ťus ra clannaigsed na maen adchualumar.

(P) Saxus mac Negúa meic Alainius meic Ibaith meic
Magóc meic Iafeth Meic Náe, is úad Saxain. Emoth mac
Magóc, is úad fine thuaiscert an domuin. Barachán, a quo
Gaeidel, mac Eitheoir meic Bai meic Tai meic Barachain
meic Magoch. Aitheachtaig mac Magóch, is dia chloind-
sein na thuatha thangadar an Erinn ria nGaidelaib, .i.
Parrthalón mac Sera meic Sru meic Esrú meic Praimint
meic Aithechtaig meic meic (sic) Magóch meic Iafeth meic
Náe : ⁊ Neimid mac Adnomain meic Paim meic Thait meic
Sera meic Srú.   Ocus adberaid aroili do lebraib corab ar
slicht an meic do ťagaib Parrthalon thair(b) do Neimead,
.i. ar slicht Adla meic Parrthaloin.   Ocus clanda Neimid,
.i. Gaileoin ⁊ Fir Bolg ⁊ Fir Domnánd ⁊ Tuaith Dé Danund.
As dóib-sin do chan an file.

Magog mac an Iafeth . . . .

(a) At first written ⅁ (i.e., *tri* three) : afterwards c e was written flanking
the i, to turn the word into *ceitre* four.
(b) The *h*-dot doubtful.

Farrsaid, he was son of Baath s. Magog s. Iafeth. Others say however that Feinius Farrsaid was s. of Baath s. Ibath s. Gomer s. Iafeth.

(N) As for Ibath, one of the two sons of Magog, his son was Alainius. He had three sons, Airmen, Negua, Isicon. Airmen had five sons, Gotus, Uiligotus, Cebitus, Burgandus, Longbardus. Negua had four sons, Vandalus, Saxus, Bogardus, Longbardus. Isicon, the third son of Alainius, had four sons, Francus, Romanus, Albanus, *a quo* Albania in Asia Minor, and Albanactus s. Britan s. Silvius s. Ascanius s. Aeneas s. Anchises, *a quo* western Alba, and Britus, from whom are called the Islands of Britain.

(O) Then was the world divided into three divisions, Europe, Africa, Asia. Seventeen years before the scattering of the languages there came the first man of the seed of Iafeth into Europe, Alainius s. Ibath s. Magog s. Iafeth s. Noe. Alainius, of him are the Franks and the Romans. And his three sons came with him, Armen, Negua, Isicon : so that on the hither side they begat those sons of whom we have heard.

(P) Saxus s. Negua s. Alainius s. Ibath s. Magog s. Iafeth s. Noe, of him are the Saxons. Emoth s. Magog, of him is the people of the north of the world. Barachan, *a quo* the Gaedil, s. Etheor s. Bai s. Tai s. Barachan s. Magog. Aithechtaig s. Magog, of his progeny are the peoples who came into Ireland before the Gaedil—Parthalon s. Sera s. Sru s. Esru s. Praiment s. Aithechtaig s.[a] Magog s. Iafeth s. Noe : and Nemed s. Agnomain s. Paim s. Tat s. Sera s. Sru. Others of the books say that Nemed was of the family of the son whom Parthalon left in the east, Adla s. Parthalon. Also the children of Nemed, the Gaileoin and Fir Bolg and Fir Domnann and Tuatha De Danann. Of those the poet sang,

Poem no. IV.

(a) Disregarding the dittography in the text.

(Q) Is iad tra na cineada sin .i. clanda Iafeth, ra gabsad ferandus ⁊ flaithus na Heorpa uili, ⁊ tuaiscert-leithi na Haissia : ⁊ is iad sin cuig prim-chinéla deg chlainni Iafeth cona fo-chinelaib : ⁊ ra sealbsadar feranda imda isan n-Aissia, .i. o Sliab Mai ⁊ o Sliab Tur a tuaid co Sruth Danai ⁊ coruigi an Sceithia tuaiscertaig : ⁊ ra selbsad an Eoraip uili, coruigi an aigen muiridi fuineada Insi Bretan ⁊ connigi an Espain treuillig budeas, .i. Tuillslicht.   Da chlannaib Iafeth meic Náe connigi sin, cona prim-chinelaib ⁊ cona fo-chinelaib, ⁊ cona ngabalaib ⁊ cona ferandaib, itir Aissia ⁊ Eóraiph.

96. Na tri meic-si tra Náe ra thuirmsemar romaind .i. Sém ⁊ Cam ⁊ Iafeth : ria ndilinn rugtha an triur sin. Ocus adberaid araili co rugad mac do Nae iar ndilinn, .i. Eoinitus : ⁊ Éthán an rand feraind do gab, ⁊ as na tri randaib aili ra teibead a ferand. Ocus rob estrolagda maith he, iar n-a foglaim o athair, o Náe.

97. Coba bean Nae, is i ra fig édach ré cách iar ndilinn.

Eua ben Adaim, is i ra fig tonag di féin ⁊ do Adam ar tus, an tress la iar teacht a sruth Tibir diaid a n-aitrigi, iar n-a forchongar do Dia fuirri.

Catafola a n-ingen, rugad araen ré Cain, seitchi Phendain meic Adaim, is i ra figh édach ria chách. Is uimpi doronad an t-ed.

Iafeth mac Nae, is e ra seind cruit ⁊ organ ar tus iar ndilinn.

(a) Sem mac Náe, an cet goba ⁊ an cet cherd ⁊ an cet saer iar ndilinn.

Nae imorro, ra thindscain tirfrecar do denum, an cet bliadain iar ndilinn : .i. dorigni ar ⁊ búain, ⁊ do chlandustair fineamain.

Cam mac Nae imorro ranig snam ⁊ aircheadal ⁊ filidecht ar tus.

Ora airig tra Cam iarsin co tiefad an dili, ⁊ na faidi cá thirchartain co tiefa dílgend chlainni Adaim, tria fingail Chain for a braithrib, do rindi tri colamna ceithir-(b)slis, .i.

(a) The initial S is of an extravagant shape; it looks as though the scribe thought that it was a ꝋ.

(Q) Now these are those peoples, to wit the progeny of Iafeth, who took the territory and princedom of all Europe and of the northern side of Asia; and those are the fifteen chief people of the progeny of Iafeth, with their subordinate people. And they possessed many territories in Asia, namely from Mount Amanus and Mount Taurus northward to the river Don, and to Northern Scythia: and they possessed all Europe to the ocean of sea in the west of the island of Britain, and to three-cornered Spain in the south, i.e. the Astures. (?) Of the progeny of Iafeth son of Noe down to this, with their chief peoples and their subordinate peoples, their takings and their territories, both in Asia and in Europe.

96. As for the three sons of Noe that we have reckoned above, Sem, Ham, Iafeth: before the Flood were those three persons born. Others say that a son was born to Noe after the Flood, named Ionitus. Ethan was the portion of territory which he received: out of the other three portions was his portion selected. He was a good astrologer, having learnt it from his father Noe.

97. Coba, wife of Noe, she it is who wove raiment for every one after the Flood.

Eua wife of Adam, she it is who first wove an apron for herself and for Adam, on the third day after coming from the river Tiber (sic : lege Tigris) after their penance, when God had commanded it to her.

Catafola their daughter, who was born along with Cain, wife of Pendan son of Adam, she it is who wove raiment before anyone else : about her was the jealousy excited.

Iafeth son of Noe, it is he who first sounded a harp and an organ after the Flood.

Sem, son of Noe, the first smith, the first wright, the first carpenter after the Flood.

As for Noe, he began to work husbandry in the first year after the Flood. He made ploughing and reaping, and planted a vineyard.

Ham, son of Noe, first attained to swimming and poetry and bardism.

Now when Ham understood thereafter that the Flood should come, and the prophets were foretelling that a destruction of the progeny of Adam should come, by reason of Cain's kin-

(b) the ṡ sprs.

columan d'ael, ⁊ colaman do criaid, ⁊ colaman do chiaraig.
Ocus do sgrib intu scela na haimsiri cora mairdis iar ndilinn.
Ra millead an colaman aeil ⁊ an colaman criadh, ⁊ ra mair
an colaman cinrach. Conad he ra indis scela na haimsiri ria
ndilinn; ⁊ mairid iartain.

Olibana a ben-sidi, ⁊ is i ra cet-cum edach iar ndilinn.

98. ¹Grēcus mac Iathfeth, is ²ūad in Grēg ³Mōr ⁊ in
Grēg ⁴Beg ⁊ Grēg na ⁵Halaxandria.   Espānus mac
⁶Iathfeth, ō tait ⁷Espāndai. Gomerus mac ⁸Iathfeth,¹
dā ⁹mac ¹⁰lais, .i. ¹¹Emoth ⁊ Ibath.   ¹²Emoth, is ¹³ūad
fine thūaiscert in domain.¹³   ¹⁴Ibath, dā ¹⁵mac ¹⁶lais,
.i. ¹⁷Bodb ⁊ Baath.   ¹⁸Bodb, ¹⁹diar bo mac ²⁰Dohe.
Elenus ²¹mac ²²Dohe, trī ²³meic ²⁴lais, .i. ²⁵Airmen,
Negūa, Isicon.   ²⁶Airmen ²⁷imorro, ²⁸cōic meic ²⁹lais,
³⁰.i. ³¹Gutus, ³²Cibidus, ³³Uiligothus, ³⁴Burgandus,
³⁵Longbardus.   ³⁶Neagūa ³⁷imorro, trī ³⁸meic ³⁹leis, ⁴⁰.i.
⁴¹Saxus, ⁴²Boarus, Uandalus.   Hisicon ⁴³imorro, ⁴⁴in
⁴⁵treas mac ⁴⁶Elenuis, ⁴⁷ceithri ⁴⁸meic ⁴⁹lais. ⁵⁰.i.
Romanus, Frangcus, ⁵¹Britus, Albanus. · Is ⁵²hē in
tAlbanus sin ⁵³rogab ⁵⁴Albain ⁵⁵ar ⁵⁶tūs ⁵⁷cona ⁵⁸chloind,
⁊ is ⁵⁹ūad ⁶⁰ainmnigther ⁶¹Albu : ⁶²co ro indarb ⁶³a
⁶⁴brāthair ⁶⁵tar Muir ⁶⁶nIcht, ⁶⁷conad ūad Albanaich
leatha Hoidia.

99. ¹Magoc ²mac ³Iathfed, is ⁴dia ⁵chloind-⁶sen na
⁷tūatha ⁸tāncadar ⁹in ¹⁰Ērinn ¹¹‡ ar tūs ‖ ¹²rīa
¹³nGāeidelaib, .i. ¹⁴Parrthalōn mac Sera meic Srū meic

98. ¹⁻¹ om. β¹²: Greacus m. Iafet, &c., β   ² uadh β   ³ mhoir β
⁴ bheg β   ⁵ Halaxandreach β   ⁶ Iafeth β   ⁷ Easpain β
⁸ Iafeth β   ⁹ mhac β⁰¹²   ¹⁰ leis β¹²   ¹¹ Eamot β¹²   ¹² om. β¹²
¹³⁻¹³ uadh finidh thuaisciort in domhain β uatha fine tuaitsciort (·ths-β²)
in domhuin β¹²   ¹¹ Iobat β¹²   ¹⁵ mhac β⁰¹²   ¹⁶ leis β¹²
¹⁷ Boidhbh β⁰¹²   ¹⁵ om. M Boidhbh β⁰¹²   ¹⁹ dar β¹²   ²⁰ Dothe β
Tote β¹²   ²¹ mhac β¹²   ²² Dothe β Dote β¹²   ²³ mic β¹²
²⁴ leis β¹   ²⁵ Armen β⁰¹²   ²⁶ Armen M β¹²   ²⁷ dono β om. β¹²
²⁸ cuig mic β¹²   ²⁹ leis β¹   ³⁰ om. .i. β¹²   ³¹ Gotus β⁰¹²   ³² om. M
³³ -gotus M β⁰¹²   ³⁴ -ntus M β⁰¹²   ³⁵ -bh- β Longabairdus β¹²
³⁶ Negua β⁰¹²   ³⁷ om. β⁰¹²   ³⁸ mic β¹²   ³⁹ lais β⁰²   ⁴⁰ om. .i. β⁰¹
⁴¹ Saesus β¹²   ⁴² Boairus β¹²   ⁴³ om. β¹²   ⁴⁴ in y/c M : an β¹²

murder against his brethren, he made three four-sided columns, one of lime, one of clay, and one of wax. And he wrote upon them the histories of the [antediluvian] age, so that they should endure after the Flood. The columns of lime and of clay were destroyed, and the column of wax remained: and this it was that related the histories of the Age before the Flood, and it survives thereafter.

Oliuana his [Iafeth's] wife, it is she who first fashioned raiment after the Flood.

98. Grecus s. Iafeth, of him is Graecia Magna and Graecia Parva and Alexandrian Greece. Espanus s. Iafeth, from whom are the Hispani. Gomer s. Iafeth had two sons, Emoth and Ibath. Emoth, of him is the northern people of the world. Ibath had two sons, Bodb and Baath. Bodb, who had a son Dohe. Elenus s. Dohe had three sons, Airmen, Negua, Isicon. As for Airmen, he had five sons, Gutus, Cebidus, Uiligothus, Burgundus, Longbardus. Negua moreover had three sons, Saxus, Boarus, Uandalus. Isicon moreover, one of the three sons of Elenus, had four sons, Romanus, Francus, Britus, Albanus. This is that Albanus who first took Alban, he and his children, and of him is Alba named: so he drove his brother across the sea of Icht, and from him are the Albanians of Latium of Italy.

99. Magog son of Iafeth, of his children are the peoples who came into Ireland at first before the Gaedil, namely Partholon s. Sera s. Sru s. Esru s.

---

[45] tres β thres β[12] [46] Heloni β[012] [47] cethri β[9] ceithre β[12]
[48] mic β[12] [49] leis β [50] om. β[012] [51] Briotus β[12] [52] e au β[012]
[53] roghabh β[012] [54] -uin β[12] [55] air β[12] [56] ttus β [57] gonadh β[12]
[58] cloind M chloinn β[012] [59] nadha β uadh β[12] [60] -ghthair β
-ghther β[12] [61] Alba β[12] [62] gor iondairb β gur hionarbadh β[12]
(-airb- β[2]) [63] ins. Britus β Briotus β[12] [64] bhr- β[012] [65] tair β[2]
[66] nIocht β[2] [67] gonadh uaidh Albanaigh β[012] (conadh β[1])

99. [1] Magoth β Magog β[12] [2] mhac β[12] [3] Iafeth β Iaphet β[12]
[4] da β[12] [5] chloinn β[012] [6] sin β[12] [7] tuathadh β[12] [8] thangadair β
tangadar β[12] [9] an β[012] [10] Eirinn β[12] [11] om. β[012]
[12] re β[13] [13] nGaedhealaibh β nGaoidhil β[12] [14-11] om. β[012]

[19]Easrū meic Gāeidil Glais meic Niūil meic Fēiniusa Farrsaig meic Bathatha meic Magog meic Iathfeth meic Nae : no[14] [15]Parrthalon mac [16]Sera [17]meic [18]Srū meic [19]Easrū meic [20]Pramint meic [21]Aitheachda meic [22]Magoth meic [23]Iathfeth[24, 25]. Ocus [26]Neimead mac [27]Adnoimin meic [28]Phaim meic Thait meic [29]Seara meic Srū [30]meic Easrū, ⁊rl.[30]. [31]Ocus Clanda Nemid, [32].i. [33]Galeōin ⁊ Fir [34]Bole ⁊ Fir [35]Domnand ⁊ [36]Tūatha Dē Danand.

[37]Ocus fineada Cloindi Beothaig meic Iarmuineōil Fatha meic Neimid, .i. Tūatha Taiden ⁊ Domnannaig dia roibi Conall Cruachain, ⁊ Clanda Umoir, ⁊ Cruithnich na Cruachna, ⁊ aicmeada Slebi Uiri, dia rabadar na riga, .i. Tindi mac Conrach ⁊ Mac Cecht ⁊ Fir Chraibi, dia roibi Tindi mac Conrach, ⁊ Eochaid Dala. Ocus airmid colaig corob d'iarsma na fincadach sin Clanna Morna ⁊ sentuatha Condacht olchena.[37]

100. [1]Conad do na gabāil sin Parrthalōin ⁊ Nemid, ⁊ do genelaigib na tūath sin olchena[1], do chanad so—

Magog mac an Iafeth . . . .

[2]Scuirem do chlannaib Nāe ⁊ dia n-imthechtaib. Adfēdsam do chlannaib Gāeidil bodesta ⁊ dia n-imtechtaib ⁊ dia ngabhālaib.[2]

Miniugad Gabal nErenn.

These two paragraphs are all that represents § I in Min.

μΛ 25 γ 40   μR 90 δ 14

101. Mīniugudh Gabal nĒrenn, ⁊ a [1]senchais, ⁊ a rēmend [2]rīgraidi, annso sīs, [3]⁊ ethre i mbēolo aissneisen, ⁊ labra ōg [4]dondni remunn, ō [5]thosuch [6]in libair [7]anūas co tici [8]so, *ut* [9]*dicit historia.* Hybernia

[15] Partholon β Pairrthalon β[12] : mhac β[12]   [16] Searra β Serra β[12]
[17] mhic β[12] (*hic et semper*)   [18] Sruth β[12]   [19] Esru β[012]   [20] Braimint β Framint β[12]   [21] Eachachta β[012]   [22] Magog β[12]   [23] Iafeth β Iaphet β[12]   [24] me Seara me Sru *ins. and erased* β   [25] *ins.* mic Naoi β'
mic Noe β[12]   [26] Neimheadh β is uaid (uadh β²) Neimhedh mhac β[12]
[27] Aghnomain β[012] (mh β[12])   [28] Paimm. Tait β[012]   [29] Sera β[12]
[30-30] *om.* β[012]   [31] ⁊ Clann Neimeadh β ⁊ is o Neimedh β[12]   [32] ⁊ M

Gaidel Glas s. Nel s. Feinius Farsaid s. Bathath s. Magog s. Iafeth s. Noe : or Partholon s. Sera s. Sru s. Esru s. Brament s. Aithechda s. Magog s. Iafeth. And Nemed s. Agnomain s. Pamp s. Tat s. Sera s. Sru s. Esru &c. And the progeny of Nemed, to wit the Galeoin, the Fir Bolg, the Fir Domnann, and the Tuatha De Danann.

And the families of the progeny of Bethach s. Iarbonel *Fáith* s. Nemed, i.e. the Tuatha Taiden and the Domnannaig, of whom was Conall of Cruachu, and the progeny of Umor, and the Cruithne of Cruacha, and septs of Sliab Fuirri of whom were the kings i.e. Tinde s. Conri, and Mac Cecht, and the Fir Chraibi, of whom was Tinde s. Conri and Eochu Dula. And learned men reckon that of the relics of these families were the Clanna Morna and the old populations of Connachta in general.

100. So that of the said Takings of Partholon and of Nemed, and of the genealogies of those peoples in general, was this sung—

Poem no. IV.

We shall leave off from the progeny of Noe and their adventures. We shall tell now of the progeny of Gaeidel and of their adventures and their Takings.

---

101. An explanation of the Takings of Ireland, and of her history, and of her royal roll, here below; and a recapitulation of the narratives, and a clear statement of the matter before us, from the beginning

---

om. β[12]   [33] Gaileoin β   [34] Bolg β Bholg β[12]   [35] Domhnaind β Domhnann β[12]   [36] Tuat β[2]   [37-37] *om.* β[012]

100. [1-1] *om.* β[012] amhuil asbeart in fili β, do reir in file β[12]   [2-2] *not in* M

101. *This and the following matter down to the poem* Gaedel Glas ótait Gáedil *missing from* μV. *The text of the missing portion printed from* μ_A, *with variations from* μR *unless otherwise stated.*   [1] séanchas   [2] -raide innso   [3] ┐ ethre *om.* μ_A: ambeolu aisneisin μR   [4] duinn remund μ_A   [5] -ach   [6] ind   [7] *om.*   [8] indso   [9] dicunt

insola [10]possita est in occidente; sicut [11]Ade Paradisus
in australi plaga orientis [12]poissitus est, ita Hibernia
in [13]septimprionali parte, apud [14]occasum sita est.
Sic similes [15]sunt natura humi[16], sicut similes sunt
ambo locis in orbe : quoniam sicut absque bestia
Paradisus est, ita periti Hiberniam non habere
serpentem uel leonem uel ranam uel murem nocentem
uel draconem uel [17]scorpium uel [18]unum noxium
animal nisi [19]lupum tantum testantur. Hibernia ergo
dicitur 'insola [20]occasus.' 'Hyberoe' Grece, 'occasum'
[21]dicitur Latine; 'nia' autem uel [22]'nyon' Grece,
[23]'insola' Latine dicitur. ‡ [24]Hybernia autem proxima
[25]Britanie insola : [26]spacone[(a)] terrarum angustior, sed
[27]situ fecundior. Hoc[(b)] ab Affrico in Boriam
porrigitur, cuius partes priores in Hiberniam,[(c)] ‡' id
est in [28]Espaniam ||' et Cantabricum Occianum
intendunt; unde et Hibernia dicta. Scotia[(d)] autem
dicta, quia a Scotorum gentibus colitur. Illic nulla
[29]anguis, auis rara, apes[(e)] nulla : adeo, ‡' non sic in
hoc tempore ||', ut aduectos inde [30]pulueris[(f)] [31]seu
lapillos, si quis alibi sparserit inter apiaria,[(g)]
examina fauos deserunt ||.   ‡ Scoti autem [32]a Scota,
filia regis [33]Egipti Pharaonis, sunt dicti, que [34]fuit
[35]Nelii uxor.   ‡' [36]Phoeni autem a Foenio [37]Fariseo
dicuntur ||'.   [38]Scoti autem idem et Picti, a picto
[39]corpore, ‡' quasi [40]scissi ||', eo quod [41]aculeis ferreis
cum atramento variarum figurarum [42]stigmate
adnotentur ||.   [43]Heriu [44]dono ab [45]heroibus nominata
est.   [46]‡ Sudet qui legit ‡.

<hr>

historici   [10] poisita   [11] Adae   [12] poisitus   [13] septim trionaili
[14] occassum, the first c sprs. yc μR   [15] om.   [16] ins. sunt   [17] scorpiam :
-puim corrected later μ₍   [18] unam   [19] lupam   [20] occassus   [21] dicunt
[22] nyaon   [23] innsola (Latine sprs. yc μR)   [24] Hibernia   [25] Britaniae,
the t sprs. yc μR   [26] spacō μ₍ spatio μR   [27] sutu   [28] Hispaniam
[29] angis   [30] pulueres   [31] seuo lapilos μ₍   [32] nearly a whole line
of writing, probably written in error, erased here.   [33] Aegipti Faraonis
[34] fuit sprs. yc μR   [35] Neli ux(or sprs. yc. μR)   [36] Foeni   [37] Faisiseo μ₍
[38] Scotiorum μ₍   [39] corpoire   [40] scisi   [41] acules ferres μ₍ aculeis
feraeis μR   [42] stimate   [43] Heri μ₍ Hereo μR   [44] daua   [45] h-ioribus μ₍

of the foregoing book down to this, *ut dicit historia*.
The island of Ireland is situated in the west; as the
Paradise of Adam is situated on the southern coast of
the east, so Ireland is in the northern portion, toward
the west. Those lands are as similar by nature, as
they are similar by their positions on the earth : for
as Paradise hath no noxious beast, so the learned
testify that Ireland hath no serpent, lion, toad,
injurious rat, dragon, scorpion, nor any hurtful beast,
save only the wolf. And so Ireland is called "the
island of the west" : "Hyberoc"(h) in Greek is called
"occasum" in Latin; 'nia' or 'nyon' in Greek is
called "insula" in Latin. [Now Hibernia is next to
the island of Britannia : in extent of territory it is
narrower, but in soil it is more fertile. This stretches
northward from Africa, and its foremost parts tend
toward Iberia, { that is, Spain } and the Bay of
Biscay; whence also Hibernia takes its name. It is
called Scotia also, because it is inhabited by the nations
of the Scots. Within it is no serpent, rare bird,
nor bees; to such an extent—{ not at this time } --
that if anyone were to scatter in any place amongst
beehives dust or gravel carried from thence, the
swarms would desert the honeycombs.] [The Scoti
are named from Scota, daughter of Pharao King of
Egypt, who was wife of Nelins : { They are called Feni
from Fenius Farsaid {. The Scots are the same as
the Picts, so called from their painted body, { as
though *scissi*{, inasmuch as they are marked with an
impression of a variety of devices by means of iron
needles and ink.] Moreover the country is called
Ériu from the heroes. [Let him who readeth
perspire !]

46 *this is a gloss, marginal in* μ∧ *expressed by initials* s.q.l. *in* μR, s.q¹.
1;. *in* μ∧

(a) Read *spatio*.   (b) Read *hacc.*
(c) Read *Hiberiam*, and omit the preceding *in*.
(d) Read *Scotia autem, quia ab Scotorum gentibus colitur, appellata.*
(e) Read *apis.*   (f) Read *pulucres.*   (g) Read *alucaria.*
(h) The final *c* must be read as a Greek *sigma*: 'hyberoc' is meant for
ἔσπεοος, as 'nyon' for νῆσον, accusative of νῆσος.

102. Ō ¹thrib macaib ²Nōi trā ro līnait trī ³ranna in talman, .i. Eorpa, ⁴Affricca, Assia.   Sem mac ⁵Nōe dana rogab ⁶ind Aissia, ⁊ secht cenēla fichit ⁷ñad innti. Cam in ⁸Affraice ⁊ tricha ⁹cenēl ñadh ¹⁰inte.   ¹¹Iafeth ¹²mac Nōi ¹³ind Eoraip ⁊ ¹⁴in tūaiscert Aissia, ¹⁵⊣ cōic ¹⁶cenēla dēc ¹⁷ñad intib : *de quibus hoc* ¹⁸*carmen*.

Sem rogab i n-Aisia n-ait . . .
Tricha mac mīn monar nglē . . .

O Iafeth dana in t-airter-¹⁹thñascert ²⁰.i. Scithecda ⊣ Armenndai, ⊣ lucht na ²¹Hassia Biece ⊣ ergabāla ⊣ ²²ciniuda nEorpa uile, co lucht na ²³n-indsi atāit frie aness ⊣ atūaidh ⊣ anīar, ²⁴⊣ ōthā Slēibe ²⁵Riphi atūaidh co ²⁶trāigh na Hespāine. Ocht meic ²⁷trā la Iafeth, ²⁸.i. Magoth—ba sē ²⁹in t-ochtmadh mac.   Dā mac ³⁰dono la ³¹Magoch .i. ³²Ibadh ⊣ Baath.   Ō ³³Ibadh īarom rīg Romān.   Mac dono ³⁴do Baadh, Fēnius ³⁵Farrsaid ō ³⁶fuilet Scithecda, ⊣ ³⁷dia sīl Gāidil.   Ō Ibad ³⁸Fraince, Romāin, Saxain, ⊣ Brettain ⊣ Albandai. Ō Magoch mac Iafeth ³⁹didiu, na tūatha rogabsat Ērinn rīa ⁴⁰nGāidelaib, .i. ⁴¹Parthalōn mac ⁴²Sera meic Srū meic Esru meic ⁴³Briamin meic Fathecht meic ⁴⁴Baaidh meic ⁴⁵Magoch meic Iafeth meic Nōe : Nemed mac ⁴⁶Adhnomain dana meic Phaim meic Thait meic ⁴⁷Sera meic Srū : ⊣ clanna ⁴⁸Nemhid, .i. Gaileōin ⊣ Fir ⁴⁹Bolgc ⊣ Fir Domnann. *De quibus* ⁵⁰*Finntan cecinit*.

Magog mac an Iafeth.

---

102. ¹ tri   ² Noe   ³ randa an   ⁴ ⊣ Africa ⁊ Assia   ⁵ Nae tra ⁶ in Assia   ⁷ uada innte   ⁸ Affraic   ⁹ gen uada   ¹⁰ *om.*   ¹¹ Iafedh μ∧ ¹² *om.* mac Noi   ¹³ in Eoraip   ¹⁴ *om.* in   ¹⁵ *om.* ⊣   ¹⁶ gn *in both* MSS.   ¹⁷ uada inntib   ¹⁸ cairmen   ¹⁹ tuaise-   ²⁰ *om.* .i. : Scithecdai ⊣ Armendai   ²¹ Haisia Bice   ²² cineda na Heorpa uili: ciniuda *miswritten* cinuida μ∧, *and a dash put over the first stroke of the* u *to correct the error*   ²³ ninnsi tainait fria anes ⊣ atuaitn

102. Now of the three sons of Noe were filled the three divisions of the earth, Europe, Africa, Asia. Sem s. Noe settled in Asia, and twenty-seven nations were descended from him therein. Ham in Africa, and thirty nations from him therein. Iafeth s. Noe in Europe and in the north of Asia, and fifteen nations from him therein: *de quibus hoc carmen,*

Poem no. II.
Poem no. III.

From Iafeth is the north east, Scythians, Armenians, and the people of Asia Minor, and the colonists and nations of all Europe, with the people of the islands that are over against it from the south, north, and west, and from the Riphean Mountain out of the north to the shore of Spain. Iafeth had eight sons, one of whom was Magog: he was the eighth son. Magog had two sons, Ibath and Baath. From Ibath afterwards came the rulers of the Romans. Baath had a son Fenius Farsaid, from whom are the Scythians: of his seed is Gaedil. From Ibath are the Franks, Romans, Saxons, Britons, and Albanians. From Magog son of Iafeth are the peoples who took Ireland before the Gaedil, Partholon s. Sera s. Sru s. Esru s. Brainient s. Aithech s. Baath s. Magog s. Iafeth s. Noe: Nemed s. Agnomain s. Paim s. Tait s. Sera s. Sru: and the progeny of Nemed, the Gaileoin, the Fir Bolg, and the Fir Donmann. *De quibus Finntan cecinit,*

Poem no. IV.

---

²⁴ *om.* ꝛ   ²⁵ Ripe atuaid   ²⁶ traig (g *sprs. yc* µR) na Haespaine   ²⁷ *om.* tra la   ²⁸ ꝛ Magoeh   ²⁹ an tochtmad (*om.* mac)   ³⁰ *om.* dono   ³¹ Bmagoe   ³² Baad ꝛ Ibad   ³³ Ibad   ³⁴ da Baad   ³⁵ Farsaich   ³⁶ fuil   ³⁷ *ins.* is   ³⁸ Fraine ꝛ Romain ꝛ S. ꝛ Bretain ꝛ Albanda   ³⁹ *om.* didiu   ⁴⁰ nGaidil- *and om.* .i.: nGail- µₐ   ⁴¹ Partol-   ⁴² Soera   ⁴³ Bramin   ⁴⁴ Baaid   ⁴⁵ Magoich   ⁴⁶ Agnomain m. Paim m. Tait   ⁴⁷ Sera m. Stera m. Stru   ⁴⁸ Nemid   ⁴⁹ Bole   ⁵⁰ hoc carmen dicitur Finntan *the last two words in marg.*

THE VERSE TEXTS OF SECTION I.

I.

R¹ ⸏ 7 (l. 1 β 8 : F 1 β 28). R² ⸏ 15 (V 1 γ 23 : E 1 β 38 :
P 1 β 32). R³ ¶ 88 (β 34, 14 : β¹ 34 . 30 : β² 10 . 15 :
M 267 γ 47 : H 102 a 30).

1.   ¹Slūag nād ²chlōe ³cūa-chel,
            ⁴Nōe ⁵nīr ⁶bo ⁷niath-lēn,
            ⁸scēl ⁹co ¹⁰ngrāin ¹¹ro glēad gēr—
            ¹²Sēm, Cam ocus ¹³Iāfēth.

2.   ¹Mnā ²cen ³mīdend, ⁴mōr-řeba,   5
            ōs dilind ⁵cen ⁶dībada :
            ⁷Coba, ⁸brīgda ⁹in ¹⁰bāin-ela,
            ¹¹Olla, ¹²Oliua, Olīuana.

1. ¹ sluaig FR³ H sluagh V sluace P   ² claoi EP chle β⁰¹² clae MH
³ gua-chel LR² ecnad chel F conad chel M conadachel H   ⁴ ins.
ac M, ag H : Naoi E Nai P Nae MH   ⁵ níor β⁰¹²   ⁶ ba L bu V
bho β bhodh β¹²   ⁷ miad-len LR³ midathlen F niath-nel VE matha-nel
P niadh-lén β⁰¹²   ⁸ sgel FE see P sceal β⁰¹²   ⁹ gan β¹²   ¹⁰ ngradh
VE ngrad P ghrádh β⁰¹²   ¹¹ ro gleaid F rongleath gen V roglē gen
E rongleadh gen P ro gleodhagh *and om.* ger β⁰¹²   ¹² S. is C. is I. F

II.

R¹ ¶ 8 (L 1 β 14 : F 1 γ 2). Min ⸏ 102 (μΛ 25 δ 23;
p. R 91 a 23). R³ ⸏ 89 (β 34 . 29 : β¹ 34 . 47 : β² 10 . 29 :
M 267 δ 15 : H 102 a 39).

        ¹Sem ²rogab ³i ⁴n-Aisia n-ait :
        ⁵Cam ⁶cona ⁷chlaind ⁸sin ⁹Afraic :   10
        ¹⁰Iafeth uasal ¹¹is a ¹²maic,
        ¹³siat rogabsat ¹⁴i n-Eoraip.

¹ Semh β   ² dogab F μΛ H rogab *dittographed* μR roghabh β⁰¹²
² rogob M   ³ ind μΛ an β H ina β¹²   ⁴ n-Assia L Aissia F μΛ β H
Asia μR β¹²   ⁵ Camh β   ⁶ gonadh β¹ .i. β²   ⁷ claind L chainn μR
cl- μΛ H cloinn β chloinn β¹ clann β² cloind M   ⁸ in μΛ μR san

THE VERSE TEXTS OF SECTION I.

I.

1. A host that a wintry death would not subdue,
Noe, there was no hero's weakness,
a story with horror has been made clear with
keenness—
Sem, Ham, and Iafeth.

2. Women without evil colour, great excellences,
above the Flood without extinctions,
Coba, vigorous was the white swan,
Olla, Oliva, Olivana.

β^{012} H   [13] Iafedh V Semh Camh (⁊ yc) Iatafen E Iaphet β^{12} (*not* β)
Iathfeth M
2.   [1] nnaa L   [2] ceōmtin P, gen β gan β^{12} can H   [3] mideng F
midhen β mhidhen β^{12} mieing H   [4] moreua F morfeba V morfeabha
E morfephai, P mór Ebha β níor Ebha β^1 nior obha β^2 moreba M
moireaba H   [5] gan EP β^{012} can H   [6] digbada VH dibhada β
diobhadha β^{12} [7] Cobba L Cobha E β^{012} [8] brighdha VP brigha β
brioghdha β^{12} brig H   [9] an H   [10] baneala FE bancla V mbaineala E
banealai P baneala β ben aladh β^{12} [11] Ola *changed by re-inker to*
Ollai, P   [12] Oliba Olibana L Olliua Oilibana E Olipa Olipā P Oliua
Oliuana β Olliva Olivana β^1 Oilliua Olivana β^2 Oliba Olibana M Oliu
Olibana H

II.

Sem settled in pleasant Asia;
Ham with his progeny in Africa;
noble Iafeth and his sons,
it is they who settled in Europe.

β^{01} H ann β^2 sa nAfraic M   [9] Affraicc L μ_Λ Adffraic F Aifraic β^1
Aifric β^2 Afraicc H   [10] Iafiath F Iafedh μ_Λ Iaphet β^{01} Iathfed M
[11] *om*. is μR   [12] mc F, mcc μ_Λ meic μR M mhac β^{012} [13] is iad
dogab sin F hite rotrebsat μ_Λ ite rotrebsat μR is iad roghabhsat Eoraip
β^{012} (roghabh in Euroip β^{01}) is iad rogob an MH (dogab an H)   [14] sin
Eoraip F: *om*. in μ_Λ

III.

R¹ ¶8 (*not traceable in* L : F 1 γ 10). Min ¶102 (μΛ 25 δ 25 ;
μ R 91 α 25).   R³ ¶ 92 (β 34 . 43 : β¹ 35 . 14 : β² 11 . 11 :
M 267 δ 38 : H 102 β 19).

¹Tricha ²mac ³mīn, ⁴monar² nglē,
⁵einsit ō ⁶Cham ⁷mac ⁸Naē,
a ⁹secht ¹⁰fichit ¹¹fil ō ¹²Sēm,   15
¹³is a ¹⁴cōic dēc ō ¹⁵Iafēth.

¹ Triocha β triothchat β¹² (-ad β²)   ²⁻² cenel comul μΛ chenel
comol μR   ³ mind F   ⁴ is rad MH   ⁵ einnsit F cinset μR β¹²

IV.

R¹ ¶ 10 (L *first two and half quatrains frayed away*
1 β 47 : F 1 δ 8).   Min ¶ 102 (μΛ 25 δ 42 : μR 91 β 10).
R³ ¶ 95, 100 (β 35 . 14 : β¹ 35 . 30 : β² 11 . 31 : M 268 α 35 :
H 99 α 50).

1.   ¹Magog ²mac an ³Iafeth,
⁴atā cinnti a ⁵chland :
⁶dīb ⁷Parthalōn ⁸Banba,
⁹ro bo ¹⁰chadla a ¹¹band.   20

2.   Ba ¹dīb ²Nemed ³nōithech,
mac ⁴Agnomain ⁵ōen :
⁶ba dīb ⁷Gand, ⁸dīb ⁹Genand,
¹⁰Sēngand, ¹¹Slāine ¹²sōer.

3.   ¹Cland ²Eladan ³imda,
⁴fa dīb ⁵Bres, ⁶can brēig :   25
mac ⁷Eladan ⁸arm-gāith,
⁹meic ¹⁰Delbāith ¹¹meic ¹²Nōit.

1. ¹ Magoth LF Magoeh Min Magoc MH   ² mhac β²
³ Iaphet β¹² Iathfeth MH (in ¶ 100)   ⁴ ata cinti F atascinnte μΛ
ataichinte μR ataithchinte β atait chinte β¹ tait cinte β² ad aithindti
M adaithinti H   ⁵ chlann F Min β¹ clann β⁰²   ⁶ ins. ropa μR :
dibh β diobh β¹²   ⁷ Parrtolonn F Parrthalon μΛ β¹² MH Partolon μR
Purtaloin β   ⁸ Banubha β Banbha β¹²   ⁹ do bo F ro po μΛ ro
ba μR do bu β⁰¹² do ba H   ¹⁰ chalma μΛ cadla μR acadla β¹²   ¹¹ bann
F Min bhand β bhann β¹²
2. ¹ dhibh β diobh β¹²   ² Nemid F μR H Nemedh μΛ Neimhendh
β⁰¹² Nemead M   ³ naethach F naitech μΛ noethech μR naetheach β⁰¹²
(-ach β¹²) noitheach M naideach H   ⁴ Agnumaid F Adnomain μΛ H

III.

Thirty sleek sons, a brilliant fact,
they sprang from Ham son of Noe,
twenty-seven who are from Sem,
and fifteen from Iafeth.

chiusiat β einsed M ciunsed H   [6] Cam μR   [7] mcc μᴧ   [8] Noe
μᴧμR β⁰¹² Nace H   [9] ocht μᴧμR seacht H   [10] fidhchet β¹ fidhet β²
[11] ar sin F nad o Sem μᴧμR (uadh μᴧ) fuil β⁰¹² dib H   [12] Sem β⁰¹ μᴧ M
[13] om. is F μᴧ M in β⁰¹² H   [14] .u. deg F dó déc μR cuig deag β cuig
deg β¹² H cuic dccc M   [15] Iafedh μᴧ Iaphet β¹ Japhet β² Iatfedh M

IV.

1. Magog son of Iafeth,
   there is certainty of his progeny:
   of them was Parthalon of Banba—
   decorous was his achievement.

2. Of them was noble Nemed
   son of Agnomain, unique;
   of them were Gand and Genand,
   Sengand, free Slaine.

3. The numerous progeny of Elada,
   of them was Bres, no untruth:
   son of Elada expert in arms,
   son of Delbaeth son of Net.

Agnomhain β¹² Agnomen M   [5] aen F μᴧ ain β⁰¹² aein H   [6] om. ba
dib μR: ba dhibh β ba diobh β¹²   [7] Gann F μR β¹²   [8] is μᴧ dibh β
diobh β¹²   [9] Genan F Genann μᴧ Gaenann μR Ganann β¹²   [10] Seangann
μᴧ Sengann μR M Scangand β H Sengan β¹²   [11] Slaigne β¹ Slaingne
β² Slaene M Slane H   [12] saer F μᴧ MH saor β⁰¹²
   3. [1] clann F β⁰¹² clanna μR clauda H   [2] Eladhan F Ealadain
μᴧ β¹ M Elatha μR Ealadhain β⁰²   [3] imdha μᴧ β iomdha β¹²: om. μR
[4] ba Min β⁰¹² H   [5] Bress Min Breas β M   [6] gan breice μᴧ cen
breic μR gan bhreig β⁰¹² (br- β²) cen breg M   [7] Eladain μᴧ M
Elathain μR Eladhain β Ealadhain β¹²   [8] Telgaith μᴧ -ghaith β¹²
[9] mhic β¹²   [10] Delbaeith μR Dealbhaidh β⁰¹ Dealbaith β² MH (-dh β²)
[11] mic β⁰¹² (mh- β¹) Neid FH β   [12] Neitt μᴧ

4.   [1]Meic [2]Indai [3]meic [4]Alldai—
       [5]Allda [6]ba [7]mac [8]Tait,   30
       [9]meic [10]Thabuirn [11]meic [12]Eno.
       [11]meic [13]Baith, [14]Ebaith [15]ait.

5.   [1]Meic [2]Bethaig, [3]meic [4]Iardain,
       [5]meic [6]Nemid [7]hūi [8]Phāim :
       [9]Pāimp [10]meic [11]Thait [12]meic [13]Sera   35
       [14]meic [15]Srū, [16]Braimin [17]bāin.[15]

6.   [1]Braimin [2]meic [3]Aithechta
       [4]meic [5]Magog, [6]mōr [7]blad,
       [8]ro-bās a n-a [9]n-aimsir
       [10]comthaidbsin [11]ri [12]Mag.   40

4. [1] mac β^{012} [2] Innui L Indui $\mu_\wedge$ Inndui μR India β^{12} [3] mac β
mic β^{12} [4] Alldui L μR Allai F $\mu_\wedge$ MH Alla β^{012} [5] Alldui L Min
Alli F Allai β MH Allaidh β^{12} [6] fa MH   [7] mēc̄ $\mu_\wedge$ [8] Taitt L $\mu_\wedge$
Taid β [9] mic β^{012} [10] Thabairnn F Tabuirn $\mu_\wedge$ Tabuirnn μR
Tabairn β^{012} Thabairn M   [11] mic β mhic β^{12} (bis)   [12] sic LF
Ceno Min, Enna β H Eanna β^{12} Enda M   [13] Baath L β^{12} Baaith $\mu_\wedge$ β
MH Baaid μR   [14] ins. meic L Min MH, mic β mhic β^{12}: Ebath L
Ebaid F Ibaith $\mu_\wedge$ Magoich μR Ebhaith β Eabhaith β^{12} [15] aitt L
$\mu_\wedge$ H Baaith μR
5. [1] om. meic Min; mac β mhic β^{12} [2] Beothaig FM Bethach Min,
Beothaigh β^{02} Beothagh β^{1} [3] ins. ba Min; mac Min mic β^{012}
[4] Iarbaneoil $\mu_\wedge$ Iarboneol μR Iarbhoneoil β Iarbonel β^{2} -boneil M
-boinel H   [5] mic β^{012} (mh- β^{1})   [6] Neimid FM Neimhidh β
Neimhed β^{1} -mhedh β^{2} [7] hó L o F hua $\mu_\wedge$ ua β^{012} hu M   [8] Paimp
LF Paim μR M Phaimp β Poimp β^{12} [9] Paim L (yc in marg.), also
$\mu_\wedge$ MH Paimp β Poimp β^{12} [10] mac β^{012} (mh- β^{1})   [11] Thaitt L

V.

R[2] ¶ 19 (V 1 δ 9 : E 1 γ 21 : P 2 a 13 : D from quatrain
10, 3 a 1). R[3] ¶ 86 (M 267 a 1 : H 101 a 36). Also collated,
copy in Book of Ui Maine (U) 38 a 24.

1.   [1]Athair [2]cāich, [3]Coimsid [4]Nime,
       [5]in Rī [6]ūasal [7]ainglige,
       ār [8]Cuingid, ār [9]Coimde, ār [10]Ceud
       [11]cen [12]tūs, cen erich, cen [13]forcend.

1. [1] atair U   [2] chaich M caith U   [3] coimsidh (the second i
and the dot of the d due to re-inker) P coimsich M coimsig H   [4] nimi

4.   S. Inda, s. Allda—
Allda who was s. Tat,
s. Tabarn s. Enda,
s. Baath, [son of] pleasant Ibath.

5.   S. Bethach s. Iardan
s. Nemed grandson of Paimp :
Pamp s. Tat s. Sera
s. Sru s. white Braiment.

6.   Of Braiment s. Aithecht,
s. Magog, great in renown :
there happened in their time
a joint appearance against a Plain.

Tait F μR β¹² H Taitt μ∧ Taid β   ¹² mic β⁰¹²   ¹³ Sera M
Seara β H Serra β¹²   ¹⁴ om. meic μ∧ : mac β mic β¹²   ¹⁵⁻¹⁵ Easru
ain β²   ¹⁶ ins. meic L μR M H, mac β : Bimbfind F Esru Min H
Easra β Easru M   ¹⁷ briaim μ∧ ain MH.
   6. ¹ ins. mac β mic β¹² meic MH : Braimid F Briamin μ∧ Briamain
μR Braimint β Fraimint β¹ Froimint β² Praimint MH   ² ins. ba
F Min : mac F Min β, mic β¹² : ba mac *dittographed*, μR   ³ Fattecht
L Aithichta F Fathecht μ∧ Baaith μR Eachachdla β⁰¹² (-dha β) Eachada M
⁴ mac β mhic β¹ mic β²   ⁵ Magoth LF β Magoch Min Magoe MH
⁶ ins. ba L : moir β   ⁷ ins. a β⁰¹² : bladh μ∧ β⁰² blath β¹   ⁸ robasa
nanamsir L ro bassa riana [i *expuncted*] naimsir μR ro pass ria naimsir
μ∧ ro ba sona a naimsir β⁰¹² (sona in naimsear β); do FM, da bas ina
H ina *also* M   ⁹ om. n- FM (amsir F)   ¹⁰ comthadbsin L comthaibsin
F co taidhbsin ria mag μ∧ oca taibsin dar mag μR com thaibhsen β gon
dubh sin a reimed β¹² comthaibsib M comtaib (*with* sin *sprs.* yc) H
¹¹ re F R³   ¹² Magh β

V.

1.   Father of all, Master of Heaven,
the noble angelic King,
our Champion, our Lord, our Head,
without beginning, end, or termination.

HU   ⁵ mac maith Muire ingine M an ri H   ⁶ nassal E   ⁷ -de E
-ghe P -dhi H -ghi U   ⁸ cuindigh V, cuinnidh E cuinge (*written over
and defacing another word*) P cuingidh U   ⁹ coimdhi V, -dhe E
-gi M -di H coimsid U   ¹⁰ cenn M ceand U   ¹¹ gan PU, can H
(*throughout the line*)   ¹² tuis E   ¹³ foireenu P foireenn M
forceand U

2.   ¹Ferr nā ²cach rī ³in ⁴Rī ⁵raith   45
      ⁶lasndernad ⁷in ⁸maiss mōr-maith.
      ⁹grāda ¹⁰Nime. ¹¹cāem in cloth,
      ¹²arāen ¹³issin ¹⁴cēt Domnoch.

3.   ¹Delbais secht ²nime ³sin Lūan,
      sin Mairt muir, ⁴talum ⁵tond-būan;   50
      ⁶sin ⁷Chētain, ⁸ēsca is ⁹grēin ¹⁰nglē;
      ¹¹neōil ¹²is eōin ¹³Dia ¹⁴Dardāine.

4.   Duine ¹ro ²delbad īarsin,
      ³debrad! ⁴isin ⁵n-Āenditin,—
      ⁶tuead, ⁷etir ⁸chois is ⁹cend,   55
      ¹⁰assin ¹¹doman ¹²cāem ¹³eoitchend.

5.   ¹Gniomrad in ²tseisedh ³laoi lāin,
      ⁴aisneidfed dūibh sin ⁵deg-dāil,
      anmann' in talman, thīar tair,
      an deilb ⁶n-ill-dathaig ⁷nAdhaim.   60

6.   ¹Cend ²Adaim ³airdire co ⁴hōg
      ⁵tuead a tir maith Malōn:
      ⁶is ⁷tairis ⁸tēgaid amach
      ⁹srotha ¹⁰Parrduis ¹¹co ¹²bladach.

7.   ¹Bruinde ²ind ³Tir ⁴Harōin ⁵aird,   65
      ⁶a ⁷bru a ⁸Baibiloin ⁹bith-gairg,
      a ¹⁰chossa a ¹¹Labain ¹²lēr-blā,
      a ¹³sliasta ¹⁴a tīr ¹⁵Gogoma.

2. ¹maraid dogres MU (-raigh U), fear H   ²gach EP   ³an P
⁴rig MU   ⁵rath U   ⁶lassnernadh V lasndernadh E lasandernad
PU (written over another word P) lasnderna MH (-san- M)   ⁷au H
⁸mais EPM om. U   ⁹gradha VPU   ¹⁰nimi EU   ¹¹coemda cloth
VEP (caemda E caomdha P), caem a cloth HU   ¹²maraen EMHU
araon P   ¹³isin E isin PHU isa M   ¹⁴chet E cedomnach H
domnach PU
3. ¹dealbais PMH   ²nimi HU   ³sind VE isin P san H
⁴talom E, -am MH   ⁵tonn- VEPH   ⁶sa VH san P   ⁷cet- PU
chedain M   ⁸escca P   ⁹grian VEPMHU   ¹⁰n- om. VEHU
¹¹neoill MH niuil EU. In U written over something else, apparently
nuiil   ¹²₇ M   ¹³om. dia MU   ¹⁴-aeine E -aoine P diard- MU
4. ¹ra H   ²dealbad EMH dhealbadh P   ³debradh EP dearbad
M deadbrad U   ⁴isind E isa M isan H   ⁵aoindidin E n-aoine didin
P aendidin HU naindidin M   ⁶tucadh V tugadh EU tuccad P
⁷itir EMH   ⁸cois EPU   ⁹cheand M chend H ceand U   ¹⁰asin
E (the a yc E) isin PMU issin H   ¹¹domhan E domun MH
¹²chaem VMH caom EP (-mh P) caem U   ¹³coitchenn VEP choitchenn
H choitchend M choiteeand U

2.   Better than every King is the King of Grace
      by whom was made the great excellent world-stuff,
      the orders of Heaven, fair the fame,
      together on the first Sunday.

3.   He formed the seven heavens on the Monday,
      on the Tuesday sea, earth with enduring surface;
      on the Wednesday, moon and bright sun;
      clouds and birds on Thursday.

4.   Man, who was formed thereafter,
      Debrad! on the Friday,—
      he was taken, from foot to head,
      out of the fair common earth.

5. The works of the full sixth day
   I shall relate to you in (this) good company;
   [I shall tell of] the beasts of the earth, west and east,
   of the form of Adam, rich in colour.

6.   The head of renowned Adam perfectly
      was taken from the good land of Malon:
      through which go forth
      the rivers of Paradise famously.

7.   The breast of the man from lofty Aron,
      his belly from ever-fierce Babylon,
      his legs from Laban, a conspicuous land,
      his thighs from the country of Gogoma.

5. *this quatrain in EP only: printed as in E, these variants from* P: ¹ gnimrad   ² -sed   ³ lai   ⁴ aisneidhfit   ⁵ deghaill
⁶ nillath-   ⁷ nAdhuim
   6. ¹ tuead (tugudh U) ceud (ceand U) Adaim co hog ‖ a fearand (-und U) molfach (molbthach U) Malon (Molon U) MU: ceand H
² Adhaim E, Aduim P   ³ oirdairee V airrdeire E airrdire P airrdhire H (*the mark of lenition scratched out*)   ⁴ hogh PH   ⁵ tucadh P
⁶ *om.* U   ⁷ *the* is *sprs. yc* E   ⁸ tee(ad) V tecaid MH tegait U
⁹ srotha V (*the* a *yc* V) srota P   ¹⁰ Parrthais V Parduis E Partais P
Parrthuis H Parrthais U   ¹¹ go E   ¹² bhladhach P blatach U
   7. ¹ bruinne E bruindi PHMU   ² an MH in U   ³ fir EPU
⁴ Haron EH Haraib M Hardon U   ⁵ ard EU *also* H, *but an* i *sbs.*
yc H   ⁶ a *sbs yc* E   ⁷ pru P   ⁸ Biblon E Lotain M Babilon U
⁹ -garg EU lan-gairg M   ¹⁰ cosa E lama MU   ¹¹ Laban EMHU
¹² leir mbla E leir bla H erbla U   ¹³ sliasda E: chosa M, lama H
cosa U   ¹⁴ i U   ¹⁵ Goghoma V Gagoma E Gogomah- (no Gomaa
sec. man. in marg.) P Gomaa M Gouma H Gogama U

8. Trī ¹trāth ²d'Adum ³cen ⁴anmain
   ⁵īar n-a ⁶chruthugud ⁷do ⁸talmain;   70
   ⁹ardāig ¹⁰Fir ¹¹do ¹²baī trī trāth
   ¹³cen ¹⁴anmain n-a ¹⁵churp ¹⁶chāem-gnāth.

9. ¹Triar ²ro ³chruthaig a ⁴chorp ⁵cāin
   ⁶īar ⁷n-ērge dō n-a ⁸bethaid,
   ⁹allus ¹⁰d'usce, ¹¹ba dia deōin,¹¹   75
   ¹²tess ¹³tened, ¹⁴tinfed ¹⁵āeoir.

10. ¹Adaig ²Adaim fīal ³in ⁴feth
    sair ⁵ar ⁶slōib ⁷Parrduis ⁸Partech;
    ⁹ro ¹⁰altuig ¹¹faiesin ¹²grēine
    ¹³tar⁽ᵃ⁾ mullach ¹⁴in mōr-¹⁵sleibe.   80

11. ¹Adraim, adraim ²thusa, a. ³Dē!—
    ⁴is ē ⁵cēt-guth ⁶do ⁷rāid ⁸sē:
    ⁹ac faiesin ¹⁰Eua ¹¹āine,
    ¹²and ¹³dorigne ¹⁴a ¹⁵chet-gāire.

12. ¹A chēt-imthecht, ²cāine guis   85
    ³co ⁴tobar ⁵Pairtech ⁶Parrduis:
    a ⁷chēt-rith, ⁸rem ⁹co ndaithe,
    do ¹⁰dechsain na ¹¹hēnlaithe.

8. ¹ thrath VMH tra U   ² d'Adamh E d'Adam M d'Adham U
² gan EPU   ⁴ anmuin H   ⁵ ar U   ⁶ cruth E chruthad P
cruthadh U chruthugud M: *other* MSS. *have* cruth-   ⁷ don M ar HU
⁸ *ins.* trom EP: thal- E talmhuin P   ⁹ -igh EPU   ¹⁰ fir PU
¹¹ ro VEP da U   ¹² baoi E boi P bhi U   ¹³ gan EPU can H
¹⁴ anmuin PH   ¹⁵ corp E chorp H   ¹⁶ caomhgnath E caomgnath P
chaemnar M chaemngnath H comgnath U
     9. ¹ ceathrar M   ² *om.* ro M; do H dar U   ³ cruth- E
cruthaidchi M cruthaidh H cruthad U   ⁴ corp EPU chuirp M
⁵ choin M   ⁶ ar U   ⁷ n-erghi V neirge dho E neirge do P
nergi M neirgi HU   ⁸ bethaigh V beathoid M bhethaid HU
⁹ *ins.* a U   ¹⁰ dusqi E duisqe P is uisqi M duisqi H   ¹¹⁻¹¹ fodein
M badeoid U   ¹² tes VEMH teass P teas U   ¹³ tenidh V teinfedh E
tineth P tinedh H tenead U   ¹⁴ tinfedh V teinfedh E timfeadh U
¹⁵ aieoir P aiger M: *the* e *written over another letter* H
     10. ¹ aiged EH aee P aidheadh U   ² Adhaim EU Adaimh P
³ a EHU   ⁴ feith P   ⁵ fri VEPH   ⁶ Sliab VEP (bh EP)
MHU   ⁷ -dhuis E -tais P -dais M -thuis H dhais U   ⁸ pairtech E
ftach P partiach U   ⁹ ra H   ¹⁰ atlaig E alt- P altaig MH
failtigh U   ¹¹ *ins.* ag EP: aigsin E aiesin P faisci U   ¹² grene

8. Three days had Adam without life
after his formation from earth;
because of a Man who was three days
without life in His ever-fair body.

9. There were Three Persons who formed his fair
body
after he arose alive;
sweat from water, it was with his good will,
heat of fire, breath of air.

10. The night of Adam, generous the repose,
eastward upon Pairtech Mountain of Paradise;
he welcomed the sight of the sun
over the top of the great mountain.

11. I adore, I adore Thee, O God!—
this was the first word that he uttered:
When he saw noble Eve,
then he made his first laugh.

12. His first walk—beauty of strength—
to the Spring of Partech of Paradise:
his first race, a course with swiftness,
to see the birds.

VMH greini P in ngreni U   [13] dar VEDUH do M   [14] an EPH
[15] sleibhe E slebe DM sleiphe P slebi H sleibi U

11. [1] adram adraim E adhrum adhrum U   [2] tu VEPMU tusa D
thusu H   [3] Dhe, *lenition mark faded* D   [4] hiss V iss ED hise P
is H   [5] toisech VEPD ced guth M toiseach H   [6] ro DU   [7] raidh EU
[8] se E   [9] hic aisein VD ic aisgin E ac faicsin PM hic aicsin H ig
faigsin U   [10] Ebha E Eba M   [11] ane V aince E aille M ailli HU
[12] ann DH   [13] dorinde E dorindi M dorine H dorighni U   [14] in D
[15] ced EDH ched PM: gairi H

12. [1] chetna V ched EM ced P: imtecht EP imdhecht U   [2] caine
guiss V cain aguis M caini niss H lith gan geis U   [3] go DU
[4] topur VE top- PDH tobor U   [5] prech PD -each V paitrech EH
pairtiach M parrtiach U   [6] partais V parrdais E pairtais P
parduis D parrthuis H parrthais U   [7] ced E cheit D ched PM
[8] rem VDM reim EP ceim U   [9] condaithi D co ndaite P conaichi M
conaithi H condhaithe U   [10] descain E dechsinn P descuin D
decain U   [11] haenlaithe P -laithi D henlaithi MH

(a) Here D begins.

178   THE VERSE TEXTS

13. ¹Cōic ²lā ³dēc, ⁴nī ⁵lūad ⁶sāeb,
d⁷Adam is d⁸Eua ⁹marāen,   90
co ¹⁰toracht ¹¹demon ¹²donīm
¹³dia ¹⁴saigid ¹⁵j ¹⁶nĀenditin.

14. ¹Dell ²nathrach, corp ³āeoir ⁴scīm
⁵tue ⁶leis ⁷diabul ⁸sin ⁹droich-rēim :
¹⁰litri ¹¹trias ¹²ro chau, nī ¹³as līach,   95
¹⁴Iae, Uau, Iae ⁊ Iath.

15. ¹Atā ²sund ³in ⁴fāth—⁵rofess—
ar a n-⁶apar : Clē ⁷sech ⁸dess :
⁹ar ¹⁰is ī ¹¹in ¹²lām ¹³chlē chrom
¹⁴ro ¹⁵riged ¹⁶cosin ¹⁷uboll.   100

16. Iar ¹n-imarbus ²dōib—nīr ³dlecht—
⁴ro ⁵laite ⁶i tīr ⁷n-aird ⁸nEgept :
⁹remes ¹⁰trī ¹¹mīs ¹²īarsin maidm
¹³rusbiath ¹⁴ruscit ¹⁵ind āen-phailm.

17. ¹Ro ²coimpred ³Cāin, ⁴nīr chīan ;   105
⁵ro ⁶coimpred, ⁷rucad ⁸Abīal ;
do Chāin ⁹chrīn ¹⁰in ¹¹cachta,
¹²ro len ¹³gnīm na ¹⁴mallachta.

13. ¹coig EP cuig H   ²laithe VE laithi PDH   ³deg EHU
⁴nocho M; *ins.* is U   ⁵luadh EP luag M slicht U   ⁶saobh E
saob P saebh U   ⁷Adum VH Adhum EU   ⁸Ebha E Eba PD
Eu H   ⁹-aon EP -oen D   ¹⁰torracht EP tanic U   ¹¹demun VH
deaman E demhan P deman M   ¹²do nimh E do nim *other* MSS.
Perhaps to be read do[g]nīm   ¹³da mellad MU   ¹⁴saighid V
saice P soig D: *om.* MU   ¹⁵ind D san MH isin U   ¹⁶aondidin E
aoinedittin P oendidin D aindidin M aendidin HU
14. ¹dealb EPH dealbh U   ²natr- EPH   ³aer U   ⁴eim
VH seim ED seimh P em M emh U   ⁵tug E   ⁶les D
⁷demin M diabal H demon U   ⁸co MH tre U   ⁹droch-reim VE
drochmen P droichrem D ndrochmen M ndrochmein H drochmein U
¹⁰littri V   ¹¹tria ro can E triarrochan D trias archan M resar
chan U   ¹²ra H   ¹³is MU   ¹⁴Ia Ae Uau ⁊ Aiath MSS.; *except*
Ainath P, ia uau ⁊ en iach M iae. uau, iaiath U
15. ¹is he sin MU (e U)   ²sunn EPD   ³an H   ⁴fat U
⁵ro-fes ED ro-feass P ro feas M ra-fess H rotfeas U   ⁶apur V
abartar E apartar P abar MU   ⁷seach MUH   ⁸des EHU deas
PM thes D   ⁹air P ardaig MHU (-gh U)   ¹⁰issi VP as i E is hi M
¹¹an EPH   ¹²lamh EP laam D   ¹³chle crom VH: ele chrom E

13.   Fifteen days, it is no idle tale,
    had Adam and Eve together,
    till a demon of misdeeds (?)
    reached them, on a Friday.

14.   The form of a serpent, a body of thin air,
    the devil took to himself on the evil course :
    the letters through which he made incantation—a
        wretched affair—
    were *He, Var, He,* and *Yodh.*

15.   There is the reason—it is familiar—
    why men say "Left beyond right":
    because it is the crooked left hand
    that was stretched to the apple.

16.   After they had sinned—it was not lawful—
    they were cast into the lofty land of Egypt :
    A space of three months after the transgression
    the one palm-tree fed and clothed them.

17.   Cain was conceived, it was not long;
    Abel was conceived and brought to birth;
    to withered Cain of the shackle
    the deed of the curse adhered.

cle crom PU (crum P) chrom chle *written first and then corrected* D
¹⁴ do MH da U   ¹⁵ righed P righeadh U   ₁₁   ¹⁶ cossin V cosind E
gusin PU cosa nuball H   ¹⁷ ubhall E nup, *expanded in marg. in
later hand* nubhuill P ubaoll D uball M ubull U
    16. ¹ ninarbus U   ² do P doibh U : *two letters (apparently* do)
erased after this word H   ³ drecht H   ⁴ ra H   ⁵ laithi VD
laiti P late M laitea U   ⁶ a MH   ⁷ nairdd V nard EHU
⁸ nEighept V nEigept EH nEigep (*sic*) P Egeptt D   ⁹ remiss V
remis E reimeas P remess D   ¹⁰ tri miss *om. in text and ins. by
late corrector in marg.* V   ¹¹ mhis U   ¹² triasin V re sin H
¹³ rossbiath V rosbiath EU   ¹⁴ roset E rosneit V rusneith P
rusneid H roseith *the mark of lenition erased* U   ¹⁵ in VEMU an
PH aon pailm E aonpa *with* ilm *added by corr. in marg.* P oen pailm
D naen-pailm M aen-phailm H aen-pailm UE
    17. ¹ ra H   ² choimp- D coimpread M coimbread U   ³ Chain D
⁴ nir cian D ni chel M ni cel U   ⁵ rucad ro coimpread M : ra H :
⁊ ru coimbread Abel U   ⁶ coimpredh V com- E   ⁷ rucadh VE rucead P
rugad D   ⁸ Aibial D Aibel M Abel U   ⁹ crin EPHU crich M
¹⁰ an H   ¹¹ eachtai P chachta DMH   ¹² roglen ED dolen M ralen
H ronlen U   ¹³ gnimh E   ¹⁴ mallachtai D

18.　¹Lotar d'²id(ⁿ)pairt dā ³reithe
　　　⁴Abēl, Cāin ⁵nīr ⁶chleithe;
　　　⁷nochor indraic ⁸leis in Rīg
　　　⁹in ¹⁰idpairt ¹¹ruc ¹²leis ¹³Cāin.　　　　110

19.　¹Tāinic rath ²ruithne ³Rīg ⁴grīan
　　　⁵forsin ⁶idpairt ⁷ruc ⁸Aibīal :
　　　⁹dē ro ¹⁰līn ¹¹formad ¹²is ¹³ferg
　　　Cāin colach na ¹⁴clāen-cherd.　　　　115

20.　(b)¹Rogab ²Cāin n-a ³lāim ⁴luind
　　　⁵lecain ⁶cintaig ⁷in ⁸chamuill :
　　　⁹co Haibēl ¹⁰lēim ¹¹co ¹²luindi,
　　　¹³conid ¹⁴ro ¹⁵marb ¹⁶d`āen-¹⁷builli.　　　120

21.　¹Tuc ²Seth a ³lāim re ⁴lecain
　　　⁵ac faicsin fola ⁶in ⁷phecaid :
　　　⁸'sē sin ⁹in fer ¹⁰cen ¹¹urchra
　　　arar ¹²fās in ¹³chēt-ulcha.

22.　¹Adberait ²rind na ³heōlaig,　　　　125
　　　lucht ⁴in ⁵ēcnai il-⁶cheōlaig,
　　　nach ⁷fāsait na ⁸clocha ō ⁹chēin—
　　　¹⁰ō`n lō ¹¹rosfer fuil ¹²Aibēil.

18. ¹ Lodar HU　　　² idbairt E edbairt U　　　³ rethe D reithi H
⁴ Aibeil MH Anel U　　　⁵ ni MH gan U　　　⁶ chlethe D cleite E
chleithi P cleithi H clethe U　　　⁷ nocho ro gab ri na rig DE (gaib D)
nochar gab ri na rig P noar gab ri na rig M nochor indraice lasin ri H
nocho rogab in rig rel U　　　⁸ lassin V　　　⁹ ind VE inn P　　　¹⁰ idpart
E idbairt PD eadbairt U　　　¹¹ rucc P rug M　　　¹² leiss V lais P
¹³ Caen U
19. ¹ tanic VU tanuig D tanig H　　　² ruithni VPDH ruitni E
ruithin M ruithen U　　　³ righ VE ri H rigrian U　　　⁴ nel M　　　⁵ for
ind VDM forand E forin P foran H ar an U　　　⁶ edpairt VDH iopairt
(sic) E inpairt P idbairt U : reithi M　　　⁷ rug ED　　　⁸ Abial VPDH
Aibel M Abel U　　　⁹ om. de M　　　¹⁰ lion E　　　¹¹ formud V format PU
¹² ꝶ M　　　¹³ fearg VMU ferrce P　　　¹⁴ claen-redhg V claon-cerd E
-redhg (no claoin-cerd in marg.) P -redg D -cheard M -cealg U
20. ¹ -gabh PU -gob M ragab H　　　² Caidin P　　　³ laimh EP
⁴ luinn E : luind om. and sprs. (D)　　　⁵ leca M lecca U　　　⁶ cintaich VD
-taigh E chinntach P chintach M chintaig H　　　⁷ an PH　　　⁸ chambaill
E camaill P chamuill H cambaill U　　　⁹ co Habial VEH co Hab. P

18. They went to offer two rams,
Abel, Cain who was not noble;
the King did not consider worthy
the offering which Cain brought with him.

19. There came the grace of the brilliance of the
King of Suns
upon the offering which Abel brought :
thence did envy and anger fill
sinful Cain of the crooked crafts.

20. Cain took in his savage hand
the guilty jaw-bone of the camel ;
to Abel he leapt with violence,
so that he slew him with a blow.

21. Seth set his hand to the jaw-bone,
on seeing the blood of the sin :
he is the man without deficiency
upon whom the first beard grew.

22. The learned tell us,
the people of wisdom of manifold melody,
that from a long time the stones grow not—
from the day when Abel's blood suffused them.

go Haibial D go Habial H co Hauel U ¹⁰ lem DHU ¹¹ go DU
¹² luinde VEP luinne D luindhi U ¹³ comadh EP -ad MHU ¹⁴ ra H
¹⁵ mharb EH marbh PU ¹⁶ do en V d'aon E d'en PH d'oen D
¹⁷ buille VED bhuilli P bulle U

21. *This quatrain is here in* EP, *follows no.* 32 *in* M, *and is absent
from all the other* MSS. ¹ tig E ² Seith EP ³ lamh EP lam M
⁴ *ins.* a E ⁵ ar bfaigsin E ag faigsin P ⁶ an P ⁷ pec. E pecaig M
⁸ sin fen (fein P) in fer (fear M) PM ⁹ an E ¹⁰ gan E can M:
in P *another word has been re-inked into* can ¹¹ urcra MSS. ¹² fas P
¹¹ ced-ulcai E cet-ulchai P

22. ¹ atberait VU adberad E atberuit D adbearaid MH ² rinn PD
³ -aigh VU ⁴ ind VD an EPH na MU ⁵ egna E egno (*written* egl-)
P' eena DH heagna M hegna U ⁶ ceolaigh E ceol- P hil-cheolaich D
-cheolaich M -cheolaigh U ⁷ hassait V na hasad E asait P assuitt
D nach fasaid M hassaid H fasait U ⁸ cloca U ⁹ cein P chen
M chein, *the* i *expuncted* U ¹⁰ o rusben riu M o da ben riu U
¹¹ rosben ED ¹² Abel VU Abeil PH

(*a*) s² M here.　　　　(*b*) s¹ M here resumes.

23. ¹Rogabsat ²secht ³cenuic ⁴īar sain
⁵for ⁶Cáin, ⁷īarsin ⁸fingail;　　　130
⁹cnoc ¹⁰cechtar a ¹¹dā ¹²chos ¹³cain,
¹⁴is dā ¹⁵chnoc ¹⁶for a ¹⁷lāmaib.

24. ¹Cnoc ²ina ³ētan, ⁴mo nūar,
is ⁵cnoc ⁶cechtar a dā ⁷grūad :
⁸tar ⁹chnoc ¹⁰a ētain, ¹¹ro-¹²līach,　　　135
¹²in ¹³t-uball ¹⁴tarlaic ¹⁵Laimiach.

25. ¹Laimīach ²dīgamus ³cen ⁴gāi
is ⁵ē cēt-fer ⁶thuc ⁷dā ⁸mnāi :
⁹leis ¹⁰dorochair ¹¹Cāin ¹²crom
¹³dia ¹⁴tarlaic ¹⁵fair in ¹⁶uboll.　　　140

26. Dā mac ¹Laimīach, ²lāechda a ³mbrīg,
Iubal ⁴is ⁵Tubalchāin :
Iubal fuair ⁶cruit in ⁷cara,
⁸Tubalchāin ⁹in cēt-¹⁰goba.

27. ¹Edpairt ²Abēil, mar ³adclos　　　145
⁴rucad ⁵dia ⁶ēis ⁷i ⁸Parrdos;
⁹is ē ¹⁰sin ¹¹in ¹²rethe ¹³rān
¹⁴tucad ¹⁵dar ¹⁶cenn mac ¹⁷nApram.

23. ¹·sad VEMH ragab- H　²seacht M　³cnuice V cnuic EPDMH cnuich U　⁴-sin EMPU -soin D　⁵ar MU　⁶Chain VMH Caidhin P　⁷isin EH iarsan P tresin U　⁸iarsindinguil, *with ï yc above the* d D bhfingail P ïingail H fingal U　⁹cnoce VH　¹⁰chechtar M cecthar U　¹¹dha VEU　¹²choss V chos E cos PU　¹²choin M chain H　¹⁴⁊ EDMU　¹⁵cnoc EPU　¹⁶na EDM ar a U　¹⁷lamhaibh VE lamhaiph P

24. ¹cnocc VH　²ara M　³edan EMHU　⁴munuar V monnuar E manuar UM　⁵cnoce H　⁶ceachtar M　⁷gruadh VEPU　⁸dar VEPH ar U　⁹cnoc VEDUM chnoce P cnoce H　¹⁰an edain E ind etuin D in edain M a ēdain HU　¹¹ra H　¹²liadh E liad D　¹²a E an H　¹³tubull V tubhall EP turchur U　¹⁴tarluie D ro thelg M ra thilg H ro theilg U　¹⁵Laimhīiach E Laimfiach P *marg.* Lamiach DU

25. ¹Lamiach VEU Laimfiach P　²dighamuiss D diamus M bigamus U　³gan PD can H: eo mbrig U　⁴goe E gaoi P　⁵he cet fer V cet fer *also* E: fear M　⁶tue VPU tuee E tug D thug H　⁷dia E　⁸mnaoi P　⁹lais VEPH les U　¹⁰adrochair M

23. After that seven wens took hold
upon Cain, after the kin-murder :
a wen |upon| each of his fair feet,
and two wens upon his hands.

24. A wen in his forehead, alas,
and a wen |upon| each of his cheeks :
through the wen of his forehead, very
wretched!
[went] the apple which Lamech cast.

25. Lamech the two-spoused, without falsehood,
he is the first man who took two wives :
by him did crooked Cain fall,
after he cast the apple upon him.

26. The two sons of Lamech, valiant their
strength,
Iubal and Tubalcain :
Iubal invented harps of music (?),
Tubalcain was the first smith.

27. The offering of Abel, as it hath been heard,
was taken after him into Paradise;
that is the very splendid ram
which was given in place of the sons (sic)
of Abram.

---

adrocair U   ¹¹ Caidhin P   ¹² cromm E crum P   ¹³ ar arde
arlaig in tubull U   ¹⁴ tarlaice E -luig D -laig H   ¹⁵ aire D
¹⁶ ind ubull E ubhull P tuboll D tuball M dub. H
26. ¹ Lamiach EU Laimh- P   ² laocdha P locchda D laech co
mbrig M laechdha U   ³ mbrigh VEPDU   ⁴ sic EU, ⁊ all other MSS.
⁵ Tupcaí P (bis) Tubalchoein D Tubalcain U   ⁶ chruit D   ⁷ charae
E carui P   ⁸ Tubalcain (a stroke through the stem of the b) U
⁹ om. E, an HP   ¹⁰ gaba VDHU gabae E gabhadh P
27. ¹ hedp- E cadhp- P hedb- PD edb- M eadb- U   ² Aibeil DH
Aibel M Abhel U   ³ atcloss V adcloss E atclos PD daclos M doclos HU
⁴ rucadn V ruccad E rucad P rugad DU   ⁵ da MU   ⁶ hes V ess
D es U   ⁷ hi VEPD a HU   ⁸ Pardos VD Pardoss E Parrtos H
Parrtus HU   ⁹ ins. ⁊ U: is hessin V isse P hise D: hessin (om. is) H
¹⁰ om. sin U   ¹¹ an PH   ¹² reithe EP reithi MH   ¹³ rain H
¹⁴ tucadh V tuccad EP tugad D   ¹⁵ ar M tar HU   ¹⁶ cend EHU
¹⁷ nAbram VDPM Abram (om. n-) EU, nApraim H

28. [1]Crocenn [2]ind [3]rethe sin rīam
     [4]riacht [5]d´Abrām īar [6]nAbīal :
     [7]itches [8]im Crīst [9]cen [10]chinaid,
     [11]ic [12]fosaic [13]dīa [14]desciplaib.   150

29. Daisia fa sead ainm [1]in chroind
     co [2]torad n-imda n-āloind,
     [3]a Muig Aron a [4]Parrdus—   155
     dīa [5]ndernad [6]in [7]t-imarbus.

30. [1]A hocht cethrachat [2]nōi cēt
     is [3]mīle, nī [4]himarbrēcc,
     ō rē [5]ind [6]Adaim [7]chētna [8]cain
     [9]co [10]Haprām. [11]cossin [12]n-athair.   160

31. [1]Tricha [2]nōi cēt [3]bliadan [4]mbān
     [5]sāegal [6]Adaim [7]ria imrād :
     deich [8]mbliadan, [9]risin [10]uile,
     [11]sāegal [12]a mnā [13]mong-buide.

32. [1]Sāegal [2]Seith [3]is eōl [4]dam [5]sin   165
     a [6]cūig dēc ar [7]nōi [8]cētaibh :
     [9]cūig bliadna [10]nōi cēt ro [11]clos
     no [12]co [13]rug [14]in [15]t-ēc [16]Enos.

28. [1]crocand V croccann E croicenn PM crocann D crocend H
croicend U   [2]in EMU an PH   [3]reithe V reithi EMHP rethi D
rithi U   [4]doriacht VEPDH do ruacht M arucht U   [5]om. d' U
[6]nAip- P nAibeil M nAbhel U   [7]atches VPU itchess EM hitchess D
atces P itcheas M adces H   [8]an P am MH   [9]gan P cin D can
MH om. U   [10]cinaid D dar eabair U   [11]hic osaice, with f sprs.
cD ig P do M   [12]fossaice E asaic M asaigh U   [13]da U
[14]deisciplaib E disgiplaib (in marg. absdalab) P apsdalaib M deiscep. H
aptalaib U

29. this quatrain om. VEDHU   [1]an croinn P   [2]dtor. nimdhu P
[3]amnigh P   [4]Parrtos P   [5]-adh P   [6]an P   [7]-bhas, in
marg. timarbus P

30. [1]a hocht ceathrachad cem [cein?] glan, | mili ar noe cedaib
bliadan, | o re Abraim chedna chain, | co Hadam, cus in athair M
[2]noe V nai ced H   [3]mili HU   [4]-breg D himirbreg HU   [5]inn P
an H in U   [6]Adhaim VEU Adaimh P Adauim D   [7]cetna VH

28. The hide formerly of that ram
came to Abram after Abel:
it was seen about Christ without fault
as He washed for His disciples.

29. Daisia, that was the name of the tree
with much and beautiful fruit,
in the Plain of Aron in Paradise—
for which the sin was committed.

30. Eight and forty, nine hundreds
and a thousand, it is no fiction,
from the time of that same fair Adam
to Abram, to the father.

31. Thirty and nine hundred clear years
was the life of Adam with its fame;
ten years, with all of those,
was the life of his yellow-haired wife.

32. The life of Seth, I have that knowledge,
fifteen over nine hundreds:
five years and nine hundred, it was heard,
until death took Enos.

chetnai E cedna P ⁸chain ED ⁹go D gu U ¹⁰Habram EU ¹¹cos in EP gussin D cusan H gusin U ¹²om. n· EDUH: athair E athauir D

31. ¹trica U ²noe M nai U ³-ain P mbliadan U ⁴om. n- MH ⁵saogh- P saedhal (no g written see. man. above the d) D soegul U ⁶Aduim D Adhaim U ⁷ria imradh EP re imrad MH re imrath U ⁸-dh- H ⁹riss sin V rissin EDH iarsin U ¹⁰huile D mile H ule H uili U ¹¹saogh- P soegal D saegul U ¹²Eua U ¹³buidhe VE budi H bhuidhe U

32. ¹saoce- P soegul U ²Seth EDMU ³as H ⁴damh VP ⁵sain V soin D ⁶do MU ⁷se DM ⁸cettaib E cetaip P cetauibh D ⁹cuie VM se EP ¹⁰nochad V nochat ED .lxxxx. at P noe eet M ¹¹closs VP chloss E: ra clos H ¹²go DU cho H ¹³rue VMHU ¹⁴an PH ¹⁵teg VEPDMH tee U ¹⁶Enoss VE

33. Deich ¹mbliadan ²nōi cēt, ³cen crāid,
    ⁴āes meic ⁵Enosa, ⁶Caināin :   170
    ⁷nōi ⁸cēt ⁹acht ¹⁰a cūic, ¹¹co ¹²mblaid,
    ¹³sāegal ¹⁴Malaleith mōr-¹⁵glain.

34. ¹Cūic ²bliadna ³sescat, ⁴nōi ⁵cēt
    ⁶do Iareth ⁷rīa ⁸ndul ⁹i n-ēe :
    ¹⁰trī ¹¹chēt sescat ¹²a ¹³cūic ro ¹⁴clos   175
    d´¹⁵Enōc ¹⁶rīa ¹⁷ndul ¹⁸i ¹⁹Parrtos.

35. ¹Ochtmoga ²bliadan ³co mblaid
    ocus ⁴nōi ⁵cēt do ⁶bliadnaib—
    ⁷is ē sin ⁸in ⁹sāegal ¹⁰seng
    ¹¹tucad do ¹²Mathasalem.   180

36. ¹Sāegal ²Laimīach, ³lūaiter ⁴lat,
    ⁵secht cēt ⁶a ⁷cūic ⁸sechtmogat :
    ⁹sāegal ¹⁰Nōe, ¹¹nōeb a ¹²blad,
    ¹³cacca ar ¹⁴nōi ¹⁵cētaib ¹⁶bliadan.

37. Trī meic ¹d´Adam ²ca mbāi ³cland—   185
    Seth, ⁴Sile, Cāin ⁵clāen-cam :
    a ⁶teora mnā, ⁷būadach ⁸brīg!
    Olla, ⁹Pip, ⸵ ¹⁰Pithīp.

---

33. *This quatrain om.* U
cet M *nochat other MSS.*
resembling u) co ngrain M
VP Enos ED   ⁶Chainean V Cain ean P Cainan D Cainean (*the i and
second a sbscr. apparently in a slightly different ink*) H   ⁷nai M
⁸cett E   ⁹ach H   ¹⁰*om.* a MH   ¹¹*ins.* bliadna MH : ar *for*
co MH   ¹²mblaidh V bloid M blaid H   ¹²saoghal P   ¹⁴Malaleth
VED Malaleit P Malalel M   ¹⁵gloin P

¹mbliadna P   ²lxxxxat cc cradh P nai
³cen crad VEDH (*in* E *an open* a
⁴*ins.* a V : aess VED aois P   ⁵Enois

34. ¹coic VED coig P da M dece U   ²mbl. U   ³sesca M
⁴*ins.* is : nai M   ⁵cett E   ⁶d´Iareth U   ⁷re MHU   ⁸dul P
ndol D nul H   ⁹adece V a dh- P adee ineg D a dee M a deg H
aneg U   ¹⁰sesca tri cet U   ¹¹cet VM   ¹²*om.* a E   ¹³coic VD
coice E coig P *om. and* cuig *ins. in bad hand in marg.* U   ¹⁴closs VE
¹⁵Enoce ED Enogh P Enog H   ¹⁶re MHU   ¹⁷ndol D   ¹⁸hi VPD a H
¹⁹Parrthoss V Pardoss ED Parrthos P Parrdus M Parrthus H Parrtus U

35. ¹-gha EP sechtmogha MU   ²-ain P   ³com mblaid V : eo
mblaidh U   ⁴noe V   ⁵cett E   ⁶-aip P   ⁷is he sin E hisse

33.   Ten years and nine hundred, without vexation
       the age of the son of Enos, Cainan;
       nine hundred save five, with renown,
       the life of Malaleth great and pure.

34.   Sixty five years, nine hundred
       to Iareth before going to death :
       three hundred sixty and five was it heard
       to Enoch before going into Paradise.

35.   Eighty years with fame
       and nine hundreds of years—
       that is the stately life
       which was given to Mathusalem.

36.   The life of Lamech, to you is it mentioned,
       seven hundred, five and seventy :
       the life of Noe, holy his renown,
       fifty over nine hundreds of years.

37.   Adam had three sons who had progeny—
       Seth, Sile, Cain perverse and crooked :
       their three wives, victorious strength!
       were Olla, Pip and Pithip.

sin D   ⁸ an H   ⁹ saog- P -gul U   ¹⁰ seang U   ¹¹ tuccadh E
tugad PD tugadh U   ¹² Mathasaileam VH Matha Salem EP (*the
second* m *dotted sec. men.* P) Mathusalem D

36. ¹ saoghal P saeghal U   ² Lamiach VU Lamech ED   ³ luater U
⁴ latt P leat U   ⁵ seacht M   ⁶ seacht mbliadna caecad M secht
mbliadna trichat U(a)   ⁷ coic VED coig H   ⁸ -moghad V -moghat E
-mogad H   ⁹ saoghal P socgul P   ¹⁰ Naoi P Naee MH   ¹¹ naeb V
naobdha P niamda MHU (-dha U)   ¹² bladh VDU   ¹³ coica D
¹⁴ nai M   ¹⁵ cettuip E cetuib D cetaibh U   ¹⁶ -dhan P

37. ¹ om. d' MU: Adum VH Adham E Adaum D Adaim M
Adhaimb U   ² coa mbae E ga mbaoi P coamboi D ga mbi U
³ clann D   ⁴ Sili H   ⁵ claon P cloen D: cham VDU chamm E
⁶ dteor P tri MHU   ⁷ buadhach VU   ⁸ brigh VPD a mbrigh
EU a mbrig MH   ⁹ Pib U   ¹⁰ Pithib EDMU Pitib P

(a) *In marg. of* U: seacht moghat seacht ccet is e so airemh is firianigh do
reir an biobla.

38.　Trī meic ¹Nōe nair ²cech ³neirt,
　　⁴Sem, ⁵Cam, ⁶Iafet ⁷aurdaire :　　　　　　　190
　　is ⁸re ⁹Cam, ¹⁰calad ¹¹cīape,
　　¹²ro ¹³scarad ¹⁴ind ¹⁵airdrīge.

39.　¹Cata ²Rechta ³ba ben ⁴Sem,
　　Cata ⁵Chasta ben ⁶Iafeth,
　　Cata ⁷Flauia, ⁸co ⁹ngrād ¹⁰ngrinn,　　　　195
　　ainm mnā ¹¹Caim, ¹²nocho ¹³celim.

40.　¹Cam ²ro gab ³i ⁴nAffraicc n-ait,
　　⁵Iafeth ⁶rogab ⁷i ⁸nEoraip ;
　　nī ⁹chelar ¹⁰duinne, dar Dīa !—
　　Sem ¹¹rogab ¹²uile ¹³i ¹⁴nAisīa.　　　　200

41.　¹Tricha ²cined, ³rād ⁴nglan nglē
　　⁵cinsit ⁶ō Cham mac Noē :
　　a ⁷secht fichit, fuil ⁸ō ⁹Sem,
　　¹⁰a cūic dēc ō Iafeth.

42.　¹I ²Slēib ³Radruip ⁴aided ⁵Sēim ;　　　　205
　　⁶bās ⁷Iafeth ⁸i ⁹Slēib ¹⁰Armēin ;
　　¹¹i ¹²Slēib ¹³Raphan, ¹⁴rād ¹⁵nglan nglē,
　　¹⁶ro-thatham Cam ¹⁷meic ¹⁸Noē.

38. *This quatrain om.* M　　¹ Nai P Nae HU　　² gaeh PU cē D cen H
³ nert U　　⁴ Seim P Semh U　　　⁵ Cham ED Camh PU　　⁶ *ins.* is U :
Iafeth PU　　　⁷ aurdairce E oirrdire P airdire HU　　　⁸ is ria
VPH his ro Cam ED　⁹ Camh U　¹⁰ caladh VEU　¹¹ ciabe EH cipe P
cebe U　　¹² do H　　¹³ scaradh VU sgarad P　　¹⁴ int D an H in U
¹⁵ ardrighe E n-airdrighe P ard- D
39. ¹ Catirasta U　　　² Reacht H　　³ fa bean M　　⁴ tSem V
tSeim P tSeim H Semh U　　⁵ Casta EDHU Gasta P　　⁶ Iafedh V
Iafet P Iathfed M　　⁷ Flaia M Flagia H　　⁸ go U　⁹ ngradh VPU
ngrain M　　¹⁰ ngrind VPHU grind E　　¹¹ Cam P　　¹² nocha PDH
¹³ ceilinm E chelim D ceilim PU
40. ¹ Camh P　　² ragab H rogabh U　　³ ind VP inn E an H
⁴ *om.* n VP : Affraic P Athfraic M Affraich U　　⁵ Iathfedh M　⁶ dogab H
regabh U　　⁷ inn V ind P an H　　⁸ nEoruiph E　⁹ cel ar P chel ar
duine D chel arduin U　　　¹⁰ duini H duine *all other* MSS. *except* U
¹¹ rogob M ragab H　　　¹² huile D nili MHU　　　¹³ inn VE an H
¹⁴ Aissia VII Assia EDU
41. This quatrain *om.* VDU ; follows quatrain 21 in E.　In M the
quatrains in this part of the poem are in the following order :—37, 40,

38. Three sons of noble Noe, of every [kind of]
  strength
Sem, Ham, glorious Iafeth:
from Ham, for all his firmness,
the high-kingship was sundered.

39. Cata Rechta, she was the wife of Sem,
Cata Casta, the wife of Iafeth,
Cata Flavia, with pleasant love,
was the name of Ham's wife, I conceal it not.

40. Ham settled in pleasant Africa,
Iaphet settled in Europe;
it is not hidden from us, before God!—
Sem settled altogether in Asia.

41. Thirty races, a pure, clear saying,
sprang from Ham son of Noe:
twenty seven, which are from Sem,
fifteen from Iafeth.

42. In the mountain of Radrap the fate of Sem;
the death of Iafeth in a mountain of Armenia;
in the mountain of Rafann, a pure, clear
  saying,
the great sleep of Ham son of Noe.

41, 39, 42, omitting 38.   [1] Fichi M   [2] cinedh E cineth P cinead M
[3] radh E   [4] glan gle EPM   [5] cinsed E -set P -sead M   [6] Cham m.
Naoie E; Naoie *also in* P, Naei M   [7] coie dec badar PM   [8] og PM
[9] Seimh EP   [10] a cuig deg o Iathfeth E Is a cuig dec ag
Iathafeit P is a undec at Iathfeth M. *The version of this quatrain in* H
is as follows:—
    Tricha cinedh Chaim colaig   cimsed on fir can olaid,
    a secht fichit fuil o Sem   a cuig deg ac Iatafet.

42. [1] hi VEPD a MH   [2] sleip P sleb MU   [3] Radhruip P Rathuiris
M Radraip H Rathuir chain U   [4] aiged VH aidedh E aighed P
bas MU   [5] Sem EDMU Seimh P Seim H   [6] bass E   [7] Iathfed M
[8] hi P a H   [9] sleb EM sleab U   [10] Armen VM Armein U
[11] hi EPH   [12] sleb M sliab U   [13] Rapan V Rafan MH Rafin U
[14] radh VP   [15] raglan gle U glan gle VPMH glan ngle E   [16] ro hatham
V ro athtam ED (*in* D *changed sec. man. by writing* th *sprs. and
expuncting the 2nd* t) ro attham P ro ratham do ratham (*in rasura*) H
ro hathim U   [17] mc V mc E mac U   [18] *written* ixe P: Naei M Nace H

43.   ¹Airde ²hairce, ³baile ⁴itá
⁵tricha ⁶cubat ⁷eutroma ;
trī chēt ⁸cubat ⁹i n-a ¹⁰fat;
¹¹n-a lethet ¹²cōica ¹³cubat.   210

44.   ¹Ōen-²chubat ³'n-a ⁴tigi ⁵thair,
⁶itir ⁷fid ⁸is ⁹bidumain :
¹⁰bidumain ¹¹uimpi ¹²cen brōn,
¹³dīa 'muig ¹⁴ꝋ ¹⁵dīa ¹⁶medōn.   215

45.   A doras ¹assan ²sliss ³sōer,
⁴amail ⁵ro ordaig ⁶Noē ⁷nōem ;
⁸dāig ⁹ro oslaiced ¹⁰a tōeb ¹¹thair
¹²ār Crīst, ār ¹³Cenn, ār n-Athair.   220

46.   Trī ¹cōecait ²mīle co ³mbūaid
⁴airde ⁵Thuir ⁶noithig ⁷Nemrūaid,
cāeca ⁸mīle ⁹tar ¹⁰cech ¹¹leth
¹²rogab ¹³in Tor ¹⁴trēn ¹⁵rīgthech.

47.   ¹Trī ²cethrair ³trī fichit, ⁴fīr,
⁵āirem ⁶thoisech ⁷is trēn-ˢrīg
⁹lasandernad ¹⁰thoir ¹¹in Tor,
im ¹²Nemrūad, im ¹³Nabcodon.   225

43. ¹ airdi PMH arde na hairce fir trath U ² ins. na M (also in H, but erased): airece VE airce P airci D hairci MH ³ baili ED bail H i fail tra M ⁴ itha V itta P ta DH (before the t an a faintly sbs. cH ⁵ caeca M ⁶ cubad MH cubhat U ⁷ cutruma VE cudruma PH cutranuma D cudrama U ⁸ cubad VM ⁹ inna D ana H ¹⁰ fad EMH ¹¹ na leithe V leithed EPM na llethe D lethat U ¹² coeca V coicca D caeca M ¹³ cubad VM cubatat E cubaat (sic √D, but in D copied like cubattt) D

44. ¹ aou P aen HU ² chubad M cubhat U ³ ina natigi U (the dittography caused by a change of line) ⁴ tighi VP tighe EP tige D ⁵ tair PU thoir M ⁶ etir V eitir EP ⁷ fidh VP fid EMH bi U ⁵ ꝋ U ⁹ bittummain E bidamuin MH bidomain U ¹⁰ uitumain VP bittummain E bitumain D bidamain M bidomain U ¹¹ impe E impi PM immpi D umpi U ¹² gan EPU can H ¹³ diamuigh VP diamuich ED imaig M immaigh U ¹⁴ occus P ¹⁵ ar MU ¹⁶ medhon VU meton P.

45. ¹ ara PMH asa D ar U ² slis EMHU slios PH ³ saer VDMH saor P ⁴ is andaid E samlaid DHU ⁵ ro ordaigh VE ro ordaigh D rosordaigh U ra for ro as usual in H ⁶ om. Noe ED (ins. sec. man. D) Naoi P Nae MH Nai U ⁷ naem VMHU noeb ED naom P ⁸ daigh VEP (also perhaps D, but the mark of lenition

43.   The height of the ark, a place in which are
thirty balanced cubits;
three hundred cubits in its length;
in its breadth, fifty cubits.

44.   One cubit in its thickness eastward,
what with wood and pitch:
pitch about it without regret (?),
outside and inside.

45.   Its door out of its free side,
as holy Noe ordained;
for He would open its side eastward,
our Christ, our Head, our Father.

46.   Thrice fifty miles with victory
was the height of the famous Tower of Nemrod;
fifty miles over every side
did the strong royal Tower contain.

47.   Thrice four men and three score, truly,
the reckoning of leaders and strong kings
by whom the Tower was made in the East,
including Nemrod and Nabcodon.

faded) ardaigh U: co ros foslaic a taeb thair M   [9] roslaicedh V
roslaiced ED hosluiced P foscail H oslaicthi (*om.* ro) U   [10] *om.* a
VEP: taeb VD taobh P thaeb H taib U   [11] tair HU   [12] ar Crist
chaem ar ar n-athair M ar Cris (*sic*) uais ar innathair U   [13] cend EH
    46. [1] coecat V choicat E la P choica (*with a* d *apparently following,
but erased*) D chaecaid M   [2] cubat EP mili U   [3] -dh EPU
[4] *ins.* fa he M, ba he U: arddi E airdi MH   [5] tuir E in tuir MU
[5] noithich VE noite P *om.* MU naithid H   [7] -dh E Neamruaid M
Neamrudid *with attempt sec. man. to turn the first* d *to an* a U   [8] mili
MH   [9] dar E for HU   [10] gach VEPDU cach MH   [11] leath M
[12] rogob M dogab H -bh U   [13] an PH   [14] trenuilleach M   [15] rigtheach V
-tech PH righeach U
    47. [1] *om.* M   [2] chetrair E cethruir P ceathrar M ceathrair HU
[3] ar fichit *instead of* tri f. M: tri .xx. fieit fir (*sic*) U   [4] co M
[5] dairim V dairem P airim EU   [6] tuissech V taoisech P toissech D
thaiseach M toisech H taiseach U   [7] in M   [8] ri E righ PU
[9] lassandernadh V -adh *also* E -earn- M lasadugadh U   [10] tair VP
thoir (*the lenition mark faded*) D thair HU   [11] an PH   [12] -adh U
[12] Nabgadon VPDU -gaton P Nabhgodon U

48. ¹Im ²Assur, im ³Ibad ⁴n-ard,
    im ⁵Laitin is ⁶im ⁷Longbard,
    im ⁸Grēcus, ⁹im Gomer nglē
    im ¹⁰Ēber mōr mac ¹¹Saile.

230

49. ¹Im ²Boidb, im ³Britus ⁴cen brath,
    ⁵im ⁶German is ⁷im ⁸Garad,
    ⁹im ¹⁰Scithus, im ¹¹Gothus nglan,
    im ¹²Dardan, Sardan solam.

235

50. ¹Rī na ²talman is na tor
    ³in Rī ⁴sīnes ⁵each ⁶sāegol,
    ⁷būanaided mo ⁸chruth, mo chlī
    cid ⁹ōen in ¹⁰t-abb sa` t-airdrī.

240

51. Ro ¹scāilti na ²bērla ³dōib
    do ⁴trāetad ⁵Nemrūaid nert-mōir;
    ⁊ ro ⁶trascrad ⁷in Tor,
    ⁸comad ⁹īsligthe ¹⁰a n-ūabor.

52. ¹Cōic ²bliadna cethrachat cain,
    ³mīle secht cēt do ⁴bliadnaib,
    ō ⁵thosach ⁶domain co ⁷n-ūaill,
    ⁸no co ⁹torchair ¹⁰Tor ¹¹Nemrūaid.

245

---

48. ¹ Amasur Amabad M ² Asir P Asur HU ³ Baad D Baadh (written like baᴄᴄōɩ E Ibath H Ibhadh U ⁴ om. n- VPH ⁵ Latin E Laidin HU ⁶ am H ⁷ -bhard U ⁸ Gregus MH ⁹ mac Gomer gle M ¹⁰ Emir V Eimer P Emer MH ¹¹ Sale U

49. ¹ am MH : Imodbh U ² Bodb VH Boid EPDM ³ Boritus (*the* o *expuncted*) V Brittus E ⁴ gan brath P co mblad MU (-dh U) ⁵ um P ⁶ Gomer H ⁷ am H ⁸ Garadh V Gharadh U ⁹ nm P ¹⁰ Garath M Scotus H Scithius U ¹¹ Scotus H Gothius U ¹² Dardarn (*but the second compendium perhaps to be read* ai) D

50. *This quatrain om.* VED, *in this place in* PM, *and in* HU *at the end of the poem, where it is more appropriate so far as the sense is concerned: the version of the last line in* H *is probably correct, as it ends with the word* athair. ¹ Rig U ² talmhan U ³ an H

48.   Including Assur and lofty Ibad,
Latinus and Longbardus,
Grecus and brilliant Gomer,
great Eber son of Sale.

49.   Including Bodb and Britus without deception,
Germanus and Garad,
Scithus and pure Gothus,
Dardan and swift Sardan.

50.   King of the earth and of the lords,
the King who prolongeth every life,
may He make enduring my form, my body
though the abbot and the high king be alike.

51.   The languages were dispersed for them,
for the subjection of Nemrod, great in strength;
and the Tower was overturned,
so that their pride was humiliated.

52.   Five years and forty fair,
a thousand seven hundreds of years,
from the superb beginning of the world,
till the Tower of Nemrod fell.

---

⁴ sineas MU sinus H   ⁵ gach PU   ⁶ saoghal P saegal H saeghul U
⁷ buanaiged mo cruth can cair, is é ar n-ab is ar n-athair H, buaidnaidh-
eadha dom chorp caiu co tuga in tab sin tathair U   ⁸ cruth mo clí P
⁹ aon P   ¹⁰ tab M in tadm (?) sa tairdrigh P

51. ¹ sgaoilti P sgailti D scailtea MU   ² berlae E   ³ doip P
doibh U   ⁴ traethad VEDH traothad P thraedad (t *sprs. over first* d
yc) M thraethad U   ⁵ -oid M   ⁶ thascrad E -grad PD -cairtea U
⁷ ar P   ⁸ comud V combad E gumad U   ⁹ isslitte V isliti E islide PD
islidi MHU   ¹⁰ annuabar PU (*first* n *expuncted* P) anuabur D
anuabar PH

52. *This quatrain om.* VMH.   ¹ Coig P   ² mile P   ³ mili DU
⁴ -aiph P -uib D   ⁵ tosach P -eac U   ⁶ -uin E   ⁷ mbuaidh U
⁸ *om.* no P : no go D   ⁹ torcair P ndorcair U   ¹⁰ ins. in P   ¹¹ -ruad
D -ruaidh U

O

53.   [1]I m-Maig [2]Senair, [3]īarsin Tor,
       [4]ro [5]tinōlad [6]in [7]chōem-scol,   250
       [8]sin [9]chathraig [10]Ibitēna,
       [11]do [12]foglaim na [13]n-il-bērla.

54.   [1]Eōlaig na [2]mbērla, [3]is [4]blad [5]bind
       ar [6]a n-ērgna [7]nostuirmim,
       im [8]Fēinius [9]Farsaid [10]co [11]rath,   255
       ⁊ im [12]Chai [13]cain-brethach.

55.   [1]Hiruath, [2]Nenual brāthair Niñil,
       [3]⁊ [4]Gāedel mac [5]Ethiñir,
       [6]Dauid ⁊ Loth [7]na land,
       [8]Saliath, [9]Nabgadou, Forand,   260

56.   [1]Talemon, [2]Cainan, [3]nī [4]chel,
       [5]Caleph, [6]Mored, Gad, [7]Gomer,
       [8]Etrochius, [9]Bel, Bobel [10]binn,
       [11]Ossi, [12]Iessu, [13]Iochim,

57.   [1]Hidomus [2]is [3]Ordmor ard,   265
       [4]Achab [5]is [6]Ruben ro-ʼgarg,
       [8]Humelchus, [9]Ionan ān,
       [10]Affraim, [11]Srū, Iar mac [12]Nemān.

53. [1]immuig V immaigh ED immaigh P hi maig M a muig H a maigh U   [2]Sennair ED (S̄ E)   [3]imon M iarsan H iman U   [4]ra H [5]-ladh E -oil- P -oilead M -oileadh HU   [6]an H   [7]chaem VE caom sccoil P mor- M tren- H trom- U   [8]isin H gusin U   [9]cathraig V cathraich E catraig PH chathruigh D chatraid M catraigh U   [10]Ibithena V Ibithenae E Ibitena P Imbithena D Hebotena M Eba tena H Gan sena U   [11]ro M dimdhaghud na nilberla U   [12]foglaim V focchlaimm E foghuim D foghlaim M fodlaim H   [13]-lae E -lai P hil- M
54. [1]-laigh EU -lach PM -luich D   [2]mberlo D   [3]as PH *om.* U [4]bladh P   [5]binn PD   [6]in ergna E a u-ergnai M   [7]rosturmim VH -tuirbim P tuirmimm D -airmim U   [8]Fenius V Foenius D Feinius M Feinius U   [9]-aidh V Farr- PH Farrsaich M Farrsaigh U   [10]go D gan U   [11]brath U   [12]Chae V Chaoi E Caidhe P   [13]-breathach VM caoin-breath (ach *yc*) E chain- M
55. [1]Iruath U   [2]Nenbhal E Noenal D Naeneal M Neanual U [3]⁊ *yc* P   [4]Gaidel V Gaoidel E Gaoidhel P Goeidel D Gaedeal M

53.   In the plain of Senar, after the Tower,
       was the fair school assembled,
       in the city of Ibitena,
       for learning the manifold languages.

54.   Those skilled in the tongues—'tis tuneful fame—
       for their cunning I enumerate them :
       including Feinius Farsaid with grace
       and Cai of the just judgements.

55.   Hiruath, Nenual brother of Nel,
       Gaedel son of Etheor,
       David, Loth of the blades,
       Saliath, Nabcodon, Forand.

56.   Talemon, Cainan, there is no concealment,
       Caleph, Mored, Gad, Gomer,
       Etrochius, Bel, tuneful Bobel,
       Ossi, Iessu, Iochim.

57.   Hidomus and lofty Ordmor,
       Achab and very rough Ruben,
       Humelchus, brilliant Ionan,
       Affraim, Sru, Iar son of Nema.

Gaeid. H Goedel U   ⁵ Eithiuir EPMHU   ⁶ Dabhi E   ⁷ nalland E
na lann PDM   ⁸ Sailiath H   ⁹ -codon E Nabgodon P Nabcadon
D Nabhcadon M -godon U

56. ¹ Tailimon P Dalamon M Talumón H Tailemon U   ² cain MH
caem U   ³ nocho MU nocha H   ⁴ cél PH   ⁵ Calep E Saleph P
Quiliph M Pilib U   ⁶ Moriath M mor iath U   ⁷ Goimher E Goimer H
⁸ Etrochius (o sprs. yc) V Etroichus P Etroichiuss D Eochrochuis M
Etroichus H Etrocus U   ⁹ Bel babebind M Belbobel U   ¹⁰ bind VEHU
¹¹ Osse ED Ose M Osu U   ¹² Iasu EU Isiu M   ¹³ Iocim E Iochimm
D Iachim M Iacim U

57. ¹ Hidomius VED Hidmius P Domu; M Idonius U   ² om. MU
³ Oirdmor E Ordinor P Ordomus M Adramus U   ⁴ Achap P Acab U
⁵ Sru MU   ⁶ Ruiben EP Rumen U   ⁷ gharb E   ⁸ Humeleus EPH
Umelchus M Imeleuus U   ⁹ ins. is U   ¹⁰ Affraim is Iar VEPH
Affram P Affraim Isiar D Efraum M Eaffraim U   ¹¹ om. Sru MH
(is Iar H) Iarinach (or -mach) is Neaman U   ¹² Nemain VDH

58. ¹Nēl mac ²Fēiniusa ³nīr ⁴bfann
⁵luid ⁶i ⁷nĒigept, ⁸co ⁹Forann;   270
¹⁰i ¹¹ferann ¹²Ēigipt ¹³īartain,
¹⁴rucad ¹⁵Gāidel ār n-athair.

58. ¹Niuil U   ²Feinus P Foeniusa D Feiniusa M   ³nar MH
⁴bfand VPH fann D fann MH fand U   ⁵luidb E luig H   ⁶an EH
⁷Eigipt EHU Eigipit P Egipt D Eigep M   ⁸go D re M iar U

VI.

R³ ¶ 28 (B 8 γ 53 : M 265 a 40).

1. ¹Tobar ²Parrduis, būan a ³blad
⁴dīanaid ainm ⁵Nuchal nīam-glan;
⁶sīnit as, nī ⁷thrūag a ⁸threōir   275
ceithri srotha ⁹sōer-cheneōil.

2. ¹Fison ²*sufflatio* arfas,
Geon ³*felicitias*,
uelocitas Tigris trēn,
is *fertilis* ⁴Eufraiten.   280

3. ¹Fison sruth ola, ²sair suaire,
Tigris in fīn, sīar ³sōer-chuairt,
⁴Eufraites in mil, ⁵fodess,
Geon in loim, ⁶thuaid ⁷tibes.

1. ¹tobur B   ²Parrtuis B   ³bladh B   ⁴dianadh B   ⁵Nuchul B
⁶sighnit ass B   ⁷truag MSS.   ⁸treoir B   ⁹saer M -cheineoil B
2. ¹Fisson B   ²suflatio B suflaitio M   ³*sic* M (*which must be
retained for the metre*): -itas B   ⁴Eofraten M

VII.

R³ ¶ 66, 89 (β 34.20; β¹ 34.39; β² 10.21; M 267 δ 6;
H 102 a 35).

¹Cēt ²aimsir ³in ⁴bethad ⁵bind   285
⁶ōthā Adam co dīlind,
sē ⁷bliadna ⁸cōicat, ⁹rād nglē,
¹⁰ar ¹¹sē ¹²chētaib ar ¹³mīle.

¹cead β   ²aimser MII aimsior β   ³an Hβ   ⁴beath H
bheatha β bhethadh β¹²   ⁵bhinn β^{m2}   ⁶ota M ató H ata o Adhamh

58. Nel son of Feinius who was not weak
went into Egypt, to P.₁arao;
in the land of Egypt thereafter,
was born Gaedel our father.

⁹ -and EPMU   ¹⁰ hi bf. E hi f. D, a f. MH   ¹¹ -nd EHU   ¹² Eigipti
V Eigipit P Egipt D Eigeipti H Egeapt U   ¹³ iardtaiu E iartoin
Diardain U   ¹⁴ rueadh V rugad EII ruce P rugadh U   ¹⁵ Gaedeal
V MH Gaoidel EP Goeidel D Gaedhel U

VI.

1. The spring of Paradise, lasting its renown,
whose name is Nuchal of clear brilliancy;
there extend from out of it, not miserable is its
strength,
four rivers of free nature.

2. Phison was revealed as *sufflatio*,
Geon as *felicitas*,
strong Tigris as *uelocitas*,
and Euphrates as *fertilitas*.

3. Phison a river of oil, gently eastward,
Tigris wine, a free circuit westward,
Euphrates honey, southward,
Geon milk, which laugheth northward.

3. ¹ Fisson B   ² saer B   ³ saerchuart M   ⁴ Eofrates M
⁵ fodhes B fodeas M   ⁶ tuaidh B   ⁷ tibhes B thibeas M

VII.

The first age of the tuneful world
from Adam to the Flood,
fifty-six years, a clear saying,
over six hundreds and a thousand.

go dilinn β^{012} ⁷ bliadhna β ⁸ caecad M caogad β^{012} ⁹ radh β
rangle β^{12} ¹⁰ air β^{01} ¹¹ se β^{12} ¹² ceadaibh β chedaib β^{12} (ced- β^2)
¹³ mili H mhile β^{012}

VIII.

R³ ¶ 66 (II 98 *a* 3).

Dia Haine docuas inti,
isa n-aire comlain chinti.   290
Dé Mairt dolodar amach
asin lestar chaem-chlarach.

IX.

R³ ¶ 68 (II 98 *a* 21).

1. Ceatrar as (s)ía saegal slán,
indisis Cánoin chomslan,
Adam, Iareth, ailli ^(a)geal,   295
Náe nar is Mathasalem.

2. Tricha ar noi cetaib can ail
saegal airmidnech Adaim ;
a dó seseat noi cet cain,
saegal Iareth abrad-chain.   300

3. A noi seseat ar noi cet
do Maithisailem, ni breg :
caoga ar noi cet, nir bo liach,
saegal Naee meic Laimíach.

(*a*) geall MS.

VIII.

On Friday there was the ingoing
into the ark complete, appointed.
On Tuesday they came out
from the fair-boarded vessel.

IX.

1. Four who are longest of complete life,
the perfect Canon hath related :
Adam, Iareth, a bright praise,
noble Noe and Mathasalem.

2. Thirty over nine hundreds without reproach
the venerable life of Adam :
nine hundred sixty and two fair,
the life of Iareth of the fair brows.

3. Nine hundred sixty and nine
to Mathasalem, it is no falsehood :
nine hundred and fifty, it was not pitiful
the life of Noe son of Lamech.

NOTES ON SECTION I.

PROSE TEXTS.

First Redaction.

(For the explanation of the asterisk see the beginning of R².)

1, 1*. *Fecit* shows that ∞ R¹ worked on an ante-Hieronymian text of Genesis. The Vulgate has *creauit*, as in R³ ¶ 20.

The gloss in R¹ is of some critical importance. It is absent from ¶ 1*, therefore it was not incorporated in the text of *Q. In LF it appears in the form ꝛ *nĩ fil . . . . fairseom*, to which F (and L *sec. man.*) add *fēin*. The version in *X is preserved in R³ ¶ 20; there we have the older *feisin*. In LF *nā foircend* precedes *fairseom*, in *X it follows *fairseom feisin*. Such a shifting about of words is practically diagnostic of the incorporation of a superscript gloss, therefore *nā foircend* must be a further glossarial addition made after the incorporation of the original gloss with the text. The history of the interpolation was therefore as follows :—

(1) The gloss existed, interlined or marginal, in √LF*X*Q in the simple form .i. *nĩ fil tosach fairseom* : a very natural comment—"In the beginning God made . . . . (note, that *He* hath no beginning)."

(2) ∞ *Q was copied, without the gloss, or at most with it in an interlineation.

(3) There must have been a MS. √LF*X in which the gloss was incorporated, and to which *nā foircend* was added glossarially. (In R³, these words must have been still interlined in √BMH, for B has them in a different place from the other two MSS. of R³.)

(4) From this MS. √LF and *X derive. But as F generally displays closer affinities with *Q than with L, we must suppose that L has undergone scribal distortion or editorial manipulation in deriving from √LF. If we had more of *X, we should probably find it nearest to ∞ R¹ : F and *Q must on the whole be good copies of √LF *X *Q,

as they are in close agreement : L is the farthest away from
∞ R¹.

2, 2*. Here again we find evidence that *Q represents an
older text; in 2* we have *cētumus, olchena, Āendidin* as
contrasted with *chētus, archena, Āine,* in 2. *Dorigne* and the
consistent spelling -*nd*- are also older than *doringne* and the
spelling -*nn*-. In these readings F shows a closer affinity to
*Q than to L.

Soillsi aingel is an attempt at a solution of the old puzzle,
as to how light could have been created before the luminaries :
see Augustine, *Civ. Dei* xi. 9.   The creation of the angels
upon the First Day is usually described in summaries of the
Creation such as this : for example, in the Arabic *Book of
the Rolls* :[1] "The Holy First Day, chief of Days : early in it
God created the Upper Heaven and the Worlds, and the
highest rank of Angels . . . and the Archangels,'' etc.   So in
Isidore, *Etym.* v. 39 : *Prima aetas in exordio sui continet
creationem mundi.   Primo enim die Deus in lucis nomine
condidit angelos.*   And in the old English *Lyff of Adam and
Eve* (ed. Horstmann, *Sammlung altenglischer Legenden,*
p. 220 ff.) : "God as his wille was behihte to make liht : and
þo he made angelus.''

Firmament.   The absence of the definite article shows
that the writer took the word, which he found in his Latin
Bible, for a proper name.

The reading in F, *neam .i. firmamaind,* is a misplacement
of a gloss, for *neam* must originally have explained the
difficult word *firmament,* and not *vice versa.*   The gloss must
also have been in *X, for in R³ ¶ 20, third interpolation,
it has displaced *firmament* altogether.   That *X, and not
*Q, is the source of this passage is shown by its use of
nem-chruthaig as against the *n-ēchruthach* of F* Q.   This
excerpt from *X is further instructive, as it shows that all
the dates are interpolations.   They *precede* the works in *X,
but *follow* them in the other MSS.   The original text was
therefore a bald list of the works of creation—"He made first
the formless mass.   He made Firmament.   He made Earth
and Seas,'' etc.   The names of the days were interlined as

---

[1] Ed. Gibson (Camb. Univ. Press), transl. p. 3.

glosses, and taken in at different times and in different places. They were not securely in the text even in L, for at least three of them have been inserted *sec. man.* in that MS.

After *tondaitecha*, the words *in mara* in LF and *na fairrge* in *Q kill one another. They are both glosses, inserted independently by readers who knew or discovered for themselves that *marine* creatures were created on the Fifth Day. It follows almost inevitably that *ind ácoir* and *in talman* are glossarial also.

Día after *ro chumsain* is correctly omitted by E; as it has entered the text before *íarom* in *Q, and after it in √LF*X, it is suspect on the principle already set down. Most likely it remained as ᵹ till late in the R² tradition. In the original text, the verb *ro chumsain*, like *dorigni*, had no subject expressed.

Oipriugad for *foirbthiugad* is another mark of affinity between F and *Q.

⁊ *uí ō follomnacht itir* may perhaps have been suggested by the OL text *requieuit ab omnibus operibus suis quae inchoauit Deus facere* (cf. LXX, ὧν ἤρξατο ὁ θεὸς ποιῆσαι)—an implication that the Divine energy continued after the accomplishment of the Creation. As it occurs in F*Q it must be original, or a very early interpolation; more probably the latter, as it is absent from *X.

⁊ *dorad bendachtain foraib* in R² must have been inserted after the incorporation of the first leaf of *Q with that text. It is unknown to LF*X, and breaks awkwardly into the sense.

Foraib is almost certainly a copyist's mistake for *fair*: he forgot that the blessing was upon the rest-day, not upon the creatures (Gen. ii. 3).

2ᴀ (in R²). A group of three late interpolations (y^1, y^2, y^3), which (like the gloss at the end of 2* just noticed) entered the *Q tradition independently, after its first leaf had been separated from the rest of R¹. The first two were borrowed by yR^3, but the third was ignored; as yR^3 was nothing if not acquisitive, we infer that *Z, his copy of R², did not contain it. Y², which is a natural pendant of ¶ 2, was the first of the three to make its way into the text; but y^1 y^2 must both have been no more than marginal notes in *Z, for yR^3

has inserted y^2 *before*, not after, the list of the works of Creation, and has taken in y^1 at a different place (¶ 25).

꞊ *a allus* is a gloss: it is not found in R^3, and therefore was unknown to *Z.

The original purpose of y^2 was to show that Adam was made from the four elements. A further interpolator has confused this by inserting the specification of the countries from whose earth Adam was fashioned. YR^3 (¶ 25) has discovered anew the purpose of the passage, and has expressed his discovery by adding the comment *is amlaid . . . in gach duini.*

For parallels to the ideas here expressed as to the materials from which Adam was made, see Stokes, *Three Irish Glossaries* p. xl: idem, *Man Octipartite* (sic), in R.C., i, p. 261. The formation of Adam from the four elements is thus described in the Syriac *Cave of Treasures* :[2] "The angels saw the right hand of God opened out flat and stretched out over the whole world : and all creatures were collected in the palm of His right hand. And they saw that He took from the whole mass of the earth one grain of dust, and from the whole nature of water one drop of water, and from all the air which is above, one puff of wind, and from the whole nature of fire a little of its heat and warmth"—and therewith made Adam. In the same work Budge quotes from a Coptic tradition preserved in *The Discourse of Abbatôn the Angel of Death*, by Timothy, archbishop of Rakoti (Alexandria), to the effect that the clay of which Adam was made was brought by the angel Mûrîêl "from the land of the East." More specific but mutually contradictory information is afforded by various Jewish Rabbis on the subject. Eisenmenger[3] quotes Rabbi Meir as saying that the dust from which Adam was made was brought together from the whole earth : ingeniously deducing the fact from a combination of Ps. cxxxix [Vulgate cxxxviii] 16 and 2 Chron. xvi. 9. Rabbi 'Oshaya declares that the body of the first man came from Babel, his head from the land of Israel, his limbs from the other countries. Other theories are given in the same place, but none so specific as the version which has reached the Irish interpolator.

---

[2] Tr. Budge, pp. 51-2.   [3] *Entdecktes Judenthum*, vol. I, p. 364.

For Garad, Arabia, Lodain, Agoria the homily on Creation in *Lebor Brecc*[4] substitutes Malon, Arton, Biblon, Agore respectively.   I can make nothing of these, unless "Agoria" be a misreading for "Moria": in some forms of Irish script capital *M* is not unlike *Ag*.   Mount Moriah is alleged to have been the site of the altars of Solomon, David, Noah, Cain, and Abel as well as of Abraham, and is specified by Maimonides (*Beit Abachria*, c. 2) as being the source of the earth from which Adam was made.   According to *The Dialogue of Salomon and Saturnus*,[5] Adam was made of eight pounds weight of materials, which are specified, but here irrelevant.

The same authority agrees with *y*³ in saying that Adam was created as at the age of thirty, but the age of Eve is not specified.   According to the *Lebor Brecc* homily, Adam was created nine months before Eve.

3. 3*. The legend of the Fall of the Angels, here introduced as a necessary preliminary to the Fall of Man, is part of the complicated angel-demon mythology that was absorbed from Persian sources and developed in post-exilic Judaism: quite likely it has its roots in the myth of the combat of Marduk and Tiâmat, which is the prologue to the Babylonian legend of Creation.   Brought to shape by false exegesis of such scattered passages as Isaiah xiv. 12, Luke x. 18, Revelation ix. 1 ff., the story was taken over into early Christian tradition.   The first of these passages, foreshadowing the downfall of the King of Babylon, and addressing him ironically as "Morning Star," has given the name "Lucifer" to the leader of the revolting angels: see Augustine *Civ. Dei*, xi. 15.   The story appears in most early paraphrases of the Biblical history, as for instance in *Saltair na Rann*, no. vi, and in the fourteenth century *Cursor Mundi*.[6]   None of the LG texts knows of the *second* fall of the infernal angels, after the temptation of Eve, referred to in the hymn *Altus Prosator*, verse G.

In both F and L this paragraph is desperately difficult to decipher: impossible indeed, at least for me, without the

---

[4] Ed. MacCarthy, Todd Lectures. iii. p. 48.

[5] Ed. Kemble (Aelfric Society, 1848), p. 180.

[6] Ed. Morris, E.E.T.S., line 473 ff.

help of ultra-violet photographs prepared by Professor Ditchburn. But the page is so badly rubbed in both MSS., that the photographs do not recover the whole text: it is, however, clear that L here stands by itself, and F and *Q, though not identical, are related. L's reading looks like a scribal guess at an illegible passage in √L. Comparison between the two texts reveals two or three minor interpolations, indicated by the marks ‡–‖ on the printed page, but not calling for special remark. *Imbe* in *Q as against *Nime* in LF is probably right. I take ⁊ *do Eua cona chlainn* to be a double interpolation. In the original, Lucifer and Adam were in partnership. Then someone, forgetting that Adam was at the time expected to be a virginal immortal, added *cona chlaind*. After that someone else slipped in ⁊ *do Eua*, and forgot to make the consequential change *cona cclaind*.

In R², *do Neimi* is anomalous, but it is certainly what it looks like in V. It is very worn and obscure in this place.

The "Nine orders" of the Angels are very frequently specified in Apocryphal literature, as in *The Book of the Secrets of Enoch*, xx. 1.[7] The following enumeration is given by Solomon, bishop of Basrah:[8] "The angels are divided into nine classes and three orders. The upper order contains Cherubim, Seraphim, and Thrones, and these are the bearers of God's throne: the middle order contains Lords, Powers, and Rulers: the lower order contains Principalities, Archangels, and Angels." Isidore (*Etym.* VII. v. 4) gives a similar enumeration, but in a different sequence.

[*Ro*]-*diumsach inti Lucifer*, though appearing both in *Q and in LF, is probably an early interpolation, seeing that the words of the Almighty are habitually reported in Latin. It is probably nothing more than some reader's personal opinion on Lucifer's proceedings.

The words *Venite*, etc., are a reminiscence of the sentence upon the builders of Babel—*Venite et confundamus linguam eorum* (Gen. xi. 7). The words *ut uideamus*, imported into

---

[7] Charles, *Apocrypha and Pseudepigrapha of the O.T.*, vol. ii, p. 441. See also Colossians i. 16: *Irish Liber Hymnorum* (Henry Bradshaw Society edn.), vol. ii, p. 155.

[8] As quoted by Budge, *Cave of Treasures*, p. 45.

the *Q tradition from the preceding verse 5 of the Babel narrative, are also found in the quotation from the Babel story in *Auraicept na nÉces.*[9] The Irish translation there given, *mutatis mutandis*, is identical with that found here in *Q. Obviously the annotator of R² was familiar with the *Auraicept*: we find further evidence of this on a later page.

4, 4*. That the envy of Satan for his supplanter was the reason for the Temptation and the Fall of Man, is the usual belief, derived ultimately from that popular apocryphon, *The Book of Adam and Eve.* The passage, which it is needless to quote here, will be found in Charles, *Apocrypha and Pseudepigrapha*, ii, 137. The Irish historian has, however, missed the contrast between the *Paradisus spirituum*, from which Lucifer was cast out, and the *Paradisus corporum* (not "heaven") which was to have been the portion of Adam: even the glossators in R³ overlooked this, though they could have learnt of it from Comestor, *Historia Scholastica*, chap. xxi. Our text knows nothing of the refusal of Lucifer to do homage to Adam: a very common incident in Creation stories. It is related in the Lebor Brecc *Homily.*

Doluid Iofer Niger. The subject of the verb must originally have been *Lucifer*, carried through from the preceding sentence. "Iofer Niger" is beyond question an intrusive gloss, written in by someone fresh from reading the *Life* of the fourth-century St. Juliana.[10] The name is there given as an alternative for Belial son of Beelzebub, *totius mali inuentor*: but so far as I have been able to find out for myself, or through enquiries which the Rev. P. Grosjean, S.J., has most kindly made on my behalf, the name does not appear to be recorded in any other text. Bespelled by Juliana, this being is compelled to confess his own misdeeds, the first of which is *Ego sum qui feci Adam et Euam in Paradiso praeuaricari.*[10a] The editors of *Acta Sanctorum* quote variant forms—Iophin, Iofet, Iofen, Tophet, and they suggest an (improbable) etymology (Hebrew שָׁחֹר, *sahōr*, "black").

---

[9] Ed. Calder, p. 12.

[10] Acta Sanctorum, February, vol. ii, esp. p. 875.

[10a] Alluding, of course, not to the original transgression, but to the subsequent subterfuges of the culprits. Our glossator has overlooked this: so has the Irish translator of the Juliana text.

The relevant passage is quoted in the glosses to *Félire Oengusso*:[11] the name there appears as Iafer, Iofer, and (in *Lebor Brecc*) Ethiar. Of all these forms, "Tophet" is the most comprehensible, but is not on that account necessarily the most authentic. The critical history of this interpolation usefully supplements that of the gloss in ¶ 1. It was absent from *X, as will be seen by reference to ¶ 31 : R³ cannot have taken this from *Z, because that MS., being dependent for its opening words upon *Q, would have included the demon's name. It is also absent from F, which here shows itself earlier in tradition even than *Q. In L it has become distorted by corruption : the form there found, *Iarngir*, may be compared with *Ifirnaig*, the form which the name has assumed in the Irish text of *Vita Iulianae* (R.C., xxxiii, p. 316) under the influence of the word *Ifernd*.

The occasional superiority of F and *X to *Q is further illustrated in this ¶; *Q contains two other interpolations, not in *XF. *I ffochraic dō* is an attempt to fill in what someone took for a lacuna after *dobērtha*; and *co curp sćim* is a cheville borrowed from Poem V, line 93.

The detached part of this paragraph, which follows ¶ 5A in R², contains an unintelligible expression ⁊ *cenn fri cotlud*. Though a guesswork rendering for it is offered in the translation, I suspect that it is really nothing but an early misreading of *cen forcend*, "without end."

5, 5*. This ¶ was no part of ∞ R¹. It must have been a marginal gloss in √R¹; it was taken into the text before the words *Conid aire sin*, etc. in *Q, and after them in √LF*X. Moreover, the differences between the texts in the two traditions cannot be explained except on the assumption that when it was in the marginal-gloss stage *it was in Latin throughout*, and that what we have are two independent attempts at a translation. The renderings into Irish of the words of the Deity are later still. Those in *Q are obviously quite independent of those in LF.

On the whole the texts are Old Latin. *Terra es et in terram ibis* is OL : Vulg. has *Pulvis es et in puluerem ibis*. Sabatier's restoration of the OL of the second quotation is *In sudore faciei tui edes panem tuum* : Vulg. has *In sudore*

---

[11] R.I.A. edition, p. 52; H. Bradshaw Soc. edition, p. 74.

uultus tui uesceris pane. Our text lies between the two; but Sabatier in his notes quotes an identical version from Hieronymus *In Isaiam.* The OL of the third quotation is *Multiplicans multiplicabo tristitias tuas et gemitum tuum; in tristitiis paries filios.* Vulg. has *Multiplicabo acrumnas tuas et conceptus tuas: in dolore paries filios.*

It is worth passing notice that the biblical order of the three texts is reversed. Almost certainly the original glossator quoted them from memory.

We note as a contribution to the genealogy of the MSS. that the unauthorized addition *et filias tuas* is omitted in F, inserted without translation in L, and inserted with translation in *Q. We have no excerpt from *X at this point, so we do not know what was in that MS.

Sasam in R¹ may also be read *sasad,* in the obscurity of the page.

5A. (in R²). I cannot find the reading *Ecce os* in any of the Latin versions, but it is presupposed by all the redactions.

Is cuma, which is absent from E, does not seem to make any reasonable sense: the suggested translation is a mere makeshift. I suspect that the words have no glossarial or other connexion with the text at all; that they were originally a marginal scribble conveying a surreptitious communication from one student to another on some subject of transient interest—"Never mind"; "It doesn't matter."

In chēt-ghaire, here adopted from P as against VE. is certainly right: the gloss was clearly suggested by line 84 of the poem no. V. The change to *choibche* is arbitrary, made by someone who did not understand the original reading.

It is obvious that this ¶ is an interpolation, quite irrespective of its absence from R¹. It makes the creation of Eve follow the Fall!

6. This paragraph is the most difficult to read of the whole obscure first page of L. Here again *Q gives a better text, though there are several interpolations, especially the alternative version of the death of Abel.

There are numerous speculations as to the instrument of Abel's murder. *The Book of Adam and Eve* does not enlighten us. *The Book of the Rolls* says that a sharp

stone was used. In the Old English versions, it is commonly
said that the instrument was an ass-bone: thus, in the *Lyff of
Adam and Eve* we read "wiþ þe cheke-bon of an asse he smot
him on þe hed"; and in *Cursor Mundi* (1073) we are told—

> Wit the chafte ban of a ded has
> Men sais þat þar wit slan he was.

This was presumably suggested by the exploit of Samson
against the Philistines. *Saltair na Rann*, which follows *The
Book of Adam and Eve*, has nothing to say on the subject:
and there does not appear to be any authority for the idea
that a camel-bone was used. Did the old Irish historians
fully comprehend the difference between an ass and a camel?
In Cashel Cathedral there is a quaint carving of an elephant,
of a much later date, which reveals a very rudimentary
conception of the appearance of an exotic animal: and as in
ancient Ireland the camel and the ass were equally
unfamiliar,[12] it is quite possible that they were supposed to
be similar or identical.

"*Lasin enáim chamaill*" is the best that I can make of
the faint traces in L. It seems to be different from the *do
lecain chamaill* of R² and the *fid chnama* of FR³ (§ 87). The
version of this paragraph in F is glossarial, and has ousted
its lemma: the original form (with some minor verbal
variations) is preserved by L*Q. The F version has been
written after R² attained its present form, in which the Flood
is stated to be a punishment for the murder of Abel. One
of the glossators of R³ has copied it in ¶ 87, directly from F
or perhaps √F; this late and corrupt version cannot come
from the early MS. *X, which is the source of most of the R¹
glosses in R³.

Fo intamail marbtha na n-idbart is a gloss which has come
into the *Q tradition after its incorporation with R²: it refers
to Exodus xiii. 13, xxxiv. 20.

7. The folio torn from *Q to complete √R² comes to an
end just before ¶ 7. The mutilated MS. still remained, to
form the basis of R³: the *Q equivalent of this paragraph
will be found in R³ at ¶ 88. The text of L is thus revealed as

---

[12] See *Proceedings*, Royal Irish Academy, xxxiii, section C, p. 530.

corrupt. *Mac Adaim* has become *imorro*: *aireagda ro bái ac* has dropped out, almost certainly by oversight of a *cor fá chasán* (these words are in a *cor fá chasán* in F)[13]: *acca mbái cland* is a gloss. In these respects F follows *Q exactly. The genealogy breaks the sense awkwardly, and is doubtless an early interpolation: it appears in all three MSS. Most likely it was first written by an annotator in the margin. The second interpolation of L is not in F, which substitutes the *Imroimadar* . . . . *Olíbana* also found at the end of ¶ 88.

The remainder of the text of this part of R¹ is genealogical, giving the following particulars—

(i) Seth to Noah, a genealogy at first assumed rather than expressed, but early interpolated into ¶ 7.

(ii) The three sons of Noah, with their inheritances (¶ 8).

(iii) The sons of Japhet (¶ 9).

(iv) The descendants in Ireland of Magog son of Japhet (¶ 10). Everything outside this brief scheme may be taken as interpolated matter.

Acca mbái claind, shown by its absence from F*Q to be glossarial in the L tradition, is interesting, as it proves the acquaintance of a glossator in that tradition with poem no. V (see line 185 of that poem). There are two quatrains from this poem quoted in R¹, from a version widely different from that which appears in R², R³.

In tAdam tánisi has grown out of a confused and inaccurate recollection of 1 Corinthians xv. 45.

The second interpolation is otiose, as it merely repeats what has gone before. F has a different interpolation here, which must come from a MS. of R² (¶ 10, 11): gR³ has copied it, like the preceding paragraph, from F or from √F. Note that the discovery that the wives of Noah and his sons were their respective sisters had not been made when the MS. of R² used by gF was written. Also note that the expression *na hairci sin*, which appears in the L interpolation, postulates a previous mention of the Ark which, in fact, does not occur in the present context.

---

[13] An illustration of the fact that the *external form* of the texts is of considerable importance in criticising MSS., and especially in determining their affinities.

The almost complete absence of the Flood story from R^1 contrasts notably with the emphasis laid upon it in R^2, R^3, and is one of several indications of the primitive simplicity of that text.

The names of the women of Noah's family were themes for endless vain speculation. According to *The Book of Jubilees* Noah's wife was called 'Emzârâ, and the wives of his sons were respectively Sêdêqêtêlĕbâb, Nê'êlâtamâ'ûk, and 'Adâtan'êsês. Various Jewish and other apocryphal authorities name Noah's wife Noria. Noema, Bath-Enos, Tithea, and Haieal; Eutychus names Salit, Nahlat, Arisisah as the wives of his sons.[14] The poem *Athair cáich* gives Cata Rechta, Cata Chasta, Cata Flauia as the sons' wives (quatrain 39). Olla, here named as Shem's wife, there becomes the wife of Seth. Comestor gives similar names—Phuarpara for Noah's wife, and Pharphia, Cataflua, Fliva as the sons' wives. Cata Flauia or Cata Flua, expanded into Cata Folofia, appears in the compilation known as *Bansenchus* as the wife of *Cain*—confusion between Cain and Cam or Ham is not infrequent—as we may see in the *Book of Leinster* facsimile 136 b 32. In the *Dialogue of Salomon and Saturnus*[15] this tradition is combined with that in the text before us. Noah's wife is there called Dalila : those of Ham and Japhet are respectively Jatareeta and Cataflunia, but, the author adds, "by other names are they named, Olla, Ollina, and Ollibana." Shem's wife does not appear : indeed, Shem himself has become the wood of which the ark was made. In the fifteenth century *Master of Oxford's Catechism* the omission was rectified : Noah's wife is called Dalida, and the sons' wives are Cateslinna, Latereeta, and Aurea, otherwise Ollia, Olina, Olybana.[16] In the Pseudo-Berossus of Johannes Annius[16a]—for what that absurd document may be

[14] Fabricius, *Codex Pseudepigraphus Vet. Test.*, p. 277.

[15] Ed. Kemble, p. 184.

[16] Ibid., p. 218. The confusion of D and L (Δ, Λ) in these last two versions of the name of Noah's wife shows that it must come ultimately from a Greek source.

[16a] On this worthy see *Proceedings* R.I.A., viii, p. 354 ff. The only reason for quoting him here is the fact that he had somehow become acquainted with these names : the use which he made of them concerns no one but himself.

worth—we read how "Noah taught astronomy, division of
time, and astrological predictions, and he was considered as
being of divine origin : therefore was he called *Olybama* and
Arsa, which mean 'heaven' and 'sun' wherefore the
Scythians of Armenia have towns Olybama and Arsa Ratha
and the like."[17] In the Caedmon *Genesis*[18] the names of these
women are given as Percoba, Olla, Oliua, Olliuani. Gollancz,
in his introduction to the sumptuous facsimile of the
Caedmon MS.,[19] considers that the passage containing these
names is an interpolation, on the ground that elsewhere the
MS. closely follows the Biblical text. He suggests that they
have been picked out more or less at random from some
Onomasticon of Biblical names, in which Aholah, Aholibah,
Aholibamah (Vulgate *Oolla*, *Ooliba*, *Oolibama*) occurred
together. This is quite admissible, assuming the early
existence (and local availability) of such an Onomasticon ;
but the compiler can hardly have taken the trouble to
look up the unsavoury connexion in which the first two
of these names are found (Ezekiel xxiii). His suggestion
that Percoba is a corruption of "Berseba" seems, perhaps,
less happy. Percoba figures in *Bansenchus* along with her
daughters-in-law, thus characterized (*Book of Leinster* facs.
136 b, 35–40).

> Percoba ben Noe co n-nāri,[20]
> Cen choi, cen gāri—ba gand![21]
> Copa sēim ba comse a eāem-ṫir,[22]
> Toirsech ea cōiniud a cland.
> Olla setig Sēim blāith bithi,
> Ben Chaim Oliuan o hāis,
> Commām Iafeth Olīuane,
> Na tarat barr for bāis.

"Percoba the wife of Noe with shame,[21] without weeping,
without laughter—how dull![22] That she was modest suited

---

[17] Fabricius, *op. cit.*, p. 245.
[18] Also in *Saltair na Rann*, ed. Stokes, lines 2485–2488.
[19] Published 1927 by the British Academy.
[20] Referring, presumably, to the episode of his drunkenness.
[21] Lit., "it was niggardly"! The translation adopted is a perhaps
supererogatory attempt to endow the cheville with some semblance of
sense.
[22] Ba comsech cā caem-ṫir MS., which is unmetrical.

her fair husband, sad in lamenting her were her children.
Olla the spouse of Sem, smooth and feminine, the wife of
Ham Oliuan of free-will: the wife of Japhet Oliuana, that
won not the goal over death.'' Epiphanius (*Adv. Haeres.*
I ii 26) gives us a long and silly story about ''Noria wife of
Noah'' who burnt the Ark while it was a-building. This is
irrelevant here: but it may not be a mere accidental coincidence
that he makes reference immediately afterwards to a certain
prophet, one *Barkabba*, whose name he describes as suitable,
Καβββᾶ γὰρ ἑρμηνεύεται ʻπορνεία' κατὰ τὴν Συριακὴν διάλεκτον.
For completeness' sake we may add that the poem beginning
Kedig dam a Dē do nim, contained in the Irish *Sex Aetates
Mundi,* has the same names, Copha, Olla, Oliua. It also gives
Olla as the wife of Seth, along with Pibb and Pithibb, the
wives of Adam's other married sons (cf. Poem V, line 188).

8. The *Q version of this ¶, much farced with glosses and
interpolations, appears in R³, partitioned between ¶ 89 *ad fin.*
and ¶ 92. Its principal contribution to criticism is the close
relationship which once more it shows between that MS. and
F, as both have a glossarial addition correcting the number
of the sons of Shem (but in different words). On the other
hand it does not show some careless omissions of F.

The world was supposed, on the basis of the data supplied
in Genesis x, to have been divided into 72 nations or linguistic
groups: see for instance Isidore, *Etym.* IX ii. The total of
30 + 30 + 15 is 75, which is three too many: the glossarial
note just referred to corrects this.

The names of Shem's sons here specified are the *first three*
of those enumerated in Gen. x. 22. It is not clear why they
should be reversed in order. ''Persius'' corresponds to the
Biblical Elam.

Cush and Canaan are the *first and last* of the sons of
Ham enumerated in Gen. x. 6.

The sons of Japhet are more disguised. Dannai presumably means *Dodanim* (recte *Rodanim*) at the end of the
list in Gen. x. 4. *Grēgus* no doubt is the same as *Javan*
(= Ionians). *Hispāinius* is *Tarshish*, the leading town in
Southern Spain. This, like ''Dodanim,'' appears in
Gen. x. 4 as a son, not of Japhet, but of his son Javan. The
equation *Gomerus* = the Biblical *Gomer* needs no comment.

9. The *Q version of this ¶ appears is R³, partitioned, owing to later interpolation, between ¶ 94 and ¶ 98. It became the common property of early historians, and appears also in *Sex Aetates Mundi*, from which another version of it has entered the text of H, in the long extract from *Sex Aetates* which forms our ⸕ 95. It is also found in Nennius. Leaving for the moment the general question of the text and its origin, let us concentrate our attention upon the LG version, as it appears in LF*Q. It is unknown to R². The irrelevance of the passage to the main purpose of LG shows that it can be no part of the original text: but as it appears in *Q it must have been an early interpolation. The oldest form of it, however, happens to be preserved by a late interpolation in H (¶ 93): *Iathféth dono mac Náe, is úad tuaiscert-leth na Haissia ⁊ lucht na Heorpa uile.* This must derive from a tradition earlier than the extant R¹ texts: in these, the obviously glossarial *.i. Aissia Becc, Airmen, ⁊ Fir na Scithia* had already become incorporated after *Haissia,* making it necessary to repeat *is úad* before *lucht.* L makes the further addition of *Media,* and corrupts *tuaiscert-leth* to *sior-deise.* *"Mac Náe"* was probably also glossarial, and I suspect that it was still interlined when ∝R³ dealt with the text: it does not appear in H in the "full-dress" form in which we find the passage in ¶ 94, though BM both contain it.

I take it that these words, and the preceding quatrain (*Tricha mac min*) were set out in √HMB as follows:—

To the margin of this MS. someone added against these words *is iad a cland-scm* I*enfamaid*, which appears in all three derivatives. M, and B as presented by its eighteenth-century copyists, follow the text with this addition, and display no more than unimportant orthographical variations. But ∝H started a vicious tradition by overlooking the words in the *cor fā chasān* (line 2 of the above figure) at the end of the quatrain. He proceeded from the quatrain to line 3; thence, misled by the continuity of the sense, to line 4; and did not notice the omitted words till he came to *Alaxandruch*. So he inserted them in his transcript at the place which he had reached, allowing the repetition of the words *is ūad* . . . . *Alax.* to remain, to save himself the trouble of making erasures. As he wrote *Greg Beg* . . . . *Greg Mōr* in the first of these repetitions (¶ 94) and reversed the order in the second (¶ 98) it follows that the scribe of his exemplar (√HMB) must have accidentally omitted *Greg Mōr*, and inserted it as an interlined correction. Large interpolations were subsequently made piecemeal in the H tradition—¶ 93 after the quatrain, and ¶¶ 95–97 before *Grecus mac Iafeth*. From this point onward the two texts, R¹ and *Q, are virtually identical, and we need notice no more than that *Q justifies the insertion of *mac* after *Hisicon imorro in tres,* where L has left it out.

Taking now the paragraph in detail: the first few lines, and probably the only original part of the paragraph, enumerate the peoples descended from Japhet in Western Asia and Europe. The first interpolation enlarges on these details, assigning various peoples to the sons of Japhet from whom they are descended. These sons are the same as those enumerated above, in ¶ 8, excluding "Dannai," who is here disregarded. *Grecus* and *Essbāinus* correspond to the Biblical *Javan* and *Tubal*. Isidore helps us to link them together: "*Iauan a quo Iones qui et Graeci, Thubal a quo Iberi, qui et Hispani*.[23] Gomer, according to Isidore (*loc. cit.*), is the ancestor of the Galatae or Galli, so it is natural to affiliate to him two personages, Emoth and Ibath, who are in the traditional Teutonic and Celtic ancestry respectively; even although these have no warrant either in Genesis or in Isidore. The important son Magog does not appear: but that is because the following interpolations have divorced him from his context. Properly speaking, ¶ 10 should follow on immediately after the first interpolation, to which it belongs.

The second interpolation is an Irish version of the Frankish "Table of Nations," published first by Grimm,[24]

---

[23] *Etym.*, IX, ii, 28–29.
[24] *Teutonic Mythology*, Eng. Tr. by Stallybrass, vol. iv, p. 1734.

and afterwards, with a much more extensive *apparatus criticus*, by Müllenhoff.[25] This document must date from about the year 520, as Müllenhoff has shown—basing his conclusions on the names included and (what is equally important) omitted. The genealogy starts from the statement for which Tacitus is our oldest authority,[26] that the god Tuisto had a son Mannus, from whose three sons are descended the three branches of the Germans, the Herminones, the Istaevones, and the Ingaevones. The Frankish Table gives eponymous names, Erminius, Inguo, Istio, clearly postulated to explain the names in Tacitus: and these are the Armen, Negua, and Isicon of the Irish version. Two MSS. of the Frankish Table give Alanus or Alaneus as the father of these three eponyms. These MSS. (E and F in Müllenhoff's enumeration) appear from the forms which the names assume to be of Irish origin. In the others, the parentage of the three brothers is not specified, though Alanus appears in the document as "the first king of Rome"! In "Alanus" Grimm recognized long ago a miswriting for the "Mannus" of Tacitus.

To Erminius the Frankish Table assigns the Goths, the Walagoths or Goths of Italy, the Vandals, the Gepidae, and the Saxons: to Inguo, the Burgundians, Thuringians, Langobardi, and Baioarii or Bavarians, who are here referred to in literature for the first time. This distribution somehow became disjointed when the document reached Ireland. There, in *Sex Aetates Mundi* (see *Book of Ballymote*, p. 3 of facsimile a 50, also LG ¶ 95 N); in LG. in the present paragraph; in the Reichenau MS. of the Table, lettered F in Müllenhoff's edition; and in Nennius, who has certainly derived his copy from an Irish source: the Burgundians and Langobardi are transferred to "Airmen" or Erminius, and the Vandals given to "Negua" or Inguo in exchange. All the versions agree in assigning Romanus, Britones, Francus, and Alamannus—the Romans of Central Gaul, Britons (of Brittany), Franks, and Alemanni, the four peoples who in or about the time when the table was drawn up were under the domination of the Frankish King Chlodwig) to Istio or

---

[25] "Die fränkische Völkertafel" *Abhandlungen* der Ak. zu Berlin, 1862, p. 532.

[26] *Germania*, § 2.

Isacon, the third of the three brothers. (Naturally Romanus, Francus, etc., in the Irish text are to be regarded as representing Latin *accusative plurals*.)

The table also appears in *Sex Aetates Mundi* and in Nennius; the latter version, as Zimmer has shown[27] must have been taken from an Irish source. But we cannot follow Zimmer in concluding that that source must have been either LG or *Sex Aetates*—Zimmer prefers the former hypothesis. In fact, all three compilations must have borrowed it from some common source unknown: for all three treat the genealogy differently. LG links it on to Gomer, son of Noah: *Sex Aetates* to Magog: and Nennius to Javan. The last named gives us a long genealogy, back to the antediluvian patriarchs, impinging in one or two places only on the much shorter pedigree in R^1: we find Nennius's version, however, in another connexion, in R^2 (see below, ¶ 16).

The peculiar pendant which is found in LG only, must be an addition by some philomath within the LG tradition itself. "Albanus" should of course be "Alemanus": the miswriting is a very simple matter. Our glossator thought of "Alba," and associated "Britus" with Britain (instead of Brittany). So he seemingly invented this story of the Britons having driven out the "Albans" across the English Channel, in order to secure the monopoly of the Island of Britain; and he seeks to account for similar ethnic names on the continent—Albanians, Alba Longa, or what not—as the result of this manœuvre. *Sex Aetates* has something similar, in saying that from Albanus come the "Albanians of Asia."[28]

10. (*Q version in ¶ 99, 100, much inflated with glosses.) As has already been noted, this paragraph is properly a continuation of the first interpolation in ¶ 9. The names in the form in which they appear here, from F, are very corrupt.

Tancatar Érinn, in which the verb of motion is used without a preposition, is a favourite construction in this text, and may possibly indicate the influence of a text originally in Latin '(as in Vergil's *Italiam uenit*).

---

[27] *Nennius vindicatus*, p. 234 ff.
[28] See Zimmer, *op. cit.*, p. 237 ff.

Second Redaction.

11. This ¶ hints that in the original form of R² there was an antecedent in which the unions of Sethites and Cainites were denounced. It is more fully preserved in R³, to which we may postpone the discussion of the subject. The three sentences, in which a singular conception of the family of Noah is suggested, are clearly glossarial interpolations. They have made no impression on R³—except in the late MS. M, at ¶ 188, where the idea implied is referred to. It is probably inspired partly by a desire to draw an exact analogy between the households of Adam and of Noah, partly to insinuate that only by such irregular unions could the contamination of Cainite blood be avoided. I have found no authority for it in apocryphal or pseudepigraphic literature. The Syriac *Cave of Treasures* says that Noah married Haykel d. Namūs d. Enoch, brother (*sic*) of Methuselah.[28a] It is referred to (probably borrowed from the text before us) by the compiler of the prose version of *Banśenehus*.

The statement that the Flood was a penalty for the crime of Cain has here arisen fortuitously, owing to the accidental juxtaposition of ¶ 6 from *Q and ¶ 11 from R². It is possible to find it elsewhere in Apocrypha: thus *The Book of the Rolls*, to give but one example, makes Adam prophesy to Seth in these words: *Know, my son, that there must come a Flood to wash all the earth, on account of the children of Cain, the wicked man who slew his brother.* But this is not really parallel: the Flood is here a punishment for the *children* of Cain [and their union with the Sethites] not for the crime of Cain.

12. Here we have definite proof of what we suspected in the preceding paragraph: that the Flood, according to R² in its original form, was the penalty for the sinful marriages of Sethites and Cainites, and not for the crime of Cain itself, as the text in its present form suggests. The theory is based upon a misinterpretation of Genesis vi. 1, 2.

[28a] Tr. Budge, p. 99, who quotes (ibid., p. 97) the Book of Enoch, ch. x, for a marriage between Noah and Enoch's daughter: I cannot find this in Charles's translation.

The copyists of R² have here and there made a bad muddle of the story: conspicuously so in this paragraph, especially in the laboured arithmetical disquisition inserted at the end. The account of the Flood was developed by the copyists of the R² tradition: the R¹ copyists took little interest in it. The R² version has carelessly admitted certain discrepancies with the biblical history. The forty days of downpour, and the 600 years of Noah's life, come from Genesis vii. 12, 11. That there were "three pairs" of clean beasts is a lapse of memory: *no sechta* is a reader's correction. The month of May is named in the Irish text: the Hebrew and all the versions say "the second month." On the hypothesis that the Creation took place at the Vernal Equinox, April would be the first complete month, and so May would be the second. That the biblical months were lunar was hidden from the compilers. The date (seventeenth) agrees with Heb. and Latin: LXX: has "twenty-seventh." A careless glossator seems to have misread the date as "seventh," and to have rushed in with the information that the embarkation took place on the nones (seventh) of May. I take the sentence beginning *In tan tarnaic* to be a gloss, as it breaks the sense: *dẽda do inglan*, etc., is a further gloss upon that: and *nõ sechta* is an additional gloss. Lower down, ⁊ *cona ingenaib* is obviously glossarial, as it is superfluous before *sẽitchib*, and indeed makes nonsense.

"Twelve cubits," which is given by all MSS. for the height of the water level above the loftiest mountain-tops, is an error: the biblical text in all versions says "fifteen," and (later in the ¶) E and P have given the correct figure. So, apparently, did √V, as is suggested by the form *cubait* for *cubat*. Early in the history of the text—or even in the history of the document from which the R² compilers derived their information—.xii. must have been misread and mis-written for .xu., as often happens. It is indeed *possible* to read .xu., as the number is written, in both V and E: but inadmissible, as it dislocates the arithmetic of the following interpolation. The Ark, we are told, drew ten cubits (there is no biblical warrant for this): its keel was two cubits above the highest summit: therefore the water-level was twelve cubits above them. This note further contradicts the orthodox

version of the height of the Ark (30 cubits, Gen. vi. 15): ten
cubits below water and fifteen above make only twenty-five.

Something has been lost from the sentence, .xii. cubat diu
ūas na slēibtib atā airdiu : I suggest diu < don usce > uas,
which would be an easy haplography.

13. The irrelevance about Enoch and Fintan is clearly
a reader's note. Of the latter we shall hear more on a later
page. On the legend that Enoch is reserved to fight against
Antichrist, along with Elijah (and even to perish in the
fighting), see *Revue celtique*, xxvi, pp. 164–5, and references
there.

14. The waters began to dry after 150 days (Gen. viii. 3),
but the Ark was floating for 7 months 27 days (Gen. viii. 4,
LXX and Vulg.: Hebrew says 17 days). The waters continued to dry until the tenth month (Gen. viii. 5). An early
loss by homoiotes at this point has affected all the MSS.:
before *dechmad miss* we must supply the words *dechmad
miss : i cẽt lō don*. The raven was sent out after 40 days
(Gen. viii. 6, all versions): the 47 of the Irish text is a
mistake. There is no Biblical warrant for sending forth the
dove *on the following day*: it is derived from ὀπίσω αὐτοῦ
(LXX) or *post eum* (Vulg.) which represent a Hebrew
original meaning *from him* (i.e. from Noah). The seven days'
intervals of the missions of the dove follow the Biblical story.

15. The date of the exodus from the Ark, in all the
Biblical versions, is given as "The twenty-seventh day of the
second month" (Gen. viii. 14). *For pridnöin Mai* must be
due to the same glossator as the author of the similar gloss
in ¶ 12, who believed that the voyage occupied exactly a solar
year, which, in fact, was approximately true.

The passage *tossuch . . . ocht cẽtaib* is an interpolation,
as it breaks the sense. It must come from some historical
treatise (not *Ser Actates Mundi*, but resembling it). The
opening words are clearly a chapter heading. The
double article NA *hāeisse* IN *domain* may be accounted for by
"age-of-the-world" having come to be regarded as an
indivisible technical term. The figures are not accurate: the
Hebrew reckoning should be 390, not 292; the Septuagint

reckoning 1170, not 842. (See the table in Skinner's
Commentary on Genesis, p. 233.)

The statement that Noah's altar was the first built after
the Flood is preceded by the mark .i., which is usually
diagnostic of an interpolated gloss. The passage *ammand mac
Nōe* to the end of the annexed poem is also no part of the
original text. It likewise interrupts the sense, which is a
description of the divisions of the world: and it gives names
for the wives of Noah's sons not in accordance with the
tradition followed by R². This tradition is summed up in
poem V, and if the original redactor had named these women,
he would presumably have followed its lead. See note on ¶ 7.
The last sentence is a relic of the original abstract of the
Biblical history, rendered obsolete by the elaborate
genealogical matter which has been superposed upon it.

16. Riphath, to whom the pedigree in this paragraph is
traced, comes from Gen. x. 3. The original meaning of the
name is obscure: in 1 Chron. i. 6 it appears as "Diphath," the
discrepancy being due to the similarity of the characters for
D and R in both the older and the later Hebrew scripts. The
addition "Scot" has of course no Biblical warrant, but
conceivably it has arisen from some copy of the Latin version
in which the name was given as *Riphaz* or *Rifatz* (as in two
of the MSS. on which the Vatican *variorum* edition is based).
The *z* we may suppose to have become separated from the
rest of the name, resolved into *sc* or *st*, and then expanded
into "Scot."

The genealogy is obviously quite different from that given
in R¹: but it is of equal if not greater antiquity, for it was
in the document used by Nennius. The ancestry of
"Alanius" as given by Nennius is practically identical with
that before us. See ¶ 9 above.

The interpolation at the end is an attack on an opinion,
presumably held by many men of learning at the time, but
now of insignificant importance! But it illustrates the
difficulty which the compilers had, in reducing their chaotic
materials to order.

17. We have here the first of the Synchronistic disquisi-
tions, chiefly founded upon the Chronicle of Eusebius, which

form an important but probably intrusive element in R², R³. The figures of Eusebius are not correctly reproduced. He allows only 853 years between the beginning of the reign of Ninus and the end of that of Tautanes (the Tutanes of our text): whereas R² has 874. As for Tautanes, we must take him as we find him. It has proved impossible to reconcile the names of Mesopotamian kings, derived by Eusebius from Berossus, with the names recovered from the monuments.

The interpolator in this paragraph reckons 40 years from the Tower to Feinius Farsaid: he must therefore be a different person from the author of the otherwise very similar interpolation in ¶ 16, who makes Feinius the sixteenth in descent from Rifath of the Tower.

¶ 17 allows two years from Feinius to Ninus, and from Eusebius we learn to consider Ninus a contemporary of Abraham. But we have already seen that on the lowest estimate there were 292 years from the Flood to Abraham: a long period must therefore be assumed from the Flood to the Tower, to be bridged by three generations only—Japhet, Gomer, Rifath.

The animadversion on the *Auraicept* is a fatuity: on referring to that text (ed. Calder, line 126) we find that the Latinus of the Tower was quite a different person from Latinus son of Faunus.

18. "Cineris" is the *Akenkheres* of Eusebius, the *Smenkh-ka-ra* of modern Egyptology. He is of no importance in Egyptian history: a mere ghost-king who reigned for a brief space c. 1360 B.C. immediately before the now famous Tutankhamun. The glossarial addition, explaining the name of Scota, has arisen from a later passage in the same redaction (see vol. ii, ¶ 129, and note thereon). It was primarily an attempt to explain the relation of Scota II, daughter of Nectanebus, to the name "Scota," and to *differentiate* her from Scota I, daughter of "Cineris," who is the person before us at the moment.

Dobreath a ingen is in all the MSS., and in the R³ appropriations of the text. It should be *dobretha a ingen*, as the corrector of E has noted in a very bad hand, which has induced the misreading, critical note (15) *ad loc.*

Third Redaction.

At the beginning of the text in B is written in an eighteenth-century hand "Accounts partly authentic and partly fabulous of the first Inhabitans (sic) of Ireland." At the top of the first page in M is written in a hand contemporary with the text *An toibrechan selaithi annso sis.* This has been partly cut through by a bookbinder, and is in consequence not perfectly easy to make out.

20. The gloss *isin Mac*, which has entered the text of M as an interpretation of *ar tūs* or *in principio* (critical note no. 5), is an exegesis as old as Irenaeus, who saw what he presumably thought was the Hebrew word *bar*, "son" (it is really Aramaic), in the opening words of Genesis, *B'rēshīth barā*, "In the beginning of creating."[29]

The Irish annotator probably borrowed the idea from Petrus Comestor, whose influence is obvious throughout the glosses in R³: *Verbum erat principium in quo et per quod Pater creauit mundum . . . Creatus autem est in principio, id est, in Filio.*[30]

With regard to the interpolations, we have seen above (note to ¶ 2A) that y^2 does not come from *Q, the MS. of R¹ used by ∞ R³, nor from *X, the MS. of R¹ used by yR^3, but from *Z, the MS. of R² used by yR^3, in which MS. it was still a recent interpolation in the margin. Y^3 comes from *X. That it was added later than the others is shown by the reversal of the blocks of material, for the matter of y^3 precedes y^2 in R². The first interpolator knew that the Creation was fully described in the following text: the second interpolator rushed in where his predecessor had thought it at least unnecessary to tread. The following differences

---

[29] See Gwatkin, *Early Church History to A.D. 313*, vol. i, pp. 196–7. The Armenian (the only extant) version of the Irenaeus text, at p. 692, translates these words "The Son in the beginning." See also Augustine, *De Civitate Dei*, xi. 32.

[30] *Historia Scholastica*, cap. i.

between this passage and its cognates in the other MSS. are noteworthy :

(i) The statements are inverted, each day being named before its work. (The significance of this has already been pointed out in the notes to ¶ 2.)

(ii) The month-dates are inserted (possibly a still later interpolation).

(iii) Adam is mentioned before the beasts in the sixth day's work.

(iv) There are some differences of Vocabulary : *neam* for *firmament* (on which see note to ¶ 2). "*muir*" *ina timchell*, *rīltanda* for *renna*, *anmanda muiridi* for *tondaitechu*. A few passages have all the appearance of intrusive glosses, and are marked as such in the text.

The date assigned to the *beginning* of Creation—fifteenth of the Kalends of April, i.e., 18th March—is obviously determined by the Vernal Equinox. The *completed* Universe is set upon its course on that day, the natural beginning of the year, solar and agricultural. Though not stated, it is presupposed by the Flood story in R²: see note to ¶ 12.

With the description of the Matter of Creation compare the following, from *Cursor Mundi* (l. 348) :—

> The mater first ther of he mad,
> That es the elementes to sai,
> That first scapless al sameu lay . . .
> This elementz that al thinges bindes,
> Four er thai als clerkes findes,
> The nethermast es watur and erth,
> The thrid es air, and fir the ferth.

The gloss *ni locdacht*, etc., may be borrowed from some commentary or homily, though I have not succeeded in tracing its origin. But it reads more like the interpolation of a copyist, anxious to reassure himself that the transcription of the words which he has just written down did not constitute an act of unpardonable sin. If this were so, we must assume that the major interpolations had already established themselves in the text, concealing from the writer the fact that he was dealing with a text which had scriptural warrant.

21. It is important, as will appear presently, to note that the words dropped by homoiotes in B (⁊ *fodlad na n-usci*) contain 14 letters.

The subject of *ro fogail* may be either *Dīa* or *firmamint*—probably the latter, as it carries on the command "let it divide . . . it divided." The ambiguity exists even in Heb.: LXX has removed it by inserting ὁ θεός. The Irish translator is not quite emancipated from the idea of his predecessors responsible for R¹, R², that *firmamentum* is a proper noun, and does not require the article.

22. Here there is another haplography in B, caused by the homoiotes of *clandaiged*. The mistake existed in √B; for sB has observed the gap in the sense, and has inserted a full stop after the *clandaiged* which has survived. His intelligence did not, however, carry him to the further step of realising that he was copying a biblical text, so that had he chosen he could have filled the lacuna by referring to a copy of the book of Genesis, and translating the equivalent of the missing words.

Note that 43 letters are lost, practically the exact triple of the loss noted in the preceding ¶: this indicates (i) that √B was written in narrow columns of short lines, with an average of 15 letters to the line, and (ii) that some of the carelessnesses for which the Book of Ballymote is notorious must be laid to the account of the exemplar from which it is copied.

23. *In grēin, ind ēsca*, which have no authority in any version of the biblical text, are evidently old glosses, interlined in √BMH and incorporated with the text after the separation of the B, M (and H) traditions, in different relative contexts.

24. *Barnimdaighter* is an illustration of the use of the possessive pronouns to supply the place of the missing first and second persons of the passive: but it is probably an artificial archaism in this place. One distinguished Celtist to whom I showed it called it "a monstrosity."

25. *In Tuismeadh* is another old gloss, earlier than √BMH. The omission of verse 25, which is almost a repetition of

verse 24, may have been intentional; but Tr. is on the whole
too conscientious for this, and it is more likely a piece of
carelessness or laziness on the part of a copyist.

On the interpolation, see notes to ¶ 2ᴀ.

27. This paragraph begins the J-source of the Hebrew
Genesis. Although Comestor calls special attention to the
critically important word *Dominus*, which here begins to
appear in the Divine name—adding an exegesis with which
we need not trouble ourselves—the glossators have not shown
any special interest in it; nor has the Irish translator made
any endeavour to maintain the distinction, which is found in
the Hebrew and all ancient versions.

The story of the finding of a name for Adam, contained
in the long interpolation at the end of the paragraph, appears
first in *The Book of the Secrets of Enoch*, written in Egypt
somewhere about the beginning of the Christian Era, and
brought to its final form by a Hellenistic Jew.[31] It survives
to-day in a Slavonic version only: but in its time it had a
considerable influence upon Early Christian literature. In
chap. xxx. v. 13 ff. we read: And I [God] appointed him
[Adam] a name, from the four component parts, from east,
from west, from south, from north, and I appointed for him
four special stars, and I called his name Adam. Charles cites
parallels from *The Sibylline Oracles* (iii. 24–6); Pseudo-
Cyprian, *De Montibus Sina et Syon* iv; Bede, *Exposition of
Genesis*, iv; which in one form or another narrate the same
story; others might be added. In *Cursor Mundi* we read
(line 592)—

> In this nam er four letters laid
> That o the four ʒates er said:
> Sua micul es Adam for to muth
> Als est and west and north and south.
> And thou mai ask, wit-outen blam,
> Qui God him gaue sua mikel a nam . . .
> It takens Adam and his sede
> Ouer al the werld than suld thai spred.

---

[31] See R. H. Charles, *Apocrypha and Pseudepigrapha of the Old
Testament*, ii, p. 425 ff.

So we find in *The Dialogue of Salomon and Saturnus* (Ed. Kemble, pp. 178, 194)—

"Whence was the name of Adam formed?—Of four stars. How are they called?—Arthox, Dux, Arotholem, Minsymbrie."

In illustration of which Kemble quotes the following elegiac couplet from MS., Harl. 3362, fol. 6—

Anathole dedit A, Disis D, contulit Aretos
Et Mesembrios M : collige, fiet ADAM.

The *Master of Oxford's Catechism* (op. cit., p. 217) gives Artax, Dux, Arostolym, Momfumbres as the names of the four stars. None of these versions of the story refers to the mission of the angels, which, however, appears in the Old English *Lyff of Adam and Eue* : this text gives us the closest parallel to the Irish version—

"þo after he made mon of erþe in flesch and bon, in þe vale of Ebron . . . þer-aftur God bad foure angelus þat heo schulden seche þulke monnes nome þat he hedde imaad. Seint Mihel wente in to þe est : he seih þer a sterre þat was swiþe briht, Anatalim was þat sterre ihote, wiþ þe furste lettre A, and soone he com aȝeyn. Gabriel in to þe west-half wente; and he seiȝ in þe firmament a sterre þat hihte was Dysus: þe furste lettre D þer-of soon he brouȝte. Raphael com to þe north : he say þer a sterre þat is iclepet Areis; anon he fleyh aȝein, wiþ þe furste letter A þat he con wiþ him bringe. Forþ him wente Vriel riht in to þe souþ. Messembrion hihte þe sterre þat he sih þere; wiþ þe furste lettre M he wente swiþe aȝeyn & brouht hit tofore God wiþ þe oþur þreo. God took þeos foure lettres & bad Vriel rede & he radde : Adam."

28. *Parrthus na Toile* is a rendering of *Paradisus Voluptatis*, the Vulgate equivalent of the Garden of Eden. OL. has simply *Paradisus*, to which the *Parrthus* of R[1] corresponds.

The Rivers of Paradise were a favourite subject for speculation: it is therefore not surprising to find this paragraph farced with glosses. The conceptions that lie behind them are set forth most simply in *Cursor Mundi* (line 1032)—

> Midward that land [Paradise] a wel springes,
> That rennes out with four strandes,
> Flummes farand in fer landes . . .
> The first es Tigre and sithen Gyon,[32]
> Sithen Eufrates and Fison.

Some hints at the characters attributed to the Rivers of Paradise are given by Comestor (borrowing from Isidore XIII. xxi. 7). *Unus dictus est Phison, qui a Gangaro rege Indiae dictus est Ganges . . . Tigris animal est uelocissimum, et ideo fluuius a sui uelocitate tigridi equiuocatus est . . . Euphrates frugifer uel fructuosus.*[32a] The *Master of Oxford's Catechism* comes close to the statements in Poem no. VI:

> "Whate hight the iiij waters that renneth through Paradise?—The one hight Fyson, the other Egeon, the iijde Tygrys and the iiijth Effraton. Thise be milke, hony, oyll, and wyne."

There is a similar passage in *Salomon and Saturnus*. These ideas are forced, in Christian tradition, into an analogy between the four streams and the four evangelists: *Cursor Mundi* at line 21.293, likens the words of the Evangelists to water, wine, milk, and honey respectively. They are, however, of Jewish origin. Rabbi Yehosha ben Levi is quoted in *Yalkut Shimoni* as saying, in the course of a description of the terrestrial paradise, "And there flow out from it four rivers, one of milk, one of wine, one of balsam, and one of honey."[33]

We have already seen that ϗ/B had about 15 letters to the line. The haplography in the last interpolation in B is evidently due to a careless copying of words arranged thus—

---

[32] In some MSS. *Ganges*.

[32a] *Hist. Schol.*, Liber Genesis, cap. xiv (all quotations from this book are from the section on Genesis unless otherwise stated).

[33] Eisenmenger, *Entdecktes Judenthum*, ii, p. 310.

ꝯoꝺeꝛꝛcānꝺiꝛiuch
cheiꝺꝛiꝺecoꝛoích
ꞇꝛelaꝛiiꝺaíbiꝫoṁe

—the central line of the three being omitted, because either
its end was similar to the end of line 1, or its beginning to
the beginning of line 3.

Bdellium was the name of a gum, used for medicinal
purposes. But Tr. or his copyists having turned the word
into *Boellium*, the glossator identified it with the Latin *opalus*.
His note is obviously a description of the opal set in the
volcanic matrix (andesite or what not) in which it is found
in nature. I have not traced the source of his information,
but what he says about the stone seems to be a confused
recollection of some description of the play of colours seen
when it is contemplated from different angles.

29. That Adam was created first and afterwards transferred to the Paradise was the general belief, following Genesis
iii. 7, 8. Damascus is named as the scene of Adam's creation,
and of his retreat after the Fall : see Comestor, ch. xiii. This
tradition is followed by gR^3, ¶ 38.

The glosses upon *oipriged* and *coimetad* are obviously
suggested by Comestor. *Tulit ergo Deus hominem de loco
formationis suae in Paradisum, scilicet terrestrem, ut
operaretur ibi. Non tamen laborando ex necessitate, sed
delectando et recreando, et sic Deus "custodiret illum,"
scilicet hominem. Vel utrumque refertur ad hominem, ut
scilicet homo custodiret Paradisum et "operaretur" ut dictum
est.* (Hist. Schol. xv.)

The interpolation y^1 is meant to explain away the
discrepancy between the threat of *immediate* death upon
eating of the fruit, and the fact of Adam's survival for over
900 years.

Comestor, again, is the source of y^2: *Praecepitque ei
dicens,* etc.; *ut homo sciret se esse sub Domino, praeceptum
accepit a Domino* (loc. cit.).

30. It is impossible to decide whether the string of adjectives after *suan* and *ben* in this ¶, which is anticipatory of the vicious style of the later romance-writers, is due to Tr. or to his copyists. But see the note to the following ¶.

The idea that Adam's sleep was mantic rather than anaesthetic seems to be another borrowing from Comestor: *Non somnum, sed exstasim, in qua creditur supernae interfuisse curiae; unde et euigilans prophetauit de coniunctione Christi et Ecclesiae, et de diluuio futuro, et de iudicio per ignem* (Hist. Schol. xvi). It was, however, a common idea: Epiphanius (*Adv. Haeres.* II i 48) ingeniously proves it by pointing out that Adam spoke of the past (*os ex ossibus*), present (*ex uiro suo sumpta est*) and the future (*homo adhaerebit uxori sui*)! In the Old English Paraphrase of *Genesis and Exodus*[34] we read—

> God dede ðat he on sweuene cam,
> And in ðat sweuene he let him sen,
> Mikal ðat after sulde ben.

Many other quotations to the same effect might be taken from various sources.

The note *is ī seo cēt faitsine* appears to be due to a dullard homiletic glossator who has made several comments of the same kind on the text, and who is also probably responsible for the silly note *arāi grāda*, etc. He did not observe that a predecessor had already called Adam's words, *Ecce os* etc., "the first *coibche* and the first prophecy which Adam made." The longer gloss is older than the shorter statement, as it comes later in the text. This is a very important critical principle, of not infrequent application in the text before us. The annotator was in such a hurry to "hold his farthing rushlight to the sun" that he had not the patience to read a line or two further, when he would have found that he had been anticipated. In fact, both wiseacres have been misled by careless reading of Comestor, who definitely asserts that the passage which follows (*Quamobrem*, etc.) is the real prophecy (*Hist. Schol.* xix).

---

[34] Ed. Morris, E. E. T. S. (1865), lines 224–6.

31. There is evidence in the beginning of this ¶ that the adjectival exuberance of the biblical translation is to some extent glossarial. The superlatives attached to the Serpent in the original text have been multiplied by an annotator : they appear in the two MSS. *in a different order*, which as before indicates the interpolation of an interlined gloss.

The interpolation y^1 appears to come from R^2, because Eve is represented as being the sole victim of the Serpent's temptation. Comparison with the text of R^2 (¶ 4*) shows that *co curp scim* is an interpolation made after the leaf of *Q had come into R^2, but before the writing of *Z, the copy of R^2 used by gR^3. The omission of *Iofer Niger* is a striking feature in this version of the passage.

The envy of Lucifer against Adam is referred to by Comestor (*Lucifer enim deiectus a Paradiso spirituum, inuidit homini quod esset in Paradiso corporum, sciens si faceret eum transgredi quod et ille ciiceretur* (Hist. Schol. xxi)). For once, however, this is not the source of the interpolation : the idea had been in the text from before Comestor's time, and LG, as we have seen, has no hint at the contrast between the spiritual and the terrestrial paradise emphasized by Comestor. The interpolation y^2 has nothing to do with y^1. It comes from a different source, and is most likely due to a different annotator.

Before these interpolations were made the text probably ran thus : *Ro bái nathair . . . ┐ ro ráid*. As the interpolation separated the subject from the verb, a later glossator interlined .i. *in athair sin* above *ro ráid*. When the gloss entered the text *is í* evolved out of .i. This glossator's spelling of *athair*, without the initial *n*, has survived the vicissitudes of his note after its incorporation.

32. This paragraph is much farced with glosses. After *ro hoslaicit* a leaf has been lost from B. Its matter is preserved in the eighteenth-century transcript β, which is a good, though not a perfect copy of the MS. The two other eighteenth-century copies, β¹, β², have been collated throughout, but (as has been shown in the introduction) their only value is as a check on β, confirming some of its readings; their own variations do not appear to possess any importance, but they are recorded in order to secure completeness.

"In the noise of a mighty wind" is a curious misinterpretation of the Latin *ad auram*.

A medhōn chrainn Pairrthus: the singular number of *chrainn* reproduces the Latin *ligni*.

33. The gloss *ō guth aingleagda* is preserved in M only, but probably is another loss in the B tradition due to the short lines of ℣B and the carelessness of *s*√B. If the text were written in ℣B thus

ꝗ
ogaiꝺme ṛč Ꝺiaaꝺa
oguꝼh aiꞟ gleagꝺa
ꝗꝺoꝓ aiꝺaaꝺacaiꝼ

there would have been homoiotes at both ends—a fatal trap for *s*√B.

On the first leaf of H, which begins in this ¶, the topmost 16 lines of each column are torn away entirely, and some of the others are injured, as the tear runs obliquely. In fact, the first few of the surviving lines are reduced in this manner to a few letters only, which would be quite unintelligible if we did not possess a perfect copy in M for comparison. If this first leaf of H had been perfect, the surviving portion of that text would have begun somewhere about verse 4 of the chapter, thus extending back to slightly before the beginning of the lacuna in B.

It may be worth mentioning that the Welsh antiquary, Edward Lhuyd, according to a letter written by him on 20 December 1702, and printed in *Archæologia Cambrensis*, 1859, p. 246, was possessed of "an imperfect copy of the B[ook] of Genesis in Irish" bestowed upon him by a priest near Sligo, who told him that "in the opinion of one of their chiefest antiquitys [*sic*]" it "was very little later than the first planting of Christianity" in Ireland. This fragment does not seem to be preserved among Lhuyd's MSS. in Oxford; and as one or more of the fragments now bound up in the miscellany which includes our manuscript H were at one time in Lhuyd's possession and bear his autograph, I am inclined to suspect that this "fragment of the book of Genesis" was no other than Π. If so, its Sligo provenance may possibly be confirmatory of the suggestion made above (p. 13) that the Π leaves had been torn out to supplement the deficiencies of the Book of Ballymote. In that case, however, the deficiency was not that caused by the loss of folio 9, which must have taken place after Lhuyd's time, but the chasm in this text described, *loc. cit.* Further, the depredation most probably took place before 1522, when the Book of Ballymote appears to have migrated from Sligo to Tir Conaill.

Dorad domh do chrann, omitting the definite article, is a literal translation from the Latin *dedit mihi de ligno*. It adds a subtle point to the story, as suggesting that Adam professed ignorance of the tree from which the fruit had come; but unfortunately the Hebrew text disallows it.

For the curious rendering *acht mī fēin*, see the notes on the Latin text.

34. The translator seems to have missed the point of the serpent's "lying in wait," and to have understood it to mean self-protection rather than hostility.

The gloss *iomad galar mīsda dhuit* is paralleled by a Rabbinic idea (Eisenmenger, i, p. 833) that this disability is due to a union between Eve and Sammaël in the guise of the Serpent.

Further confirmation of our conclusions as to the nature of $\mathfrak{P}/B$ is here forthcoming. As the words *d'indcarna Dia* . . . ⁊ *do thalmain* are absent in β^{012} we may take it for certain that they were also absent in B. They just amount to two of the short lines of which we have already found indications—

cencon aᴈaᴅᴄuịꞃꝝō
ᴈaᴌᴆinᴆepꞃꞏᴆiaᴈu
oịꞃịꝛᴆoᴌúaịᴈꞃꞃᴆo
ᴈaᴌᴆoꞃonaᴆꞏịꝛꝛae

The eye of $s\sqrt{}B$ wandered from the beginning of the second
of these lines to the beginning of the fourth.

35. Our worthy glossator seems to fear that subsequent
readers, if not warned, would take Eve to be the mother of
animals as well as of men!

How *g*H ascertained that the garments made for Adam
and Eve were *of one colour* does not appear.

36. The perverse exegesis in the interpolation in this ¶
is from Comestor: *Ironia est, quasi noluit esse ut Deus, sed
in euidenti est modo quod non est* (Hist. Schol. xxiv).

37. Y¹ is clearly an incorporated gloss, the lemma of which
is the sentence *following*. It filled the whole interlinear space
above that sentence in the MS. from which it entered the
body of the text, and thus it was taken in before the words
which it ought to have followed. That Adam and Eve
remained virgin in Paradise was a notion suggested by the
fact that Eve's name of universal mother is not recorded till
after the Fall. Something of the idea will be found in
Augustine, *Civ. Dei* xiii, 13, 14: and it was emphasised in
the *Revelationes* of Pseudo-Methodius, according to which,
*Sciendum est quod exeuntes Adam et Eua de Paradiso
uirgines fuerint*: or as the Old English paraphrase expresses
it,

> ȝet owt of Paradyse when þey paste
> clene vyrgenys were þey both—

Our glossators, however, show no direct acquaintance with
that singular production, and probably took the idea from
Comestor, who gives a paraphrase of the words of Pseudo-
Methodius in his chap. xxv. According to the Syriac *Book
of the Bee*, Adam and Eve remained virgins for 30 years after
their expulsion (ed. Budge, chap xviii).

The interpretation of the name of Cain is borrowed in
the first instance from Isidore: *Cain possessio interpretatur,
unde etymologiam ipsius exprimens pater eius ait "Cain"
id est "Possedi hominem per Deum." Idem et lamentatio,
eo quod pro interfecto Abel interfectus sit, et poenam sui
sceleris dederit. Abel luctus interpretatur* (Etym. VII.

vi. 7). We must regard *no lamentacio* as a gloss, although Isidore gives the alternative interpretation, partly because, though in a Latin context, it is introduced by an Irish conjunction, and partly because it is ignored in the subsequent matter. Both etymologies are of course wrong. *Cancithi* is the Hebrew קָנִיתִי *qanīthī*, "I have gotten," *Lamentatio* looks back to the quite independent Hebrew word קִינָה *qīnāh* "a dirge." All these early commentators overlook the fact, which a little knowledge of elementary Hebrew grammar would have taught them, that it was Eve, not Adam, who said *Possedi hominem*. But they are in the good company of Augustine, *Civ. Dei* xv. 15.

The idea expressed in y^3, following many ancient commentators and versions, that the acceptance of Abel's offering was indicated by fire from heaven, seems to go back to the version of Theodotion, in which יִשַׁע (*respexit*) is translated ἐνεπύρισεν. It is, of course, developed under the influence of the narrative in I (III) Kings xviii (Elijah on Carmel). As usual, Comestor is the proximate source of the glossator's information: *Quia placuit Deo Abel et pro ipso placuit oblatio eius, quod quomodo cognitum fuerit, alia translatio aperit. "Inflammauit Deus super Abel et super munera eius." Ignis enim de coelo oblationem eius incendit.* (Hist. Schol. xxvi).

There is no authority for the words *a ttoirsi* ⁊ *in dubha*, which must be a glossarial expansion.

38. The simple account of the murder of Abel in B (as preserved in the derivatives of that MS.) is clearly the original version, being based on the Genesis text. The interpolation in M, *ro iad a dā lāim fō brągait cor ba marb* (H here unfortunately fails us) is as clearly borrowed from R². This introduces us to a further complication in the history of the text—the borrowings from earlier redactions at late stages of development. This cannot be one of the borrowings originally made from *Z, as in that case it would have been in B also.

Y¹, in one form or another, must have been in √BMH. The family had returned to Damascus where Adam was created—we need not vex the shades of the glossator by insisting that Damascus could hardly have been a *cathair* at this stage of the world's history, as he conceived it. Comestor says of the expulsion from Paradise: *Emisit eum Dominus de Paradiso Voluptatis . . . in agrum scilicet Damascenum, de quo sumptus fuerat, in quo Cain Abel suum fratrem interfecit* (Hist. Schol. xxiv).

Y² seems to be an extract from some homily upon Abel. The haplography attested by β⁰¹² must have been in B. It was easy for a scribe to commit (*Abel dō cĩt marb . . . Abel in cĩt martir*) but for once it cannot be laid to the account of √B, for the omitted words are too long for the 15-letter lines of √̇B.

The variant of the question *Quid fecisti* in M is curious. Presumably it is due ultimately to a reader who, having read *Cid doroinnais?* was moved to write in the margin *Pecad gnīm n-adbal*! (He was of the spiritual kindred of Lucifer's critic in ¶ 3.) The loss of *cid*, which might easily happen after the preceding *Cāin* (especially if it were written *Caidin*, as in P) would result in the absorption of this note by the text.

Y⁴ seems to come from another homily, in which reference was made to Genesis iv. 10, xviii. 20, and Luke xviii. 7, 8.

39. Once more we have a paragraph filled with glossarial fatuities. The MS. from which ∞H, ∞M, and ∞B were copied, in this order (as shown above, p. 14) must have had *ro oslaic a bēl*, probably with an open *a* in *oslaic*. Both ∞M and ∞H independently misread this as *ro sluic Abel*: but ∞B copied it correctly, and in the derivatives from B the reading has been put beyond a doubt by inserting the prefixed *f*. We have already seen that we cannot assume a ⁿ/MH differentiated from ⁿ/B; the mistake must therefore have been made twice. In the M tradition a number of interpolations—three in this paragraph alone—have entered the text, not found in H or in B. Y¹ has been inserted by some one who did not take the trouble to observe that it contradicts the biblical story, related a few lines above. But it must have entered the M tradition before the story about Abel's being strangled with Cain's hands (¶ 38) was inserted. For we may lay it down as a general principle that when we have two contradicting interpolations (*a*) and (*b*), if they

ıun consecutively they may be contemporary, the glossator
setting down two opposing views between which he makes
no choice; or else (b), the second, may be later than (a),
having been interpolated by a second glossator to contradict
what was already in the text. But if the two are separated
by some lines of text, then the probability is greatly in favour
of (a) being the later of the two, having been inserted by a
reader who has not yet reached (b) and does not anticipate
it.

The perverse notion that the mark of Cain was designed
to secure a prolongation of his punishment is borrowed from
Comestor. "*Omnis quis inuenerit me occidet me.*" *Ex timore
hoc dixit, uel optando dixit, quasi diceret: Utinam occidant
me. "Dixitque ei Deus: Nequaquam ita fiet." Non cito
scilicet morieris, "sed omnis qui occiderit Cain"—supplendum
est, liberabit eum a timore, a dolore, et miseria—"septuplum
punietur." Id. est, punitio fiet de eo dum uiuet in poena.*

There have been many speculations on the mark of Cain.
For once Comestor is jettisoned by our glossators, who say
nothing about the theory adopted by him, that the mark was
a perpetual shaking of the head—that "he wagged alwey forþ
wiþ his heued" as the Old English *Lyff of Adam and Eue*
puts it. The 'lump in his forehead' goes back to a lost *Book
of Lamech*, which told how Lamech, under the guidance of his
son Tubalcain—for he was blind—shot an arrow at a wild
man covered with hair, and with a horn growing out of his
forehead, who proved to be Cain. Lamech was so distressed
by the discovery that he killed Tubalcain. The additional
"lumps" are added by *y*M under the influence of poem no. V
(quatrain 23). That Cain had no beard comes indirectly from
the same authority, which states (lines 123, 124) that Seth
was the first man who grew a beard.

40. A glossator has doubtless introduced the appellation
diamus, in order to distinguish the Cainite from the Sethite
Lamech. The interpretation of the word is most likely the
work of a still later annotator.

41. That Naamah was a weaver or embroideress was a
commonplace of mediaeval apocryphal speculation. Probably
our glossator borrowed the fact from Comestor—*Soror uero*

Tubalcain Noema, quae inuenit artem uariae texturae (Hist. Schol. xxviii). So also *Cursor Mundi* (line 1523)—

> A sister had this brether alsua,
> And sco was heiten Noema :
> Scho was the formest webster,
> That man findes o that mister.
> That fader was the first o liue,
> That bigam was, wit dubul vijfe.

Ro chĕt-chum is a favourite construction in this text : the composition of *cĕt* with a verb, to denote "he was the first to" perform whatever action is specified.

42. The difficult Song of Lamech has given trouble to the translator, and apparently also to his copyists. The rendering as we have it does not even make reasonable sense, to say nothing of its relation to the original text. *Ro mharbus fer emuigh aniu* seems to have arisen out of *Ro mharbus fer am guinib* (the last word perhaps written *guiniu*), thus representing the Latin *occidi uirum in uulnus meum*. The sentence which follows is apparently a gloss, the original form of which was most likely *.i. is inund ⁊ "ro chrechtnaiges" annsin*.

The word *sechtoll* does not seem to occur elsewhere in Irish literature.

It is curious that none of our meddlesome glossators have come forward with the information—known to the author of poem no. V. and universally believed—that Lamech's victim was Cain.

43. Adam's speech is thus written in β : *air Adhamh,* |*ar*| *.i. siol*, etc., indicating that the scribe was puzzled by the word *ar*. It can scarcely be equated with the Irish *ar*, "ploughing" : it is perhaps a degeneration of the Hebrew זרע, *zer'a*, "seed"—read backwards, like the Tetragrammaton in poem no. V. This word appears in the original of the passage, and may have reached the Irish translator by some circuitous route.

At the end of this paragraph there comes the lacuna in the B-tradition (see p. 13) which was there even before B lost its leaf. The eighteenth-century copyists were conscious of a gap in the sense, and each in his own way made a makeshift

stop-gap, here printed as ¶ 43a. H resumes in the course of
the following paragraph, and until M fails us at the end of
¶ 52 H and M are the only authorities for the text. It is
here printed from M, with variants from H.

44. Y² like y³, was in M only. H is here defective, but a
count of words shows that there was no room for it.

According to a belief recorded by Comestor, Adam was
only seven hours in Paradise (*Quidam tradunt eos fuisse in
Paradiso septem horas*—Hist. Schol. xxiv). With this *Cursor
Mundi* more or less agrees (line 985)—

> For he [Adam] was wroght at undern tide,
> At middai Eue draun of his side.
> Thai brak the forbot als sun,
> That thai war bath don out at none.

A poem contained in the *Book of Ui Muine* specifies $13\frac{1}{2}$ hours :
but the *Master of Oxford* makes the time seven years. The
writer of y² must have copied it from some other *literary*
source, as is indicated by the spelling *Eba*, by the here
superfluous specification of the nature of the sin, and by the
description of the forbidden tree as *Crand na Haithne* (not
Fessa).

Of the transfer of Adam's head to Golgotha, Comestor,
with a critical judgement which he does not as a rule
encourage us to expect in him, writes as follows : *Ambrosius,
in Epist. ad Romanos uidetur uelle quod ibi sepultus fuerit
Adam, et a capite eius dictum Caluariam: et ei dictum ab
apostolo: Surge qui dormis, exsurge a mortuis, et illuminabit
te Christus. De qua opinione dicit Hieronymus quod
fauorabilis est interpretatio, et mulcens aures, non tamen uera.
Unde credimus hoc a falsariis positum in Ambrosio.* (Hist.
Schol. in Euangel. clxx). Of the burial of Adam in Hebron
we read in *Cursor Mundi* (line 1415)—

> Doluen he [Adam] was thoru Seth his sun,
> In the dale that hat Ebron :

and in Comestor: *Locus in quo luxerunt* [Adam and Eve,
after Abel] *dicitur Vallis Lacrymarum iuxta Hebrom* (Hist.
Schol. xxv, doubtless suggested by Ps. lxxxiii [Hebrew lxxxiv]

verse 7). This geography is a commonplace of the Adam apocrypha. The interpolation y³ is peculiar to M, and probably came from the same literary source as y². The glossators have apparently never heard the Eastern story, told in *The Cave of Treasures*, that the body of Adam was part of the cargo of the Ark, where it served the useful purpose of keeping the men and the women apart; and that it was afterwards buried by Shem in Golgotha.

45 ff. Worthy of passing notice is a commentator, possibly of ethnological or psychological interest, who was apparently unable to conceive of large numbers except in *scores*, and had to reduce the hundreds to that unit, in order to understand them.

50. Enoch was the central figure of a vast mass of folklore and apocryphal literature. His existence "in desert places and away from common life" is doubtless an expansion of the Biblical *et non apparuit*, but it may have reached the Irish glossator from some special source.

The ten names of God are thus enumerated by Isidore (*Etym.* VII. i. 1): El, Eloi, Eloe, Sabaoth, Elion, Eie, Adonai, Ia, Tetragrammaton, Saddai. The list given by Epiphanius (*Adv. Haeres.* I, iii, 40) is Sabaoth, Eli, Eloi, Israel, Sadadai, Ellion, Rabboni, Ia, Adonai, Iabe. On their magical use, see Budge. *Amulets and Superstitions.* pp. 369 ff.

From *ō anmandaib īcsamlaib* in this paragraph to the end of ¶ 52. M is our only authority for the text.

52. With the end of this paragraph the great lacuna begins in M. Unlike *s*B, *s*M was conscious of the gap in his exemplar, and left the remainder of the column, upon which he was writing, a blank, in the hope of filling in the missing matter afterwards. This neither he nor the subsequent owners of M were ever able to do: and H, which now carries on the story, shows us that the space provided (32 lines in a column of 50 lines) was absurdly small.

We are still in the mutilated first leaf of H, which has lost the top lines of all its columns. The missing portions of the two texts slightly overlap, so that at this point there are a few lines of the text which are altogether lost, as well as

portions of the beginnings and endings of others—covering
verses V. 31 (last clause) and VI. 1, 2, of the biblical text.

In the gloss explaining the name of Noah, *is Noe* is doubtless to be corrected to .i. *Noe*.

53. From here on to ¶ 87 our only authority is H. The
first two verses of chap. VI, lost from our text, contain the
fragmentary tale of intercourse between *filii Dei* and *filiae
hominum*. This tantalizing story was for long the subject of
speculation : and some copyist seems to have considered these
speculations more interesting than the barren biblical
narrative. That the "sons of God" were the Sethites, and
the "daughters of men" the Cainites, was the normal
mediaeval solution of the enigma. It is set forth in Pseudo-
Methodius as well as in Comestor, ch. xxxi, the Old English
Lyff of Adam and Eve, and many other authorities. The
full story, as related in *The Cave of Treasures*, is to the effect
that Adam, when dying, had commanded Seth and his
descendants to remain on the holy mountain of Hermon, apart
from the offspring of Cain, and that this injunction was
repeated by each succeeding patriarch till the days of Yârêd
(Jared, which means "descent"), when the Sethites broke
their oaths and went down to the encampment of iniquity of
the Cainites. The glossator has based his interpolation, with
which the text resumes after the lacuna, upon the detailed
paraphrase of this story in the Irish *Sex Aetates Mundi*.
The MS. is here much injured. The inner edge of the leaf
has been made ragged by tearing the fragment from its
proper place (as described, p. 13 *ante*), and in consequence
parts of several lines are lost. Some of the gaps can be filled
up by a collation of *Sex Aetates* (Rawl. B 502 facsimile) ; but
not all, for the texts, though similar, are not identical.
Restorations of the text are here contained within square
brackets.

The alternative explanation of the origin of the monsters,
recorded here by a later glossator, will be found below, ¶ 81.

54. The glossator has forgotten that the descendants of
Seth had their share in the production of the giants.

R

55. Here again an extract from *Sex Aetates Mundi* has been interpolated, and has ousted verses 5, 6, of the biblical text: a process facilitated by the fact that the two passages began with the same words. The passage as it appears in Rawl. B, 502, reads *Otchonaire Día imorro tictain dóib dar a thimna, ro chinnistar na dóini do huili-dilgenn, coni do tucad in diliu.* This has been expanded in our text by glossators.

The interpolation at the end of the paragraph is from another source.

57. Y² is obviously suggested by Comestor's *fuit haec arca in fundamento quadrata* (Hist. Schol. xxxii).

The interpolations y³ a, b, are parts of a single marginal note that has become bisected, and has entered the text in two different places—in the second place breaking very awkwardly into the sense. The information is derived in part from Comestor: *Bitumine intus et extra linita est, quod est gluten feruentissimum quo ligna linita non dissoluuntur aliqua ui uel arte nec materia uel maceria bituminata solui potest . . . In lacubus Iudaeae supernatans colligitur. In Syria limus est a terra aestuans.* Comestor in his turn seems to have taken this from Isidore (*Etym.* XVI. ii. 1): *Bitumen in Iudaeae lacu Asphaltite emergit, cuius glebas supernatantes nautae scaphis adpropugnantes colligunt. In Syria autem limus est passim aestuans a terra . . . Natura eius ardens et ignium cognata, et neque aqua neque ferro sumpitur . . . utilis ad conpages nauium.*

I can find no authority for the two persons who altruistically contributed to the success of an enterprise from which they themselves derived no benefit: the carpenter with the improbable name Epiphenius, and the mixer of pitch whose name, in the absence of auxiliary evidence, cannot be certainly read in the text: evidently sH could not read it clearly in √H, and did his little best to copy it as it stood.

ɦuıɒıá aꝥloıce

The curved line over the *n* is turned the wrong way for the usual *m* contraction. It is a little to the right of the middle of the *n*, and is attached to the top of the following *l*. The only expansion that I can think of is *Dia-anarlaoite*, as printed in the text, or perhaps *Anarlarte*. By a perverse fate the name of the father of these brethren is torn away except the end, 13, in which the minim is most likely part of an *n*. This gives -*nus*, a termination that will not fit any antediluvian name in history or legend that I ever heard of. These names, and the details of the construction of the Ark here set forth, and the prayers of Noah and his sons, appear to come from some lost homily or apocryphon.

58. Here again a glossator tells us of the peculiar matrimonial relationships of Noah and his sons, presumably borrowing them from some late ms. of R².

59. On the importance of the discrimination between clean and unclean *birds* in this paragraph, see p. 9 *ante*. The adjectives *siltcach saidbir* may be original or glossarial, it is uncertain which, and matters little.

60-65. There is little in these paragraphs to call for notice other than what is referred to in the notes on the biblical text. The glosses are more than usually naïve : note especially the expression of admiration for the Ark at the end of ¶ 61, and the description of the proceedings of the dove in ¶ 65. If the latter is not an invention, it would be difficult to say whence the glossator obtained his information. Someone has acutely observed that glosses like this express and partially satisfy a natural craving for an *illustrated* history-book. In the absence of pictures, the annotator jots down picturesque details, which fill in the mental picture suggested by the words.

That the first emission of the dove took place seven days after that of the raven is a glossator's discovery, with no biblical authority.

66. The chronology of the Flood according to the inter-polation forming this and the following paragraph is not easy to follow, and the attentions of glossators have added to the confusion. But the following is clear (paying due attention to the corrections, p. 127)—

	year	month	day
Noah enters ark	600	2	10
Flood begins	600	2	17
Flood lasts 150 days = 5 months of 30 days each. Therefore grounding of ark at the end of that time takes place on			
	600	7	17
Mountain tops appear	600	10	1
Raven sent forth 40 days afterwards (1 month and 10 days), and therefore on			
	600	11	11
Noah opens ark	601	1	1
Noah leaves ark	601	2	27

Noah has therefore been in the ark 1 year 17 days—in the
Irish reckoning 1 year 16 days.

The interpolators (or one of them) apparently supposed
that the expression "second month" implies that the May
in which Noah entered the ark was an interealary May (*Mai
atharrach*). This is interesting, as it seems to indicate the
recollection of a lunar calendar like that of Coligny.[35] The
calculation that he entered the ark on a Friday and left it
on a Tuesday presupposes a lunar calendar with 12 months
of 30 days: $12 \times 30 + 16 = 376 = 7 \times 53 + 5$. The first
of these five extra days being Friday, the last would be
Tuesday: on this assumption therefore the calendar works
out.

It is unknown to me on what basis or authority the number
of species of birds and fishes in the ark is reckoned—or for
that matter, why fishes were included in the calculation at all.

67. The reference to Enoch is rendered obscure by the
state of the MS.: ᚉᚑᚄᚑᚇᚐᚋᚏᚑ comes at the end of a line, after
which a blob of the very opaque purplish colour, with which
a capital letter on the other side of the page had been
decorated, has penetrated through the vellum. Underneath
this disconcerting obstruction the eye of faith can discern
very faint traces of a letter like an ɫ or a b. The ép begins
the next line; but ᚏᚐ*ép is more difficult to comprehend than
ᚏᚐép, the reading here adopted. The general sense is
presumably that as Adam and Noah were the founders of

---

[35] Unlike those responsible for R², who thought of solar months: see
notes on ¶ 12 above.

human physical life, the pious Enoch was the founder of
human spiritual life.

78. The gloss ⅂ ōna huilib ċnaib is a good illustration of
the haste of a reader, too impatient to read to the end of the
sentence, where he would have discovered that the birds had
not been forgotten.

80. Comestor says (on earlier authority) that the rainbow
shall cease to appear forty years before the Last Judgement :
*Et tradunt sancti quod quadraginta annis ante Iudicium non
uidebitur arcus, quod etiam naturaliter ostendet desiccationem
aeris iam incoeptam* (Hist. Schol. xxxv). This paragraph is
greatly influenced by the corresponding passage in *Sex
Actates Mundi*, from which also the long passage on the
history of the rainbow comes. The absence from *Sex
Actates* of the anticipation that the bow will not appear before
the Judgement indicates that this is a later intrusive gloss
on the LG text.

81. Here again the translation has been contaminated by
an extract from *Sex Actates Mundi*. The glosses also come
from that work, so that the obvious interruption of the former
by the latter is old. R^3 interpolates the mutual slaying of
"the children of Dardan and Ioph," which does not refer to
the Trojan war, as might appear at first sight,[36] but to the
destruction of the Midianites (Judges vii. 19 ff.) : *Dadan* and
Epha appear in the Latin version of the account of the family
from which this people is said to have descended (Gen. xxv.
3, 4).

We are not, however, to suppose a simple cross-copying
from one book to the other. The curse on Ham, and the
destruction of his descendants, were written in first : the
further note, here printed in smaller type, attributing the
existence of monsters to the curse on Ham, must have been
added as an interlined and marginal afterthought. This is
shown by its dispartition (compare the fate of the note on
the composition of pitch, ¶ 57.)

---

[36] Notwithstanding the occurrence of these names, in Trojan
connexion, among the descendants of Ham in *Sex Actates Mundi*.

The word *gid* (in *tucad gid dilgend*) does not appear in the corresponding place in *Sex Aetates Mundi* (see Rawl. B, 502, facs. p. 71 *b*, line 49). I take it that the words in √H were *tucad aigid-dilgend* "a death-destruction was brought" (on the persons of the Canaanites, and confiscation on their land). The missing letters were in a *cor fá chasán* at the end of the preceding line, and were overlooked by *s*H.

The accompanying diagram shows what must have lain before *s*H in the MS. (√H) which he was copying. The preceding MS. ($\sqrt[2]{H}$) had nothing but the matter of the first and last of these lines in sequence (omitting, of course, the letters after *Iafcih* in line 1). Later, someone wrote into the margin of $\sqrt[2]{H}$ the note about the consequences which the curse upon Ham had brought upon his Canaanite descendants. After this, √H was copied from $\sqrt[2]{H}$; and the copyist took this note into the text, the writing being disposed as in the diagram. Still later, another scribbler, writing partly between the lines and partly in the margin, enriched √H with the further details about the monsters descended from Ham—an item of special interest, apparently, as another glossator inserted it again in √H, at ¶ 53.

When our MS. H was copied, history repeated itself. The new paragraph was incorporated in the text at what was obviously the most convenient place, the period preceding *Iarsin* in line 2. The scribe pursued it as far as *dainib*, in the margin at the end of line 5: but he failed to observe its conclusion, tucked into the blank space at the end of the short line 6. He then returned to *Iarsin*: but the interlineation which he had already copied, and at which he did not look again, screened from his vision the *cor fá chasán*, which must have concluded the first line and contained the beginning of the obviously imperfect word "gid." There

must have been no more than a short sentence before *larsin*
originally: a longer sentence would have filled up the
preceding line to the end, leaving no space for the indispens-
able *cor fá chasán*. This is an additional argument for the
secondary nature of the "monsters" gloss.

It is most fortunate that sH possessed in abundant
measure the most valuable of all endowments for a scribe—
un-intelligence. He copied by rote what lay before him: its
meaning, if it had any, was not his concern—that was the
affair of his betters. Owing to this admirable quality, he
failed to identify, in the words at the end of line 6 when at
last he reached them, the end of the "monsters" note which
he had copied only a few moments before—although he had
already copied out its whole text some time previously, when
writing ¶ 53. He therefore transcribed them just as they
stood, and made no attempt to insert them in their proper
place. It never occurred to him that "gid dilgend" was
incomprehensible nonsense. Had he realised these things, he
would infallibly have made disastrous efforts after emenda-
tion, and would thus have destroyed all the clues!

R², while copying these details, omits a censure upon the
Gaedil for ascribing the monsters to the Cainites, this being
a violation of the scriptural truth that all life perished in
the Flood. Augustine (*Civ. Dei* XVI. 8) discusses at length
whether the monstrous races of men (in which there was in
his time at least a half-belief: he gives a list of these
deformities of folklore) were descendants of Noah, and answers
in the affirmative. He does not, however, call in the curse
of Ham to account for them.

82. The genealogical chap. x is lost. The heterogeneous
paragraphs which follow the Biblical translation represent
various attempts to fill its place.

83. The story of the Tower of Babel is very diffuse, and
departs widely, in its language at least, from the biblical
text. The lacunae near the beginning are due to a tear which
mutilates the inner margin of the leaf.

"Hebrew," says Augustine (*Civ. Dei* XVI. 2), "was the
common language of the race of men till the time of Heber
father of Peleg, when the earth was divided. Till then it did

not require a distinctive name, but after that it was called Hebrew, after Heber." Nowhere can the origin of the name *Gorthigern*, given to this primitive language by Irish historians and grammarians, be discerned: we might guess that it is a corruption of some sort of rendering of the *Vox Domini* of the Psalter, the language being assumed to be the speech of Heaven.

[It may be desirable to explain here, in condonation of the use of the symbol Δ for the Latin manuscript which lies at the basis of the biblical text which we have been studying, that it has been chosen simply because it is one of the very few symbols not already pre-empted by the elaborate *apparatus criticus* of the Vatican edition. There is not the slightest fear of its ever being confused with the St. Gall MS.]

---

86. The biblical extract is followed by a miscellaneous collection of snippets, with the basal text *Q acting as framework. For an analysis of this part of the compilation see the introduction to the present section. In these paragraphs, the parts belonging to *Q are printed in ordinary type, the stratification of interpolations being roughly indicated by two varieties of smaller type. This paragraph is in H only, but the lacuna of M ends at the beginning of the poem. The particulars as to the place of death of the patriarchs are doubtless taken primarily from poem no. V, quatrain 42: but from what source it reached that authority I have not discovered, and until it is found attempts at explaining Rafán and Radruip would be mere guesswork. *Formcinia*, of course, = *Armcnia*, and the mountain intended is no doubt Ararat.

87. In H and M, apparently from R², or from some text depending thereon. The comment regarding the age of Adam seems to come from this passage of Comestor, quoting Pseudo-Methodius: *Et anno creationis uitae Adam decimo quinto natus est ei Cain et soror eius Chalmana. Et si enim factus est Adam quasi in aetate triginta annorum tamen fuit unius dici et anni* (Hist. Schol. xxv).

88. This comes from *Q. See the notes on R¹, ¶ 7. The appended gloss, though containing the same substance as the corresponding gloss in ¶ 7, is differently worded and must have been introduced independently.

89. The last sentence and the appended quatrain continue the matter from *Q: but before it a passage from *Sex Aetates Mundi* has been interpolated. This includes the first verse of a poem (given in full in *Sex Aetates*) and the tabular statement of the ages of the Patriarchs. These figures agree with *Sex Aetates* against all versions of the biblical text (except the Irish translation printed above) in the case of Seth: against all versions *including* the Irish translation in the case of Mahalaleel: and with all versions against the Irish translation in the cases of Methuselah and Lamech.

90. In H only, of unidentified origin. But see below ¶ 92. Two successive readers have appended speculations on how the Goidelic language came to be.

91. Also in H only. It is mutilated by a tear from the inner margin of the leaf, and would be unintelligible if it were not borrowed from *Sex Aetates Mundi*, with the aid of which text it can be partly restored—though with some slight verbal differences—from the copies in Rawl. B. 502 and in B. The words *acht a leigind a fo-tasgor na cinel* appear in Rawl. (41 d 20) from which B differs only in some orthographical trifles, in the form *acht a lecud hi fothechdas na genel n-aile.* The following passage from Isidore (IX ii. 39) appears to be the basis of the paragraph: *Nam quod ex filio Cham qui vocatur Mesraim Aegyptii sunt exorti, nulla hic resonat origo uocabuli, sicut nec Aethiopum, qui dicuntur ad eum filium Cham pertinere, qui Chus appellatus est. Et si omnia considerentur, plura tamen gentium mutate quam manentia uocabula apparent, quibus postea nomina diuersa dedit ratio.* See also Augustine, *Civ. Dei,* XVI, 6.

92. The beginning of this ¶ is in BM as well as H, but it is a continuation of the matter in ¶ 90; ¶ 91 being a later interpolation. The text of *Q then resumes: note how the correction about the number of the sons of Shem has been taken over. The passage is much farced with interpolations. The formula *cia ainmigter ... ni tabar a n-airem* comes from

Sex Aetates Mundi, as also does H's note, which has ousted its lemma, to the effect that the unnamed sons had descendants, but of no importance. The summary enumeration of the sons of Shem and of Japhet in R¹ has been expanded by reference, not to the Biblical source, but to Isidore (IX ii 26 ff.). He enumerates the sons of Japhet thus: *Gomer* (ancestor of Galatae i.e., Galli), *Magog* (supposed ancestor of Scythians and Goths), *Madai* (supposed ancestor of Medes), *Iauan* (ancestor of Ionians, who are the Greeks, and eponym of the Ionian Sea), *Thubal* (ancestor of Iberi who are the Hispani, by some supposed ancestor of the Italians), *Mosoch* (*ex quo Cappadoces, unde et urbs apud eos usque hodie Mazaca dicitur*), *Thiras* (ancestor of Thracians). By some misunderstanding the city of Mazaca (Caesarea in Cappadocia) has become an unauthorized additional son, Maisechda, whose descendants a later interpolator naturally sought in vain: see below ¶ 95 L. The variant in H (⁊ *ni tabar . . . . tabairt forro*) is an adaptation of a similar passage in *Civ. Dei*, XVI. 3.

93. This paragraph in H only. It is borrowed from R² (¶ 15). It is not clear why the order of the sons of Noah has been reversed.

94. This paragraph, more or less mutilated, is in all the MSS. It comes from R¹, but there are some traces of the influence of R². The version before us gives some good readings. It is more probable that *Fir na Scithia* should decline into *Farsacca*, and that this, owing to the constant association of "Medes and Persians," should develop a prefixed *Media*, than that *Farsacca* (protected by the associated *Media* from misunderstanding) should evolve into *Fir na Scithia*. The phrase *Is ūad lucht na Heorpa uile* is now exposed as a marginal gloss, taken into the text in different places: and "Grēcus mac Iafeth" is likewise shown to be an intruder into the text of R¹.

95. For convenience of reference this very long paragraph is broken into sections, denoted by capital letters. Most of it comes from *Sex Aetates Mundi* (here referred to as SAM): it is found in H only.

A.—The gloss *no Eōnae* and the secondary gloss *.i. an scindser*, are not in SAM. But the additional son of Japhet appears, there named Masseca.

B.—The interpolated explanation of the name Gallograeci is based on Isidore, *Etym.*, IX, ii, 68. (*Galatae Galli esse noscuntur, qui in auxilium a rege Bithyniae euocati regnum cum eo parta uictoria diuiserunt: sicque deinde Graecis admixti primum Gallograeci, nunc ex antiquo Gallorum nomine Galatae nuncupantur.*)

C.—Also based on Isidore, *Etym.*, IX, ii, 69 (*Graeci ante Thessali a Thessalo, postea a Graeco rege Graeci sunt nuncupati*).

D.—This section only repeats well-worn etymological speculations with neither value nor authority behind them. The harmonistic identification of Rifath with Ibath is perhaps worth a passing acknowledgement.

E.—Taken direct from the list of Japhet's descendants in Isidore *Etym.*, IX ii, 26 ff. (*Filii Gomer nepotes Iaphet, Aschanaz a quo Sarmatae quos Graeci Rheginos uocant, Riphath a quo Paphlagones, Gotorna a quo sunt Phryges*). "⁊ Ilia" must be a gloss.

F.—*Madai, a quo Medos existere putant*: Isidore, *loc. cit.* We shall hear of the eight Medians who ruled the world, in due course, in some of the later synchronistic insertions.

G.—A combination of Isidore and SAM. According to the former: *Filii Iauan Elisa, a quibus Graeci Elisaei, qui uocantur Aeolides. Unde et lingua quinta, Graece Aἰολίς, appellatur*; and again, *Iauan, a quo Iones, qui et Graeci; unde et Mare Ionium*. In SAM we read: *Iaban a quo Ioni sunt, et a quibus nominatur Ionicum Mare, ⁊ is uadib rogenatar Eolldai ⁊ a quibus nominantur Iolici. Oeus is uaidib ainmnigthir in cuiced berla na Greci .i. Berla Eolla.* There is no reference to Alexander the Great in either source.

H.—Isidore, *loc. cit.*: *Tharsis a quo Cilices, ut Iosephus arbitratur. Unde et metropolis ciuitas eorum Tharsus dicitur Cethim, a quo Citii id est Cyprii, a quibus hodieque urbs Citium nominatur. Dodanim, a quo Rhodii.* I cannot find

any justification for the quoting of *Civ. Dei* as an authority,
unless it be this sentence from XVI, iii, *ad init.*: *Coeptae
sunt enim commemorari a minimo filio qui uocatus est Iapheth.*
A poor latinist, with an ill-written MS., might mix up
"Coeptae" with "Scithim," and "Iapheth" with "Ioif," and
produce the reading presupposed. An absurd reading, but
probably most of us have heard or perpetrated equal
absurdities in our own schooldays.

I.—This comes from some other source. The islands are
admittedly enumerated from memory, and the names appear
to be distorted: *Rōid, Sicil* and *Creid* are the only ones whose
identification is clear. *Corbdith* and *Ceithiria* are presumably
the Cycladic islands *Carpathos* and *Cytherea*. *Rodain* I
conjecture (with fitting hesitation) to be the Balearic Islands,
which were colonized by Rhodians, and are roughly speaking
opposite the mouth of the Rhône (*Rhodanus*).

K.—*Thubal, a quo Iberi qui et Hispani: licet quidam ex
eo et Italos suspicentur.* The Irish compiler is less cautious
than Isidore. The remainder of this section apparently
comes from Augustine (*Civ. Dei*, VII, 4).

L.—*Mosoch, ex quo Cappadoces, unde et urbs apud eos
usque hodie Mazaca dicitur; Thiras, ex quo Thraces,*—Isidore,
loc. cit. The Irish writer does not trouble himself with the
Cappadocian city of Mazaca, which, as we have already seen,
has become "Maissegda" son of Japhet. SAM, while briefly
enumerating the descendants of the sons of Japhet, though
mentioning this fiction in the preliminary text, does not, like
the author of the interpolation before us, confess that
information about his progeny is missing. It gives us the
extra-biblical information that Thiras had seven sons: and
then enumerates the children of Gomer, as they appear in § E
above. But it does not, like the text before us, duplicate the
personality of Rifath.

M.—*Magog, a quo arbitrantur Scythas et Gothos traxisse
originem*: Isidore, *loc. cit.* The identification of the Goths
and the Gaedil follows from the historical sojourn of the
former, and the legendary sojourn of the latter, in the land
of the Scythians, of which we shall hear later. The matter

of this section, in shorter form, appears in SAM: Isidore remarks further: *Gothi a Magog filio Iaphet nominati putantur de similitudine ultimae syllabae, quos ueteres magis "Getas" quam "Gothos" uocauerunt* (IX, ii, 89).

N.—This repeats matter which has already appeared in R¹ (¶ 9) and will be found again in ¶ 98, taken from *Q. The text here is different, and more closely in accordance with that in SAM. The paternity of Baath is differently given, and the genealogical steps between him and Elenus or Alanus are omitted. Longbardus has been duplicated, and his double has been made into a fourth son of Negua. SAM differs from R³ as to the geographical connexion of Albanus: we there read .i. *ota ind Albain airtherach isind Assia Moir.*

O.—Borrowed from SAM, with an interpolation on the descent of the Franks and the Romans from Alanus.

P.—Only the beginning from SAM. The rest is the orthodox LG tradition, though the family of Barachān is new.

Q.—Mostly from SAM but with some expansion. "Sliab Mai" can be identified with *Amanus* by the help of Comestor (*Filii Iaphet tenuerunt septentrionalem regionem a Tauro et Amano montibus Ciliciae et Syriae usque ad fluuium Tanaim*—Hist. Schol. xxxvii). Isidore testifies to the same distribution: *Haec sunt gentes de stirpe Iaphet, quae a Tauro monte ad aquilonem mediam partem Asiae et omnem Europam usque ad Oceanum Brittanicum possident.* The sentence relating to Spain appears to be corrupt. In SAM it reads: ⁊ *in Espain n-uilidi co huilinn talmain* (Rawl) or ⁊ *conice in Easpain uilide fodcis .i. treuilleach,* which is nearer our present text. Tre-uilleach is written ᚦuilleᚦé, which suggests a possible origin for the mysterious word ᚦuillᚦlichᚦ; but *tre-uillig* also appears in the text before us, and if this excludes the explanation suggested, I can only conjecture that it is a corruption of *Astures.*

96. In H only. Ionitus, the fourth son of Noah, has obviously reached our text through Comestor. *Centesimo anno tertiae chiliadis natus est Noe filius in similitudinem*

*eius, et dixit cum Ionithum.   Trecentesimo anno dedit Noe
donationes filio suo Ionitho, et dimisit eum in terram Ethan,
et intrauit cum Ionithus usque ad mare orientis, quod dicitur
Elioschora, id est, "solis regio."   Hic accepit a Domino
donum sapientiae, et invenit Astronomiam* (Hist. Schol.
xxxvii).   Comestor here follows Pseudo-Methodius,[37] whose
alleged ''Revelations'' popularized this personage in Europe.
He passed into the traditions of the founding of Rome, the
greatness of which he was said to have foretold.   See G. A.
Graz, *Roma nella memoria e nelle immaginazioni del medio
eve,* Torino, 1882, I, p. 86.[38]   The legend is of oriental origin.
According to the *Cave of Treasures* Nimrod learned wisdom
from Yôntôn son of Noah, but the devil afterwards perverted
the teaching, which accounts for the mixture of good and evil
in astrology, magic, etc.   The *Book of the Bee* gives Yônatôn
as the name of the post-diluval son, whom Noah loaded with
gifts and sent forth "to the fire[39] of the sun" in the east.

97. In H only.   A history of the beginnings of the arts,
clearly an imitation—almost a parody—of the inventions
attributed in *Genesis* to the sons of the Cainite Lamech.   Eve's
penitence in the Tigris is the central incident in the *Book of
Adam and Eve* and related apocryphal documents.   The twin
sister of Cain is usually (following Pseudo-Methodius) called
Calmana.   *Is uimpi doronad an t-ed* refers to the story that
the real cause of Abel's murder was the desire of both brethren
to marry this sister: a dispute in which Adam took the part
of Abel, as he considered that Cain's twin consanguinity was
too close for an admissible marriage.   The brother 'Pendan'
appears in the later redaction of *Tenga Bith-nua* (*Revue
Celtique,* xxviii, p. 300) as a second victim of Cain's jealousy.

Two long interpolations have divorced Oliuana from her
husband Japhet.

The erection of the pillars is attributed to Seth by
Josephus, who is apparently the source of this frequently-

---

[37] See C. D'Evelyn, *The Revelations of Methodius* (Mod. Language
Assoc. of America, xxxiii (1918), p. 135.)

[38] I have had no opportunity of verifying this reference.

[39] "Fire" should be "land."   The corresponding Syriac words in
their native script have some superficial resemblance, which might mis-
lead a careless or astigmatic copyist.

repeated story (Antiqq. I, ii, 3). The Irish writer has missed the point of the difference in the materials of the pillars. According to Josephus, there were two pillars, one of brick and one of stone. If the anticipated destruction came by water, the stone pillar would survive, if by fire the pillar of brick.

98. On this paragraph see notes to ¶ 9.

99. This is from *Q. It is instructive to compare the two genealogies of Partholon with the corresponding text in F, ¶ 10, the only other R¹ text which has preserved this passage.

*Q (1)	*Q (2)	F
Parthalon	Parthalon	Parthalon
m. Sera	m. Sera	m. Sera
m. Sru	m. Sru	m. Sru
m. Esru	m. Esru	m. Esru
m. Gaeidil Glas		
m. Niuil	m. Praimint	m. Bimbind
m. Feiniusa Farrsaig	. . .	. . .
m. Bathatha	m. Aitheachda	m. Aaithecha
m. Magog	m. Magog	m. Magoth
m. Iathfeth	m. Iathfeth	m. Iafeth

Most likely the genealogy marked *Q (1) is the original, and was the only one in *Q. In the LF*X tradition, the shorter genealogy became substituted for the *Q genealogy; and this alternative form was inserted into the tradition from some MS. of that group. When two variant forms of a statement are given, united by a conjunction which means *or*, in the overwhelming majority of cases we may assume that the first is the original form, the second an interpolated alternative.

The concluding part of this ¶, which is certainly no part of the original text, is a condensed (and confused) genealogy of the Aitheeh-Tūatha of Connacht. Tindi s. Conri, Eochu Dala, and Fidheg s. Fēg, who is not here mentioned, divided Connacht between them after the coming of the Fir Bolg, taking respectively the East, West, and South of the Province. See *Genealogical Tracts*, i (ed Ó Raithbheartaigh) under the various names in the index, where further aspects of the

relationships of these communities will be found. They are
there derived from the Fir Bolg, not, as here, from the
Nemedians. One or other of the two references to Tindi s.
Conri in the paragraph before us, must be intrusive : it is
not certain which, as the *Genealogical Tracts* assign him to
the *Fir Taiden*. These, with the Domnannaig and the Fir
Craibe, constituted the "three original Connachta." Sliab
(F)uirri is in Galway, near the Roscommon boundary, and
close to Ballygar.

101. This paragraph, as is explained in the introduction,
begins a translation of the early Latin text. It was headed
Miniugud Gabal nErenn "An explanation (i.e. translation)
of the 'Takings of Ireland'." The following words were
doubtless added when the text (originally independent) was
tacked on to R², to supplement the deficiencies of that version.

Ethre i mbcolo aissncisen "an end (or tail) in a month
of relation" rendered by Thurneysen (*Zu ir. Handschr. u.
Lit.* ii, 5) as "recapitulation" perhaps might rather be
supposed to refer to the end of a chain of oral transmission,
and be translated "tradition."

Ō thosuch in libair anūas : an editorial note, inserted to
link the text to R² to which it is now appended.

Hybernia insola, etc., down to "*insola*" *Latine dicitur*, is
probably the preface of the original text.

Then follows an interpolation derived from Isidore (XIV,
vi, 6) as Thurneysen has already observed : it is not reproduced quite correctly in our MSS. : the true readings of
Isidore are given here in footnotes to the text. There are
two glosses, one explaining the corrupt *Hiberniam* (for
Hiberiam) and the other contradicting the oft-quoted
statement, disseminated by Solinus, as to the absence of bees.

Scoti autem a Scota . . . . . . adnotentur is an additional
interpolation, suggested by the reference to the *Scotorum
gentes* in the excerpt from Isidore.

The sentence beginning *Phoeni autem* is a further interpolation, interrupting the remarks about the Scots. Their
identification with the tatooed Picts in this passage is
contrary to all the orthodoxy of the LG tradition.

With *Heriu dono* the original passage resumes : this
follows on naturally to the etymological speculations

interrupted by the intruded excerpt from Isidore.   Here again an unusual idea is suggested.   The comment s. q. l. is a frequent formula of complaint regarding a passage which a reader found it hard to understand.   It is equivalent to the *difficilis est haec pagina* of the Saint-Gall *Priscian*.

Quasi scissi is another etymological interpolation, a guess by some wiseacre at the origin of the word *Scoti*.

VERSE TEXTS.

I.

Metre : the two quatrains forming this composition are probably, in origin, independent compositions, as is suggested by their diversity of metre.   The second is in *casbairdne* ($7^3 + 7^3$) with trisyllabic rhymes between lines 2 and 4 ; the first is in *snām sebaic*, a variety in which the third line ends with a monosyllable.

The text has been greatly corrupted by scribes, who tinkered with it unrestrainedly in the vain hope of extracting more sense out of it than the author or authors ever put into it : as the verses are mere displays of metrical gymnastics, the meaning is of minor importance in an endeavour to restore the text.   In addition to the rhymes, there is assonance between the first two lines of each stanza, and an alliteration in every line, which the attentions of the scribes have to some extent suppressed.   This is the chief help toward restoring the text.   The MS. P has been re-inked unintelligently.

1. *Slūag* has evidently been changed to the plural after the incorporation of the second quatrain, bringing another "host" into view.   Both alliteration and meaning help us to choose *cūa-chel* "a winter (or rainy) death" as the true reading, although it happens to be found only in the three inferior derivatives from B.   *Conad* has arisen from a misreading of a mark of prolongation as an abbreviation for *n* : the same mistake is probably at the base of F's *ecnad*.   In *snām sebaic* there is no necessity for vowel-assonance between lines 1 and 3, and therefore we can read *cel*, "death, fate" instead of the less tractable *cīl* "an omen."

S

2. The insertion of *ac* in MH (not in B) is an attempt to mend the metre, after Noë had come to be pronounced as a monosyllable, Nāi. The alliteration decides for *niath-lēn* against rival readings.

3. The evidence for the infixed pronoun (*ronglēad*) is hardly strong enough to justify us in adopting it, though it may be right.

4. *Ialafen* in E is an attempt to mend the metre, the name having sunk into a dissyllable.

8. The rhyme with *dībada* teaches us the pronunciation *Olīuǎna*.

II.

Metre: *debide imrind.*

Apparently a variant of poem V quatrain 40, not found in any complete text of the poem—or more probably from another poem on similar lines, as V is in *debide scāilte*, and has only two quatrains (23, 49) in *debide imrind.*

III.

Metre: *debide scāilte.*

A variant of poem V quatrain 41, likewise not found in any complete text of the poem. In Min these two quatrains run continuously, as though forming one extract: this may be original, the matter which separates them in the other Redactions being editorial. Naĕ is here still a dissyllable, but Iafōth is no longer trisyllabic. The variant *do dec* in the last line has obviously arisen from a misreading of the numeral sign .u.

IV.

Metre: *crā cummaise etir casbairdne ┐ lethrannaigecht.* There should be alliterations in the first two lines at least, but in a poem so full of proper names this is impossible to maintain consistently. The language is Middle Irish.

20. This cheville may also be translated something like "well seen was his authority," but the rendering chosen makes little difference to the sense.

22. *Ōen* used absolutely, as a rhyme to *sōer*.

32. *Meic*, inserted before *Ebaith* by numerous MSS., though desirable, is hypermetric and must be rejected.

33. *Iardain* must be read instead of *Iarboneil*, for metrical reasons, though the last is the more orthodox form.

36. *Esrū* and *meic* must be omitted, for metrical reasons. Compare line 32.

39. This refers to the magical apparition of the Tūatha Dē Danann : the "plain" is Mag Tuired.

V.

Metre : *debide scāilte*. The versifier began by making alliterative linkages (*conachlann*) between the end of every quatrain and the beginning of the next, but after the seventh quatrain abandoned the effort : no re-arrangement of the quatrains can establish the device after this point, and we must assume that the few cases to be found in the latter part of the poem are accidental.

There are two versions of this long composition, contained in not a few modern MSS. I have collated several of these in the Royal Irish Academy[40] without finding anything of importance : no version contains the isolated variants which

---

[40] 23 A 40, F III 2, 23 M 18, C vi 1, 24 P 13. Of these 23 A 40 23 M 18 and C v 1 belong to the M group and show nearly all of its peculiar readings and arrangements of the quatrains. Except for scribal mistakes (as *abartar* for *abar*, line 98 (23 A 40)) or the peculiar spelling *Caidin* for *Cain* in 23 M 18, they show no particular individuality. A later hand has inserted into 23 A 40 an attribution of the poem to Eochaid ua Floind : 23 M 18 is content to say *Ollamh eigin cct*. F III 2 and 24 P 13 are closer to the printed version. F III 2, which attributes the poem to Colum Cille, closely follows EP in its readings. The following variants may be worth noting : line 58 (this spurious quatrain is present, as in EP) *dib gan Chaim*: line 68 *Agānta* (for *Gogoma*): line 89, *tri trāth go leith, nī lūad saobh*: line 129, *ro fāsadh .uii. ccnoic*: line 142, *Tubadh Caoin*. Stanzas 28–30, 34, 37, 39, 45, 46, 50 are omitted. The city in line 251 is called *Imbītena*, as in D; in 263 we find *Etrosius*—one of many proofs afforded by Irish MSS. that although *c* was always pronounced hard in Irish, it was pronounced as *s* before *i* and *e* in Latin. 24 P 13 has also close affinity with EP, but has nothing of importance to tell us.

we have seen in nos. II, III above. In the MSS. before us, M
may be taken as the type of the one text, R² of the other.
H, on the whole, follows R², but U (*the Book of Ui Maine*),
which has a fine copy in a different context, follows the M
version. Referring back to the diagram, p. 14 *ante*, I am
now inclined to think that the two folios, 2 and 7, disappeared
together, and had both gone when ∞M transcribed the text.
He recognised the torso of the poem, and found another copy
from which to supply the missing quatrains (1–30). M and
H appear to agree against R² more frequently in the second
half of the poem than in the first.

42. *Mac maith Muire ingine* (an unconscious lapse into
the heresy of Sabellianism!) is peculiar to M among the
manuscripts here used. Though not in U, it is a reading of
the M version of the text.

43. None of the MSS. indicate the nasalization after *ār.*

46. *Maiss,* the chaotic material out of which the universe
was fashioned.

52. The "clouds" (*neōil*) are introduced to make an
assonance with *cōin.* The poet takes advantage of the
freedom in *debide* rhyme to unite the long vowel in *glē* with
the short vowel in *Dardāine.* Some peculiar minor verbal
differentiations appear in the M text in this quatrain.

54. The assertive interjection *Debrad* is here left
untranslated, in view of the uncertainty attaching to its
etymology. As everyone knows, an over-indulgence in this
expletive was one of St. Patrick's few human weaknesses.

57. This stanza breaks the *conachlann,* which has not yet
been abandoned; and as it appears in two MSS. only it is
probably spurious, even although it is a necessary supplement
to the preceding stanzas, which describe the works of creation.
It is here printed as in E, with the addition of punctuation
and prolongation marks only. *Deg-dāil,* the company
listening to the narrative. *Anmann* must be for *anmanna*
(the a elided before the following vowel): this, and the
accusative *deilb,* are governed by *aisneidfed.* Note the article
with a noun depending on a proper-name genitive in the last
line.

61 ff. The poet is here dealing with a body of apocrypha differing from that followed in the prose text, as may be shown by the following table :—

	Prose (¶ 2A, 25)	Verse
Head from	Garad	Malōn
Breast „	Arabia	Arōn
Belly „	Lodain	Babylon
Legs „	Agoiria	Laban, Gogoma

—disregarding the variant forms in the different MSS.

This, however, does not bring us nearer to discovering the origin of the Irish version of the story. Verses which appear to be a rather remote variant of these quatrains, found in *Codex Palatino-Vaticanus* (Todd Lectures, III. p. 24) revert to the prose version (Garad, Arabion [or Aradon, or Adilon], Laban, and Dagaria [or Gagaria]). The poet has also his own views as to the course of the rivers of Paradise. *Tairis* is the reading of all the MSS., but we should doubtless emend this to *tairse* : the rivers ran through the (fem.) *land*, not the (masc.) *head*. In this stanza we note an important deviation in the M text.

69. *Trāth*(*a*) means "days," as is more usual in this text, not (canonical) hours, on account of the reference to Christ's three days in the tomb. The first couplet of this quatrain is metrically faulty, as both lines end in a dissyllable. That Adam was for some time without life is a popular belief in apocryphal literature : but it is quite independent of the three-days' sojourn of Christ in the tomb, with which it is here typologically connected. In fact, the stories vary as to the length of time which elapsed before the body of Adam was quickened. A Muslim legend shows some affinity with the ideas here expressed. "Allah formed Adam out of a handful of dust . . . which . . . had been collected from different parts of the world, and consisted of various kinds of soil, which accounts for the divers colours of men and women. When Allah had formed Adam, He left the figure lying lifeless forty days—some say forty years—while notice was sent to the Angels, the Jinn, and the Jan, to be ready to worship and do him honour as soon as Allah had put breath into his nostrils.[41]

73. *Triar* presumably means the three Persons of the Trinity, who are represented as collaborating in the creation of Adam—another variant from the conception in the prose text. To make any sense of the cheville at the end of line 75 we should have to read *ba dia ndeōin* "by Their good will": but no MS. supports this.

77. An abridged translation of quatrains 10–13, 15 will be found in Archdeacon Seymour's paper, *The Book of Adam and Eve in Ireland*,[42] which should be in constant reference in studying the apocryphal Adam matter in this compilation. Pairtech, the "great mountain" of Paradise, is new: it appears again in the form *Pariath* in the *Lebor Brecc* history of the creation (Todd Lectures. III. p. 48). Adam's hymn of praise is a commonplace of apocrypha. In *Pirqe Rabbi Eliezer*, chap. II. we read "And as [Adam] saw the creatures which God had made he began to praise God his Creator, and said: O Lord, how great and many are Thy works!"

81–2. Another metrically faulty couplet, both lines ending in a monosyllable.

83. According to the Syriac *Cave of Treasures* "God took a rib from the loins on the right side of Adam and He made Eve: and when Adam woke up and saw Eve he rejoiced in her greatly. And Adam and Eve were in Paradise, clothed with glory and shining with praise, for three hours." (Tr. Budge, pp. 59–60).

87–8. This apparently refers to the naming of the birds; at least I can find no other story connecting Adam with birds. Syncellus, *Chronography*, gives the dates of the incidents of Adam's life thus: 1st day of week [3rd day of Creation of Adam, 8th of Nisan, 1st of April, 6th of Phamouthi] Adam named wild beasts: 2nd day, named cattle: 3rd day, *named fowls*: 4th day, named creeping things, etc., etc.

---

[41] J. E. Hanauer, *Folklore of the Holy Land* (London, 1907), p. 9.
[42] *Proceedings*, R.I.A., xxxvi, section C, p. 121.

91. All the MSS. read *do nim*, which is unmetrical, and incidentally nonsense. It seems best to emend it to *do-gnīm* (gen. plur.) "of evil deeds," the complementary formation to *so-gnīm*, "a good deed."

96. These words spell the letters of the Tetragrammaton יהוה the Hebrew divine name *Yahweh*, inaccurately rendered "Jehovah" in European popular speech. The notion that the Devil was the first to invoke the name of God reappears in *Salomon and Saturnus* (*ed. cit. antea*, p. 191)—

"Who first named the name of God? the devil first named the name of God."

We find the statement repeated in the *Colloquy of Adrian and Ritheus* (ibid., p. 204), and also by the *Master of Oxford*—

"Who cleped first God?—The devyll."

The basal idea doubtless is that the devil acquired power over the Deity by knowing and using His secret name.[43] The poet's knowledge of Hebrew was limited to the letters of the alphabet and their names, possibly learnt from the section-headings in Ps. cxix (Vulgate cxviii); and to the external appearance of the Tetragrammaton. He did not even know that Hebrew is written and read from right to left, so that when he spelt out the letters of the divine name he enumerated them in the reverse order—the left-to-right order in which he was accustomed to read or write Latin or Irish.

97. An aetiological myth to account for the superiority of the right hand to the left. In an account of the Creation and subsequent events in T.C.D. MS. H 2 5, most of which follows LG closely, I find this: *Ro hiomuil imorro Adamh an t-ubhall ⁊ ro bad tarnocht dū eis, ⁊ les ta lamh chle seochus lamh dheas ann, mar as ī an lamh chle sineadh chum an ubhaill.* "A. ate the apple and became naked thereafter [compare *Cod. Pal. Vat.*, p. 54] and therewith the left hand comes after the right hand, for it is the left hand that was stretched to the apple." I have not come across the idea elsewhere in apocrypha, though doubtless it exists.

---

[43] For analogies see Frazer, *Taboo and the Peril of the Soul*, p. 387 ff.

101. The expulsion of the errant pair to *Egypt* is unorthodox : Damascus is the usual place of their exile. The "one palm" suggests that the poet did not know the difference between dates and figs.

105. Throughout the poem the name *Cain* is treated as a dissyllable. P sometimes emphasises this by spelling it *Caidin.*

109. The poet, writing presumably from memory, has forgotten that Cain's offering was "of the fruits of the earth." Once again we see a faulty couplet, with the end words having the same number of syllables.

124. Seth was the first man to *grow* a beard, for Adam was presumably created with his beard, Abel died a beardless youth, and it was part of Cain's punishment to have no beard (as in the prose text ¶ 39). But no ancient authority known to me explains how Seth was a witness of the murder of Abel (which took place before he was born), why he "put his hand to the jawbone," or what he did with it.

127. That stones "grow" is still an article of popular belief : I have been shown, by a Co. Meath farmer, a stone with a mark upon it which, he believed, was produced by the pressure of another stone, while the marked stone was "growing." *Salomon and Saturnus* agrees with our poet that this growth had been stopped by the flow of Abel's blood. We there read—

> "Tell me why stones are not fruitful?—Because Abel's blood fell upon a stone when Chain his brother slew him with the jawbone of an ass."

Also in *The Master of Oxford's Catechism*—

> "Why bereth not stonys froyt as trees?—For Cayne slough his brother Abell with the bone of an asse cheke."

139. The tale of how Lamech accidentally slew Cain is one of the most familiar legends of Apocrypha. It is of Jewish origin, and as stated above, in the notes to ¶ 39, was probably imported into Christian tradition from a lost "Book of Lamech." See Seymour, *op. cit.,* p. 130, for references to which add the quotation from Rabbi Solomon Jarchi in

Eisenmerger's *Entdecktes Judenthum*, vol. i, p. 470. The weapon used by Lamech was, however, an arrow; not an apple, as in the text before us.

142. The name Tubalchain must be scanned as a tetrasyllable, to give a rhyme for *brig*: we must therefore follow E in reading *is*, as against the *ocus* of other MSS. On the other hand it is a trisyllable in line 144, unless E is right in omitting the following article. But D emphasizes the difference by a difference of spelling.

143. The words *in cara* are difficult to deal with. See Meyer, *Contribb.* s.v. *cor* for the meaning suggested in the translation.

145. I know of no other version of the almost nauseatingly silly story of the subsequent adventures of Abel's ram, narrated in this and the following quatrains.

148. It is common sense that this must refer to "the ram caught in the thicket," which provided a surrogate for Isaac: and that the original version ran *dar cend meic Aprām* (not *Aprāim*, which is forbidden by the rhyme: Aprām is indeclinable). Some meddler, however, older than the existing MS. tradition, oblivious of the story of the sacrifice of Isaac, assumed vaguely that the event must have been something or other in the history of the Children of Israel; so he changed the genitive singular to genitive plural.

153. This quatrain seems out of place: it probably should follow quatrain no. 15. The name of the tree is given as *Sezen* in the Ethiopic *Book of Mysteries of Heaven and Earth*. (See Budge, *Cave of Treasures*, p. 66); as *Deachuimhan* ["tithing"] in the late version of *Tenga Bithnua* (*Rev. Celt.* xxviii, 300).

155. We have heard of "the plain of Aron" before, as the region over which the rivers of Paradise flow. This looks like a confusion based on some old misreading of the Hebrew source (the ד, *d*, in "Eden" being misread as ר *r*). The contrary mistake is made in the Greek version of Numbers xxvi. 36.

163. *Deich mbliadan risin uile,* i.e., ten years in addition to all the 930 years of Adam's life. That Eve survived Adam is generally agreed in apocryphal literature, but the actual length of her widowhood is very variously stated.

166. The poet has misread .d.cccc.xii. in his authority, substituting .xu. for the last letters. On the other hand, he has not docked Seth's life by three hundred years, as the prose texts have done. The M text has altered the verse text to conform with the prose.

173. Jared's life was 962 years long. Here again .ii. has been misread as .u.

177. Most of the MSS. agree on *ochtmoga,* but the variant *scchtmoga* is historically correct.

182. Lamech's life was 777 (Hebrew) 753 (Septuagint). The figure in the text 775 and H's correction 757 are both unauthorized. An owner of U has taken the trouble to look the matter up : see the footnote.

186. Adam's son Sile, and the three wives in line 188, reappear in *Sex Aetates Mundi,* but whence they reached that text I have failed to discover. Olla was Seth's wife, Pip was Cain's, Pithip was Sile's. Evidently there is some confusion between Seth and Shem, just as Cain and Ham (Cham) are sometimes interchanged. Pip and Pithip must therefore have some kinship with Oliva and Olivana, but the nature of the kinship is not clear.

193. On the names of these women see the note on the prose texts ¶ 7.

205. On this quatrain and its mysterious geography, see the notes on the prose text ¶ 86, where we find the interesting back-formation *Formenia* > *Armenia* on the basis of *ar* < *for.*

212. D spells this word *cubaat,* and writes it thus (as nearly as can be represented in print) cubaττ, the first two τ's being really a fantastic *a.* The same peculiarity was probably also in √D, and has influenced E's *cubatat.* E was certainly not copied from D, but might well have come from

√D. This is a good illustration of the way in which the *external form* of the MSS. and their handwriting may sometimes give us some crumbs of information as to their relationship; see ante, p. xxvii. It must be admitted that this peculiar way of writing a sequence of *a*'s and *t*'s, in any combination, is a trick of Muirges ó Maoil Conaire, the scribe of D, and that it reappears in the *Book of Fenagh*, another of his productions. It is not, however, a regular habit: it looks more like an artificial affectation, in which he indulges whenever he remembers to do so, and he may have made it his own after learning it from √D.

215. The cheville *cen brōn* is more than usually meaningless here if we give to the word *brōn* its ordinary meaning "sorrow." K. Meyer, *Contribb.* gives (with a query) an alternative meaning "burden" which helps slightly, but not much. But we need not expect a poet in metrical difficulties to be intelligible all the time : our present poet is better in this respect than many of his colleagues.

218-219. In both these lines the *o* of *ro* is metrically elided. Several of the scribes have failed to notice this, and have endeavoured to emend what they took to be the faulty measure of the rhythm.

221. I know of no authority for the extravagant dimensions here ascribed to the tower.

228. The list of the heroes of Nimrod's Tower agrees with that in *Auraicept*, except that Peleg and Rabiath (= Rifath) Scot are here omitted. Dardan appears in *Auraicept* as "Bardanius." The names are selected, on some random principle which it is futile to try to determine, from a list of the immediate descendants of Noah; with such incongruous additions as Nabcodon, Latinus, and Longbardus. The first of these comes from an Ogham alphabet of names : see Calder's *Auraicept*, p. 20, and also below, line 257.

240. The sense of the couplet seems to be "though God be no respecter of persons—though the abbot and the king be all one in His sight—may He grant me the favour of a long life."

251-2. These lines appear in the order as printed in all the MSS., but as the tetrasyllable *Ibitēna* should follow the trisyllable *il-bērla* they should be transposed. The city of Ibitēna is apparently an echo of the name of the Median city of Ecbatana. As the table of *variae lectiones* shows, this name assumes a variety of forms. Keating gives another version, Eathēna, and quotes this quatrain as from *Cin Droma Snechta*—which seems to suggest that this poem was contained in that important manuscript.

257 ff. This is the Ogham-alphabet list of the chief persons of Nimrod's Tower, from which one set of names for the Ogham letters was derived. For metrical reasons the alphabetic order has been disturbed (see for the proper arrangement Calder's *Auraicept*, p. 20) and some of the names have been modified. Mored, Gad, Hidomus correspond respectively to Muiriath, Gotli, and Iudonius. Ordmor (possibly meant for *Ord Mōr*, but the *variae lectiones* suggest that it is one word) corresponds to Ordines (Ordomus in M). Srū, the Stru of the Ogham list, has been lost from all the MSS. except M; and additional names have been interpolated (Nenual, Gaedel, Cainan, Ionan).

VI.

Metre: *debide scāilte.*

273. On the characters ascribed to the rivers in this poem, see the note on the prose ¶ 28.

274. The name Nuchal here given as the fountain-head of the four rivers, can hardly be dissociated from Nuchul, given as the name of an African river in the Geographical Poem of Ros Ailithir (*P.R.I.A.*, xvi, p. 241). Its (probably erroneous) identification with the Nile, and the identification of the latter with Gihon, may have led to the transference of the name to the well-spring of Paradise.

278. We must read *felicitias* for the sake of the metre.

284. I suspect that *tibes* is wrong, but I take it as I find it in the MSS.

VII.

Metre: *debide scāilte.*

VIII.

Metre: *rannaigecht becc.*

This quatrain, and the following poem, found in H only, are printed exactly as they appear there, with the addition of punctuation marks only.

IX.

Metre: *debide scāilte.*

296. In this poem Nāe has become a monosyllable; a fact emphasised by the spelling of the genitive Nāee in line 304.

IRISH TEXTS SOCIETY

—:□:—

THE IRISH TEXTS SOCIETY *was established in* 1898 *for the purpose of publishing texts in the Irish language, accompanied by such introductions, English translations, glossaries and notes as may be deemed desirable.*

The Annual Subscription is 21/- *(American subscribers,* $5*), payable on* 1st *January. This entitles members to receive, post free, the current volume. There is no entrance fee.*

Members whose subscriptions are not in arrear may, where necessary, complete their sets by obtaining back volumes up to Volume XXI inclusive at the reduced rate of 10/6 *a volume. Volumes XXII and XXIII are* 12/6 *and all subsequent volumes are* 21/- *each. The current subscription of* £1 1s. 0d. *should be paid for the year in which any application is made for back volumes under this arrangement.*

The payment of a single sum of £12 12s. 0d. *(colonial or foreign members,* £13 0s. 0d. *; American members,* 65 *dollars), entitles to life membership. Life members will receive one copy of each volume issued subsequently to the receipt of this sum by the Society. All remittances should be made payable to the Society, not to individual Officers.*

Vols. I. II. III. and XIV. are now out of print and others are rapidly becoming scarce. The ordinary sale price to non-members through Messrs. Simpkin, Marshall, Ltd., 4 *Stationers' Hall Court, London, E.C.4., is* 25/- *per volume (post free).*

The Council makes a strong appeal to all interested in the preservation and publication of Irish Manuscripts to join the Society and to contribute to its funds.

Please Note Address.

All communications should be addressed to the Hon. Secretary, Irish Texts Society, c/o National Bank Ltd., 15, *Whitehall, London, S.W.1.*

IRISH TEXTS SOCIETY.

THE THIRTY-FOURTH Annual General Meeting of the Irish Texts
Society was held on Saturday, 11th February, 1933, in the Library
of the Irish Literary Society.

Dr. Robin Flower, chairman of the Executive Council, presided.

The Minutes of the last Annual General Meeting, held on the
13th February, 1932, were taken as read. Mr. Maurice O'Connell,
Assistant Secretary, read the

Thirty-Fourth Annual Report

Duanaire Finn. The Council are glad to report that all the
poems and translations forming Part II of *Duanaire Finn* are
through the final proofs. Arrangements are now being made for
binding. This volume will be followed by Part III, consisting of
the Preface, Notes to the Poems, Glossary, and Index of Persons
and Places, etc. Both volumes are being edited by Mr. Gerard
Murphy, M.A. Part I, edited by Professor Eoin MacNeill, D.Litt.,
was issued by the Society in 1907, and is now nearly out of print.

Instructio Pie Vivendi (Holy Life and Heavenly Thought). The
first part of this interesting theological work is now nearing
completion. It will consist of the Latin original and Irish
translation, with a short glossary of the rarer Irish words. The
Irish is a very good specimen of the early modern language. The
work will be in two volumes, and volume two is in active
preparation.

The Great Blasket. The Council regret that owing to illness,
the result of an accident while on a visit to the Aran Islands, Dr.
Flower was obliged to suspend his work on this volume for some
time. He has now resumed. The volume will consist of a collection of tales dealing with the life of the Great Blasket Island, Co.
Kerry, in the nineteenth century. A number of poems by a poet
of the locality will also be included, with stories illustrating their
subjects.

NOTE.—Part II of *Duanaire Finn* was distributed in September of this
year.

6

The number of back volumes disposed of during the year was 94. The Rev. P. S. Dinneen's edition of the Society's revised and enlarged Irish-English Dictionary is now nearly exhausted. The Council have under consideration the question of a reprint.

During the year an edition of the Society's smaller dictionary in Roman type was completed, and a new edition in Irish type has also been printed. Both editions are now obtainable at 3/-.

The Council regret to report the deaths of the following :— Right Rev. Dr. Shahan, Vice-President of the Society ; Lady Gregory, Col. J. W. MacNamara, Dr. Goddard Orpen.

Members who joined during the year were :—Dr. Gerard Coyne, Ballinasloe ; Miss Anna Irene Miller, Baltimore, U.S.A. ; Maire Ni Locain, Dublin ; Fergus Patterson, Putney, London ; Convent of St. Louis, Monaghan ; Minnesota University Library, Minn., U.S.A.

J. C. Sprott, Esq., Glasgow, resigned.

The adoption of the Annual Report was moved and seconded. During the discussion which followed, Dr. Joyce referred to the slow rate of production of the Society's books. It was explained that the delay in every case was occasioned by illness or pressure of other business that obliged the editors to postpone their work on the Society's volumes. On a show of hands the Report was adopted.

The Financial Statement was explained by the Treasurer and adopted on the proposal of Mr. Buckley, seconded by Dr. Joyce.

The re-election of the Officers and outgoing members of the Council, Mrs. Banks, Mr. Buckley and Dr. Flower, was proposed by Mr. O'Keeffe, seconded by Mr. FitzGerald, and carried.

A hearty vote of thanks was accorded to Mr. R. W. Farrell, F.L.A.A., for auditing the accounts, and his appointment as auditor for the year 1933 was agreed upon.

7

IRISH TEXTS SOCIETY.

RECEIPTS AND PAYMENTS ACCOUNT FOR THE YEAR, 1932.

Dr.	£	s	d	Cr.	£	s	d
Brought forward from 1931 ...	1115	12	1	Trade Distribution ...	7	3	1
Donations to Editorial Fund ...	1	11	0	Storage	7	10	0
Sales of Larger Dictionary ...	398	8	9	Printing and Binding ...	275	17	1
Sales of Smaller Dictionary ...	82	19	0	Postage, etc.	12	1	4
Interest, etc.	167	1	7	Income Tax	27	10	0
Postage			6	Insurance	4	10	0
Subscriptions and Sales of Volumes	191	13	10	Investment, 5% War Loan ...	1016	14	3
				Royalty ...	53	2	6
				Editors' Expenses ...	20	0	0
				Sundry Expenses ...	72	13	2
				Balance, being Cash in Hand and at Bank ...	460	5	4
	£1957	6	9		£1957	6	9

BALANCE SHEET AS AT DECEMBER 31st, 1932.

Liabilities.	£	s	d	Assets.				£	s	d
Sundry Creditors ...	449	10	6	Cash at Bank ...	455	0	1			
Reserves :—				Cash in Hand ...	5	5	3			
Printing and Binding of Volumes under Contract	670	0	0	Cash on Deposit ...	850	0	0	1310	5	4
Income Tax ...	30	0	0	£2900 3½% Loan at 99⅛				2874	12	6
Binding of Larger Dictionary	66	13	4	£250 C.N.R. at 91 ...				227	10	0
Printing of Annual Reports	20	0	0	Sundry Debtors				355	18	2
Editorial Expenses ...	540	0	0	Insurance paid in Advance				1	2	6
Subscriptions paid in advance for Vols. not under Contract	226	16	0	Office Furniture	11	13	1			
Reprint of Larger Dictionary	600	0	0	Less Depreciation ...	4	10	6	7	2	7
Balance	3324	15	3	Stock				1151	4	0
	£5927	15	1					£5927	15	1

(Signed) M. C. LYNCH, Hon. Treasurer.

The undersigned, having had access to all the Books and Accounts of the Society, and having examined the foregoing statements and verified them with the Books, Deeds and Documents, etc., relating thereto, now signs the same as found to be correct.

(Signed) ROBERT W. FARRELL, F.L.A.A., Certified Accountant.
28th January, 1933.

GENERAL RULES

——:0:——

OBJECTS

1.—The Society is instituted for the purpose of promoting the publication of Texts in the Irish Language, accompanied by such Introductions, English Translations, Glossaries and Notes as may be deemed desirable.

CONSTITUTION

2.—The Society shall consist of a President, Vice-Presidents, an Executive Council, a Consultative Committee and Ordinary and Life Members.

OFFICERS

3.—The Officers of the Society shall be the President, two Honorary Secretaries and the Honorary Treasurer.

EXECUTIVE COUNCIL

4.—The entire management of the Society shall be entrusted to the Executive Council, consisting of the Officers of the Society and not more than ten other Members, to whom the Executive Council may add by co-optation not more than two members, who shall retire annually.

5.—All property of the Society shall be vested in the Executive Council, and shall be disposed of as they shall direct by a two-thirds majority.

6.—Three members of the Executive Council shall retire each year by rotation at the Annual General Meeting, but shall be eligible for re-election, the Members to retire being selected according to seniority of election, or, in case of equality, by lot. The Council shall have power to co-opt Members to fill up casual vacancies occurring throughout the year. Any Member of Council who is absent from five consecutive Ordinary Meetings of the Council to which he (or she) has been duly summoned, shall be considered as having vacated his (or her) place on the Council.

CONSULTATIVE COMMITTEE

7.—The Consultative Committee, or individual Members thereof, shall give advice, when consulted by the Executive Council, on questions relating to the publications of the Society, but shall not be responsible for the management of the business of the Society.

MEMBERS

8.—Members may be elected either at the Annual General Meeting, or from time to time, by the Executive Council.

Subscription

9.—The Subscription for each Member of the Society shall be £1 1s. 0d. per annum (American subscribers, $5), entitling the Member to one copy (post free) of the volume published by the Society for the year, and giving the right to vote on all questions submitted to the General Meeting of the Society. Regular members, whose subscriptions have been paid up to date, may, however, fill up gaps in their sets of back volumes, prior to volume 22, at 10/6 a volume. The payment of a single sum of £12 12s. 0d. (Colonial or foreign members £13 0s. 0d., American members 65 dollars) entitles to life membership. Life members will receive one copy of each volume issued subsequently to the receipt of this sum by the Society.

10.—Subscriptions shall be payable in advance on 1st January in each year.

11.—Members whose Subscriptions for the year have not been paid are not entitled to any volume published by the Society for that year, and any Member whose Subscription for the current year remains unpaid, and who receives and retains any publication for the year, shall be held liable for the payment of the full published price, viz. 25/- of such publication.

12.—The publications of the Society shall not be sold to persons other than members, except at the advanced price of 25/-.

13.—Members whose Subscriptions are in arrear shall not have the right of voting at the Annual General Meeting of the Society.

14.—Members wishing to resign must give notice in writing to the Honorary Secretary, before the end of the year, of their intention to do so; otherwise they will be liable for their subscriptions for the ensuing year.

Editorial Fund

15.—A fund shall be opened for the remuneration of Editors for their work in preparing Texts for publication. All subscriptions and donations to this fund shall be purely voluntary, and shall not be applicable to other purposes of the Society.

Annual General Meeting

16.—A General Meeting shall be held each year in the month of January, or as soon after as the Executive Council shall determine, when the Council shall submit their Report and the Accounts of the Society for the preceding year, and when vacant seats on the Council shall be filled up, and the ordinary business of a General Meeting transacted.

Audit

17.—The Accounts of the Society shall be audited each year by an auditor appointed at the preceding General Meeting.

Changes in these Rules

18.—With the notice summoning the General Meeting, the Executive Council shall give notice of any change proposed by them in these Rules. Ordinary Members proposing any change in the Rules must give notice thereof in writing to the Honorary Secretary seven clear days before the date of the Annual General Meeting.

LIST OF IRISH
TEXTS SOCIETY'S PUBLICATIONS

—☐—

(Out of print)

(1.) ᵹ⁊oʟʟᴀ ᴀn ⸝ιuᵹᴀ. [The Lad of the Ferrule]
eᴀᴄᴄⱜᴀ Cʟoιnne Rⱜ nᴀ h-ʟoⱜuᴀⱜꝺe. [Adventures of the
Children of the King of Norway]
Edited by PROFESSOR DOUGLAS HYDE, LL.D., D.LITT., M.R.I.A.

(Out of print)

(2.) Fʟeꝺ bⱜⱜcⱜenꝺ [The Feast of Bricriu]
(From Leabhar na h-Uidhre).
Edited by GEORGE HENDERSON, M.A., PH.D.

(Out of print) See Volume 3a New Edition.

(3.) Dᴀncᴀ ᴀoꝺᴀᵹᴀιn Uí Rᴀcᴀⱜʟʟe [The Poems of Egan
O'Rahilly]
Edited, chiefly from MSS. in Maynooth College, by
The REV. P. S. DINNEEN, D.LITT.

(Volume for 1909) *(See No. 3)*

(3ᴀ) Dᴀncᴀ ᴀoꝺᴀᵹᴀιn Uí Rᴀcᴀⱜʟʟe [New Edition of the Poems
of Egan O'Rahilly]
Revised by PROFESSOR TADHG O DONNCHADHA and
The REV. P. S. DINNEEN, D.LITT.

(Volume for 1901)

(4.) Foⱜᴀⱜ Feᴀⱜᴀ ᴀⱜ Éⱜⱜⱜnn [History of Ireland.]   By
GEOFFREY KEATING. Part I. (See Vols. 8, 9, 15).
Edited by the late DAVID COMYN, M.R.I.A.

(Volume for 1902)

(5.) Caiṫréim Conġail Claiṗinġniġ [The Martial Career of Conghal Clairinghneach].
Edited by
The REV. P. M. MacSWEENEY, M.A.

(Volume for 1903)

(6.) Virgil's Æneid, the Irish Version, from the Book of Ballymote.
Edited by The REV. GEORGE CALDER, B.D., D.Litt.

(Volume for 1904)

(7.) Duanaire Finn. The Poem Book of Finn. [Ossianic Poems].
Part I.
Edited by PROFESSOR EOIN MacNEILL D.Litt.

(Volume for 1905)

(8.) Foras Feasa ar Éirinn [History of Ireland]. By Geoffrey Keating. Part II.
Edited by The REV. P. S. DINNEEN, D.Litt.
(See Vols. 4, 9, and 15).

(Volume for 1906)

(9.) Foras Feasa ar Éirinn [History of Ireland]. By Geoffrey Keating. Part III.
Edited by The REV. P. S. DINNEEN, D.Litt.
(See Vols. 4, 8, and 15).

(Volume for 1907)

(10.) Two Arthurian Romances [Eaċtra Macaoiṁ an Iolair aġus Eaċtra an Ṁaḋra Ṁaoil] Adventures of the Eagle Boy and Crop Eared Dog.
Edited by PROFESSOR R. A. S. MACALISTER, M.A., D.Litt.

12

13

14

(Volume for 1922)

(24.) The Pursuit of Ᵹꞃuⱥıᵭ Ᵹꞃıⱥn-ꝼoluꞃ.
Edited from a MS. in Trinity College, Dublin, by
CECILE O'RAHILLY, M.A.

———

(Volume for 1923)

(25.) Rosa Anglica. An Early Modern Irish Translation of
Part of John of Gaddesden's Text-Book of Mediæval
Medicine.
Edited by WINIFRED P. WULFF, M.A., Ph.D.

———

(Volume for 1924)

(26.) Cⱥıꞇꞃéım Ꞇoıꞃᵭeⱥlbⱥıᵹ [The Triumphs of Turlough].
Edited by DR. STANDISH HAYES O'GRADY. (Vol. I.
Text).

———

(Volume for 1925)

(27.) Cáıꞇꞃéım Ꞇoıꞃᵭeⱥlbⱥıᵹ [The Triumphs of Turlough].
Edited by DR. STANDISH HAYES O'GRADY (Vol. II.
Translation).

———

(Volume for 1926.)

(28.) Duanaire Fhinn. The Poem Book of Finn. Part II. The
last part of the Poems with translations.
Edited and translated by GERARD MURPHY, M.A.

———

(Volume for 1927.)

(29.) Instructio Pie Vivendi—Holy Life and Heavenly Thought.
Part I. Latin and Irish versions with Glossary of Irish
words.
Edited by The REV. JOHN MacKECHNIE, M.A., B.D.

15

(Volumes in Preparation)

The Great Blasket. A Collection of tales told by Comár O Cṅoṁċáṁn and recorded by ROBIN FLOWER, D.Litt, with poems by Seán O Ḋuṁnṗleiḃe (*in the Press*).

Duanaire Finn. Part III. Containing Notes to all the Poems, Glossary, Indices, etc.
Edited by GERARD MURPHY, M.A.

Instructio Pie Vivendi—Holy Life and Heavenly Thought. Part II. English translation of the Irish version, with Notes, etc.
Edited and translated by REV. JOHN MacKECHNIE, M.A., B.D.

The Harrowing of Hell and other New Testament Apocrypha.
Edited and translated from Irish Manuscripts of the 15th century, with a critical study of the sources and with notes. By ROBIN FLOWER, D.Litt.

Irish versions of three tales by Montalvan, with the original Spanish text and synopsis in English.

Cinn-Lae Amhlaoibh Uí Shúilleabháin. Humphrey O'Sullivan's Diary, 1827-1835. Two volumes.

The revised edition of the Society's Larger Irish-English Dictionary (1340 pp.), edited by REV. P. S. DINNEEN, D.Litt., (price 12/6 net ; post free 13/-) can be purchased from The Educational Company of Ireland, Ltd., 89 Talbot Street, Dublin. The Smaller Irish-English Dictionary (240 pp.) by the same editor, can be had of Messrs. M. H. Gill & Son, 50 Upper O'Connell Street, Dublin, and of Messrs. Simpkin, Marshall, Ltd., 4 Stationers' Hall Court, London, E.C.4. (price 3/- net.).

LIST OF MEMBERS.

(N.B.—Members are earnestly requested to send Notice of any Change of Address to the Hon. Sec., Irish Texts Society, c o National Bank, Ltd., 15, Whitehall, London. S.W.1., to avoid loss of books and notices).

Honorary Life Members :

NAMES.	ADDRESSES.
Hull, Miss Eleanor, D.Litt.	... 2, Gloucester Gardens, (58) Richmond Hill, Richmond, Surrey.

Life Members :

Bradley, The Rev. Michael, P.P.	Knockloughrim, Co. Derry.
Braunholtz, Prof. G. E. K., M.A.	22, Old Road, Headington, Oxford.
Byrne, G. P.	... 24 College Square North, Belfast.
Byrne, The Rev. J. ...	... Castlehead, Grange-over-Sands, Lancs.
Crotty, The Rev. Michael, P.P.	Abbeyside, Dungarvan, Co. Waterford.
Curran, The Rt. Rev. Monsignor M. J.	Irish College, Rome, 24.
Dalton, J. P.	... 19 Belgrave Square, Monkstown, Co. Dublin
De Paor, Eamonn ...	... Fatha, Eadarghoil, Bantry, Co. Cork.
Diolun, Maolra, M.A., Ph.D.	... University College, Dublin.
Donnellan, J. P. ...	... Killeany, Aran Isles, Co. Galway.
Doolan, Thomas ...	... 31-32 Great George's Street, Waterford.
Dowling, Frank	... 950 South Street, Roslindale, Mass., U.S.A.
Farrell, R. W., F.L.A.A. ...	... Clonbrone, Arundel Road, Durrington, Worthing, Sussex.
FitzGerald, T. D., B.A. ...	... c/o National Bank, Ltd., 15 Whitehall, London. S.W.1.
Fleming, The Rev. R., PH.D.	... Rathmines, Dublin.
Gahagan, F. Evatt	... 31, Harrington Sqr., London, N.W.1.
Goblet, Professor Yan M.	... 178 Rue de la Pompe, Paris, xvi.
Gourley, C. E.	... 70 Claremont Road, London, E. 7.
Hackett, J. D.	132 East 16th Street, New York, U.S.A.
Harley-Walker, The Rev. C. T.	The Yews, East Hanney, nr. Wanstead, Berks.
Havard-Jones, The Rev. H. T., M.A.	The Vicarage, Spaldwick, Huntingdon.
Haynes, Miss Muriel Sturgis	... 22, Embankment Road, Boston, Mass., U.S.A.
Horsford, Miss C. ...	... 27 Craigie Street, Cambridge 38, Mass., U.S.A.
John, E. T.	... 63 Warwick Square, London, S.W.1.

NAMES.	ADDRESSES.

Kelly, Paul Herrick ... ... 132 Cheapside, London, E.C.2.
Kennedy, Chief Justice Hugh ... Newstead, Clonskeagh Road, Dublin.
Kennedy, Patrick J., M.A. ... 17 Irishtown, Clonmel, Co. Tipperary.

Lewis, The Hon. A. L. ... ... The Hill, Abergavenny, Mon.

MacErlean, Andrew A., LL.B. ... 119 East 57th Street, New York, U.S.A.
MacFhinn, An t-Athair Pádraig Coláiste na h-Ollsgoile, Gaillimh.
Eric, D.D.
MacLoughlinn, James L. ... 60, Waterloo Road, Pembroke, Dublin.
McInnes, Wm. MacArthur ... c o McLaren, 55, Randolph Road, Broom-
hill, Glasgow.
Malone, Prof. Kemp. ... ... Johns Hopkins University, Baltimore,
Maryland, U.S.A.
Mitchell, The Rev. Joseph, Canon President, St. Mary's College, Galway.
OBuacalla, Micheál ... ... 108, Rock Rd., Booterstown, Co. Dublin.
OCarroll, Jos., M.D. ... ... Lynwood, Dundrum, Co. Dublin.
OCasaide, Séamus, M.A., B.L., Bóthair Lorcáin, Clontarf, Dublin.
M.R.I.A.
OCianáin, S. F., M B. ... ... Ballinalee, Edgeworthstown.
OCorcura, Micheál ... ... 2 Mulgrave Road, Cork.
ODubhgaill,The Rev. T.,B.A.,B.D. St. Columb's College, Derry.
OSullivan, The Rev. T. ... 173 Botanic Road, Dublin.

Perry, Miss A. M., M.A. ... ... 79 South End Road, Hampstead, N.W.3.

Sheehan, The Most Rev. M., D.D. Archbishop of Sydney, Juverna, Homebush,
Sydney, N.S.W.

Ua Concheanáin, Tomás ... Lios na Mara, Bothar na Tragha, Galway.
Ua Corcra, Domhnall ... ... 1 Auburn Villas, Ashburton, Cork.
Ua Cuileamháin, Seán ... ... Dun Cormac, Wexford.

Van Hamel, Dr. A. G. ... ... 19, Prins Hendriklaan, Utrecht.

Walker, Charlton, B.A. ... ... 16 Seaton Avenue, Plymouth,

Ordinary Members :

Andrews, Mrs. Edmond ... 561 Surf Street, Chicago, Ill., U.S.A.
Ashbourne, Lord... ... ... 17 Rue des Domeliers, Compiègne, Oise,
France.

Banks, Mrs. M. M. ... ... 16, Hornton Court, Kensington, W.S.
Bartholomew, J. ... ... Nunholm, 9 Victoria Circus, Glasgow, W.2.
Béaslaí, Piaras, Major General 8, Eden Park, Sandycove, Co. Dublin.
Bell, S. ... ... 3, Southdean Gardens, Wimbledon.
Bergin, Prof. Osborn J., D.LITT. 10, Grosvenor Place, Rathmines, Dublin.
Beynon, The Rev. E. D. ... 8475 Dearborn Avenue, Detroit, Michigan,
U.S.A.
Boland, John P. ... ... 4, Stone Buildings, Lincoln's Inn, W.C.2.
Boswell, C. S. ... ... Gatcombe, nr. Seaton, South Devon.
Boyd, E. A. ... ... 131 East 19th St., New York City, U.S.A.

18

NAMES.	ADDRESSES.
Bradley, W., M.D. ...	... Nevonstown House, Navan, Co. Meath.
Brady, Very Rev. J. Canon, P.P.	Keady, Co. Armagh.
Breathnach, Caitlín ...	... 23 Main Street, Carrick-on-Suir.
Breathnach, Cormac	... Central Model Schools, Dublin.
Breen, The Rev. D. ...	... Dingle, Co. Kerry.
Bright, William, LL.D., T.C.D.	... Willowdale, Glenageary Rd., Dunleary, Co. Dublin.
Briley, W. P.	... 18, Temple Park, Blackrock, Co. Dublin.
Brophy, Michael M. ...	... 48, Approach Road, Margate.
Brown, Professor A. C. L.	... Northwestern University, Evanston, U.S.A.
Brown, Thomas ...	... 20, Nassau Street, Dublin.
Brown, Prof. W. Edward	... Lafayette College, Easton, Pa., U.S.A.
Buckley, James, M.R.I.A.	... 11, Homefield Road, Wimbledon, Surrey.
Burns, Samuel	... 13 Warrington Road, Newcastle-on-Tyne.
Byrne, O. A.	... Villa Faraldo, 3, Rue Bel Respiro, Beau Soleil, A M., France.
Calder, Rev. Geo., B.D., D.LITT.	4, Oakfeld Terrace, Glasgow, W.
Clarke, John J.	... 57 St. Aubyn's Place, Lr. Newtown, Waterford.
Coffey, Brian MacMahon, M.D.	12, Denny Street, Tralee, Ireland.
Cohalan, The Most Rev. Dr.	... Bishop of Cork, Farranferris, Cork.
Costello, Thomas, M.D. ...	... Bishop Street, Tuam, Co. Galway.
Coyne, Dr. Gerard ...	... Mount Pleasant, Ballinasloe, Co. Galway.
Cox, Prof. Edward G., PH.D.	... University of Washington, Seattle, Washington, U.S.A.
Creed, The Rev. C. M. ...	... Durrus, Bantry, Co. Cork.
Crone, J. S., M.D., J.P., M.R.I.A.	Castlereagh, 34 Cleveland Road, Ealing, London, W.13.
Cross, Professor Tom Peete	... Dept. of Comparative Literature, University of Chicago, Ill., U.S.A.
Cullinan, Rev. Thos. ...	... P.O. Box 89, Cradock, S. Africa.
Curran, C. P., M.A. ...	... 15, Garville Avenue, Rathgar, Dublin.
Curtis, Prof. E.	... 37, Trinity College, Dublin.
De Barra, Liam ...	... Beech Walk, Roscrea, Co. Tipperary.
De Bhál, An t-Athair Tomás, S.P., PH.D.	Cill Curnáin, Co. Limerick.
De Bharra, Seán ...	... 61, Patrick St., Drumcondra, Dublin.
De Blacam, Aodh ...	... Lios Gréine, Artane, Co. Dublin.
De Blaghd, Earnán ...	... 6 Temple Villas, Palmerston Road, Dublin, S.W.1.
De Lury, Alfred T. ...	... University of Toronto, Canada.
Digby, Everard W. ...	... 47, Charleville Rd., London, W.14.
Diolún, Thomas ...	... Teach an Daingin, Galway.
Dobbs, Miss M. C. ...	... Port na Gabhlann, Cushendall, Co. Antrim.
Donnellan, P., M.D. ...	... St. Mary's, 13, Mayfield Rd., Terenure, Dublin.
Dowley, Miss Brigid ...	... Westgate, Carrick-on-Suir, Co. Tipperary.
Dowling, Mrs. D. ...	... Ard na Gréine, Ballymacelligott, Tralee.
Doyle, Miss M.	... 56 Hunter St., London, W.C.1.
Dunn, Professor Joseph...	... Catholic University, Washington, D.C., U.S.A.
Dunne, The Rev. J. ...	... Rathroe, Tullow, Co. Carlow.

19

NAMES.	ADDRESSES.
Eadie, Lieut.-Colonel J. Inglis, D.S.O.	c/o. Messrs. Grindlay & Co., 54, Parliament Street, London, S.W.1.
England, Thomas A., LL.D.	... 11a Caithness Rd., London, W.14
Enschedé, M. Johannes	... Huize, Ipenrode, Heemstede, The Netherlands.
Esmonde, Sir T. Grattan, Bt.	... Ballynastragh, Gorey, Co. Wexford.
FitzGerald, M. J.	... 18, King St., Snow Hill, London, E.C.1.
FitzGerald, Rev. Wm., c.c.	... Thurles, Co. Tipperary.
FitzSimmons, B.	... Sheepshead N. School, Kilcrohane, Bantry.
Fitzsimons, Patrick J.	... 48, Longstone Street, Lisburn.
Flower, Robin, D.LITT.	... Dept. of MSS., British Museum, London, W.C.1.
Flynn, Francis	... 4, Avon Place, Bothwellhaugh, Bothwell, Scotland.
Franklin, M.	... 74, St. Lawrence Rd., Clontarf, Dublin.
Freeman, A. Martin	... 166, Lauderdale Mansions, London, W.9.
Fynes-Clinton, O. H.	... Weirglodd Wen, Bangor, N. Wales.
Gaffney, J. S., B.A., Solicitor	... 86, O'Connell Street, Limerick.
Gaidoz, Professor Henri	... 22 Rue Servandoni, Paris vi.
Gates, H. C.	... 24, Bayswater Terrace, Skircoat Green, Halifax, Yorks.
Gill, Mrs. M.	... Castle Street, Carrick-on-Suir, Ireland.
Gogan, L. S.	... 373, North Circular Road, Dublin.
Green, J. S., Lt.-Col., R.A.M.C., M.R.I.A.	Air Hill, Glanworth, Co. Cork.
Griffen, Harold D., M.A.	... William Woods' College, Fulton, Missouri, U.S.A.
Griffin, Henry Farrand	... Barnstable, Massachusetts, U.S.A., per Stevens & Browne, Ltd.
Grosjean, The Rev. Paul, S.J.	... 24, Boulevard St. Michel, Brussels.
Gwynn, Dr. Edward	... Provost's House, Trinity College, Dublin.
Haran, Dr. J. A.	... 15, Shelley Road, Beechen Cliff, Bath.
Hayden, The Rev. E. M.	... St. John's Rectory, Clinton, Ill. U.S.A.
Headlam, M. F., c.b.	... 5, Tedworth Square, London, S.W.3.
Healy, A. Collins, B.A.	... 521 West 124th Street, New York City, U.S.A.
Heggarty, The Rev. J. M.	... 114E, 2nd St., Los Angeles, Cal., U.S.A.
Henry, Prof. Robert Mitchell, M.A.	Queens' University, Belfast.
Hickey, The Rev. B.	... St. Mary's, Wellington Road, Ashton-under-Lyne.
Hodges, Figgis & Co.	... 20, Nassau Street, Dublin.
Hogan, John	... 7 Prince Arthur-Terrace, Leinster Square, Rathmines, Dublin.
Hogan, The Rev. Stanislaus, O.P.	Holyrood, East Camberwell, Melbourne
Houlihan, The Rev. M. J.	... 43 Maple St., Hyde Park, Mass., U.S.A.
Hull, Vernam E.	... 29 Randolph Hall, Cambridge, Mass., U.S.A
Hurley, The Rev. T. A.	... The Monastery, Killarney, Co. Kerry.
Hyde, Professor Douglas, D.LITT.	65 Adelaide Road, Dublin.

20

NAMES.	ADDRESSES.
Jarcho, Saul W.	... 303 West 106th Street, New York, U.S.A.
Jennings, Rev. T. A., M.A.	... St. Jarlath's College, Tuam, Co. Galway.
Johnston. J. P., SC.D. ...	... Royal College of Science, Upper Merrion Street, Dublin.
Joyce, Francis, M.B. ...	... 190 Camberwell Road, London, S.E.5.
Joyce, Wm. B., B.A. ...	... 1 Et ra Road, Rathmines, Dublin.
Joynt, Ernest E.... ...	... Kingston, Tyrconnell Road, Inchicore, Dublin.
Keappock, The Rev. Thomas ...	Parochial House, Collinstown, Co. Westmeath.
Keenan, L. F., M.D. ...	... 58 Upper Clapton Road, London, E.5.
Keliher, Thomas ...	... 134 Upper Thames Street, London, E.C.4.
Kiernan, T. J., M.A., PH.D.	... Office of the High Commissioner, Irish Free State, 33-37 Regent St., London, S.W.1
King, Michael J., B.A. ...	... Borrisone, Co. Limerick.
Lankford, J. R.	... 7 Ashburton Hill, St. Luke's, Cork.
Leshe, Shane	... Glaslough, Co. Monaghan.
Lewis, Timothy	... University College, Aberystwyth, Wales.
Liddell M. F.	... 35, Trinity College, Dublin.
Lloyd, Joseph H., M.R.I.A.	... Buaile na Gréine, Stillorgan Park, Dublin.
Lynam, E. W., B.A., M.R.I.A.	... British Museum, London, W.C.1.
Lynch, M C.	... 20 East Bank, Stamford Hill, London, N.16.
Lynch, Timothy ...	... Sun Lodge, 65 Sunday's Well, Cork.
Macalister, Prof. R. A. S., M.A.	18 Mount Eden Road Donnybrook, Dublin, S.E.1.
MacAoidh, Ian	... 33 Curzon Rd., Muswell Hill, London, N.10.
MacAoidh, Micheál ...	... Teach Druim, Drum Amharc, Dún na nGall.
MacBhloscaidh, P. ...	... 17 Sráid Caitrin, Limerick.
MacBride, A., M.D. ...	... Infirmary House, Castlebar, Co. Mayo.
MacBride, Joseph M. ...	... Mallow Cottage, Westport, Co. Mayo.
MacCana, Peadar ...	... 25 Mary Street, Drogheda.
MacCarrthaigh, Tadhg ...	... N.S., Kinnegad, Co. Meath.
McCarthy, P. J., N.T. ...	... Shannon View, Glin, Co. Limerick.
MacClintock, Major H. F.	... Red House, Ardee, Co. Louth.
MacColuim, Fionán ...	... Department of Education, Dublin.
MacCosgair, Liam T. ...	... Beechpark, Templeogue, Co. Dublin.
MacDermott, The Very Rev. J. Canon	Croghan, Boyle, Co. Roscommon.
MacDiarmuda, An t-Athair M.	Keady, Co. Armagh.
MacDomhnaill, F. S. ...	... c o. Barclays Bank, 9 Russell Square, London, W.C.1.
MacDonald, The Rev. Archibald	Kiltarlity Manse, Beauly, Invernesshire.
MacEochagáin, Stiobhán Pádraig	Lorne House, Coleham, Shrewsbury.
MacGauley, P. T.	... 108 Drumcondra Road, Dublin
MacGiolla Seannaigh, an t-Athair	Spiddal, Galway.
McGrath, Patrick ...	... 20 East Essex Street, Dublin.
MacGreevy, Thomas ...	... 15 Cheyne Gardens, London, S.W.3
MacGuanna, D. ...	... 69 Lindsay Road, Glasnevin, Dublin.
MacKay, Donald ...	... c o Miss M. MacKay British Bank of South America Ltd., Caixa Postal, 83 Sao Paulo, Brazil.
MacCarvill, Mrs. Eileen...	... 8 Fitzwilliam Square, Dublin.

21

NAMES.	ADDRESSES.

McKenna, The Rev. L., S.J. ... Rathfarnham Castle, Co. Dublin.
McLees, William H. ... ... 379 Grant Avenue, Brooklyn, New York, U.S.A.

MacLennan, The Rev. Malcolm, 6 Polwarth Terrace, Edinburgh.
D.D.
MacLeod, The Rev. Malcolm, M.A. United Free Church Manse, Lochgilphead Argyllshire.

MacLoingsigh, The Rev. Peadar St. Columb's College, Derry.
MacLysaght, E. ... ... Raheen, Tuamgraney, Co. Clare.
MacMurnaigh, Micheál ... ... St. Anne's, Anne St., Dundalk.
Macnaghten, The Hon. Helen ... Runkerry, Bushmills, Co. Antrim.
MacNeill, James ... ... Dundrum, Co. Dublin.
MacNeill, Patrick Charles ... 27, Edenvale Road, Rathmines, Dublin.
MacNiocaill, S. ... ... 46 Oakley Road, Ranelagh, Dublin.
MacSeáin, The Rev. Seán ... Omagh, Co. Tyrone.
MacSuibhne, Pádraic ... ... 5 Highfield Avenue, Cork.
MacSwiney of Mashanaglass,
The Marquess, M.R.I.A. ... 39 Upper Fitzwilliam Street, Dublin.
MagFhloinn, Liam ... ... Newtown School, Waterford.
Mahony, J. J. ... ... Suite 608, Ashland Block, Chicago, U.S.A.
Meaghar, The Rev. J. R. ... St. Thomas of Canterbury, Waterloo, Liverpool.

Meehan, Francis ... ... Leitrim, Ireland.
Merriman, Professor P. J., M.A. President, University College, Cork.
Mhic Chathmhaoil, Mairéad, Bean Westpoint House, Strand Rd., Sutton, Co. Dublin.
Micheál, an t-Athair, O.S.F.C. ... Fr. Mathew Hall, Queen St., Cork.
Miller, Miss Anna Irene ... 2426 Eutaw Place, Baltimore, Maryland, U.S.A.
Miller, C. R. D. ... ... 301, Craigie Hall, Cambridge, Mass., U.S.A.
Miller, The Rev. W. ... ... Braganza House, Carlow.
Moloney, Francis ... ... 74 State Street, Boston, Mass., U.S.A.
Moynihan, James ... ... 34 Dunbar St., Cork.
Mühlhausen, Prof. Docktor Rudolfstr, 48, Hamburg, 34.
Ludwig
Mulcahy, Timothy, B.A.... ... 2 Tivoli Terrace, Clonmel.
Mullen, The Rev. E. J., C.C. ... Carrick, Tirconaill.
Munn, Dr. James Buell ... 58 Garden St., Cambridge, Mass, U.S.A.
Murphy, F. T. ... ... 4 Highland Park, Roxbury, Mass, U.S.A
Murphy, J. J. Fintan ... 16 Extra Road, Brixton Hill, London, S.W.2
Murphy, William, N.T. ... 53 Harbour Row, Cobh, Co. Cork.
Murphy, Dr. Philip ... Main Street, Carrick-on-Suir, Co. Tipperary.
Murray, Sir Hubert ... Government House, Port Moresby, Papua.
Murrin, James B. ... Carbondale, Pennsylvania, U.S.A.

Nesbit, Mrs. M. K. ... ... Montilly, Sion Mills, Co. Tyrone.
Newlin, Nicholas... ... ... 1804 Pine St., Philadelphia, Penn., U.S.A.
Ní Bhruadair, Gobnait ... Baile an Chongnaimh, Cuan an Chaisleain, Cill Airne, Co. Ciarraíghe.
Nic Dhonnchadha, Lil. ... 116, Lower Baggot St., Dublin.
Nic Eochagáin, Seosaimhín ... 87 Upper Dorset St., Dublin.
Nic Mhathghamhna, Lil. ... Listellick, Tralee, Co. Kerry.

NAMES.	ADDRESSES.
Ní Dhunlainge, Sighle ...	... 19 Finglas Rd., Glasnevin, Dublin.
Ní Locain, Máire...	... 136, Upper Drumcondra Rd., Dublin.
Nilsen, Eugene ...	... 20, Ekebergueren, Christiania, Norway.
Ní Raghallaigh, Máire	... 87 Upper Dorset Street, Dublin.
Ní Shuilleabháin, Eibhlín	... Baile h-Éil, Co. Kilkenny.
Nolan, P. J.	... 624, Roosevelt Avenue, York, Penna., U.S.A.
OBeagáin, R. S.	... 2, Wilmont Avenue, Sandycove, Dublin.
OBraoin, D.	... 5 Ennismore Villas, Magazine Road, Cork.
OBriain, Art.	... 15 Mecklenburgh Square, London, W.C.I.
OBriain, Pádraig ...	... Ballyferriter, Dingle, Co. Kerry.
OBriain, Seán, B.A., B.COM., H.D.E.	... Céimín, Dorgan's Rd., Glasheen, Cork.
OBrien, The Rev. Denis, D.PH., D.D.	Effin, Kilmallock, Co. Limerick.
OBrien, Michael	... Ballymakeera, Co. Cork.
OBrien, Edward, M.A. ...	... Falmore House, Moville, Derry.
OBrolcháin, Pádraic ...	... Dún Bride, Nashville Park, Howth, Co. Dublin.
OBrosnacháin, an t-Athair D. ...	Colaiste Bhreannáinn, Cill Airne, Co. Chiarraidhe.
OByrne, William ...	... Eascrach, Cruimghlinn, Co. Bhaile Atha Cliath.
OCadhainn, Liam ...	... Les Buissonnets, Bridgemount, Castlebar, Co. Mayo.
OCadhlaigh, Cormac, M.A.	... 5 Hill View, Cross Douglas Rd., Cork.
OCallaghan, Jeremiah ...	... 121 Duke Street, Sheffield.
OCaoimh, Micheál... ...	... 3 Ashbourne Villas, Limerick.
OCarroll, J., B.A. ...	... 2 The Terrace, Arklow, Co. Wicklow.
OCarroll, J. T. ...	... 129 Queen's Road, Richmond, Surrey.
OCeallaigh, Seán ...	... Ros Cathaill, Cill Mhine, Westport.
OCeallaigh, Seán T. ...	... c o. The Nation, 91 St. Stephen's Green, Dublin.
OCeileachair, The Rev. Seán	... Coláiste Naoimh Eóin, Portláirge.
OCeocháin, Domhnall ...	... Coolea, Macroom, Co. Cork.
OCinnéide, An Bra. S.M.	... Mainistir na mBrathar, Dún Dealgain.
OConchobhair, Diarmuid	... Carrignaveeah, Sunday's Well, Cork.
OConchobhair, Risteárd	... 7, George's Quay, Cork.
OConnell, Maurice, A.C.I.S.	... Hill View, Marion Rd., Mill Hill, London, N.W.7.
OConnor, Denis Hayes	... Monster House, Charleville, Co. Cork.
OConnor, Michael ...	... Clooncurra N.S., Lispole, Co. Kerry.
OCriocháin, an t-Athair Brian ...	Grange, Sligo.
OCuill, Seán	... 44 Mountjoy Street, Dublin.
OCuinn, The Rev. Seamus	... Bessbrook, Co. Armagh.
OCúrnáin, The Rev. Tadhg	... The Presbytery, Dingle.
ODalaigh, R.	... 63 Handside Lane, Welwyn Garden City, England.
ODea, The Rev. D., B.A.	... Newmarket-on-Fergus, Co. Clare.
ODomhnaill, an t-Athair M.	... Teach na Sagart, Castlerea, Co. Roscommon.
ODonachu, an t-Athair D.	... Tracton, Co. Cork.
ODonnchadha, Prof. Tadhg, D.LITT.	Croata, Glasheen Road, Cork.

23

NAMES.	ADDRESSES.
ODonnell, The Rev. M.	... Kilronan, Aran, Co. Galway.
ODonnghaile, an t-Athair N.	... Galway.
ODonovan, J. J. ...	... 2 Eden Terrace, Limerick.
ODonovan, T. J., B.A. ...	... An Cappach, Bréan Traigh, Co. Cork.
ODubhda, Peadar ...	... Bothar Dealgan, Dún Dealgan.
ODubhshlaine, F. ...	... Customs and Excise Office, Glenamaddy, Co. Galway.
ODuibhir, Antoine ...	... Roinn Josef, Coláiste Phádraig, Maynooth.
ODwyer, Professor R. ...	... 9 Upper Leeson Street, Dublin.
OFionnachta, S.	... 6, Warrenpoint, Clontarf, Dublin.
OFlaherty, The Rev. Michael	... Summerhill College, Sligo.
OFlynn, John	... Kirwan's Hotel, Carrick-on-Suir, Co. Tipperary.
OFearghaill, Rev. A., s.J.	... Coláiste Iognáid, Gaillimh.
OGabhláin, Pádraic ...	... Cloongoonaugh, Aughamore, Co. Mayo.
OGallagher, M.	... 1430 Plaisance Court, Chicago, U.S.A.
OGlasáin, Séamus ...	... Barry's Hotel, Rath Droma, Wicklow.
OGorman, The Rev. J. J., D.C.L.	193 Fourth Avenue, Ottawa, Canada.
OHalloran, The Rev. P., C.C.	... St. Mary's Nenagh.
O h-Annracháin, Peadar	... Dun Aoibhinn, an Scibrin, Co. Cork.
OHanrahan, T. W. ...	... Altamount, Kilkenny.
O h-Aodha, Seamus, M.A.	... Ive-Le-Bawn, Fermoy, Co. Cork.
OHegarty, P. S.	... Highfeld House, Highfeld Road, Rathgar, Dublin.
OHegarty, The Rev. T., C.C.	... Quigley's Point, Derry.
OKeefe, The Rev. David	... St. Colman's Cathedral, Queenstown.
OKeefe, J. G.	... 1, Dynevor Rd., Richmond, Surrey.
OKelly, Thomas ...	... 40 Hilldrop Road, London, N.7.
OKiely, Laurence, M.A. ...	... Crehana, Carrickbeg, Carrick-on-Suir.
OLoughlin, Colm	... 5-6 Fleet Street, Dublin.
OMahoney, D., M.B. ...	... Glasnevin Lodge, Glasnevin, Dublin.
OMáille, Prof. Tomás, M.A., PH.D.	Roigne, College Rd., Galway.
OMaolcathaigh, Pádraig	... Coláiste Chnuic Mhelleri, Ceapach Chuinn, Co. Waterford.
OMaolchatha, Séamus	... An Ghráinseach, Clonmel, Co. Tipperary.
OMaoldhomhnaigh, an t-Athair Mairtín	Killaloe, Co. Clare.
OMeachair, Pádraig ...	... 2184, Valentine Avenue, Bronx, New York, U.S.A.
OModhráin, The Rev. S.	... St. Jarlath's College, Tuam, Co. Galway.
OMoghráin, Pádraig, M.A.	... Knockloughra N.S., Westport, Co. Mayo.
OMoráin, The Very Rev. P. S., Canon	Claregalway, Ireland.
OMuimhneacháin, Conchubhair	Béal Atha an Ghaorthaidh, Co. Cork.
OMuirthile, An Br. D.L.	... Coláiste Cacimhghin, Glas Naoidhean, Baile Atha Cliath.
OMuimhneachain, Aindrias	... Coláiste Caomhghin, Glas Naoidhean, Baile Atha Cliath.
OMurchadha, Colm ...	... Leinster House, Kildare St., Dublin.
OMurchú, Micheál ...	... 33 Home Farm Rd., Drumcondra, Dublin.
ONeill, Seán	... Customs and Excise, Swinford, Co. Mayo.
ORaghallaigh, Criostoir, M.A.	... 269 Clonliffe Road, Drumcondra, Dublin.
ORahilly, Professor T. F., D.LITT.	Ballincurrig House, South Douglas Road, Cork.
ORayla, Proinsias ...	... 19 Munster Street, Phibsborough, Dublin.

NAMES.	ADDRESSES.

OReilly, The Rev. J. M. ... Bekan, Ballyhaunis, Co. Mayo.
OReilly, The Rev. Robert ... Prior, Ballinskelligs.
ORiam, Liam P. ... ... 15 Kempshott Rd., Streatham, London, S.W.16.
ORiain, The Rev. Nioclás ... Tipperary.
ORiain, Art. ... ... 3, Páirc Cille Muire, Dublin.
ORioghbhardáin, Domhnall, o.s. Tamhain, Oran Mor, Co. Galway.
ORioghbhardáin, M., B.A., F.R.G.S. N.S. Abbeydorney, Co. Kerry.
ORiordan, E. F., M.A. ... ... Suite 608, Ashland Block, Chicago, U.S.A.
ORiordan, J. P. ... ... 59, Harberton Rd., Highgate, London, N.19.
Ormond, The Rev. W., Adm. ... Carrickbeg, Carrick-on-Suir, Co. Tipperary.

OSeaghdha, Muircheartach, o.s. Ard na Gréme, Eadar Goil, Bantry.
OSeochfhradha, Pádraig ... 119, Morehampton Road, Donnybrook, Dublin.
OShaughnessy, J. ... ... Gifford Park, Bronxville, N.Y., U.S.A.
OShea, The Rev. John ... Carrick on Suir, Co. Tipperary.
OSuilleabhain, Seán ... Kinnard, Lispole, Co. Kerry.
OSullivan, D. J. ... ... Cairn Hill, Foxrock, Co. Dublin.
OSullivan, D. K. ... ... 89 Emmet Rd., Dublin.
OSullivan, Jerh. ... ... St. John's, Port Glasgow.
OSulhvan, John ... ... Beni Suef, Egypt.
OSuilleabhain, Tomas, Cigire ... 9 Geraldine Villas, Traghli.
OTighearnaigh, P. S ... ... 57 Palmerston Road, Dublin.
OTreasaigh, an t-Athair M. ... St. Michael's, Pery Square, Limerick.
OTuathail, Eamonn, M.A. ... 15, Lower Kenilworth Park, Harold's Cross, Dublin.
Parker, The Rev. P., P.P. ... Cushenstown, Ballynabola, Co. Wexford.
Patterson, Fergus ... ... Stella Polaris, Westleigh Avenue, Putney, London, S.W.15.
Perry, The Rev. J. F. ... ... Hern's Nest, Rugeley, Staffs.
Phléimoinn, Máire Bean ... An Sgoil, Sil Eiligh, Co. Wicklow.

Porter, Mrs. Valentine Mott. ... Box 211, Carmel, California, U.S.A.
Probsthain, A. ... ... 41, Great Russell St., London, W.C.1.
Purcell, Joseph ... ... 2 Glenmalure Villas, Castleview Gardens, Limerick.

Redmond, Owen J. ... ... 13 Lomond Avenue, Fairview, Dublin.
Reinhard, J. R. ... ... 328E. Huron St., Ann Arbor, Michigan, per B.H. Blackwell, 50 and 51 Broad St., Oxford.
Rice, The Rev. James ... St. Joseph's, Headley Road, Hindhead, Surrey.
Rice, Ignatius J. ... ... Roselawn, Ballybrack, Co. Dublin.
Robinson, Prof. F. N. ... ... Harvard University, Cambridge, Mass., U.S.A.
Roche, Miss K. ... ... Mater Dei Gymnasium, 59 Batavierenwe, Nijmegen, Holland.
Rohan, T., M.A. ... ... 84, St. Lawrence Road, Clontarf, Dublin.
Ross, The Rev. Neil, M.A., B.D. The Manse, Laggan, Kingussie.

NAMES.	ADDRESSES.
Saurin, C. J. ...	... 23 Grosvenor Road, Ilford.
Seton, Sir Malcolm ...	... 26 Upper Park Rd., Haverstock Hill,N.W.3.
Sheehan, John ...	... William Street, Fermoy, Co. Cork.
Sloane, C. Gordon ...	... Platten Hall, Drogheda, Co. Meath.
Smith, J. A., LL.D. ...	... Magdalen College, Oxford.
Smith, Prof. Roland M.	... Dept. of English, Wesleyan University, Middletown, Conn., U.S.A.
Smyth, F. Acheson ...	... 71 Harcourt Street, Dublin.
Suipéal, an t-Athair T., B.D.,B.A.	Lixnaw, Co. Kerry.
Taylor, Barry	... 5124 Calumet Avenue, Chicago, U.S.A.
Thompson, Lady ...	... 39, Steele's Road, Hampstead, N.W.3.
Thurneysen, Prof. Dr. L. Rudolf	Bonn. Mechenheimer Allee 55, Germany.
Tierney, Rev. John, D.PH.	... Edenderry, Offaly.
Town-end, E. R., Paymaster-Lieut., R.N.	Boundary Oak, Waterlooville, Cosham, Hants.
Ua Buachalla, Domhnall	... Maynooth, Co. Kildare.
Ua Ciaráin, Rev. A. ...	... Ballincondan, Ballina, Co. Mayo.
Ua Fearachair, D. ...	... 17 Grattan Square, Dungarvan, Co. Waterford.
Ua Gadhra, Proinsias ...	... Ceibh na gCeannaidhe, Limerick.
Ua Mathghamhna, Seosamh	... Patrick Street, Listowel.
Ua Tuama, D.	... Kincora, Moreton, Cheshire.
Ui h-Ainnin, Máire, Bean	... Crecora, Patrickswell, Co. Limerick.
Ui Chuinn, Máire, Bean...	... National School, Killala, Co. Mayo.
Vendryes, Professor J. ...	... 85 Rue d'Assas, Paris.
Walsh, The Rev. Paul ...	... Stamullen, Co. Meath.
Walsh, The Rev. R. F., C.C.	... Draperstown, Co. Derry.
Walshe, M. C., J.P. ...	... 2b, Bickenhall Mansions, Gloucester Place, London, W.1.
Walsh, Miss Róisín ...	... Cypress Grove, Templeogue, Co. Dublin.
Walshe, Rev. J. A. ...	... Rossmuck, Maam Cross, Galway.
Waters, Eaton W., M.D.	... Brideweir, Conna, Co. Cork.
Webster, K. G. T. ...	... Gerry's Landing, Cambridge, Mass., U.S.A.
Weisweiler, Dr. Phil. Josef.	... Frankfurt a.M., Kurhessenstr, 68.
Whitehill, Walter Muir, Jr.	... c/o Barclay's Bank. (France), Ltd., 33 rue du iv Septembre, Paris.
Williams, Professor Ifor.	... Y Wenllys, Menai Bridge, Anglesey.
Williams, T. W. ...	... Woolcombe, St. Mary's, Uplyme, Lyme Regis.
Woulfe, The Rev. Patrick, C.C.	Kilmallock, Co. Limerick.
Wulff, Miss Winifred P., M.A., PH.D.	Cypress Grove, Templeogue, Co. Dublin.
Young, Miss Rose M. ...	... Portnagolan, Cushendall, Co. Antrim.

Libraries, Societies, Colleges, and Schools

Aberdeen, University Library ... per Librarian.

Aberystwyth, Library of University College of Wales — per Librarian.

Albany, U.S.A., New York State Library — per Stevens and Brown, 28-30, Little Russell St., London, W.C.1.

Baltimore, Maryland, U.S.A., Enoch Pratt Free Library ... per E. G. Allen & Son, Ltd., 14 Grape St., Shaftesbury Avenue, W.C.2.

Baltimore, Maryland, U.S.A., Johns Hopkins University Library — per E. G. Allen and Son, Ltd.

Belfast Central Public Library — per G. H. Elliot, Chief Librarian, Royal Avenue, Belfast.

Belfast, Clonard Monastery ... per The Rev. Fr. Rector, C.SS.R.

Belfast Library and Society for Promoting Knowledge (Linen Hall Library) — per F. J. P. Burgoyne, Librarian, Donegall Square North, Belfast.

Berlin, Indogermanisches Seminar (Indo-germanic Department) of the University of Berlin. — per Dr. Pokorny, Berlin, Charlottenburg, Stuttgarter Platz. 21.

Birmingham Public Library ... Librarian, Reference Dept., Ratcliff Place, Birmingham.

Boston Public Library, Mass. ... per Bernard Quaritch, 11 Grafton Street, New Bond Street, London, W.1.

California University Library ... per Stevens and Brown, 28-30 Little Russell St., London, W.C.1.

Cardiff Central Library ... ... per Harry Farr, Librarian, Cardiff.

Carnegie United Kingdom Trust — See under Coleraine, Dublin, Kilkenny, Lifford, Sligo, and Wicklow (below).

Carrick-on-Suir, Convent of Mercy — per The Reverend Mother.

Chicago, Newberry Library ... per Stevens and Brown, 28-30 Little Russell St., London, W.C.1.

Chicago Public Library ... per Stevens and Brown.

Chicago University Library ... per Stevens and Brown.

Cleveland Public Library ... per B. Quaritch, 11 Grafton St., London, W.1.

Clongowes Wood College ... per Rev. C. Mulcahy, s.j.

Coláiste Bhrighde, an Fálcarrach, Tir Chonnaill — per An Priomh-Oide.

Coláiste Caoimhin. Glas Naoidhean, Baile Atha Cliath — Do.

Coláiste Einne. Teach Talbóid, Baile Atha Cliath — Do.

Coláiste Ide, Baile an Ghoilín, Daingean — Do.

Coláiste Moibhi, Glas Naoidhean, Baile Atha Cliath — Do.

Coláiste Muire, Leitir Ceanainn,   per An Priomh-Oide.
Tír Chonnaill
Coláiste na Mumhan, Magh Ealla,   Do.
Co. Chorcaighe

Coleraine, Co. Derry, Carnegie   County Book Repository, Coleraine.
Libraries
Concord State Library ...   ... per Arthur H. Chase, Librarian, Concord,
                                     N.H., U.S.A.
Copenhagen, Royal Library   ... per Haase and Son, Levstroede, 8, Copen-
                                     hagen.
Cork, Public Library   ...   ... per Librarian, James Wilkinson, F.L.A.
Cork Co. Council Carnegie   25, Patrick St., Cork.
Library Service.
Cork, University College Library per Librarian.

Derry, Convent of Mercy   ... per The Superioress.
Dresden, Saechsische Landes-
bibliothek   ...   . Dresden, Saxony.
Droichead Nuadh : Co. Kildare, per The Very Rev. The Prior, O.P.
Dominican College
Dublin, " An Fáinne "   ...   ... per An Rúnaidhe, 25 Parnell Sqr., Dublin.
Dublin, Carnegie United King-   32, Merrion Square, Dublin.
dom Trust
Dublin County Council Library   The Courthouse, Kilmainham.
Dublin, King's Inn, Hon. Society per Hodges, Figgis & Co., 20 Nassau Street,
                                     Dublin.
Dublin, National Library of   per Hodges, Figgis & Co.
Ireland.
Dublin, Oireachtas Library   ... per Controller, Stationery Office, Dublin.
Dublin, Royal Irish Academy ... per Hodges, Figgis & Co.
Dublin, Royal Dublin Society ... per Hodges, Figgis & Co.
Dublin, Trinity College Library per A. de Burgh, Librarian.
Dundalk, Free Library   ... per Town Clerk, Town Hall, Dundalk.
Dundalk, St. Joseph's   ...   ... per The Rev., The Rector, C.SS.R.

Edinburgh Public Library   ... per E. A. Savage, Principal Librarian.
Edinburgh University Library   per J. Thin, 54-55 South Bridge, Edin-
                                     burgh.
Esker, Athenry, St. Patrick's   ... per The Rev., The Rector, C.SS.R.
Evanston, Ill., U.S.A., North-   per Stevens and Brown, 28-30 Little
western University Library   Russell St., London, W.C.1.

Galway, University College Lib- per Hodges, Figgis & Co., 20 Nassau St.,
rary   Dublin.
Glasgow, The Mitchell Library... per S. A. Pitt, City Librarian, North St.,
                                     Glasgow.
Glasgow University Library   ... per Jackson, Wylie & Co., 73 West George
                                     Street, Glasgow.
Gottingen University Library ... per Librarian, Prinzenstrasse 1 Gottingen,
                                     Germany.

Hamburg, Seminar für Verg-   Hamburg, Universität.
leichende, Sprachwissenschaft
Harvard College Library   ... per E. G. Allen & Son, Ltd.

Iowa City, Ia, U.S.A., The Library, Library Annex, State University of Iowa.   per Stechert & Co., 2 Star Yard, Carey Street, London, W.C.2.

Ithaca, N.Y., U.S.A., Cornell University Library   per E. G. Allen & Son, Ltd.

Kilkenny, Carnegie Free Library   per Ed. McSweeney, Librarian, John's Quay, Kilkenny.

Kilkenny Carnegie Library Service   Book Repository, John's Quay, Kilkenny.

Leeds, Central Public Library ...   per T. W. Hand, Librarian.

Leipzig, Börsenverein der Deutschen Buchhändler   Königstrasse, 35, Leipzig.

Leipzig, Universitäts-Bibliothek   Beethoven Strasse 6, Leipzig, Germany per A. Probsthain, 41 Gt. Russell Street, London, W.C.1.

Lifford, Tirconaill, County Library   The Librarian, County Book Repository, Lifford Co. Donegal.

Limerick, Carnegie Free Library   per J. P. McNamara, Director.

Limerick, Connradh na Gaedhilge   per The Secretary, 17 Thomas Street, Limerick.

Limerick, Mary Immaculate Training College   per The Principal.

Limerick, Mount St. Alphonsus   per The Rev. Fr. Rector, c.ss.r.

Listowel, Co. Kerry, Presentation Convent   per Sister Michael.

Listowel, Carnegie Free Library   per Veritas Coy., Ltd., Dublin.

Liverpool Public Library ...   per G. H. Parry, Librarian.

London, Connradh na Gaedhilge   per The Secretary, 31 Red Lion Square, London, W.C.1.

London, Irish Literary Society   per The Hon. Secretary, 39 Grosvenor Place, London, S.W.1.

London Library   ... ... per C. J. Hagbert Wright, Librarian, St. James's Square, London, S.W.1.

London University College ...   per Librarian, Gower Street, W.C.1.

London, University Library ...   per The Goldsmiths' Librarian, University Library, South Kensington, London, S.W.1.

Los Angeles Public Library ...   per Stevens & Brown.

Louvain, Belgium, Bibliothèque de l'Université Catholique   per Dr. E. Van Cauwenbergh, Chief Librarian.

Louvain, Collège de Saint-Antoine   per Rev. Fr. Guardian.

Lund, Sweden, University Library   per A. B. Gleerupska, Universitets Bokhandeln.

Manchester Reference Library ...   per Librarian, Piccadilly, Manchester.

Manchester, John Rylands Library   per H. Guppy, Librarian, Deansgate, Manchester.

Manchester, Victoria University of   per Librarian.

Maynooth, Co. Kildare, Cuallacht Cholm Cille St. Columba's League   per The Secretary, St. Columba's League, St. Patrick's College, Maynooth.

Meadville Theological School Library   per Stechert & Co., 2 Star Yard, Carey Street, W.C.2.

Melbourne, Public Library ... (E. C. Armstrong, Librarian), per Sotheran, Ltd., 43 Piccadilly, W.1.

Michigan University Library ... per Sotheran, Ltd., 140 Strand, W.C.2.

Minnesota University Library ... Minneapolis, Minn., U.S.A., per Stechert & Co.

Monaghan, Convent of St. Louis per Sr. M. Laurentia.

Munich, Bavarian State Library per Asher & Co., Behernstrasse, 17, Berlin.

New York Public Library ... per Stevens & Brown, 28-30 Little Russell Street, W.C.1.

New York, Columbia University Library per Stevens & Brown do. do.

North Carolina, University of, Chapel Hill. per Stevens & Brown, London, W.C.1.

Nottingham Public Reference Library per Librarian, Central Public Library, Sherwood St., Nottingham.

Oslo University Library ... per Cammermeyers boghandel, Oslo.

Ottawa, Library of Parliament... per E. G. Allen & Co., Ltd., 14 Grape St., Shaftesbury Avenue, W.C.2.

Oxford, Meyrick Library, Jesus College per L. B. Cross, Librarian, Jesus College, Oxford.

Oxford, Taylor Institution ... per L. F. Powell, Librarian.

Paris, Bibliothèque de l'Université à la Sorbonne per C. Klincksieck, 11 Rue de Lille, Paris.

Paris, Bibliothèque Nationale ... do. do.

Pembroke Urban District Library, Ballsbridge per City Treasurer, Dublin.

Philadelphia Free Library ... per Stevens & Brown, 28-30 Little Russell Street, London, W.C.1.

Philadelphia, Mercantile Library per T. Wilson Hedley, Librarian, 10th St., above Chestnut Street, Philadelphia, Pa., U.S.A.

Philadelphia Philo-Celtic Society 1504 N. Gratz St., Philadelphia, Pa., U.S.A.

Princeton University Library ... per Sotheran, Ltd., 140 Strand, W.C.2.

Rathmines, Co. Dublin, Public Library. per Librarian.

Ring, Co. Waterford, Iol-Scoil na Mumhan per Seumas Ó h-Eochadha.

San Francisco Public Library, Civic Centre per Stechert & Co., 2 Star Yard, Carey Street, London, W.C.2.

Sligo, Carnegie United Kingdom Trust County Book Repository, Sligo.

Stanford University Library, California per Stechert & Co., 2 Star Yard, Carey Street, London, W.C.2.

Strasbourg, Bibliothèque Universitaire et Regionale per M. Le Directeur.

Swansea Public Library (Welsh and Celtic Dept.) per Librarian.

Swansea, University College Library. Singleton Park, Swansea.

Thurles, Co. Tipperary, Carnegie Libraries	per Librarian, County Book Repository, Thurles.
Toronto Reference Library ...	per Messrs. Dawson & Son, Cannon House, Pilgrim Street, E.C.4.
Uppsala Kungl. University Library	Uppsala, Sweden.
Urbana, University of Illinois, U.S.A.	per Stechert & Co., 2 Star Yard, Carey Street, London, W.C.2.
Washington, Library of Congress	per Stechert & Co., 2 Star Yard, Carey Street, London, W.C.2.
Waterford Public Free Library	per Librarian, Lady Lane, Waterford.
Wicklow, Carnegie Libraries ...	County Book Repository, Wicklow.
Yale University Library ...	per E. G. Allen & Co., Ltd., 14 Grape St., Shaftesbury Avenue, W.C.2.

CPSIA information can be obtained
at www.ICGtesting.com
Printed in the USA
BVHW030229030721
610877BV00005B/646

9 789354 036323